D0146595

The Powerful Bond between People and Pets

**Recent Titles in
Practical and Applied Psychology**

Meta-Physician on Call for Better Health: Metaphysics and Medicine for Mind, Body and Spirit
Steven E. Hodes, M.D.

The Powerful Bond between People and Pets

Our Boundless Connections to Companion Animals

P. Elizabeth Anderson

Foreword by Gerald P. Koocher

Practical and Applied Psychology
Judy Kuriansky, Series Editor

Westport, Connecticut
London

Library of Congress Cataloging-in-Publication Data

Anderson, P. Elizabeth.
   The powerful bond between people and pets : our boundless connections to companion
animals / P. Elizabeth Anderson ; foreword by Gerald P. Koocher.
         p.   cm. — (Practical and applied psychology, ISSN 1938–7725)
     Includes bibliographical references and index.
     ISBN 978–0–275–98905–7 (alk. paper)
     1. Pet owners—Psychology.   2. Pets—Psychological aspects.   3. Pets—Social aspects.
4. Human animal relationships.   I. Title.
   SF411.47.A66   2008
   636.088′7—dc22   2007039209

British Library Cataloguing in Publication Data is available.

Library of Congress Catalog Card Number: 2007039209
ISBN-13: 978–0–275–98905–7
ISBN: 1938–7725

First published in 2008

Praeger Publishers, 88 Post Road West, Westport, CT 06881
An imprint of Greenwood Publishing Group, Inc.
www.praeger.com

Printed in the United States of America

The paper used in this book complies with the
Permanent Paper Standard issued by the National
Information Standards Organization (Z39.48–1984).

10 9 8 7 6 5 4 3 2 1

For Grace,
Amazing Grace Anderson
September 6, 1989–June 7, 2004

The Grace Anderson Memorial Fund was established at the veterinary hospital where Grace died, and is the place where this plaque hangs.

Contents

Preface   ix

Foreword by Gerald P. Koocher   xiii

Acknowledgment   xvii

Note to the Reader   xix

Introduction: A New Era for Companion Animals   xxi

1   Companion Animals in America and Around the Globe   1

2   Genesis and Nature of the Bond   18

3   Why We Choose Certain Animals As Companions   44

4   Roles That Animals Play in Our Lives and How We Influence
    Each Other   66

5   Embedded with Humans—Animals in the Human World   82

6   Pets As Medicine   119

7   Protecting Our Companion Animals   142

8   When Love Hurts   162

9   Love Gone Bad   181

Series Afterword by Judy Kuriansky   201

Notes   207

Bibliography   229

Index   239

Preface

I have been drawn to animals for as long as I can remember. As is the case with many animal lovers, my fondness translated into my being a *pet owner*. I grew up with dogs, who primarily lived in the yard, and I incorporated a dog into my first home after college. I do not remember being alive without a dog around, and I hope never to live without one in my family.

Unfortunately, my two earliest memories of animals are traumatic. First, I watched my grandfather decapitate one of the chickens he raised for eggs and meat. Later, my childhood was marred by watching a stray dog maul an innocent, frail kitten, after their paths crossed on a neighbor's yard.

More than fifty years later, the sad horror of those moments are vivid reminders of the cruel fates that beset animals in our society. They are at our mercy and, more often than not, are the victims of poor human choices and behaviors. Watching that dog kill the kitten informed me that when animals receive inadequate care and protection, they suffer. I consider both the kitten and the dog as victims. That experience congealed into a promise that my life must somehow benefit animals. Over the course of my life, I have learned that whether we realize it or not, when animals suffer, we suffer with them. I believe that disregard and indifference for their lives is contagious, fueling a similar lack of caring and compassion for our own lives and the lives of other humans.

For the past few years, I have spent more time with my dogs than with anyone else—one of the challenges and benefits of being a writer. As they, my devoted and constant companions grew old and died, (concurrent with my own mortality becoming more salient), I became more introspective and curious about the nature of the relationships. I became aware that a lot more was going on between us than I realized; that I really cared about these animals immensely; that I was the beneficiary of a remarkable relationship; and that I was not alone in my admiration for and appreciation of living with an animal.

My curiosity about the origins of and implications for human relationships with animals led to journalistic research, where I discovered materials primarily in two places. One, in scientific books and peer-reviewed journals that examined the relationships we form with animal companions; the other, in subjective popular press publications that reflected personal experiences. I observed that people in each realm often held each other at arm's length. For instance, I sensed that some academics scoffed at people who approached the relationships with sentimental, unsubstantiated anecdotes. On the other hand, people with companion animals seemed to scoff at the academics for being stubborn and unappreciative of the obvious benefits and advantages of companion animals.

Through my research, I began to recognize that the different perspectives can and are finding common ground and, in the process, developing respect for what each has to offer the other. My goal with this book, which was motivated by my lifelong love for animals and the trauma of losing a special animal companion, is to expand the conversation and attract new voices. This book represents an amalgamation of my deep desire to make a difference for animals, my appreciation and understanding of the investigative process (which was honed during seventeen years in the pharmaceutical industry), and my journalistic training and experience. My goal is to augment the common ground between the people on the front lines of academic research, those on the front lines in the animal care community, and those whose front line is in their home with their beloved animals. Respect and appreciation of each other's work and interests are vital to furtherance of knowledge.

Our scientific and medical systems insist that knowledge must be based on solid, empirical evidence, and that takes time. Nonscientists waiting for scientific breakthroughs and revelations are often frustrated that apparent common sense has to be demonstrated and then validated. However, we are obliged to understand the scientific process and encourage research and broad-based funding. Those of us outside of academia must also keep sharing our rich and revealing anecdotal evidence, which could become the catalyst for new research.

Often public interest in a topic, combined with political pressure, translates into increased scientific interest and enhanced research funding. Unfortunately, in the current climate, even well-designed studies in traditional fields by prestigious investigators with proven track records are being rejected by major funding sources. This means that scientists involved in human-animal research—and other nontraditional fields—face especially difficult times. Yet, these studies must be done and pass scientific rigor for the results to get the respect they deserve. Only then can the field progress and generate results that can translate into improved animal care and understanding.

Armed with a respect and appreciation for the scientific process, I was determined to base every word on as much scientific evidence and justification as I could find. My journalistic research for this book left me in awe of what scientists have been discovering, while I was just trying to housetrain my dog (unwittingly using methods established by a scientist, no doubt). I offer this book in appreciation for what they are teaching us about our relationships with animals, in hopes that others will seek out their work and help them move the field forward with interest and appreciation of their own.

Any conversation about companion animals is dominated by talk about cats and dogs, who represent the majority of all companion animals. As this book is based on the latest available literature, it can be no different because the preponderance of the research and writing on companion animals is about dogs. Consequently, most of what follows is about dogs. This is not to suggest that people who select other animals as companions do not reap similar benefits or face the similar hardships associated with dogs as companions. My understanding is that the object of your affection matters not as much as the affection itself. You will read about people who get as much out of their relationship with a reptile or a rodent as others get from a dog, for example.

Regardless, let me apologize now to those of you who live with a non-canine or non-feline companion and feel just as strongly about your animal as those who live with the highly regarded and oft-discussed dog. The science has to catch up with you. It had to catch up with dog and cat people, too, so please be patient. I have no doubt that you can identify with the information that follows and learn a lot about the relationships between people and whatever animal they happen to call companion. Because of their prevalence, I must examine why cats and dogs are so overwhelmingly popular, but I will discuss other companion creatures and the people who prefer them.

Even if you do not have a dog or a cat, you will find commonalities as you read about one of the most enduring and crucial relationships in existence: the powerful bond between people and their companion animals.

Foreword

As I read this book, Elizabeth Anderson's writing inspired me to retrace the evolution of my own relationships with nonhuman animals. My first two memories of such encounters could potentially have set me up for a diagnosis of posttraumatic stress disorder.

At the age of four, I accompanied my father on a visit to a "poultry processing" plant owned by my uncle in Maine. The concept of "free range" chickens had not entered the lexicon of poultry producers, and as far as I could see were row upon row of stacked cages each containing groups of chickens in close confinement. At the end of the long, large feeding room, workers roughly snatched the birds from their cages and hung them by their feet on overhead conveyor racks that carried them mysteriously out of my range of vision. About a 100 yards away they emerged as headless, featherless carcasses, dropping into vats of chilled water.

Some of the birds managed to flutter out of the cages and strutted about. Workers intermittently chased them down, grabbing them by the feet, and headed for the conveyor. One of the chickens headed in our direction, and my uncle encouraged me to catch it. As I reached out, it pecked my finger, drawing blood. Someone else grabbed the animal and sent it off to the conveyor. As if to comfort me, my father scooped me up and carried me along to see the animal mechanically decapitated.

At the age of five, a neighbor's dog bit my hand as I played on my front stoop in the city. The subsequent emergency room visit, stitches, and tetanus shot seemed worse than the bite itself. The dog vanished—quarantined and euthanized, I later learned.

These early experiences may explain why my first venture into animal care focused on guppies and other small freshwater fish. After several years of overnight camp, I took a nature counselor training course at Boston's Museum of Science. I began alternating volunteer work at the Museum during the school year, and teaching nature classes to campers during the summer. At various points the Museum would run out of space in the "animal room," and give me creatures to care for at home, with the idea that they would go off to camp with me in the summer. Over the years these included an assortment of reptiles, a young raccoon, and an elderly docile porcupine (sic: Mr. Ouch). My parents demonstrated reasonable tolerance of the menagerie, as long as the nonhuman family members stayed mostly in the garage.

During the early years of our marriage, my spouse, Robin, and I seemed to move up the phylogenetic ladder as we considered becoming parents to a human animal. We started with one of the more challenging freshwater fish from the cichlid family (my choice) and later added a couple of gerbils (my spouse's preference). Later we decided to "practice" our parenting skills on a more demanding species and discovered a common affinity for birds.

We adopted an African gray parrot from a pet shop and named him Omar (from the root word, meaning "talkative"). It turned out that Omar had been "wild caught" and came to the pet shop through quarantine, where he had spent several weeks confined in the company of barking dogs. We knew this because he barked and growled quite a bit during our early years together. Omar remained a member of our family for close to thirty years (more about that later), but never did show much interest in mimicking human speech, apart from a pronounced "Nooooooo!"

The birth of our daughter seemed only mildly interesting to Omar. She found him fascinating, and her first word skipped the traditional "Mommy" or "Daddy," for "Birdie." When she began to walk and became a more active presence around his cage and perches, Omar began to pluck his feathers—the parrot equivalent of human nail-biting. Bare pink skin appeared on his chest and shoulders as mounds of tiny feathers accumulated on the floor of his cage overnight. Showering him with extra attention and vitamin supplements didn't help. We thought perhaps a companion might help.

We learned of an "older bird" in need of a new home and adopted a very sweet orange-winged Amazon parrot hen, named Joey, twenty years Omar's senior. Her plumage is mostly green, but bright orange patches appear when she spreads her wings. Suspicious at first, Omar soon became friendly with Joey and stopped plucking. After all, how can one expect to impress the ladies without nice plumage? Joey would frequently groom Omar, gently breaking the stiff new feather shafts on his neck with her beak, although we never saw him return the favor (males can be like that). Within a year they had taken up residence in the same cage and lived together for twenty-six years.

Our flock of parrots grew to four, but Omar and Joey were the only "couple" in the group. Whenever a trip to the vet or nail trimming adventure necessitated removal of Omar from the aviary, Joey would clearly become agitated, climb in circles, and call out until he returned.

Late one November, Omar's health began to deteriorate; the diagnosis—degenerative liver disease. We did our best to care for him at home by making his cage easier to navigate and hand-feeding him when he could no longer make his way to the food dishes. One morning in late December he could no longer stand without rolling to one side. My daughter, age twenty-five at the time, was home for a holiday visit and the whole family sadly accepted the veterinarian's recommendation to euthanize Omar. As we prepared a shoebox lined with tissue to transport him to the veterinarian's office, we realized that we needed to bring Joey too. We all sat close to Omar as the vet, who had cared for him more than two decades, connected an intravenous line to administer the lethal drugs. Joey groomed him gently until his breathing stopped, and then looked up at the rest of us. She knew he was gone. In the car on the drive home, my daughter (an only child) said that she felt as though she'd lost a sibling. When we returned home Joey went back to her cage, but did not pace in circles or sound her familiar, "Where's Omar?"

In the early years of my training as a psychologist I learned the importance of thinking like a scientist. My professors took great pains to emphasize the importance of not ascribing human attributes, such as feelings, to the animals we studied. Such beliefs, the professors asserted, involved anthropomorphic thinking, the attribution of uniquely human characteristics and qualities to nonhuman beings. Such thinking comes naturally to us. People confronted with novel experiences will generally attempt to understand them from the framework of what they already know. When we observe nonhuman animal behavior, we cannot possibly grasp the animal's perspective. Instead, we filter what we see though our own experiential and emotional lenses.

Although I once accepted these perspectives as scientific realities, I no longer feel so certain. I now see many uncritical assertions of anthropomorphic thinking as little more than human arrogance. My own experiences, and those so well chronicled by Elizabeth Anderson in the following pages, demonstrate the complex and wonderful reality of humankind's relationships with the other animals that live among us.

In addition to containing many real life and touching examples of the special bond between humans and their companion animals, this book is also a work of careful scholarship that provides a fascinating overview of the growing body of literature on this topic. Elizabeth covers such topics as the historical origins of the connection between humans and animals; the basis of the special bond between humans and their companion animals; the incredible lengths and expense many people will go to pamper and protect their companion animals; and the tragic and heartbreaking side of this bond. The sheer breadth of the information addressed is truly impressive, which at times can be intriguing, surprising, shocking, uplifting, and even disturbing, but always thought-provoking. Elizabeth Anderson clearly has a passion for her subject matter, and whether you are a longtime animal lover, a scholar of animal behavior, or merely curious about the topic, after reading this book you will never view animals the same way again.

Gerald P. Koocher, Ph.D.
Former President, American Psychological Association

Acknowledgment

An almost magical convergence of talent, luck, and support, with a good tail wind is required to get a book from an author's head into a reader's hands. By the end, the author is almost too crazed (surely, I am not the only one) to remember each person who made it happen. On some days heavy lifting was needed to keep me going, but other times the encouragement of a stranger in the post office did the trick. No one writes a book alone—writing is lonely, but collaborative work. Following are people who performed amazing feats of magic to help put this book in your hands.

"Dr. Judy" for shifting the axis of the earth with her enthusiasm, and for introducing me to Debora Carvalko, senior acquisitions editor for psychology, health, and social work at Praeger/Greenwood Publishing. I have waited so long to refer to someone as MY book editor, and Debora Carvalko filled my every dream with her unwavering optimism, support, and patience.

Max Padon, president of the Virginia Macintosh Users Group, Inc., who graciously chaperoned me through a hard drive crash. Jordana Schmier, who performed such a *mitzvah* when the Endnote software program became threatening. Tomiko Smith for her assurances. Michelle Moglia, who proved herself to be an indispensable Endnote diva and the Energizer Bunny of references.

CT Woods-Powell, a treasure, for asking me a probing question at a pivotal juncture that made all the difference. My niece Deborah Harvey Mathes, who came through in a major way for her old auntie.

My husband Norman B. Anderson, who in spite of his demanding mistress, the American Psychological Association, finds time to delight and inspire me. Thank you, Norman, for my wonderful life and yet another success that would have been impossible without your unconditional love and support.

Note to the Reader

Early in the process of writing this book, I had to make two key decisions. First, how to refer to the animals—as *pets, animal companions, companion animals,* or *nonhuman animals*? Second, how to refer to the humans with whom the animals live—as *owners, guardians,* or some other term?

The decisions were crucial because words have power. You know that the "sticks and stones" cliché is wrong. Words *can* hurt, and sometimes more than your feelings suffer. Words reflect our biases, impacting our worldview. They also have the power to influence our behavior toward, and perceptions of, others.

I realized that the words I selected would have the power to engage or repel potential readers and would communicate my orientation toward the topic. Given the nature of my subject matter, the words would also influence whether I would be taken seriously or dismissed.

How we define animals—and ourselves in relation to them—is an academically, politically, and socially charged issue, and people feel very strongly about the position they take. For example, many people bristle at the word "pet," considering it a pejorative term that reflects—and, worse, promotes—a deep misconception about animals, contributing to their abuse, and restricting their rights as sentient beings. Others find *companion animals* and its derivatives unnecessary drivel. These people are usually the ones who think that it is silly not to refer to ourselves as animal *owners.* They lean toward the "animals-as-property" concept, while the former group of people feel that calling ourselves owners is as acceptable as admitting you own slaves. For them, words like *guardian* and *caretaker* are more acceptable. However, the term guardian has implications in our legal system that can make the word troubling.

As I write, no consensus has been reached on which term is best, but plenty of healthy debates are ongoing, in various professional and social organizations, with sensible and nonsensical evidence on every side.

I have to admit that I like the word "pet," as I consider it a term of endearment, which connotes the precious status that many animals enjoy. However, I prefer not to use it publicly because I believe we need to be nudged toward a greater appreciation for the lives of animals, and change begins with how we think and speak about elements of our world.

Consequently, in hopeful anticipation that expanded thinking about the animals with whom we share our homes, and about whom we care so deeply, can translate into widespread acknowledgement that all animals deserve full lives, which are devoid of intentional harm, I choose to refer to animals as companions when that role applies, and as nonhuman animals otherwise. Some people reject the term nonhuman animals because they feel it implies speciesism, a suggestion that the companion animals are less desirable than humans. That is neither my point in using the term, nor my perspective. Ultimately, I had to make a choice from imperfect options. Nonhuman animals may be a new term to you, but it is an accepted term in human-animal research, referring to animals that are not *Homo sapiens*. In spite of my preferred descriptors, I agreed with the publisher that including the word "pet" in the title of the book would facilitate electronic searches and make the book more accessible to readers not familiar with the term companion animals. As a compromise, from this point on, the word *pet* is usually shown is italics, unless contained in a direct quote.

You will notice that I use personal pronouns when referring to animals for whom a gender can be easily identified by an untrained eye. Conversely, not that I write much about them here, but I would not refer to a bug as him or her. I also use the word "have," rather than "own," when referring to the relationship we have with companion animals. Some would criticize this usage, but I consider the phrase, "I *have* a dog," akin to saying, "I *have* a brother" or "I *have* a child."

When referring to the human side of the human-animal relationship, I decided on the word *guardian*, but without an implication of legal responsibility. Rather, I refer only to what I firmly believe is our obligation: To do no harm; only defend, protect, and keep safe the animals with whom we share our homes, our lives—our earth. No less should be expected of us, the animals who consider themselves the most advanced, civilized beings on the planet.

Introduction: A New Era for Companion Animals

Acquiring a dog may be the only opportunity a human ever has to choose a relative.

—Mordecai Siegal (b. 1934)

Companion animals have become essential to "the new American family." They are reliable, responsive, available, and reportedly give the kind of unconditional love typically attributed to supreme beings. They have become not only our companions, but also our teachers, our children, our confidantes, our healers, our friends, and sometimes, our raison d'etre.

Pet-human partnerships are at an all-time high, according to the American Pet Products Manufacturing Association (APPMA).[1] More companion animals than people live in the United States: 382 million companion animals in a population of nearly 300 million people, as estimated by the U.S. Census Bureau for 2006. Sixty-three percent of Americans—representing more than 71.1 million households—now live with a companion animal. That is an increase from 64 million homes in 2002 and 51 million in 1988, which was the first year of APPMA tracking. American households contain 74.8 million dogs, 88.3 million cats, 142 million freshwater fish, 9.6 million saltwater fish, 16 million birds, 24.3 million "other" small animals, and 13.4 million reptiles. The APPMA reported in 2005 that approximately 45 percent of Americans live with more than one companion animal.

The recent surge in the population of companion animals is indicative of a distinct paradigm shift in the way we think and feel about them; we cannot get enough of them. Companion animals are not required to work for their keep, as is the historical custom for animals associated with humans. For the most part, there is neither livestock to herd, ranch to guard, nor mouse to catch. We simply want to *be* with them. What is behind this phenomenon?

One factor is that Americans have become increasingly isolated from one another, and basic social units have changed.[2] Perhaps technology is stripping us of the ability to genuinely connect with other people. A quick phone call here or an e-mail there does not a relationship sustain. Our social contacts are characterized by the Internet, iPods, Blackberrys, cell phones, or television. In

2006, the *New World College Dictionary* bestowed Word of the Year honors on the term "crackberry," which refers to our incessant need to check our Blackberry or other electronic device for messages. The need borders on addiction.

To make matters worse, standard methods for developing social contacts are underutilized. For instance, in many places, excessive traffic is a deterrent to socializing with colleagues and friends. Attendance at worship services, a primary way to meet people, is declining in the main denominations.[3] Social facilitation is not helped by the increasing transience of our populations, such that we no longer know many people outside of our jobs, and we have superficial relationships with coworkers. Neighborhoods where families live for generations, sharing history, culture, and social activities are rare.

In fact, we are learning to be wary of each other, constantly vigilant against crime and other threats. With terrorism as the new watchword, Americans have never felt so fragile, so exposed, or so threatened. Many of us do not have another person in our proximity: Census 2000 revealed that the number of people in America living alone is growing. Single-person households were shown to outnumber married couples with children.

Consequently, companion animals are the only family that some people have. Many young, single adults often acquire a companion animal to complete their first home away from home. Many "DINC" families (pronounced dink and stands for dual-income, no children) are established with companion animals, and many single divorcees build new families around their animals. We are not shocked even to see a homeless person with a faithful dog or cat, and we should not be. We may think that life for these companion animals is harder, but not necessarily. "Most homeless people will put their pets before themselves," said Robert Leslin, a homeless man who, with his wife Karla, has been homeless for two years after losing his job as a cook. Sharing their meager resources is not a sacrifice for homeless people who say that what the animals give them in return is priceless. That sounds pretty familiar, yes? In fact, companion animals may mean more to this segment of our population. Karla Leslin said that their cat, Stormy, has kept her from going over the edge and is sometimes the only thing in the world that makes her feel human.[4]

Animals have become integral to the family, on par with humans or in an established separate category: a family member who *happens to be an animal*. More to the point, the family simply would not be complete without them. The new American family unit consists not only of parents and children, but also companion animals. Sometimes, the companion animal is the only *other* that creates the immediate family. For example, I had the amazing privilege to meet Craig Peel, an older gentleman who survived Hurricane Katrina, but was separated from his beloved dog, Sassy. When Red Cross volunteers asked him about surviving relatives, he gave Sassy's name.

Before I met my husband, I described my family as "Muffin and me," referring to the miniature Schnauzer I raised from a puppy. Peel and I are not alone in our attitudes about our animals. Unquestionably, companion animals have risen to a new level in our society.

Forty percent of respondents to the American Animal Hospital Association's 2004 Pet Owner Survey said they would select a dog if allowed only one companion on a deserted island. An equal percentage thought that their companion animal listened better than their spouse or significant other. Fifty-four percent of the respondents said that they thought about their animals a few times a day when separated from them, while 21 percent said they think about them "all the time." Ninety-four percent added that their companion animals have "human-like personality traits."

As a family member would, animals frequently become our emissaries in the neighborhood. Many of us do not know our neighbor's names, but we know the names of their animals, especially their dogs. One of my neighbors, who is married, but she and her husband do not have companion animals, remarked proudly while we were socializing over dinner that she could amass a jury of peers for a dog who had received a ticket for jaywalking.[5] She knew the names of twelve dogs in the neighborhood, and she does not even have a dog.

MAKING SENSE OF IT ALL

This book examines why our relationships with companion animals have become paramount in our lives. It examines the complex relationships between humans and companion animals from the beginning to the bitter end, while revealing and explaining as many associated conundrums and contradictions as possible.

Chapter 1 begins with the origins of the relationships, beginning with human dependence on wild, then domesticated animals, for food, clothing, and most frequently, safety. The early relationships, even those with animals destined to become our companions, were *all* about the humans. Now, the relationships are about what we do *for them*.

One of the great contradictions of the human-animal connection is how humans care so much for certain species of animals, treasuring them as constant companions, while other species remain sources of food, clothing, entertainment, or sport.

In his unprecedented book, *In the Company of Animals*, Dr. James Serpell,[6] offers interesting, provocative insights into "why on earth, out of all the species available to us, we choose to lavish so much affection on two medium-sized carnivores...."[7]

What makes them so special? When it comes to animals, each person has a place where we draw a line between "us" and "them." In America the dividing line is usually behind cats and dogs. But why?

For one thing, we are suitably matched to dogs and cats—the most popular animals with whom we choose to live. We share with them a proclivity for sociability, at which dogs excel over cats because they are pack animals, as are we. As such, dogs prefer to live in groups, so joining *our* family groups is not a great leap for them or for us. Fortunately, the groups do not have to be large to be rewarding. Many families are essential "packs of two": a dog and his or her person.[8]

Clearly, a shared preference to live among others does not account for the impressive increase in the quantity and quality of relationships between humans and companion animals—dogs and cats in particular.

THE HEART KNOWS

In Chapter 2, I will examine what motivates our great attraction to cats and dogs. It could be that the relationships we have with our companion animals simply make perfect biological sense. Humans are quite possibly "hardwired" with an innate tendency to care about animals and nature. *Biophilia*[9] suggests just that, as you shall read.

Whatever the reason, we take certain animals into our hearts, but why? The answer, like most truths, is pure and simple: Love. We love them. My premise is that love is the operative word behind the oft-described insanity about companion animals—behaviors that some people without companion animals have trouble understanding. Sometimes we love them more than we love the people in our lives, and frequently companion animals are credited with teaching us how to love at all.

Trying to prove love sounds like a fool's errand because love is hard to define and even harder to measure. This is especially true when referring to a feeling between two particular species—one human and one composed of individuals who happen to be primarily dogs or cats.

Psychology is my field of choice when trying to decipher individual behavior, but psychological models of relationships are designed for human-to-human connections and presuppose, among other factors, a shared mode of communication through language. Adding to the complexity of proving that love applies is that most psychological research on love pertains to romantic love, which if applied to human-animal relationships indicates a pathology that is beyond the reach of this book.

In spite of the difficulties in connecting how love applies to relationships with our companion animals, love is the word most people use when asked to describe how they feel about them, as they do when asked to describe how they feel about cherished family members. In Chapter 2, I will look at several theories of love and apply certain of their aspects as a litmus test to the unique bond we have with our companion animals.

My goals, you see, are to address the ever-present question of why we bestow such attention and status on companion animals and to enlighten those who "don't get it." They do not get what the rest of us understand—we love our companion animals, and maybe, just maybe, they love us. In spite of the naysayers,

I maintain that the value we place on our relationships with our companion animals is manifested in how we treat them, and those behaviors are indicative of love.

Most people who love animals, *know* that they love them, and are not concerned about science and statistical analyses to justify their feelings, but we are all best served if we appreciate the importance of the research that validates these impressions. If the capacity that humans have to love companion animals made sense to more people, I believe that both humans and animals could benefit. A more generalized awareness and appreciation of our relationships with companion animals is crucial for the full potential of the relationships to be realized. Consider the quote by M. Gandhi, "The greatness of a nation and its moral progress can be judged by the way in which its animals are treated."

Whether you accept love as the appropriate descriptor or not, it is clear that people feel very strongly and react dramatically about animals. What is the nature of the relationship that makes people feel so attached to their *pets*? How is it that people form such powerful bonds with *creatures*, bringing them into their homes and treating them, well, like family?

My intention is to provide sufficient scientifically based information to substantiate the validity of the relationships, thereby eliminating the shame associated with caring so much for companion animals and grieving so profoundly when they die. This is the heart of the book.

You see, I agree with the French novelist, Emile Zola, founder of the literary naturalist movement, who said, "The fate of animals is of greater importance to me than the fear of appearing ridiculous." Through the ages, people who love animals have been accused of everything from witchcraft to bestiality. Some of the most damning criticism is that we care less for other human beings because we love animals so much, a notion I can easily debunk. Megan Daum said, "those of us who fret over animals must cope with a social stigma that suggests we're all a bunch of friendless oddballs."[10] I intend to provide evidence that contributes to ending the shame and also confirms and affirms these authentic, meaningful relationships.

THE CONSEQUENCES OF OUR AFFECTION

Even if we accept that we love them, the question of "why?" still begs an answer. Whether we ask our companion animals to sing for their supper or simply sit by the fire, *why* do we treat them the way we do? Why do we bring them into our homes and let them into our hearts? What are they doing for us? *To* us?

Sometimes my husband picks up our adopted five-pound Maltese, Máni, and says to her, "Who are you and what are you doing in my house?" He is asking the question in jest because Máni joined us unexpectedly after the death of Grace, our beloved dog for fourteen years, to whom this book is dedicated.

Although he was being flip, good psychologist that he is, my husband raised a valid question. Who are these creatures we call companion animals, and what *are* they doing in our houses? In Chapter 3, I will explore some of the reasons and the roles they play. Along the way, you will meet animals who act as rescuers, social workers, and matchmakers.

Because people select dogs as companions more than any other animal, you will read a lot about dogs, then cats. Other animals, such as birds, pigs, fish, horses, smaller mammals, and reptiles fill companion duties, as well. The populations of more uncommon animals as companions, such as rabbits, ferrets, and reptiles are also increasing, and I will extrapolate why some people prefer creatures not typically considered candidates for companionship.

Conclusive evidence exists that various animals can have a positive impact on the social and emotional development of humans. There is no limit to what can be achieved and learned from our relationships with companion animals, as you will read in Chapter 4. The possible influences that we have on them will also be covered in this chapter.

PAMPERING AND PROTECTING

No holes are barred when it comes to our companion animals. We treat them like beloved people and we share every benefit of human living. In Chapter 5, you will read how we have embraced companion animals into our human world, lavishing them with all our world has to offer.

Turns out that we take care of them—and they take care of us—in unexpected ways. Science has shown that companion animals can improve our lives, even beyond the obvious social support. They can be therapeutic and have been part of interventions with children and adults, particularly the elderly. In Chapter 6, you will read how certain animals offer palliative care, and I will introduce you to dogs who have been trained to detect bladder cancer, low blood sugar, and seizures.

In return for the many benefits, we do everything we can to not only pamper, but also protect our companion animals. They get a day at the spa, and they get their day in court. Ours is a litigious society, and we employ legal remedies to protect our faithful companions and their assets, as you will read in Chapter 7. Issues related to management of trust funds are just one of the reasons companion animals are appearing on judicial dockets.

There are many ways to extend protection. At the core of our democratic society is the ability to implement and utilize laws for justice and safety. It probably never occurred to the founding fathers that animals would influence political platforms, but people are working at grassroots and national levels to promote laws to establish what they see as the rights for animal companions. Our relationships with companion animals are fueling local and national government policy and influencing elections. In Chapter 7, you will read about the important work of activists for companion animals and the first political action committee that identifies "animal friendly" politicians.

BROKEN HEARTS

Impermanence is an unavoidable and tragic fact of life—nothing lasts forever. Where our pets are concerned, the end comes all too soon. The lifespan of most companion animals is painfully short. Even those who give us twenty or so years leave us desperate for more. Horses, some birds, and many reptiles enjoy a longer natural lifespan, but many dogs live less than ten years.

What, then, do we do when our hearts are broken? Many of us face this heartbreak more than once, never learning how to effectively deal with the enormous grief. Sometimes the only sympathy comes from people who have also suffered the death of a companion animal. Otherwise, the bereaved are forced to keep their grief to themselves, carrying on in the face of a monstrous emotional upheaval.

Regardless of how it happens, the loss can be profound. In Chapter 8 you will read about the grief associated with the death of a beloved animal companion and methods of healing and recovery.

BROKEN HONOR

Our companion animals are completely innocent of the tragedies that befall them because of their association with us, as happens in natural disasters and accidents. However, they seem proud to stand by us. This makes it all the more shameful that they often suffer at our own hands. Having established how we benefit from our relationships with our companion animals, I will examine whether *we* are good for *them*? In Chapter 9, I will examine how our animal companions fare in their relationships with us and look at some of the ways in which we fail to live up to being the kinds of people they think we are. You will read about issues such as animal abuse, pet-overpopulation, target breeding, and puppy mills.

Finally, I will look to the future, for us and those creatures we hold so dear—our companion animals.

1

Companion Animals in America and Around the Globe

Our perfect companions never have fewer than four feet.
—Sidonie Gabrielle Colette

Relationships between people and animals date back to the Paleolithic era, which is commonly referred to as the "Old Stone Age." The stage had been set during the previous Mesozoic era when dinosaurs walked the earth, and a diverse group of long, slim, predators, called *miacids*, lived in the trees. Over millions of years, *miacids* evolved into two distinct groups: (1) *viverravidae*—ancestors of cat-like creatures, and (2) *miacidae*—ancestors of the wolf, bear, raccoon, weasel, and the dog, among others.[1] Eventually those two lines would lead to the domestic cat and dog, who are undisputedly the most popular companion animals, in America, and perhaps in the world.

Most research indicates that animals were first kept for the work they could do or for the services they could provide. That could have been helping to corral errant cows or sheep, guarding the homestead while the people were away, laying eggs, catching mice, or becoming bacon.

Historical documents confirm that during the nineteenth century even the exalted dog pulled small wagons or walked on treadmills to power small machines, such as cooking spits, butter churns, or cider presses.[2] Cats had to work outside for their keep longer than dogs because cat litter was not invented until the 1940s. A friend who lived in California at the time confirmed that as late as 1944, she had to get sand for her Siamese cat's litter box from the beach or from a nearby construction site.[3]

Wild creatures that transitioned into working animals who lived and worked alongside humans sparked some of the most important events in human history. Moreover, the transition from working animals to companion animals has been no less significant. Today, the majority of companion animals are not required to work for their keep—unless you consider being the object of constant adoration and affection a job.

FEED ME? YES! DOMESTICATE ME? MAYBE.

Across the animal kingdom most animals were not suitable as companions because they could be neither domesticated nor tamed—two essential criteria for companion animals.

Out of 148 possible candidates for domestication, only fourteen large herbivores (plant-eating animals) and three small carnivores (meat-eaters) were domesticated by the time of the Roman Empire. Of those, only seven animals—cats, cows, dogs, goats, horses, pigs, and sheep—were domesticated successfully enough to propagate around the world.[4] Not surprising when you understand what domestication requires.

Domestication is the most demanding category because the entire species must meet a complete list of rigid criteria to be eligible. First and foremost, the species must *easily* and successfully reproduce in captivity. If you cannot persuade animals to reproduce in your environment without a lot of technologic support, domestication is unlikely. When animals have elaborate mating rituals captive breeding is difficult.

For example, although an extreme illustration, a cheetah will never become a cuddly, domesticated companion animal because several males must chase a female cheetah over many miles to win a mate. Again, this one disqualifier (no need to mention the predatory nature) is an important reason why cheetahs will never qualify for domestication or become companion animals. To further understand the difficulty associated with captive reproduction, you need look no further than pandas, whose captive breeding record alone assures that, in spite of their enormous charm and physical appeal, they will never become domesticated. Cats and dogs have become the most popular animals kept as companions throughout the ages. One advantage is that they reproduce easily in captivity, maybe a little too easily, when you consider the problems associated with "pet overpopulation." Several other animals, primarily farm animals, also reproduce reliably in captivity, but are not suitable as companions for other reasons that will soon be clear.

Further, for animals to become domesticated, they must survive on food found near or provided by humans. Modern technology facilitates the production of food that would sustain most animals in captivity, but slow maturation is another stumbling block for domestication. This criterion alone eliminates animals such as elephants, sweet though they may be, who are born eighteen to twenty-two months after conception and take an average of fifteen years to reach adult size. Cows, on the other hand, take only nine months to gestate and mature in about three years. Longer gestations usually produce stronger babies, able to hit the ground running, which is crucial to the survival of wild animals. Consider again the panda, who add to their fragility and lack of domestication-potential by being born blind, furless, about the size of a stick of butter, and helpless for weeks. Yes, much of this can be said about domestic kittens, but unlike pandas, the mother cat does not weigh more than 200 pounds and is unlikely to accidentally crush her babies, which significantly reduces infant survival rates.

A good temperament and no appetite for human flesh are obviously essential characteristics for domesticated animals. You cannot have a successful relationship with an animal who considers you a meal. Thus eliminating the apparent cuddliness of animals such as the grizzly bear and the lion. An outrageous illustration I admit, but one to help you appreciate that some animals might have otherwise been candidates for companionship were it not for the crucial, rigid elements of domestication. It is imperative for an animal to meet every criterion for domestication before being considered a companion. The criteria were likely established through unfortunate trial and error for all parties. For instance, who would not want a *pet* Bambi, but animals that panic or stress easily, especially when handled, cannot respond well to domestication, and deer can die from "capture myopathy" when handled or immobilized. Deer may seem bold because as their habitats diminish, they are forced into the open, revealing themselves to find food. Despite appearances, deer are timid, fragile creatures. Certain birds are also highly susceptible to capture myopathy.[5]

As popular as horses are as companion animals, it is ironic that some animals from their *Equus* line are completely unsuitable for domestication. Zebras, for example, are nearly impossible to train and become vicious and prone to bite as they age. Imagine how agriculture in areas native to zebras would have been enhanced if zebras' help could have been engaged?

Size is another important factor when considering domestication. Small animals are obviously more adaptable to domesticated life. Large animals, regardless of temperament, pose a constant threat to humans and they are hard to house and contain. Size alone would eliminate animals such as the gorilla, the polar bear, the moose, and—not to dwell on them, the panda. Any attempts at domestication of would have been tragic.

Finally, domestication is easier if the animal is accustomed to operating in a social group that features a strong leader, which is referred to as a dominance hierarchy. Then a human can insert himself or herself into the group, hopefully in the strongest position to ensure compliance.[6] Cats may represent one glaring, yet successful, exception to this last criterion. You see, some scientists insist that cats do not form dominance hierarchies and should not be considered social creatures as a consequence. Others argue that living in packs is not a requirement for a social hierarchy and maintain that cats form the necessary social connections with their mothers and littermates to qualify as social creatures. Still other scientists, offering a third perspective, insist that the debate is useless because dominance hierarchies are not required for social groups anyway. Regardless of your interpretation of this criterion, there is no denying that cats are domesticated.

In immediate contrast to domestication, the term "tame" can apply to just one animal within a species, not the entire species itself. Tame applies to a single animal, conditioned to live comfortably and without fear among humans.[7] A tamed animal typically does not, or learns not to, see humans as prey and will not attack them. Clearly, not all members of every domesticated species are tame. Consider feral cats or wild horses. Both come from domesticated species, but as individual creatures and distinct colonies, are not tame. Tamed animals can also revert to natural, fierce behavior, but incidents are usually isolated, and their causes are often never known, as is the case in the following example.

When magician Roy Horn's beloved 600-pound tiger, Montecore, seemed to attack him during a performance, many people thought the animal *snapped*. Both Horn and his partner, Siegfried Fischbacher, better known as "Siegfried and Roy," insist that Montecore was trying to protect a fallen Roy. It is hard to argue with the logic that if the majestic and powerful tiger had intended to kill Horn, he could have easily succeeded. However, whether Montecore attacked Horn or tried to protect him by lifting him as a mother tiger would a cub, the big cat apparently acted on instinct. Chris Rock, an irreverent comedian who is famous for his controversial perspectives may have a point in his analysis of Montecore during an HBO special when he said, "People say that tiger was acting crazy. He was just acting tiger."

Whatever the reason, the tiger's behavior was incompatible with human–animal interactions. When that happens—when instinct overcomes training—the animal is no longer considered tamed.

In some cases the behavior seems a momentary lapse of character, as was the case when Sonya Dailey's pit bull[8] of fourteen years fatally bit her grandson. The dog had no history of aggression, and the child often played near the dog. Even the sheriff on the scene said, "The dog was extremely docile, even when we arrived." Also out of character, the dog had been fighting with a small terrier when he attacked the boy.[9] Perhaps that fight was the impetus for the attack on the boy, but whatever the reason, the tamed dog reverted to instinct over training.

The tiger and the pit bull represent an undomesticated and a domesticated animal whose instincts suddenly ruled their actions, putting humans at grave risk. My intention with the example of the pit bull is not to further persecute this misunderstood and oft-maligned species. They are not necessarily more prone to reverting than are other types of dogs. Years ago, I may have thought so myself, but that was before I made the acquaintance of Ziggy, a doll baby of a pit bull, who was raised by a family with three young daughters and a host of extended family. Ziggy let his *sisters* paint his nails and put bows in his hair. He reminded me that animals, like people, are products of both heredity and environment. Even a Maltese could revert to wild behavior, albeit without severe consequences. However, any so-called tamed animal has that potential—some species more than others and some with greater consequences to humans than others.

When your well-fed cat brings a dead bird to your door, maybe that is an example of reverting to instinct. When your collie nips at your heels or herds you into the house, maybe that is reverting to instinct. Fortunately, these insignificant behaviors do not put you at risk.

It is logical to think that undomesticated, but tamed animals are more likely to revert to instinct over training than a domesticated animal. In spite of this possibility, some people prefer undomesticated—and even untamed animals—as companions. Typically, these are not the warm and fuzzy animals—unless you define a tarantula as fuzzy—and are usually considered exotics. Other arachnids and reptiles are the usual choices, followed by boa constrictors, geckos, turtles, iguanas, and pythons. You may think that those animals are undesirable companions. However, one man's phobia may be another man's *pet*.

In spite of the difficulty and the rigid criteria involved in domestication, throughout the ages people around the world have successfully domesticated—and tamed—a diverse collection of animals to keep as companions.

Dr. Serpell says that domestication is the result of biological and cultural processes woven together over successive generations in such a subtle manner that the genetic changes almost seem natural as the animals become less and less like their forbears in response to interactions with humans.[10] The evolution of the ancient wolf to the modern dog, the dog of the New World (*Canis familiaris*), was one of the smoothest transitions in history.

HISTORY OF COMPANION ANIMALS IN AMERICA

Dogs Rule

Any history of the bond between people and companion animals must begin with the dog, the first domesticated animal. Dogs are so commonplace that their history almost seems common knowledge, but we have much to learn about them and about ourselves in relation to them.[11] Fortunately, several scholarly, well-researched texts have been published specifically to explore the history of domestic dogs, and most popular press books on companion animals cover the history of dogs. This book would be incomplete without a survey of their history because the evolution of their domestication offers insight into how animals become companions.

Historians and scientists agree that dogs were domesticated approximately 15,000 years ago when prehistoric humans likely formed symbiotic relationships with them because dogs could run faster than humans and had keen noses and strong jaws to track and take down prey.

According to scientific nomenclature, dogs belong to the *Canidae* family or phylum. Members of this family, referred to as canids, include the fox, the jackal, and the coyote, in addition to the wolf and the dog. Canids are hunters and fast runners, who prefer giving birth in dens, and communicate with "facial expressions, body postures, tail-wagging, and vocalizations."[12]

When we use the term dog in a historical context, we are not referring to the animal of today. *Canis familiaris*, although part of the original phylum, is the product of millions of years of evolution resulting from natural selection and, in modern times, from imposed breeding standards. Even the "tamed wolves" of the Ice Age were countless generations apart from the earliest domesticated dogs.[13]

The origin of the dog has been a topic of scientific debate, but scientists confirmed recently that the wolf (Canis lupis) is the unequivocal ancestor of the dog.[14] The first wolves to develop from the miacid line were the Dire Wolf and the Gray Wolf. This was not a direct descendency because early canids predated even the wolf by thirty million years. The Dire Wolf (Canis dirus) evolved first and was larger and heavier, but not as fast a runner. They coexisted with the Gray Wolves, but succumbed to an extinction that mysteriously wiped out many mammals at the end of the Pleistocene era. Hence, the modern wolves and dogs hail from the Gray Wolf.[15] In fact, some studies suggest that just one or two wolves are the ancestors of all dogs.[16]

No matter the size of the dog, all are equal amounts of wolf. All dogs share 99 percent of the same DNA. It may be hard to believe, but a Maltese is just as much wolf as a Mastiff. Raymond Coppinger refers to dogs as "shape shifters" because of their amazing diversity. Indeed, dogs display a dizzying and, because of imprudent breeding, sometimes a dangerous array of sizes, shapes, and characteristics. Regardless, all dogs share a common origin. Therefore, no matter what they look like on the outside, all breeds share common characteristics.[17]

Theories about exactly how dogs and humans got together differ primarily in who took the first step. Some suggest that curious, clever wolves made the first contact, approaching settlements of people to forage for food. Then, the wolves that took to humans, stayed close and began to breed at the outskirts of the camps. Alternatively, some theories suggest that humans, particularly women, adopted cute orphaned wolf pups, which they reared and tamed.[18] Pups of tamed wolves were then easily incorporated into the human family unit. Whoever made the first bold step, dogs proved themselves to be good hunters and guardians, and humans proved they could provide food scraps and warm fires. A partnership was born.

Archaeologists have confirmed early relationships between humans and dogs by unearthing evidence of dogs living with man from carvings and paintings in tombs and ancient campsites. A small subspecies of wolf, once native to much of China and the Near East, was probably the ancestor of the first dog[19] and was a large canine that would have been very difficult to control.

All recorded history includes evidence of dogs: Artifacts indicating their early incorporation into "family life" have been found across all continents, in both civilized and "primitive" societies.[20]

What follows are just a few examples: Burial sites in Israel older than 12,000 years contain people buried close to their dogs.[21] Prehistoric Spanish caves show "doglike animals" hunting with humans, and dogs are shown in artifacts in ancient Greece. Homer mentioned dogs in the Odyssey, and Greek mythology incorporates a monstrous dog with three heads, Cerberus, who guarded Hades. Ancient Egyptians worshipped a god of death, Anubis, who had the head of a dog. Egyptians are said to have developed dog breeds by crossing them with foxes and jackals. So many dogs lived in ancient Rome that homes with watchdogs were required to post signs, "*Cave Canem*," translated "Beware the dog." Pottery from China's Han Dynasty included pictures of dogs, and toy dogs became very popular because they could fit in the sleeves of the elaborate silk attire worn primarily by the wealthy of that era.

Early dogs came to North America when nomadic hunter-gatherers migrated from Asia. However, DNA from ancient dog bones indicates that indigenous peoples of the Americas (i.e., American Indians) probably "independently domesticated" dogs. In fact, dogs were the "only domestic animals present in the majority of American Indian groups," who were "largely untouched by outside influences" before the "fateful voyage of Christopher Columbus."[22] Dogs were a significant part of the American Indian belief system and acted as guardians, hunters, and companions before European settlers appeared with their dogs, who primarily served the same purposes.

Regardless of how it began, dogs eventually warmed their way into our hearts and homes, perhaps because of their flexibility and desire to please. Throughout history preferences for companion animals has changed, but cats and dogs are the perennial favorites.

Cats Are Crowned

Cats have been loved, loathed, idolized, and vilified since they were discovered between 4,000 and 10,000 years ago, having originated from the same prehistoric *miacid* family tree that spawned the dog. Cats belong to the family *Felidae* (known as felids), and like dogs, belong to the order *Carnivora*.

Early ancestors of the domestic cat (*Felis catus*) include a number of wild and vicious hunters that became extinct along with their prey. Felidae has not changed much since appearing thirty million years ago because unlike dogs, cats have not been bred for particular tasks or for particular physical characteristics.

Domestic cats still have very much in common with wild cats. Both are solitary hunters that like to ambush their prey before grasping it with sharp claws and teeth. They move quietly with uncommon grace, like to hunt in the dark, have long tails and camouflaging markings on their fur, and possess keen hearing and sight. Researchers strive to determine how modern *Felidae* species are related to one another, using the latest techniques that go beyond the customary method of comparing morphology of the species.[23]

Most scholars have agreed that Egyptians domesticated the cat around 3950 B.P. (before the present), as evidenced by artifacts. This is logical because when you think of ancient Egypt, one of the first things that comes to mind after

Cleopatra is Egypt's signature product, grain. Ancient Egyptians consumed and stored large amounts of grain, which attracted rat colonies, which attracted cats. You can imagine that it did not take long for early Egyptians to see the wisdom of keeping cats around.

In fact, one of the reigning Pharaohs had so much grain that he pronounced that all cats were demigods, raising their status above that of humans. (Something people who live with cats suggest cats have never forgotten, contributing to cats' *bad press* for being aloof.) The Pharaoh imposed a death sentence on anyone who killed a cat, and when a cat died, one of the Pharaoh's priests had to confirm that the death was natural.

The Egyptians may have been the first to exalt and revere the cat, but they may not have been the first to domesticate the cat, according to an accidental and surprising discovery during an archaeological excavation in Cyprus, a Mediterranean island.

Here, French archaeologists shattered long held beliefs about the origin of cats when they unearthed the remains of a Neolithic cat in a grave of a Cyprus village, which was inhabited nine to thirteen thousand years *before* the Pharaohs.[24]

In Cyprus, no ancient embellished tombs exist to suggest how people felt about their cats, but the orientation and preservation of the cat's body and its proximity to the human's indicate the burial was intentional and purposeful—suggestive of a relationship. Remains of domesticated cats have been excavated from ancient settlements across the world, including Rome, Russia, France, China, and the Middle East. Sailors apparently helped cats migrate across the world by welcoming them onboard to kill stowaway mice.

Cats became popular symbols of health, good fortune, and longevity. Ancient gods and goddesses from various cultures bore feline characteristics or were protected by cats. For instance, Freya, a Norse goddess, was shown on a chariot pulled by cats. Bastet, an Egyptian goddess, was shown with the head of a cat and the body of a woman.

Ironically, cats' association with religion ultimately led to their persecution and torture. Admonitions about false gods were part of the early and expanding doctrine of Christianity, and cats, having been worshipped, were regarded as a manifestation of evil. Cats were also declared disciples of the devil because of their close association with the Pagan religion. The cat population in the United States and abroad was drastically reduced as many cats were killed, often burned at the stake with their human companions. By 1400, cats were almost extinct, contributing to wider spread of the plague, which was originally and inappropriately blamed on cats and dogs. Cats were redeemed when rats were revealed as the real vector of the plague.

Mystique and mystery still surround cats. People prone to superstition believe that a black cat is bad luck, and the ill-informed maintain that a cat can suck the breathe from an infant. Because cats appear to some people to endure rather than welcome human companionship, they are accused of remaining wild and aloof, but science is revealing that some of the misconceptions about cat behavior are the result of ancient and urban legend. Cats may remain an enigma, but they reign as the most populous companion. As you read earlier, cats outnumber dogs, 88.3 million to 74.8 million.

Cats have not changed much through the ages and the basic relationship people have with them has also remained constant, according to Jay Bisno, retired archaeologist of the Los Angeles County Museum of Natural History: "You sit with a cat on your lap, and maybe sometimes he takes a swipe at you and maybe he doesn't. But he's cuddly and friendly and attractive, and I think it was pretty much exactly the same thing in ancient times. For the average person, it was just 'nice cat.'"[25]

Horses Place a Hoof on History

Cats and dogs may be crowned the most popular animals to enter human's lives, but there is no denying that the horse was the most influential animal, not just in America, but throughout the world. Man's relationship with the horse dates back 50,000 years, with their domestication beginning in Asia approximately 6,000 years ago. As is the case with most companion animals, the first relationships were skewed to the benefit of humans. The horse was first a source of food. Not an easily obtained source, for sure, which explains the bones of approximately 10,000 horses uncovered below a cliff at a French archaeological site, where the horses are theorized to have been chased by Cro-Magnons.

Concurrently serving as food, horses became pack and draft animals before becoming modes of transportation. Archaeological research suggests that horses were first ridden as early as 4000 B.C., based on excavations of horse teeth that show possible signs of bit wear. The horse transformed the history of mankind, and their power and elegance have affected everything from casual transportation to war. Even today, engine performance in everything from cars to lawn mowers is expressed in horsepower. It is hard to imagine what humans would have become without the horse.

Horses were ubiquitous in the American landscape until cars became accessible around 1910, but actually owning a horse was a luxury most could not afford. The sound of horse's hooves was the backdrop of early American history, but unbelievably many people were not familiar with horses and had no idea what it took to keep one. Yet, when suburban sprawl began near the end of the nineteenth century, people who had not been able to afford a horse in the city could do so in the outlying areas, and a "suburban equine appeared."[26] This phenomenon coincided with the surge in popularity of keeping companion animals, and the horse as worker transformed into horse as family friend and companion. Actually, a backlash against horses emerged in the city when cars were introduced as a more economical way to travel.

When you consider what the horses have contributed to us, we have treated them egregiously. In fact, inhumane treatment of horses sparked some of the most visceral animal protection activism in America, and horses remain in a precarious position today. Because of their general status as companions, horses have been spared some of the horrors of factory farming. In spite of "glue factories" becoming things of the past, three horse slaughterhouses still exist in America. Although eating horsemeat is taboo in America, making money by selling the meat to other countries is not. Adding insult to injury, most horses are relegated now to entertainment or competitive sport, both with inherent dangers, as evidenced by the death of Barbaro, the famous 2006 Kentucky Derby winner, whose leg was shattered during the Preakness that same year. Some experts in equine development say that racehorses are too young and have insufficient bone development to take the pressure and great speeds that racing demands. Our current efforts to protect wild and domesticated horses in this country have produced mixed results.

One by One, Some of the Rest

I am confident that a child somewhere in the world has tried to make a *pet* out of almost every little animal he or she could carry or entice home. My acquisitions began one summer, when I conned my grandfather into buying me a duckling from a "feed store" in North Carolina. I stowed the duckling in a shoebox punched with tiny holes for air for the trip back to Washington, DC. I delighted in nudging the box from time to time to make the duckling peep. After living long enough for his yellow down to transform into white feathers, my charge was attacked and killed by an unrestrained dog. Later, I kept a chick from an ill-advised seventh-grade science project; he turned into a crowing rooster for whom my parents had to find a home outside the city. I am not proud of these accounts, but they speak to a child's inherent desire for animal family. Unfortunately, history supports my experience—animals inappropriately made into *pets* meet tragic ends.

Preferences for companion animal candidates have changed throughout history. Cats and dogs have remained the perennial favorites, but in early America, animals such as chickens, pigeons, and rabbits were raised purely as "pet stock." These "fancy" animals were bred and collected as ornamentals or hobbies, but could become food sources.[27] However, research indicates that most animals who became companions were domesticated purely for the "social and emotional rewards," and used only for food because of shortages.

Birds indigenous to North and Central America had an early appeal. In fact, Christopher Columbus reportedly gave Queen Isabella of Spain two parrots when he returned from Cuba, and he dubbed them "Amazon" parrots.

Colonists emigrated with songbirds as companions, and soon birds became popular companions in America. Canaries were among the first birds, arriving in the 1820s, and they quickly became the most popular bird companions. Later, bird dealers imported various species from other countries, including the parakeet from South America.

Canaries, parakeets, and parrots remain the most popular companion birds. Humans find that parrots are amazing companions because of their longevity (40–100 years), their ability to "talk," and their unwavering loyalty. You will read more about modern birds as enduring family members in later chapters.

By the 1860s, small mammals, such as mice, rats, squirrels, and guinea pigs had become popular pets for children because they were "gentle, easy to care for and short-lived."[28] Hamsters and gerbils, arriving in America first as laboratory animals, were not introduced until the mid-1900s. In 1930, a zoologist from Jerusalem discovered a small family of hamsters in the Syrian Desert. Three survived for the trip to his laboratory and most of today's hamsters are descendants of that tiny family.

Since at least 1870, companion animals have had a stronghold on American society and the population of companion animals was similar to what we see today, with the exception of fish—and robotic pets. Tropical fish became popular in the 1900s, when they were first sold in pet stores and collected by the wealthy. Electric heaters and pumps were invented around this time in response to the fishes' need for warm water and oxygen. Goldfish were first bred in Asia, arriving in America in the early 1800s, but were prohibitively expensive until the early 1900s, when they became common enough to sell in dime stores.[29]

Virtual animals and robotic dogs and cats are a logical product of the technology revolution and its cultural influences. A bit more like toys or tools than a *pet*, I doubt that robotic companions will become as omnipresent as Ipods. In spite of their appearance, niches may exist that only they can fill. For example, studies show that the elderly—who will comprise 80 million people by the year 2050 according to Census Bureau projections—benefit from interacting with animals, but many elders live in conditions not conducive to caring for a live animal. If Drs. Alex and Elena Libin have anything to do with it, a robo-cat such as NeCoRo—nicknamed Max—will be available and perfectly suited to "purr and whirr" his way into their hearts. The Libins are "robotherapists," psychologists whose research focuses on a new field: robotic psychology, which examines human-robot interactions.[30]

Robotic companions have come a long way since the early designs that looked like a collection of paper cups and moved with the dexterity of C3PO, who is famous to *Star Wars* fans.

Many robotic animals are still prototypes, unavailable to the public, but they are becoming more realistic. For example, a life-size miniature horse that responds to touch is on the horizon.

Animals with more sophisticated responses and physicality that mimic the animals they represent are backed by artificial intelligence and built-in sensors. These warm and fuzzy machines may become successful companions for specific populations, including the elderly and children with allergies or uncompromising

NeCoRo, nickname Max, is a robotic cat (robo-cat), the creation of psychologists Alex and Elena Libin, Max has visual, auditory and movement-sensitive sensors and weighs less than four pounds. The robot stretches, paws, moves its tail, opens and closes its eyes, meows, and cuddles when touched. Photo courtesy of Drs. Elena and Alexander Libin.

parents, but I doubt they will ever replace live animals. At least not in this lifetime.

However, the Libins and others are actively involved in research that so far suggests that the health benefits associated with live animals just might apply to Max and the rest of his *species*.[31]

NOTABLE COMPANION ANIMALS

Although we all feel that our companion animal is remarkable, popular and famous companion animals perform a great public service. Importantly, they can demonstrate to a wide audience how animals should be treated and the rewards of living with an animal, particularly if their guardians model responsible animal *and* human behavior. Otherwise, the humans can serve as examples of what not to do. Recently, some celebrities have been caught and publicized for bad behavior with regard to their companion animals, such as using the animals as toys or accessories and not making a commitment to the animal's welfare. These can become teachable moments where savvy animal organizations involved in humane education take advantage of the publicity to promote proper animal care.

Fame wields mighty influence. Consider what Lassie did for dogs. In her (actually his) many incarnations, Lassie showed the world how clever dogs could be and was an American hero for seventeen years. The revelation that one of the dogs who portrayed Lassie knew between 150 and 250 commands proved to a general audience how capable and intelligent dogs are.

Just based on sheer numbers, the most famous companion animals are usually dogs and cats, but others have garnered our attention. Arnold has to be the most famous pig, and his fame grew through a television show, *Green Acres*, on which he enlightened us to the true nature of pigs. Lassie and Rin Tin Tin are the two most famous dogs, and Trigger, Roy Rogers' popular horse, had such spectacular skills that even Lassie sometimes seemed a bit dim by comparison. No one really thought about the horse beneath the cowboy before Trigger rode in, via our television screens.

Many famous companion animals make significant contributions to history. You may have read about Laikia, a dog who was the first astronaut, sent into space by what was the Russian government in 1957.

Companion animals also have helped shape the public images of some of the most powerful men and women in government. For example, almost every presidential administration has included companion animals and more than 400 animals have lived in the White House over the years. In fact, once or twice, companion animals have been credited with helping win presidential elections. Eleanor Roosevelt believed that her husband secured his fourth term when he mentioned Fala, a Scottish terrier, in a critical campaign speech to the teamsters. Fala is said to have received so much fan mail that he required a secretary and was probably the most involved companion to live in the White House. He accompanied President Franklin Roosevelt on many official trips and was once rescued by a Navy destroyer when he was left behind. President Roosevelt is memorialized in statuary with Fala at his side in Washington, DC, testament to their enduring bond. No other dog is so honored.

People have visceral responses to the way politicians treat their companion animals, and the declining popularity of President Lyndon B. Johnson took a mortal blow when he was lambasted in the press for picking up his beagles by their ears to make them howl for a White House photographer.

The administration of President John F. Kennedy may have had the most diverse population of animal companions, including ponies, a rabbit, cats, dogs, birds, a hamster, and a horse. The most famous of the Kennedy animal clan would be Pushinka, who was given to young Carolina Kennedy by Soviet premier Nikita Khrushchev.

Whether on the grand stage of international politics, a small television screen, or the printed page, famous—and infamous—companion animals often open our eyes to the world of possibilities when we entwine our lives with theirs.

COMPANION ANIMALS IN OTHER COUNTRIES

The fact that no place on earth is free of pain and suffering for either people or animals is a sad commentary on humanity. If the *people* are suffering in a locale, you can be sure the animals are suffering exponentially. Yet, rich countries are not necessarily more fair and humane to its inhabitants. Wealth does not equate to humanity.

Countries, including our own, comprise people with distinct social differences based on their personal experiences, religious practices, and social customs. Even within families, people have an array of attitudes, beliefs, and behaviors related to animals.

The lifestyle that most American companion animals enjoy, especially dogs, is not as privileged or pervasive in most other countries—developed or undeveloped. Most of this book examines the widespread heralded position of companion animals in America. However in many other countries, animals struggle just to be considered *pets* rather than food or trash.

How animals are treated reflects a nation, and I firmly believe that "So long as we harm animals, we are savages."[32]

What follows are *examples* of how animals are treated or have been treated in selected parts of the world—just a sampling of problems and possibilities for companion animals where they live.

England

Companion animals in England now live in a world resembling that of their American cousins, but that has not always been the case. I mention this because England has such an infamous animal history (including cruelty to horses and dogfights) that the animal welfare movement was born there.

As part of the United Kingdom, which belongs to the European Union (EU), England has certainly redeemed itself. The EU, a political collective of fifteen countries,[33] establishes common practices and policies for member countries. It developed a "European Convention for the Protection of Pet Animals," which mandates humane treatment and proper care of "pets."[34] The Convention recognizes that companion animals have a certain status and encourages humans to provide them proper and responsible care.

The Convention evinces that U.K. denizens have high regard for their companion animals. Support for legislation to protect companion animals is not surprising when you consider that almost every other household in the United Kingdom has companion animals (52.7 percent), according to a 2003 report from the London-based Pet Food Manufacturer's Association. Homes with cats (6 million) outnumber those for dogs (5.12 million), housing 9.2 million cats, compared to 6.8 million dogs. Four million fish, 2.5 million rodents, and 1.37 million birds round off the pet population.[35] Twice as many dogs live in the United Kingdom as preschool children.[36]

Italy

Some countries in the EU legislate provisions for companion animals that exceed those required by the Convention, thereby promoting even better treatment for companion animals. For instance, in November 2005, Rome's Office of Animal Rights gained approval from its citizens for an historic and precedent-setting 59-point statute to protect all companion animals. Citizens now face severe fines of up to 500 euros ($685 US dollars) if the dogs they live with are not walked daily, and choke and electrical collars are prohibited. Pet stores are forbidden to display pets. Declawing cats and docking the tails and ears of dogs is a crime.

Goldfish must be housed in aquariums, not bowls, and they cannot be used as prizes. Italy had a pre-EU national law against the abandonment of companion animals. However, this does not prevent Italians from dumping 150,000 dogs and 200,000 cats, annually; curious behavior considering that the shelters have stopped euthanizing animals."[37] You cannot legislate or enforce compassion, but the fact that these laws exist indicates how the populace regards its animals.

Greece

Enforcement of established laws is always the second major obstacle to protecting animals. Treatment boils down to human behavior, which is why appalling conditions for companion animals, especially dogs, seem to prevail in Greece. Before the 2006 Olympics, massive numbers of animals were poisoned to "clean" the street and the government has refused to enact laws to prevent cruel treatment.

China

China has no national animal welfare law. Protection exists only for endangered wildlife species, but it does not go very far because the law does not apply to captured wildlife.

Many national and local animal advocacy groups around the world have pressured China to pass and enforce laws to protect animals, especially dogs and cats. Yet, China has become notorious for skinning dogs and cats, sometimes while alive, to produce products from or adorned with fur. German undercover investigative journalist, Manfred Karreman, who worked on an eighteen-month investigation, described the conditions for China's dogs and cats as, "worse than a concentration camp." Estimates indicate that at least 5,400 cats and dogs die horrible deaths in China each day.[38]

Japan

Japan has not been known for its animal lovers, but that is changing as more women seem unwilling to have children and are looking to companion animals for comfort and companionship. In spite of cramped housing and few parks, 10.4 million dogs and 8.5 million cats live in the country, according to the Japan Pet Food Association. The population of dogs is growing at the rate of 2.4 percent a year, while the fertility rate for humans is declining at a rate that jeopardizes Japan's ability to maintain its human population. Fertility has fallen to an all-time low of 1.28 percent, far below the 2.1 percent needed to maintain the human population of 127 million. At this rate, the Japanese human population will fall to 100 million by 2050.[39]

Thanks to commercial television, Chihuahuas are the most popular dogs in Japan. The petite pooches are obviously perfect for Japan's heavily populated cities, and demand for them exceeds supply. The small dogs are worth thousands of dollars and are becoming hot property for thieves who find them easier to fence than jewels.[40]

An industry has accompanied the growth of companion animals in Japan where people pamper companion animals with pricey gifts and outrageous services such as "Catwan," used to send photos of excrement via email to assure vacationers that their cat is remaining "regular."[41]

South Korea

Dogs do not fare well in South Korea, where their consumption has a "long history" and is "strongly linked to national identity." Consequently, criticisms about the practice from the West are viewed as an attack on their culture. Eating cats is a more a recent phenomena. Bewilderingly, "pet ownership is [also] a recent phenomenon and growing." Recent figures indicate that two million "pets" live in South Korea.[42] I am told that two distinct types of dogs live in South Korea—those kept as pets (usually small, pure breeds such as Maltese and Shih Tzu) and those raised for food (mid-sized, yellow-furred dogs raised on farms in rural areas). I was relieved to learn that the South Koreans reportedly do not eat dogs they consider "pets."[43] In 1991, Korea passed the Animal Protection Law, prohibiting human consumption of dogs and cats and considering them "domestic pets," but no penalty exists for violating the law. International humane organizations report that many cats and dogs suffer cruel deaths. Companion and stray cats are put in sacks, pounded against the ground, and then boiled—sometimes while still alive. Their liquefied remains are then sold as a cure for rheumatism. Two million dogs are slaughtered each year, according to the Animal Welfare Institute's Web site. Dogs slaughtered for consumption are transported to the markets in tiny cages, then electrocuted, strangled, or beaten to death. An estimated 6,484 stores in Korea participate in the dog meat trade.[44]

Foreign Aid

Many local and national American organizations allocate resources to improve the lives of all animals in other countries, and most have specific projects for companion animals.

A perfect example is The Humane Society of the United States, arguably the most powerful animal protection organization, which founded an international division, Humane Society International (HSI), in 1991. According to its website, HSI addresses inhumane practices and egregious cruelty around the world in a manner sensitive to the local cultures and jurisdictions. One of its many projects has been to stop the abuse and abandonment of Spanish Galgos, a dog native to Spain and similar to greyhounds. HSI has remained at the forefront of efforts to ban cat and dog fur in Europe.

The International Fund for Animal Welfare (IFAW) also works across the globe to prevent cruelty to companion animals, often using Community Led Animal Welfare (CLAW) projects. CLAW relies on the community to participate directly in programs, thereby fostering ownership of problems and promoting success. IFAW utilizes its network of fifteen international offices and many experts to create new laws and animal education programs, which aid and rescue countless dogs, cats, and other animal companions each year. CLAW has improved life for companion animals in South Africa, the Caribbean island of Dominica, Turkey, and indigenous parts of Canada. In a separate program, IFAW teamed with the North Shore Animal League America in 2005 to rescue thirty dogs from a Chinese shelter for adoption in the United States. IFAW is also a force behind the International Companion Animal Welfare Conferences, which have been held in various sites around the world, including Budapest, Istanbul, Prague, and Warsaw.

When these organizations and others draw attention to the plight of companion animals beyond our shores, they demonstrate an understanding that the future of humanity depends on the survival of all its part.

2

Genesis and Nature of the Bond

Everything ideal has a natural basis, and everything natural has an ideal development.

—George Santayana (1863–1952), philosopher

THE BOND IS BORN

The phrase human-animal bond (HAB), introduced in the late 1970s, refers to the relationships resulting from human-animal interactions.[1] As interest in the relationships grew, a new field emerged, and leaders in veterinary medicine and academic researchers were primarily responsible for scientific investigations of the bond. The Delta Society, whose mission is to "improve human health through service and therapy animals," is attributed with recognizing the need for widespread research. Historically, HAB research was funded by pet food manufacturers, but as the field advanced and public interest intensified, funding from foundations and federal agencies became available. Prior to publication of Serpell's *In the Company of Animals* in 1986, literature related to human-animal relationships was nonetheless scarce. Serpell says that most "psychologists and social scientists restricted themselves to the human domain." He also suggested that the early "taboo" associated with seriously considering companion animals impeded scientific investigation.[2] By the time he released the 1996 edition of his book, the stars had aligned, and established scientific disciplines had become aware of the neglected, uncharted potential of the human-animal bond.

Social scientists have been in the forefront of scientific interest in the human-animal bond, revealing important information about the health benefits for humans of living with companion animals. The American Sociological Association (ASA), the national member-driven organization for sociologists, created a special section "Animals and Society," with the stated purpose "to encourage and support the development of theory, research, and teaching about the complex relationships that exist between humans and other animals."[3]

The American Psychological Association (APA)—a professional membership organization similar to ASA, but for psychologists, rather than sociologists—does not have a special division on human-animal interactions. Nonetheless, in 1981, it was psychologists who formed the first and most visible professional organization dedicated to observing and improving the treatment of nonhuman animals: PSYETA (Psychologists for the Ethical Treatment of Animals). PSYETA, which was renamed Society & Animals Forum in 2004, is responsible for the vanguard research publication, *Society and Animals Journal of Human-Animal Studies*, which is available through ASA membership and is a welcomed source of information.

In 2005, the Society and Animals Forum merged with another respected organization, the Institute for Animals and Society, to form The Animals and Society Institute: a nonprofit, independent research and educational organization that advances the status of animals in public policy, and promotes the study of human-animal relationships.[4]

Research on connections, interactions, relationships, and bonds with animals is known as anthrozoology. The etymology or origin of the word is from two Greek words: *anthropos*, which means human and *zoion*, which means animal. Many fields of research, crossing many scientific boundaries and a broad range of scientific disciplines comprise anthropology. In addition to the psychologists and sociologists mentioned previously, the field includes research by political scientists, physicians, and veterinarians, for example. All of the research referenced in this book was done under the auspices of anthrozoology.

Anthrozoological research has a long and distinguished history, and furtherance of this important research is vital to our survival and development as human beings. Fortunately, anthrozoological institutes and centers are being maintained and new ones established in academic and private organizations around the world.

Anthrozoology researchers have a professional organization, International Society for Anthrozoology (ISAZ), which was formed in 1991 and publishes a prestigious quarterly, peer-reviewed journal titled *Anthrozoos*.[5] ISAZ supports and convenes members from around the world from diverse disciplines who are eager to explore the unique bond between humans and companion animals.

Use of the word *bond*, when referring to human-animal relationships is attributed to Dr. Konrad Lorenz, corecipient of the 1973 Nobel Prize for Physiology or Medicine for discoveries related to individual and social behavior patterns.

In his autobiography, written for the Nobel Foundation, Lorenz confesses that as a child growing up in Austria, he had what he describes as "an inordinate love for animals." Even as a child, he was an expert on animal behavior, becoming fixated on waterfowl. He admits that he "yearned to become a wild goose and, on realizing that this was impossible, I desperately wanted to have one and, when this also proved impossible, I settled for having domestic ducks." An early love of animals is a common trait of adults who share their homes with animals. Most of us can recall an early memory, an early animal that we loved. Exhibiting the keen observation skills of a budding scientist, young Lorenz first recognized imprinting—when a young animal learns to recognize another person or animal as trustworthy—when he was given a day-old duckling by a neighbor. Lorenz was thrilled when the duckling began following him around, having transferred its inherent following response to him.[6]

Demonstrating great personal and scientific insight, prophesying what subsequent scientists would confirm, Lorenz is quoted as saying, "The wish to keep an animal usually arises from a general longing for a bond with nature.... This bond is analogous with those human functions that go hand in hand with the emotions of love and friendship in the purest and noblest forms."[7]

In her seminal treatise, *If You Tame Me*, Dr. Leslie Irvine reviews various theories about why we form such strong relationships with animals. The first theory she refers to is the "deficiency argument," which indicates that relationships with companion animals exist because people lack the ability to enjoy human companionship. She exposes two flaws in this argument. First, studies do not support that people who favor animals have social-interaction deficiencies. Second, she points out that if people were simply using animals as human substitutes, then companion animals would live with single people more often than not, and that is not the case. Further, studies suggest that our relationships with companion animals actually enhance our relationships with people.

She discusses another theory that "equates animal companionship with economic prosperity." We need look no further than New Orleans in the aftermath of Hurricane Katrina to prove that affluence has nothing to do with the love of a companion animal. Moreover, the affluent are not automatically the best animal caretakers. If that were true, animal shelters would be void of expensive purebred dog and cats. As you might expect, people at lower socioeconomic levels are not guaranteed to neglect proper care.[8]

The final theory she presented, *Biophilia*, offers the most accepted explanation of why we want animals as companions and form such strong bonds with them. Famed biologist Edward O. Wilson developed this theory and published a book by the same name in 1984. *Biophilia* maintains that people have an "innate tendency to focus on life and life-like processes." A bold concept, *Biophilia* posits that we are "biologically based" for animal interactions as a part of our "evolutionary heritage." Basically, we are hardwired to desire kinship with animals. The *Biophilia* hypothesis includes all natural elements, but focuses strongly our "need" to incorporate animals into our social environments.[9]

People are undisputedly attracted to nature. We strive for homes in or overlooking natural environments; we decorate our homes with photographs of nature; and we enjoy watching animals more than we enjoy watching sports, according to Irvine. Children—humans in the purest, most unsullied form—absolutely adore animals and develop natural friendships with them. Irvine explains that children "pretend to be animals; they talk to animals; and animal characters populate their toys and cartoons."[10]

As Irvine points out, it is difficult to believe that we are biologically programmed with directives to care for nature, including animals, when you consider our tendency to damage and overuse it. Still, this is my preferred explanation, and the one I believe can save us—plant and animal alike—if we will simply heed the call. If we return to what may be our prime directive, we will certainly improve the lives of countless animals and perhaps realize the benefits that nature intended to impart.

Daily evidence suggests that our DNA is coded to appreciate animals. Many of us would move to jungles or forests in an attempt to live near animals, if we could do so without incurring harm. We are envious of people with the means to live on large expanses of land devoted to animals and their natural habitats. We create parks, preserves, and zoos to confine animals for viewing and interaction. We endanger ourselves and our children to interact with wild animals, getting out of cars in National Parks to commune with nature. Visitations at many National Parks have increased so greatly that the grounds are damaged or threatened to the extent that temporary closings may be required. We never lose our desire for nature, and find ways to bring nature into our homes as much as possible, often by cohabitating cats and dogs—the animals to whom we most often bond.

PSYCHOLOGY EXPLAINS THE ATTRACTION

Clearly, companion animals are important to us, but why? What needs do they satisfy? Psychological research offers the best explanation because it reveals insights into the human mind and behavior—why we think and act the way we do.

I have selected one psychological school of thought—self psychology[11]— which provides compelling evidence to support a solid theory about the importance of the human-companion animal bond.

Self psychology has a psychoanalytic basis and was spawned from traditional Freudianism, but excludes Freud's emphasis on sexual drives to explain behavioral development. This is not a new approach. In fact, the benefits of modern psychoanalysis are attributed to the principles behind self psychology because it recognizes that relationships and their associated experiences are the keys to healthy self-development. Self psychology posits that if three important needs are not met, especially during critical early growth and development, problems will develop. Experiences, people, animals, ideas, and other objects can meet the required needs and are referred to as "self objects" serving "self object functions." The needs themselves are divided into three categories: Mirroring Needs, Idealizing Needs, and Alterego Needs. A complete discussion of self psychology is beyond the scope of this book and unnecessary for you to understand how the categories apply to the human-animal bond. Suffice it to say that when Mirroring Needs are satisfied you feel understood and appreciated. When Idealizing Needs are satisfied, you feel emotionally stable and attached. When Alterego Needs are satisfied, you are able to identify with other beings, especially those you identify as being like you. It makes sense that companion animals can satisfy these needs, as evidenced by the following simple examples. Consider a young child alone in her room with only her dog for company: She reads stories and poems that she has created to the dog, who is an attentive audience. She asks the dog if he likes them, and the dog enthusiastically wags his tail and licks the little girl's face. The little girl receives what she perceives as appreciation for her creativity. The dog's reaction mirrors what the girl saw in herself: an interesting, worthwhile, expressive little person. Using this model, you can probably think of countless other scenarios where an animal's reaction can be interpreted in ways that fills the Mirroring Need.

What the dog is really feeling is not as important as how his behavior is perceived. The subjective, psychological reality—the inner experience—is more important than the external realities of the situation in this case. For instance, is your dog really *that* happy to see you when you come home? Doesn't matter. The dog's reception makes you feel good about yourself and that satisfies a psychological need.

Companion animals provide opportunities for us to feel proud and worthwhile, which satisfies Idealizing Needs. Consider people who devote a lot of time, energy, and money breeding and showing dogs. When the dogs win competitions, the reflected glory satisfies this need. Finally, the Alterego Need is easily satisfied when an animal mimics your behavior. I find that dogs are good at mimicking stretches and bows. Other yoga enthusiasts will recognize that their dogs execute two popular asanas: downward and upward facing dog. Most companion dogs will bow in the play position if you get down on your hands and knees in front of them; it appears as if they are mimicking your behavior.

Although the behavior of companion animals can fulfill the needs as established by the psychoanalytic theory of self psychology, their actions are not expected to instigate structural changes that result when you interact with other people or with trained psychotherapists. However, companion animals can help "restore the self and maintain it." A simple example: daily interaction with your dog can bring out a playfulness that can sustain happiness.

Self psychology tells us that having the three basic needs satisfied is important across the lifespan. Dogs can act as the "self object"—something or someone who responds to these needs, and self objects are "oxygen" for the psyche.

When self-psychology is applied to the human-companion animal bond, it provides great insight into why the relationships are of such great value. It offers one explanation as to what our companion animals mean to us and why we treat them the way we do: The animals mirror the joy and love we want to see in the world; they become an integral part of our being and help us present ourselves to the world.

WHY CATS AND DOGS?

Cosmic Destiny Set It Off

Dr. James Serpell, the preeminent researcher mentioned earlier, says that the popularity of dogs and cats is partially attributed to their being in the "right place at the right time," an "accident of history."[12] He maintains that dogs and cats just happened to be in proximity to humans when humans realized that animals could contribute to human survival and prosperity.

Perhaps the reasons cats and dogs initially teamed with humans *are not* profound. Perhaps it was nothing more than evolutionary kismet. Regardless, the reasons the relationships endured and have become so powerful exceed happenstance, and that is what I want to examine here.

You read that cats and dogs excel as companions because they excelled at being tamed, domesticated, and trained. Serpell explains that dogs and cats possess other characteristics, inherited from their wolf or wildcat predecessors, which also make them prime companions for humans. Foremost, they are territorial and clean— they like to stay close to home and are reluctant to soil the area where they sleep. Importantly, dogs and cats also share our circadian rhythm and are most active during the day. If we are going to be companions, it helps if we are awake at the same time. Admittedly, cats are more nocturnal, but not sufficiently so to prohibit humans from adjusting.

After cleverly questioning our affection for "two medium-sized carnivores,"[13] Serpell admitted that the size of cats and dogs contributes to their appeal. Being small and able to subsist on meager handouts was a boon for prehistoric canines and felines. More to the point, their manageable size is critical because they are carnivores after all, and we are *carni*. For the most part, dogs and cats are not large enough to pose a threat, and their size makes them perfect objects of affection. Regardless, given their predatory nature, one theory holds that humans should maintain the dominant role, even with miniatures.

Dogs, and cats, too, but lesser so, have a biological proclivity to respect a pack leader. Therefore, they are inclined to yield power to a higher-ranking human, which also contributes to their success as companions. According to that theory, if humans do not establish themselves as the leader, behavior problems can manifest, which could make everyone unhappy and often result in abandoned animals.

Social Dynamics Sweeten the Pot

Dogs and cats have behaviors that invite social interaction, which suits the human need for social contact. Dogs go out of their way to let us know they want to be near us, and what person does not enjoy being wanted? They are highly social and companionable creatures who have no problem joining the social packs that humans form called families. They assertively seek physical contact with people. Anyone who has been around a dog is familiar with the strategically placed paw or head on the lap, the nudge to the leg, or the undeniable muzzle-under-the-palm maneuver to get attention and make you feel pretty special. Cats, too, will rub their faces, heads, or their torso against your leg to make their desire for contact known. Once in your lap, they may give you a gentle, prickly kneading, which indicates the cat is content.

Humans delight in these demonstrations and interpret them as requests for social contact. Perhaps they have evolved into social signals, but it should be no surprise that most of these behaviors originally had more practical functions. For instance, dogs often jump, twirl, and wag their entire bodies when their people return from extended absences. (The definition of "extended" being solely in the eye of the beholder.) The "Boy, did I miss YOU!" behaviors are observed in wolf pups, who, when being weaned are taught to "solicit the regurgitation of solid food from parents and other pack members" by jumping up and licking their faces, while performing ritualistic movements similar to the performance you get when you return home. So you think your dog is trying to *kiss* you, but he or she is initially reverting to type and begging for food. However, dogs have learned that you like the *kisses*, and dogs like to please. They have an innate desire to cooperate with humans that was enhanced by selective breeding during domestication. They are rewarded by your pleasure and are happy to give *kisses*, upon request or spontaneously. Face-to-face greetings are not natural for either canines or felines, so this is an example of something they have learned to do just for us.

As an example of another behavior that has been translated into something that suits humans, dogs and cats have learned that if they roll on their backs they can engage us socially. This is the ultimate submissive behavior for dogs, and we interpret it as an invitation for a belly rub. However, wolf and dog pups do this for their mothers to clean their urogenital areas. Of course, the dog is not expecting that from you. Again, this behavior has become translated for the dog. The dog turns over; you rub the belly. Now, that is what the dog expects.

When cats rub your leg they may be doing it only for themselves, activating glands around their head to get a pleasurable sensation. Kneading is a kitten's way of stimulating the flow of milk while nursing. The blissful expression on their faces tells you that the behavior is *not for you*, but cats have learned that it provides a social connection. Similarly, cats are rewarded for purring, which originated as a suckling behavior.

We share a natural proclivity with cats and dogs that greatly enhances our interactions and needs no translation: we love to play. Most mammals play as juveniles, but humans and dogs and cats are among the very few who continue to play as adults. Better yet, we all love to play with balls and like the same kinds of games, particularly those that involve chasing and "keep-away."

Essentially, cats and dogs are genetically predisposed to exhibit certain behaviors that communicate and promote physical contact with us. We have given the behaviors meaning, and we interpret and respond to them in ways that reinforce the social connection between us.

Overall, dogs—and perhaps cats—apparently acquire these abilities not through acculturation, but through evolution, as suggested by the fact that puppies as young as nine-weeks-old can perform similarly with aplomb and near perfection.

Beyond Words

Being able to hang out and play games is certainly good, but the kind of social connections that precede relationships are forged and sustained by the ability to transmit and receive information, especially thoughts, feelings, and ideas. Dogs communicate primarily with sight, sound, and smell. Humans communicate with sound, sight, and touch. Somewhere along the evolutionary trail, humans began to depend heavily on body language and cues: 93 percent by some calculations. Research has widely validated the importance of nonverbal communication, which suits our interactions with dogs perfectly because they have an almost uncanny ability to read human cues and gestures. Humans speak volumes without uttering a sound, and dogs hear every word.

"All dogs are brilliant at perceiving the slightest movement that we make," says Patricia B. McConnell, Ph.D., a renowned applied animal behaviorist, dog breeder, trainer, and author.[14] Dogs pick up on our cues and gestures quickly, to say the least.

Some say that cats, observant predators that they are, could do just as well, but are not inclined. Most of the published literature on cats and body language focuses on *our* learning to read *their* body language, which brings to mind a saying that is bandied about on the Internet, "Dogs see people as family. Cats see people as staff." Yet, more than a lack of interest may be at work. Remember that cats did not join households as early as dogs. Consequently, they may have missed out on an important evolutionary process that facilitates understanding human gestures and cues.

Research suggests that dogs may have developed the ability to read human social and communication cues through a process known as convergent evolution. When two distantly related species share a similar trait or ability, it is possible that the similarity resulted from a proximal evolutionary process. One hypothesis is that dogs' enhanced social skills "represent a case of convergent evolution with humans." This may account for the fact that dogs read our communication cues as well as infants and better than our closest biological ancestor. We share 96 percent of our DNA with chimpanzees, so you would expect them to excel at cue-driven tasks, such as finding food hidden under a container that is pointed out by a human. After about fourteen months of age, human infants find this type of task a breeze. However, chimpanzees are stumped. Dogs are so good at this that they can find the hidden object even if the tester walks toward a dummy container, but points to the correct one. Dogs are able to find an object without a "test run," which suggests they already knew how to interpret the cues.[15]

Dogs also perform better in food-finding tests than wolves who were reared like puppies by humans. Even puppies, as young as nine weeks of age, some with rare human contact, tested well.[16] Ancient dogs possibly mastered their ability to find food by reading human cues as part of their successful collaboration with humans.

Interest in animal social cognition, ways that animals adapt that facilitate social interaction, has been increasing recently, with carefully designed studies that eliminate positive outcomes from "smell cues," and inadvertent human signaling. Investigators are validating the domestication theory by studying undomesticated animals (e.g., dolphins and seals) and other domesticated animals (e.g., goats) with successful cue-reading abilities.[17] Research is conclusive that dogs understand cues so well that they accurately interpret cue variations, such as cross-pointing, reverse directions, and different arm extensions.[18] Although all scientists are not convinced, study after study supports the conclusion that dogs do not learn social and communication skills from us, but that the skills are genetically imposed.[19] Dogs have adapted so successfully to human social life as to effect profound changes in their communication and social behaviors.[20]

It makes sense that communication works between our two species. Both are visual, social, and biologically predisposed to pay attention to others in our social group. Dogs are brilliant at handling their end of it, reading our cues and body language. On the other hand, we are so unaware of our movements that we are constantly sending what Dr. McConnell calls a "stir-fry of signals." She explains that while we are thinking about what we are going to say, the dog is watching the signals, which are usually incongruent with the words we are speaking. This is the basis of many behavioral problems. We do not understand why the dog will not comply, but the reason is that we are not saying what we think we are saying.

Apparently dogs are trying everything they can to get through to us, even talking. Many newspapers and television broadcasts carried the report that Barbara Walters said on national television (to much ridicule) that her dog says, "I love you." A video of several dogs mimicking speech made the rounds of the Internet a few days later. It does not look doctored to the untrained eye and shows some intriguing possibilities. I have seen firsthand the *potential* for dogs to talk. A Tibetan terrier in my neighborhood, Luna, comes as close to mimicking the cadence of human speech as I have ever seen in a dog. She only does it when she is upset, but there is no mistaking from her tone that she is displeased. Luna is not the first dog I have witnessed making sounds similar to words: our dog, Grace, a miniature terrier mix, would occasionally look at us and make a deliberate sound that phonetically was similar to "Num. Num. Num . . . " She had to use her tongue to make the sound and would always make it three times in succession, while looking directly in our eyes. We responded with such excitement when she did it that I believe we scared her from doing it.

Lydia Nichols who lives with a Yorkshire terrier named Deliah says that when Deliah wants to go outside, she shakes her head with her tongue out and makes a sneezing noise to get attention.[21] Hearing that reminded me of Máni, the Maltese we rescued, who occasionally gets my attention by making a similar sound; it is as if she is blowing air out of her mouth in a kind of low, mock bark. I know how crazy that description sounds: a dog *pretending* to bark? Maybe not pretending, but trying to *transform* her bark into something she hears all the time: words.

Those of us who think dogs *could* talk may not be so crazy after all, according to Capt. A. J. Haggerty, former head of the U.S. Army K-9 Corp and author of *How to Teach Your Dog to Talk*. He says that some dogs with a "brachycephalic head—wide head and short muzzle—are good candidates for talking." He says that with patient training, certain breeds are capable of vocalizations such as "wa-wa" or "ma-ma."[22]

Permit me a little leap here: We know that domesticated dogs have evolved into creatures very different from wolves with unique skills and abilities to suit humans. For example, wolves do not bark as a primary way to communicate with each other; they use more body language. In fact, only two basic wolf barks have been identified, and their vocal communication relies heavily on howling, whining, and grunting. Dogs all over the world, on the other hand, have a propensity to bark,[23] and the latest findings suggest that dogs began barking, probably in response to early human encouragement, as a sophisticated way to communicate with humans. So my leap is this: if dogs developed barking to communicate with us, is it reasonable to believe that a dog could be taught to, or might acquire the ability to, make a sound that mimics speech, even a sound that expresses a feeling?

Dogs are trying to communicate with us in the best ways they know and in ways they know we will understand—and the messages are getting across. A group of Hungarian investigators demonstrated that people could correctly interpret situations associated with recorded barks at twice the rate possible by chance.[24] Dogs, observant creatures that they are, can also correctly interpret the emotional content (affect) of their guardian's voices.[25] So far, the ability to use verbal language is the only communication advantage we seem to have over dogs.

There is no question that dogs have developed remarkable interspecies-communication skills. Hungarian investigator, Dr. Vilmos Csáyni, who has been studying canine cognition for the past decade sums it up: "They easily accept a membership in the family, they can predict social events, they provide and request information, obey rules of conduct and are able to cooperate and imitate human actions." "His research even suggests that dogs can speculate on what we are thinking."[26]

Eye Contact Seals the Deal

Eye contact is not a metaphor. When two mammals gaze at each other, the "two nervous systems achieve a palpable and intimate apposition."[27] The proverb, "The eyes are the windows to the soul," is another interpretation of this same concept. We are so accustomed to gleaning insight into another's thoughts and feelings by looking into their eyes that we find it unsettling to interact with people or beings whose eyes are covered or frozen in a static stare. Think about how difficult it is to talk to someone who has on mirrored sunglasses.

Eye contact and facial expressions are the most important elements of human-to-human communication. Eye-to-eye contact communicates an array of emotions from aggression to desire. From the moment the delivery-room nurse hands us over to our mothers, shocked and screaming, we demonstrate our genetic predisposition to understand the world by gazing into another's eyes. For the rest of our lives, we depend on feedback from faces, especially eyes, to find our way.

Both dogs and cats also use eye contact for communication and socialization within their species. For instance, using behavior passed down from their wolf ancestors, dogs use eye contact to establish dominance over another dog. Subordinate and submissive dogs yield power by looking away or down. Cats, not having the same range of motion in their eyes as dogs or humans, completely or partially close their eyes before looking away to communicate submission.

The Hungarian researchers also recently confirmed that the dog's eager willingness to look at human faces is what makes them such exceptional companions. Apparently, even when wolves are raised as dogs, they do not learn to value the human face, demonstrating the specificity of this behavior to dogs.[28] The researchers observed two groups of puppies, wolf and dog, raised similarly. After being trained to perform a task, then challenged with a similar but harder task, the dog pups gazed at the humans for support. The wolf pups did not. Researchers speculate that the dog's divergent behavior is also passed through their genes.

Gaze, looking steadily at another with intent, is an important component of social interaction and may be hardwired into the brain, involving the amygdala, the temporal regions, and the frontal cortex. Anyone who has lived with a cat or dog knows they seek to establish eye contact with people and devote a lot of time simply watching us. Sometimes they look into our eyes with such intensity, it is as if they are trying to burn a message into our minds. Some dogs use functional referential communication (FRC) to communicate with us. I noticed that our Grace did this regularly, but I had no idea it is a real phenomenon. My husband and I labeled it "You: That." First, she would look directly at either him or me, and once that contact was made ("You"), she would look at the item ("That") she wanted. Then she would look back at us and back and forth between us and the object of her desire until we complied. FRC or "showing" is "communicative action consisting of both a directional component related to an external target and an attention-getting component that directs the attention of the perceiver to the informer or sender."[29]

Dr. Csáyni, working with Dr. Adam Miklóski, demonstrated this behavior in the laboratory by allowing dogs to see where food was hidden when their guardians left them alone in a room with researchers. When the guardians returned, the dogs ran to the hiding place or looked back and forth between the guardian and the hiding place, "clearly signaling the location."[30]

In study after study, dogs demonstrate how smart they are about using and understanding eye contact. They use gaze cues the same way as humans. For example, they discriminate gaze cues from other cues and ignore a gaze if the person is staring into space.[31] Demonstrating that they understand the importance of the human face and eyes, dogs in one study were shown to prefer begging from a person whose face was visible and would not approach forbidden food when a person's eyes were open. If thrown a ball by a person who then turned his back, the dog consistently walked to the front of the person to return the ball, looking up at the person's face for feedback.

We take this kind of behavior for granted. Yet, it is pretty remarkable that dogs do these things at all, even more remarkable that they can consistently demonstrate their abilities in scientific investigations. We are accustomed to a dog's behavior being so congruent with ours that we ignore their behavioral heritage. For instance, dogs are biologically programmed to interpret direct eye contact as a sign of dominance, but many of our dog companions have learned to associate eye contact with a treat. (Regardless, many animal behaviorists still suggest that you not engage unfamiliar dogs in direct eye contact lest they perceive it as a threat.)

Our Grace loved to stare into my eyes, but Máni will not. She diverts her eyes or turns her head to the side. I felt rejected (How funny is that?) until I learned that she is politely accepting my role as leader of our pack. She wants to make it clear that she is not challenging me.

The bottom line is that many animals can be trained to respond to their name, even if they will not gaze into your eyes, but if you want a staring partner, get a dog.

Face It

The ability of dogs and—to a lesser degree—cats, to simulate facial expressions uniquely contributes to the other exceptional characteristics that make them perfect companions. In the absence of a shared verbal language, which is so crucial to social relationships, the ability to make facial expressions further bridges the gap between their species and ours, allowing for interspecies communication—and relationships.

Accurate assessment of facial expressions is one of the most important aspects of human social interaction. Humans identify each other and interpret emotional states by looking at faces. Using magnetic resonance imaging (MRI), researchers have identified the areas of the brain that are active when we look at faces. They discovered that we look for the same facial cues on a dog's face as on a human's face, and the same areas of our brains are active whether we are looking at the face of a dog or another person. The reason may be that dogs have the facial structure required to produce expressions which humans comprehend, and their facial fur and hair patterns enhance our ability to discern and interpret facial expressions. Naysayers believe we read too much into these expressions, but I agree with people such as Chris Behrens who said of his Australian shepherd mix, Pasha, "She has a very expressive face, and when I pack to go on a trip, I can tell she is worried."[32] One of my doggy nieces, Latte, is an Aussie mix, whose face clearly expresses her feelings.

Cat fur can have patterns that evoke expressions, but their facial muscles do not allow for them to be as expressive as dogs. Unless they are angry, scared,

Latte, whose face has the kind of markings that enable dogs to simulate facial expressions. Photo by John Staddon, used courtesy of CT Woods-Powell.

or yawning, cats usually maintain a vacant and detached look. However, people associate this face with bliss and contentment, finding it relaxing and comforting. The cats look happy, so we think the cat is happy. It works.

DOES THE INTERACTION WITH COMPANION ANIMALS QUALIFY AS A SOCIAL RELATIONSHIP?

The dynamics of relationships are difficult enough to understand when two *people* are involved. Attempting to unravel interspecies relationships that constitute the human-animal bond is a wicked puzzle.

Social and personal relationships result from a delicate interplay of tangible and intangible factors, including personality, emotional stability, familial history, timing, and "gut feelings." Predicting which relationships will work and which will not is difficult to impossible. We all have friends or acquaintances who seem like perfect companions, but their relationships end in divorce or some other type of acrimony. Conversely, others amaze us by being deliriously happy in relationships that seem to make no sense. Identifying an exhaustive list of characteristics for a good relationship is impossible—too many of those intangibles that I mentioned earlier.

Still, certain conditions must be met for any relationship to be even marginally successful. At a minimum, the individuals in a relationship should have the following qualities:

- Like each other
- Trust each other
- Enjoy shared activities
- Express affection in mutually acceptable ways
- Support each other emotionally.

Basically, we seek to have relationships with those who like us, who will be there for us when we have needs, who let us know they want to be around us, who make us feel needed, and who enjoy doing what we do. In return, we get to reciprocate and satisfy our human need to interact and care for another.

By almost any assessment from various biological, psychological, or social theories, our interactions with companion animals indeed satisfy the basic criteria for a relationship.

Come Hell or High Water

One indication of an extraordinarily strong relationship is the willingness of one partner to risk danger, even death for the other. How many people are there for whom you would "take a bullet?" Think about that for a moment. Then think about this: 93 percent of people responding to the American Animal Hospital Association's 2004 Pet Survey said they were either "very likely" (53 percent) or "somewhat likely" (37 percent) to risk their own lives for their companion animals.

In 2005, during the monumental tragedies surrounding Hurricane Katrina, the largest hurricane to hit the U.S. Gulf Coast, people revealed, as in no other event in our country's history, how far they would go to save their companion animals. They risked their lives not only in violation of what some people considered common sense, but also in violation of the prevailing authorities. The sociopolitical landscape of America was forever changed by the risks that victims of Hurricane Katrina demonstrated they were willing to take for the sake of their companion animals. The outcome should not have been a surprise because studies had shown that people would be reluctant to evacuate during natural disasters when companion animals were present and could not be evacuated with them. The reasons for "evacuation failure," some of which are described in the Katrina profiles that follow, include (1) not wanting to abandon the animal because of the strength of the bond; (2) a perceived risk associated with evacuation for guardian and companion animal; (3) insufficient time to prepare; and (4) an absence of housing for evacuated animals.[33]

Valerie Bennett, a Louisiana nurse, pleaded with police to take her two dogs on a rescue boat. She offered them her wedding ring—and her mother's wedding ring—but they would not relent. Bennett evacuated and left her two dogs with an anesthesiologist who promised to care for them, along with animals from about thirty other staff members. Bennett poured food on the floor at the hospital for her cat and left her guinea pig in its cage in a patient's room. She could not provide water because the hospital's plumbing had failed. Bennett, believing she had left her animals to die, cried while telling her story, "I just hope they can forgive me."[34] Turns out they did not have to forgive her. Bennett discovered that her animals were airlifted from the hospital and transported to a Mississippi hospital four days after she evacuated. A television crew happened to film the rescue, and Bennett spotted her dogs, Lady and Oreo. A generous couple later delivered Bennett's animals to her in Atlanta, her evacuation destination.[35]

Another woman concealed a parakeet in her bra. People hid dogs who would fit in purses or duffle bags. One man appeared for his evacuation with nothing for himself—only food, toys, and bedding for his beloved companion dog. Stories abound about people who were forced to leave animals on the highway or forfeit rescue.

One chilling news account made vivid the horror that both animals and humans suffered at being separated: A camera captured a small boy being forced to surrender his little white dog, Snowball, before boarding a bus out of New Orleans. The boy and dog had survived the wretched conditions of the Superdome only to be tragically separated. A policeman wrenched the small dog from the boy, who cried out the dog's name repeatedly before he was so overcome with distress that he vomited. The doors of the bus closed, and the boy was gone. The little white dog ran after the bus before being carried away by the officer, never to be seen again. In spite of offered rewards, both dog and boy disappeared into the diaspora of Katrina survivors. Mercifully, in response to public outcry after this incident was broadcast, authorities relaxed restrictions on companion animal evacuations with their families.

I had the pleasure of meeting Craig Peel, an older gentleman who was evacuated to Washington, DC, and fortunate enough to be reunited with his eleven-year-old Lhasa apso, Sassy. Throughout the storm Peel remained in the French Quarter of New Orleans, where he had lived for forty-three years, resisting evacuation rather than leave Sassy. He survived on bottled water and canned food and walked Sassy every day even though he had to traverse five flights of stairs darkened without electricity. Running out of food, he agreed to leave Sassy with a longtime friend and neighbor. As he was being settled into the DC Armory, a Red Cross volunteer asked him about any missing relatives. Peel responded, "Yes, my dog Sassy, . . . the only family I have left in the world." He evacuated without getting his friend's phone number. However, through a set of events worthy of a good detective novel, which include the neighbor being tracked with leads from an article in a San Diego newspaper and a providential trip to New Orleans by the executive director of the Washington Animal Rescue League, Sassy and Peel were reunited. He said, "Got my baby back."[36]

It is no secret that the majority of people unable to self-evacuate, those who were left behind awaiting evacuation assistance, were the poorest people of the regions. These were not people with expendable income who had the ways and means perhaps to pamper their companion animals. Regardless, the bond they felt for their companion animals was evident, their convictions strong.

For Better or Worse

The human-companion animal bond is not a function of a person's career, achievements, race, or ethnicity. Perhaps that contributes to its richness.

Companion animals do not care whether you are coming home from a job in a corporate office or a visit to the unemployment office. Likewise, most people do not care whether their companion animal qualifies for American Kennel Club registration, can perform tricks, or fetch the paper. They will overcome enormous challenges to remain committed to the relationships. Their feelings for the animal are pure and unconditional.

In 1996, the concept of being committed to a companion animal was introduced as "a resolve to keep a pet in spite of challenges that require expenditures of personal resources," calculated by survey responses to questions related to circumstances under which people would "get rid of" a companion in areas such as destroying furniture, requiring extensive veterinary care, and having problems with housetraining.[37]

Consider Ed Mulrenin, who promised his ten-year-old German shepherd Sonntag that he would not euthanize him after the dog became a paraplegic following a freak accident in 1998. Mulrenin tried various therapies to repair the damage, from acupuncture to surgery. When nothing worked he bought Sonntag a canine wheelchair, replaced the front passenger seat of his Land Rover with a custom bed and rearranged their lives so that Sonntag could go everywhere with him, including a forty-two-day, 12,500-mile trip to Alaska. Mulrenin, an attorney, was planning to relocate to Russia where an important job was waiting, but Sonntag's health began to fail, so he refused the job. After Sonntag developed painful arthritis and could barely move, Mulrenin relented and authorized his euthanasia. Grief-stricken, but satisfied that Sonntag had not been denied "a moment of pleasure," he said, "I made it to the finish line. I kept my promise." He whispered to the dying dog, "We made it, buddy; we made it."[38]

Consider Margie Durney and Michael Kuhse. Durney refused to let religious faith stand between her and her dog, when she stopped going to church because she did not like leaving her dog home alone to attend services.[39] When Kuhse had to relocate his family from Virginia to Moscow for his wife's job, arrangements were made for Florin and Guilder to make the trip. He briefly considered leaving them behind because of the uncertainty of such a long trip, a common dilemma for animal guardians, but he was adamant that they had to stay together. They had been in the family as a pair since they were puppies, and no trip to Moscow was going to change that. Turns out, the trip went well. "They probably had a better trip than us; they got to spend a night in Amsterdam," said Kuhse. He arranged for a veterinarian to meet them at the Moscow airport, where they were held for about five hours before going home. They had to adjust to Moscow, but had grown up in Colorado, so the weather was no problem. They may have a bit less space and do not get to run freely as much, but they have the most important thing in their lives: the Kuhse family. "I think they are glad to still be with us," said Kuhse. That is a bet I will take any day.

Think about people such as Stephanie Scott and her boyfriend Troy Bloom, who packed up and moved across state lines, out of Denver, Colorado, to keep their pet pit bull, Reilly Roo—by all accounts a big love muffin and an exuberant

These photos demonstrate the lifelong commitment that responsible guardians, such as Mike Khuse, make to their companion animals. He kept Florin (a pointer mix) and Guilder (a black Labrador mix) even when he had to relocate to Russia. Photos courtesy of Michael C. Kuhse.

face-licker—from being confiscated and euthanized because of a city-wide ban on the much-aligned breed.[40]

Mimi Scott gave up the luxurious New York condominium that had been her home for nearly ten years when the homeowner's board disallowed her four small dogs. Scott, an active widower, who counts Hollywood royalty among her close friends, said that the dogs made her feel complete. She started out with one Lhasa Apso, Kramer, who was getting older, So, she increased her family by three, but none weighed more than eight pounds. The board told her to "dispose" of three dogs to comply with the new rules. She said, "They are part of me. There's no way I would abandon them." Like most animal lovers would have done, Scott tried reason, "I tried to help them understand what it's like, but none were parents or dog owners, and all were single." Not that it mattered, but Scott also tried to make a case for the greater good, "It wasn't just me who enjoyed them. When I took them out in the cart everyone wants to pet and talk to them. Those adorable faces. You just can't help smiling." Scott offered to find another home for one, explaining that Kramer "wouldn't last that long," and she would then be left with only two dogs, one weighing less than five pounds. The board would not relent and threatened to charge her a $500 initial fine and $25 per day, per dog, until she was in compliance. She considered legal action, but decided against taking that expensive chance. When the board mandated that she had five days to get rid of three dogs, moxie kicked in. "Screw them. I'm keeping my dogs and I'm moving," she decided.[41]

Not nearly as big a sacrifice as forsaking a Central Park condo, but when my allergist ordered me to get rid of my dog, Grace, I got rid of my allergist.

Valerie Cheatham lost a long held job at an Atlanta Neiman Marcus for trying to give water to two poodles, who were sitting in a locked car in the store's parking lot, sweltering in the ninety-degree heat of Georgia's summer sun. While waiting for animal control to respond to her call, Cheatham attempted to give the dogs water through the sunroof. The owner of the car returned and berated Cheatham for climbing, albeit in stocking feet, on the roof of the car and threatened, "I'm going to have your job." Two days later, Cheatham was fired. She responded, "I'm forty-six, and I've never been fired before, but I'm going to sleep like a baby because . . . those dogs were in danger."[42]

When Gary Prentiss awoke in Wilmington, North Carolina, after more than two months in a coma, he immediately asked about his dogs. You see, every winter, Prentiss would travel south from Maine, seeking work as a landscaper and stonemason. He always slept on a cot in his van, with the dogs nearby. One afternoon, he was assaulted and left for dead. He seemed beyond recovery, so the local animal shelter found new homes for his dogs. Prentiss hoped to be reunited with his dogs, he said, "They were definitely family. I love them as much as people love their children."[43]

Where Thou Goest

We not only participate in bona fide relationships with companion animals, but the relationships also have dimensions typically observed only in intraspecies interactions (i.e., within the same species, as between two people). One particular dimension elevates relationships to a unique level—the formation of attachments, defined as "affectional bonds between two individuals [formed] over time.[44] Traditionally, psychologists considered only people when examining unique attachments that develop in relationships. Only recently have they applied attachment theory to the unique interspecies relationships between people and their companion animals.[45,46] What we know about attachment theory started with early research that focused on mothers and their children, beginning with the seminal work of Dr. J. Bowlby in 1958.[47] That same year, Dr. Harry Harlow also demonstrated attachment theory using baby rhesus monkeys, deprived of their mother in exchange for the choice of either a terry cloth or a wired surrogate. His results were dramatic, but the methods seemed harsh to me, and I have always wondered how many Psychology 101 students ran for the hills in search of another major after being exposed to his study. Could I have been the only one? I still remember the black and white movie of traumatized rhesus babies crying out in despair and running in sheer terror from corner-to-corner of a tiny confinement before finally huddling against a contraption that resembled the maid on the *Jetsons* cartoon. If you are too young to know about the *Jetsons*, think wire cage, shaped like a milk carton with big coke-bottle eyes, and no arms. The babies had a strong preference for the terry cloth *mother* despite the fact that the wire one dispensed food. When frightened, the monkeys ran for the terry cloth surrogate and spent as much time with *her* as possible. Even when not being tormented, they stayed close to the surrogate and did not investigate their environment.

Attachments serve to promote survival of the species (e.g., nursing mothers). Yet, the rhesus babies demonstrated that food is not everything. Attachments also offer protection and security, and an unparalleled, preeminent feature—comfort—which is psychologically critical for an attachment to form. Comfort is more important than the attachment figure's ability to do anything. They just have to be available, and visual proximity is better than nothing. Those poor little monkeys proved that comfort and affection are more important than food, safety, or the opportunity to explore your surroundings.

The biological and evolutionary inheritances we share with dogs may explain why we form attachments with one another, and why the relationships can be so profound and satisfying, at least for us. The kind of animals we prefer and the kinds of attachments we form may tell us a lot about ourselves. One thing for sure, the attachments we develop with our companion animals are profound. A recent survey showed that people found relationships with their companion animals more secure and positive, on every measure, than relationships with their significant others.[48]

The well-worn advice that moderation is key applies again because people who devote moderate amounts of attention to either animals or people reported being the happiest. The attachments we form with companion animals contribute to emotional and social well-being throughout our lives.

I ran across a charming account of a psychologist's remembrance of her sister's attachment to the family's horse, Shadow. It is a perfect example of the strength of the bond:

> My mom likes to tell the story about when my sister went away to college and didn't have much time to spend with Shadow. My dad decided to give Shadow to a family friend who wanted him. My sister came home one weekend and caught wind of my father's plans. I am not privy to the conversation that followed between my sister and my dad, but my mom says that when my dad walked out of the room he said, "It's very clear to me that if anyone is leaving, it's not going to be the horse."[49]

Is It Love That We're Feeling?

The question of love as it relates to companion animals has been considered since the early 1970s, when the primary focus was on whether there was any association between loving companion animals and loving humans. Specifically, were people who loved animals capable of greater warmth for other humans? Conversely, were people with great affection for animals incapable of sustaining relationships with other humans?

It is no secret that many people profess to like animals more than they like most people they know. However, research does not support that animal lovers have social pathologies or that they relate poorly to people.

To the contrary, people with companion animals are frequently regarded as more socially accessible. In both American and British cultures, the majority of people live with pets and are viewed as having positive, or at the least, harmless, personalities. This could simply mean that we like people who are like us, but maybe people with companion animals really are more pleasant.[50]

Scientifically speaking, the love of companion animals has not been correlated to the love of people. That means scientists have not proven that one relates to the other. However, there is a sufficient degree of association between two particular emotions—love and empathy—to suggest a correlation. Let me explain: By studying and comparing the level of empathy that people feel for animals to the level of empathy these same people feel for other people, psychologists have found that people who show empathy for animals also show empathy for people. People who show empathy are referred to as empathetic people and are described as people who show an interest or become involved with others; they show concern. They are the ones, for instance, who reach out to help people who are in distress, and they spend their time and money on worthy causes. Their feelings and actions are not wasted, as some reason, on the animals because their feelings and actions are not restricted to animals. These are the people most likely to respond to other people in need as well.[51]

Obviously our relationships with companion animals, cats and dogs especially, involve profound emotional attachments, but do we really *love* them?

Not many people give much thought to defining love. You know if it *hits* or not; end of story. Once people *fall in love* with each other, the cogitation typically goes no further than recognizing how limited the word is to describe such an enormous, complex experience.

Yet, the question of exactly what love is demands attention because how can we say with certainty that we love our companion animals, if we do not understand what love is? Armed with the knowledge of what constitutes love, and an acceptable application of love to the relationships we share with our companion animals, we can face the world unashamed with scientifically based evidence that what we feel for the animals in our lives is love—authentic love that deserves recognition, appreciation, and understanding—not scorn or ridicule.

Love's complexity has fascinated poets, novelists, musicians, and other artists for centuries as they applied their craft to unravel the mystery. Lately, distinguished scientists have also turned their attention to love. Biologists, cardiologists, neurologists, psychologists, and sociologists, to name a few, are directing the beam of their scientific expertise on love. Each is describing, if you will, the part of the elephant in the room that they see. Some of the resulting theories seem more like geometry than emotional dynamics of love. Yet, each reveals a unique part of the mystery.

Love's conundrum opens with a dichotomy: Love begins in the brain, but we speak of it in terms of the heart. In *The Science of Love*, Dr. Anthony Walsh confirms, "Love is not ineffable spirit that is just 'out there' awaiting discovery; it exists in a fully corporeal sense in the . . . brain."[52]

When reptiles crawled out of the water, morphing into the earliest mammals, their brains set them apart. Paul Broca, a French surgeon discovered in the 1800s that the human brain is divided into three parts: (1) the brain stem; (2) the limbic brain; and (3) the neocortex. What distinguishes a mammal from a reptile is the limbic brain—the center of emotions. With a newly sprouted limbic system, the mammal began to take care of its offspring, form families, and play. It made them *care*, not lay an egg and walk off.[53]

The limbic brain initiated the biological imperative to give and receive care and affection. It gave us the capacity to love.

Only for Love

The universe is governed by specific and observable, but unchangeable laws and principles. Love, as part of the universe, is no exception, and therefore, love must contain certain observable elements.[54] Yet, most researchers who investigate the topic admit that insufficient data make it difficult to construct a scientific description of love. Love remains "elusive vapors" difficult to "tether to verifiable facts."[55]

However, some facts are established. For instance, we know that love stems from an evolutionary obligation to survive, given that newborn humans are helpless longer than any neonate.

> If no one feeds a human infant it will starve; if no one moves it, it stays put; if no one shelters and protects it, it will die.
>
> —*Science of Love*, page 42

Rearing a baby is no short-term proposition, as you know. A human infant takes years to achieve the self-sufficiency that most mammals reach in days or months. Without the biological imperative, our species would quickly become extinct. We have no choice, but to love.

> Only a strong biologically based tendency on the part of the mother to care for the infant unconditionally will see it successfully through its period of dependency. The human adult's willingness to invest time and energy in someone else's goals, even at the expense of one's own, is called love—an active concern for the well-being of another.
>
> —*Science of Love*, page 42

Sometimes you can figure out what a thing is by looking at what it is not, which Dr. Stephen Levine does in a recent article, "What Is Love Anyway?" He says, "Love is not a single feeling" and that even in its "ordinary use" (e.g., "Didn't you love that movie?"), love involves at least two feelings: "pleasure and interest," which may evolve into joy that includes "happiness, pride, gratitude and awe." Whereas some have tried to distill love into either an emotion, a feeling, an attitude, or a combination of behaviors, Levine says that love is a complicated emotion, which is layered with many aspects that create a continuum of "transient emotional experiences, complicated by past, present, and future considerations."

He makes another point about love that I find particularly applicable to our relationships with companion animals: "love is a moral commitment" that "instantly restructures life and generates a new set of obligations."[56]

In *The Psychology of Love*,[57] Drs. Robert Sternberg and Michael Barnes present an impressive array of theories and research on love, each with valid, provocative points, and I encourage you to explore that book. To make my point, I selected from their text *agape* love as the primary love we have for companion animals. I did so primarily because the term is likely familiar. Renowned author C.S. Lewis distinguished and popularized four types of love, including *agape*, in his treatise, *Four Loves*.[58] Originating in Greek literature, *agape* love is an unconditional, selfless love given with no anticipation of compensation or payoff. This is the love that allows us to love those who may be considered unlovable for some reason. Two other types of love in the Lewis' work also apply to our relationships with companion animals: *storge* and *phila*. *Storge* is the love of affection, which involves attachment and is the kind of love expressed in families. *Phila* is the love of friendship, which expects rewards from another, such as support, admiration, mutual respect, or understanding. In the quartet, Lewis included *eros*, romantic love, which is not applicable and unacceptable in these relationships.

We are human, and love is an essential human emotion, the capacity for which is part of our biochemical inheritance. Now you can add to your evolutionary and biological entitlement the evidence I presented to unabashedly assert your feelings to friends, family, and colleagues that love is what you feel for your companion animals. As if you needed a permission slip, there it is.

THEY LOVE YOU? THEY LOVE YOU NOT?

Okay, we love them. Now, the question is do they love us in return? Does your companion animal even have the capacity to love? Most people who live with companion animals, especially indoor animals, feel that the animal not only loves them, but that the love is unconditional and everlasting. Supportive anecdotal evidence has filled many a volume. Other people, including some animal behaviorists, maintain that when we attribute emotions to animals, we are either delusional or projecting our feelings onto the animals. In contrast, a good deal of empirical research has been done on the emotional life of animals, demonstrating not only reciprocal feelings directed at humans, but also feelings directed at one another.

Charles Darwin was the first scientist to focus on emotions. However, in keeping with his philosophies about evolution, he distilled emotions to a "body function that persisted because of inherent usefulness."[59] In his quest to discover the purpose of emotions, Darwin studied and catalogued expressions in both humans and nonhuman animals, providing the basis for an intriguing supposition. If animals have facial expressions, which we know some do, does that mean they can feel?

You know the answer, but let me tell you *why* it is possible for them to feel. The most popular companion animals are mammals, and they share our brain composition, including the all-important limbic brain. Most cats and dogs, for instance, have limbic brains that are as mature as an infant's. They have the same biological imperative and capacity for love as we.

For decades, psychologists and other scientists have discounted the idea that companion animals have emotions and are capable of loving us back. They maintain that animals who appeared to express emotions were merely "reacting to hormonal rushes triggered by outside stimuli." Thankfully, researchers from disparate fields are providing evidence that all kinds of creatures "experience surges of deep-seated fear, jealousy, grief—and most important, love." Five years ago, my colleagues would have thought I was off my rocker," says biologist Marc Bekoff. "But now scientists are finally starting to talk about animal emotions in public. It's like they're coming out of the closet."[60] Not surprisingly, dogs, who read our communication cues better than primates, have shown the widest range of emotions in scientific investigations. They are likely similarly skilled at expressing their emotions and personalities. Yes, personalities. Dr. Samuel Gosling's published research demonstrates that dogs have at least four distinct canine personality factors—energy, affiliativeness, emotional reactivity, and competence—that are remarkably similar to the five major factors in the best-known tests of human personality: conscientiousness, extraversion, neuroticism, openness, and agreeableness.[61] His work proves, "personality differences do exist and can be measured in animals other than humans."[62, 63] Gosling shared with me that more rigorous analyses of his data indicate there may be as many as five major dimensions of canine personality.[64]

COMPANION ANIMAL MIRACLE WORKERS

I am not sure whether particular personality types account for the miraculous feats, but a profusion of books, newspaper articles, internet sites, and television broadcasts extol companion animals who exhibit amazing behavior, demonstrating uncanny abilities to understand when humans are in danger, pain, or some other distress. Stories of dogs and cats who dial phones to call required emergency services or who alert people to fires in the home, and dogs who save near-drowning victims are so commonplace as to almost be mundane. Other times the accounts seem almost mystical, such as an animal who performs completely out of character or in a preordained way, such as an animal who resembles a recently departed companion animal, or joins a family just days before the incident to which the animal responded. "There is a mysterious solidarity between people and animals," says Dr. Rupert Sheldrake.[65] He explains that the connection we have with companion animals is "not just metaphorical, but real literal connections." The connections are a product of the social bond *between* our two species and is similar to the bonds formed *within* species, like those between a mother cat and her kittens or a wolf and its pack. He says that the bonds exist within a "social field" and "connect the members of a group and influence the way they relate." Social fields, unlike "known fields of physics, evolve and contain a kind of memory," and he classifies these particular social fields as "morphic fields." Morphic fields, he says, hold collective memories in ways that allow ancestors to influence the behavior of the present in conscious and unconscious ways. This is one of the ways that habits, beliefs, and customs are passed down in human culture. Individual animals are also linked through their social fields, and the connections contribute to habitual patterns, according to his theories. Because of our unique bond with companion animals, we share a social field, and we are the beneficiaries of the phenomena he describes. Dogs especially are tuned in to us and are, if you accept his theory, able to pick up on our intentions and know when we need comforting, healing, and protecting. Sheldrake's theory is a possible explanation for the miraculous, almost telepathic behavior of companion animals.[66]

Take Zion, a two-year-old Golden Labrador, who had not shown any proclivity for basic training, much less saving lives, but who surprised everyone by saving the life of a boy he had never seen before. The eight-year-old, Ryan Rambo, fell from a kayak during a white-water rafting trip in Colorado. Zion was playing on the bank of the river with his young custodian, Chelsea Bennett, when Ryan bobbled by on the currents yelling for help. Bennett said that Zion "usually does not go into the river until someone throws a ball or stick." However, Chelsea's mother says Zion must have sensed something was wrong because he swam out to Ryan and dragged him to shore. Ryan's family had moved to Colorado after Hurricane Katrina damaged their home, where they had been forced to relinquish their own yellow Labrador, named Zoe—a dead ringer for Zion.[67]

Butch, a Labrador who lives with Bill Burns in Indiana, held a flashlight in his mouth to signal for help while another Labrador, Dusty, lay on Burns's chest to keep him warm after he collapsed one night while walking for exercise to control his diabetes. An observant deputy noticed the light while on patrol and found Burns, who was unconscious. Deputy Steve Hoffman said, "I would never have found them if not for the light."[68]

Honey, a Cocker Spaniel, not quite 5-months-old at the time and adopted from the shelter only two weeks prior, summoned help one morning from a neighbor when the SUV Michael Bosch was driving plunged down an embankment, trapping him in the vehicle. The pup traveled a quarter of a mile to the nearest neighbor, Robin Allen, who spotted the SUV when she returned Honey home. She said, "She was obviously trying to tell me something."[69]

Bob, an eighty-pound, chow-lab mix, threw himself in front of an alligator to save Cindy Hernandez, who was swimming in Tampa, Florida. They had been playing a game of fetch, and Hernandez decided to cool off in the water. Hernandez heard the alligator immediately, "He was moving so fast, he was cutting the water, making a sound." Bob heard the commotion, and dropped his toy to get between Hernandez and the alligator. Within seconds the alligator rolled over and Bob was gone. He sacrificed himself to save her.[70]

The next profile seems more like a fictive headline than a real event, but I communicated with the editor of the magazine who assured me that the headline is true: "Faithful Dog Saves Boy Who Tried to Drown Him." *Russian Life* magazine reported that thirteen-year-old Tudor Mura, from Moldova, took his "aged, near-blind dog to a lake to drown him, but fell in and was saved by him instead."[71]

A stray dog in Nairobi, Kenya, demonstrated that thousands of years of domestication were not wasted on her. The dog apparently happened upon an abandoned newborn girl, later named Angel, who had been wrapped in plastic and left for dead in a Nairobi forest. The dog carried the baby to her den and nestled Angel amongst her litter of newborn puppies, where passersby heard the infant's cries.[72]

Dogs are not the only heroes. Daisy, a 150-pound potbellied pig saved her pal, seven-year-old Jordan Jones, from an unprovoked attack by a neighbor's pit bull by putting herself between the dog and the boy. Daisy recovered from her wounds, including a severed ear and bites on her face and jowls. Had it not been for Daisy, little Jordan would likely not have survived.

Only ten days after a bunny named Robin joined her family, she saved the lives of two people: Darcy Murphy and her unborn daughter Brenna. Around 3 A.M. one morning, the rabbit made such a frenetic fuss in her cage that she awoke Darcy's husband Ed, who discovered that Darcy was bright red and barely breathing. She had gone into an insulin shock from gestational diabetes. Darcy believes that if the rabbit had not awakened her husband, she would have died.

Robin may have been using her animal emotional intelligence to sense that something was amiss. A less metaphysical explanation is that the rabbit's frenzy was in response to the odorous ketones Darcy was producing because of her impending diabetic coma. Like most of the people saved by companion animals, Darcy does not care about the explanation.[73]

Finally—in more ways than one—Oscar the Cat, as he is known, has demonstrated an "uncanny ability to predict when residents are about to die." He has "presided over the deaths of more than twenty-five residents," only curling up next to people during their final hours. "This is not a cat that's friendly to people," said Dr. David Dosa, who has been observing Oscar closely since his "13th correct call." Oscar's mere presence at the bedside is now viewed by the doctors and nurses as an almost absolute indicator of impending death, giving staff time to notify family members, who seem grateful for the notice. Oscar also provides companionship to people who might otherwise have died alone.[74] By the time the cat visits, the people are so ill they are not aware that the cat is a harbinger of death. Whether Oscar's behavior is scientifically significant or related to other causes is yet to be determined. Perhaps he simply notices certain smells associated with impending death or something in staff behavior clues him.[75]

We may never know why or how animals accomplish these apparent *miracles*. Who could attempt to explain how Butch knew that a flashlight emitted a substance that could be used to get the attention of other humans—who could then bring help? I am confident that scientists will eventually reveal all of the mysteries of animal behavior.

"Limbic resonance" is one explanation for an animal's apparent ability to tap into human feelings, becoming attuned to another's inner stated. You see, the limbic brain specializes in "detecting the internal states of other mammals," and the limbic ancestry we share with other mammals may allow them to read and respond to our emotional states.[76] This is the same process that wild animals use to sense danger in their environments and to alter behavior as much as possible to avoid confrontation or prepare for challenge.

This is possible because "limbic activity of those around us draws our emotions into almost immediate congruence." It is as if limbic states leap between minds to make feelings contagious. Ever been to a college or professional sports playoff game? Limbic resonance sends "waves of emotion rolling through a throng," and generates the "communal, multiplied magic." It is what also makes crowds run for an exit, and fuels the mentality behind mob activity.[77]

A cat, dog, or other nonhuman mammal with a limbic brain is just as capable of tuning into our emotional states as human babies, who excel at detecting emotions. Although babies have an immature neocortex, which prohibits acquisition of language and other skills, their limbic brain is mature. Consequently, even newborns have an instinctive ability to read the complex and varied emotional array of their mothers. Good skill to have when you cannot even stand on your own for eight or nine months after birth, and your complete survival depends on one or two people. In a classic demonstrative study, infants were shown to seek information from their mother's face for an assessment of danger when confronted with a "visual cliff."[78] The bottom line here is that humans, even in an infant state, and dogs and cats share an innate curiosity about facial expressions and a limbic system to process what they see—and then act on it.

We accept that animals, cats and dogs especially, have the ability to care. Understanding the similarities between our brains and theirs helps us appreciate that animals can also detect when we are in danger or distress—and act accordingly to *care* for us.

I will let you know when someone figures out how Butch knew about the flashlight.

3

Why We Choose Certain Animals As Companions

Animals are such agreeable friends—they ask no questions, they pass no criticism.

—George Eliot

That which is neither plant nor mineral is animal—scientific classification *Animalia*. Some of us walk on two legs; others on four, six, or eight legs; while still others circumnavigate the world on a multitude of legs. We have bodies that are covered with either skin, hair, fur, scales, or feathers. Some of us share history, evolution, culture, and biochemistry. Yet, *Animalia* is such a diverse and encompassing class that some animals in it share little more than the air and water on the planet.

The human primate is regarded as the most successful animal on earth. Some might say that is because we do the regarding. What is not in question is this: humans dictate the destiny of other animals on earth. We decide which animals will be eaten, which ones will entertain us, which ones will work for us, which ones will be displayed in zoos, and so forth.

Consequently, we also decide which ones will be our companions. Once so designated, we often choose to bestow on them everything that we feel is good about life. Earlier chapters examined and explained from an evolutionary and historical perspective why cats and dogs became the most popular companion animals. But why do they *continue* to entrance us, and what attracts us to other types of animals? Once chosen as a companion, what roles do the animals hold, and how do we influence each other's lives?

Actually, many factors are in play when we decide which animal we will call companion, and what follows is a look at the most common elements.

The most popular companion animals are chosen because they recognize and respond to humans in meaningful ways. Adults will often gather information about breed and temperament before making choices. We consider practicalities such as size, care requirements, and allergenicity. Intangible factors also are influential, such as the animal reminds you of one favored from your childhood or helps you fulfill a lifelong dream—to have a horse for instance. My early childhood experiences certainly shaped my choices. My first love was GeeTa, a dignified, aging, shepherd-collie mix, who offered me unparalleled comfort as the youngest sibling transplanted alone to a new home in a new city when my divorced mother remarried. As an adult, I am still drawn to dogs with GeeTa's markings, her soulful eyes, and her nurturing personality. After GeeTa's death, I saw Toto in *The Wizard of Oz*, and a new longing was born. Decades passed before I could fulfill my dream, but the first animal I sought was a cairn terrier, like Toto. A colleague at work had cairns, so I learned quickly that they were not all like Toto, and actually not the dog for me. Regardless, I stayed in the terrier family, adopting a miniature German schnauzer. My lifestyle remains more appropriate for dogs less than ten pounds, and I focus on small mixed breeds. However, if I had the chance, I would add a German shepherd or a collie-mix because of the lasting impact GeeTa had on me.

PRACTICALITIES, PERSONALITY, AND PSYCHOLOGY

Beyond practicalities and wish fulfillment, the determinants for which animals become part of the family, and which do not, are intriguing. A few of the determinants are programmed into our DNA and we are pretty helpless to their power. Regardless, the care with which we select a species for a companion animal, as well as a particular animal within certain species, is important to the survival of the relationship, and often to the animal. Living with the right animal can create a life enhancing experience for you and the animal; living with the wrong one can create a type of hell for both of you.

As is the case with humans with whom we associate, animals we choose as companions, can provide insight into our personalities. For example, where our "pets" are concerned, some of us have strict requirements for training and control. Others want to show off our companions in competitions. Some of us ask only for a friend. I have asked three things of each of my little dogs: do not pee in the house, do not chew the furniture, and do not bite others.

The study of personality falls primarily under the purview of the field of psychology, which considers personality a "configuration of characteristics and behavior that comprises an individual's unique adjustment to life."[1]

I have high regard for psychology, having been married to a psychologist for more than twenty years and being inherently curious about what makes people do the things they do, especially as relates to choices they make. Our personalities are often reflected in our choices; this is especially true in respect to major life decisions, which applies to selecting a companion animal. Unfortunately, qualified research that examines the relationship between human personality and preferences for specific companion animals is scarce. Consequently, much of the "evidence" is anecdotal and based on generalizations. For instance, people often assume that we prefer certain types of animals because we share personality traits attributed to that particular animal. Unfounded stereotypes about these connections abound, such as cats are self-sufficient and aloof, and so are the people who live with them. Conversely, people with dogs are considered more outgoing and social. More than any other factor, people make assumptions about other people based on *their breed* of dog. They view people with certain dogs as having the specific traits associated with their dog. For instance, Labradors connote fun and a family orientation, while miniature poodles seem fussy and high-maintenance, and Chihuahuas are viewed as high-strung and very active. Dogs may have this affect on other people's impressions in a way similar to that of other companions. Certain breeds of dogs are associated with positive traits that may enhance the impressions of their guardian. Similarly, dogs associated with negative traits may stigmatize their guardians. For example, we tend to think that golden retrievers are intelligent and give their guardians credit for being the same. Pitbulls are associated with violence and aggression, and so are people who have them.[2] One of the biggest divisions in *dogdom* are between guardians who prefer mixed-breeds to "pure-breeds," with the mixed-breed camp thought to have more of a sense of adventure and be more accommodating. Although these perspectives might be viewed as cocktail party psychology, some studies are finally emerging that demonstrate a connection between human personality and preferences for specific companion animals. Other studies have concluded that the personalities of "pet owners and non-owners" are not different, but that people with various preferences have "become victims of stereotyping by both the general population and scientific researchers."[3]

One of the first investigators to examine personality differences among "pet" owners, considered people with horses, birds, snakes, and turtles. He found that male owners of horses were "aggressive and dominant," but females were "easy-going and non-aggressive." The people with birds were "socially outgoing and expressive," while people with snakes were "relaxed and unconventional." People with turtles were characterized as "hard-working, religious and upwardly mobile."[4]

Based on observation and personal experience, another investigator, Canadian psychologist Stanley Coren developed a rather conservative, mildly unflattering view of people with cats. He says they are not very extroverted, slightly trusting, and lacking in warmth and caring. He sees them as more likely to live alone than people with dogs and live in an apartment rather than a house twice as often. People with dogs, he added, are more likely than cat people to be married and have children. Dog people, he observed, are willing to spend twice as much to save their companion animal from a life-threatening illness. His descriptors of cat people apply to people who live only with cats. He found that people who live with cats *and* dogs are more similar to people who have only dogs as companions. He uncovered some interesting statistics related to people and cats: he found that only 47 percent of people who grew up with cats, continued to have cats as adults. However, 11 percent of people who had only dogs as children, choose to have only a cat as an adult.[5] Translated: Even people who grow up with cats, usually end up with a dog at some point. Less than half remain consistent cat people as adults. Plus, very few people who grew up with dogs end up as cat-only people.

The preponderance of research on the human-animal bond relates to dogs, so more information is available on human personality and choice of dog breeds.

Not surprisingly, one study found people with toy breeds were the "most nurturing and least dominant of all." This makes sense because very small dogs were bred specifically to be companions, lapdogs if you will, and they usually demand a lot of affection and a strong personality type is not required to train them. People with herding breeds of dogs, which includes Border collies and German shepherds, were found to be the "most aggressive and orderly," while people who favored sporting breeds were the "least orderly." I suspect that in this application, aggressive is more about being assertive and bold, rather than confrontational and violent. People who lived with hounds were the "friendliest." People with terriers were the "least aggressive, but the most dependent on others for emotiona support."[6]

Coren's primary research was with dogs, and he developed a classification system to determine which dog is best for a person, given that person's personality. He used four personality markers—Extroversion, Dominance, Trust, and Warmth—based on a version of the Interpersonal Adjective Scales (IAS). The full IAS measurement was designed by Jerry Wiggins, who also designed a portion of the widely used and well-known Minnesota Multiphasic Personality Inventory (MMPI). Coren observed compatibility between extroverted women and independent (defined as personable and strong-willed) or protective dogs (territorial and dominant), which by his definition includes Siberian huskies and Samoyeds, in the former category and Akitas and Rottweilers, in the latter. Extroverted men were compatible with clever (observant and trainable) and self-assured dogs (spontaneous and often audacious), which includes poodles (clever). Dominant men and women both liked steady (good-natured and tolerant) and self-assured dogs, which includes Newfoundlands (steady) and silky terriers (self-assured). Not surprisingly, people high on the warmth scale were most compatible with friendly dogs (affectionate and genial), which include dogs such as collies and golden retrievers. Men and women with high scores in the trust category both like protective dogs and those low in trust liked dogs that Coren categorized as steady.[7]

Social psychologists inform us that familiarity and exposure affect attraction and behavior, and Coren was one of the first psychologists to demonstrate that, at least when it comes to dogs, some people prefer animals who are so familiar that they resemble them. He asked a group of women college students to select from four breeds of dogs and found that the women with long hair preferred the dogs with floppy ears, and the women with short hair chose dogs with perked ears. He said the floppy ears framed the dog's face in the way that long hair framed the women's face. Short or pulled-back hair produced a facial facade similar to that of dogs with perked ears.[8]

Another published study involving dogs confirmed and complemented Coren's findings. Two psychologists from the University of California at San Diego confirmed that "resemblance between person and pet exists," and may be based on physical attributes or similar styles. For instance, a person who is "tall and elegant," might select wolfhounds and a person who is "warm and friendly," might select a retriever. Similarities are based on multidimensional qualities—it is not

Margay has the quintessential "cute" characteristics that humans fall for. Photo courtesy J.C. Campbell.

as simple as a hairy person preferring a hairy dog or a big person wanting a big dog, according to the investigators.[9] This study also demonstrated that resemblance between people and their dogs is based on selection, not "convergence," which explains why married people begin to resemble each other after many years of marriage.[10] Not surprisingly, resemblance between dogs and people was found only in purebred dogs, simply because people could select particular characteristics. It is hard to tell just by looking whether a person prefers dogs, cats, or reptiles, but the authors conclude that "as in the case of selecting a spouse, people want a creature like themselves."

SURVIVAL OF THE CUTEST

Human brains are genetically predisposed to respond to "cuteness," an elusive quality that many of us take for granted, but scientists who specialize in identifying the types of visual stimuli that evoke a response have discovered that cute has specific characteristics, and most of them resemble infantile appearance and behavior.

Jeffrey Kurland, associate professor of biological anthropology and human development at Penn State University says that humans are attracted to "large, symmetrical heads with large eyes, small mouths and small noses."[11] Cute also involves a look of youthfulness and helplessness, such as unsteady limbs. Because human babies remain helpless, vulnerable, and demanding for such an extended time, Mother Nature coordinated babies' physical features with a desire in women to cuddle, coo, and sacrifice everything to protect infantile characteristics, and cuteness was unleashed. Natural selection ensured that the mother's preference for cute and the increasing cuteness of the babies reinforced each other and saturated the gene pool, affecting men, too.

We are genetically drawn to almost anything with characteristics that fit our definition of cute—from Mickey Mouse to King Kong—and the attraction is

Siberian researchers bred brown foxes who developed "cute" characteristics after several generations. Photo courtesy of Irina Plyusnina.

innately strong with a hair-trigger. With this primal mandate, we had no chance against the epitome of cuteness, as reflected in puppies, kittens, and other baby mammals. Over the years, selective breeding of animals has insured that cuteness not only prevails, but also persists into adulthood. Hence the appeal of miniature sizes and crossing breeds to enhance cute characteristics.

We are cute junkies: Brain scans reveal that the ventral striatum and the amygdala show increased activity when the brain is exposed to images of cuteness. These areas of the brain are commonly referred to as the pleasure centers and also become activated in response to chocolate, sex, and drugs.[12]

A group of Siberian researchers have shed light on the evolutionary develop-ment of cuteness. They bred foxes to determine how many generations it would take to create tamed animals. The only selection criterion for the foxes was that they respond well to humans. It took forty-five years to produce tamed animals who wag their tails and greet humans with excitement; that was the outcome. These foxes are more curious than other foxes, understand humans better, and are less frightened of new experiences. The astounding result is that the original foxes all had black fur, but the new foxes acquired "cute" characteristics, including white patches on their faces, big floppy ears, and curly tails.[13]

PASSING FANCY

At the illogical end of the continuum for reasons to select a companion an-imal is that the breed or species is faddish. One of the worse reasons for getting an animal is that it starred in a popular movie and seemed so adorable. Yes, I remember what I said about Toto, but remember I did not impulsively get a cairn terrier before researching the breed and evaluating our suitability for each other. People who plunge in after seeing an animal in a movie often have problems, and some popular movies make certain animals desirable. Remember Benji? More than thirty years have passed since the first Benji movie, but the dog remains so popular that Benji is almost a breed name. How many times have you heard someone refer to Benji dog? The Benji phenomenon was unusual in its influence because Benji dogs are mixed-breeds, and to get one people had to go to an animal shelter. Consequently, adoptions from shelters increased dramatically. The American Humane Association reported that more than one million dogs were adopted from shelters across the country after the movie. Statistically speaking, this effect is an outlier—a unique result very different from what usually happens. You see, television programs and movies usually trigger large consumer demand for a particular breed of dog, and the results are tragic. Notably, when the Walt Disney Studios released its non-animated version of *101 Dalmatians* in 1996, the demand for Dalmatian puppies soared. Regrettably, a record number of families ended up surrendering the animals to shelters after discovering the dogs to be completely unsuitable for their lifestyles and personalities. Within six months of the release of the movie, Dalmatian surrender increased by 25 percent, resulting in thousands of abandoned adolescent Dalmatians.[14] We will never know how many Dalmatians were euthanized as a result of their brief, movie-driven popularity. Aware of the power of movies, the Walt Disney Company partnered with the American Kennel Club to insert informational leaflets in the DVD releases of *Eight Below* and *The Shaggy Dog* to discourage people from making "spontaneous" purchases by warning them with the following kind of message: "The Siberian husky is a beautiful and intelligent dog, but not right for everyone.[15]

Problems arise whenever people try to model their lives on what looks good, easy, or fun in film or print. Sadly, our society has never been so celebrity-driven. We are consumed with watching and imitating stars. We want to be stars ourselves, which I believe gave rise to "reality TV."

The celebrity-driven popularity of small dogs is a blatant example of animal exploitation. They have not been so popular in decades, due in part to their ever presence on the arm or in the purse of a celebrity. In 2006, beating out the German shepherd and the beagle, the Yorkshire terrier became the third most popular dog breed in America, its highest ranking since the American Kennel Club (AKC) recognized them in 1885.[16] Officially known as toy breeds, the AKC also uses unfortunate monikers such as "petite pooches" and "portable pets," which some celebrities seem to translate into "disposable." They use the dogs as fashion accessories and widely model bad examples of animal care. When an important decision is based on superficial parameters, outcomes are likely disastrous.

AND THE WINNERS ARE . . .

Dogs are the most popular companion animals in America, but more cats than dogs are companion animals, primarily because people with cats often have multiple cats. Although 44.8 million homes have dogs, compared to 38.4 million homes with cats, there are 74.8 million dogs living in American homes compared to 88.3 million cats.[17]

Authors have written thousands of books about dogs as companion animals, and most of the information in this book stems from dog studies. Consequently, in this section, I will not repeat what I, and others before me, have already said about cats and dogs. Here, I want to discuss some of the other animals who dutifully behave as companion animals and why people are drawn to them. They may be less popular than cats and dogs with fewer of their species in our homes, but they do not know that, and they deserve recognition, as do the people who love and care for them. To keep this manageable, I will focus on the eight most popular companion animals identified by the Pet Product Manufacturer's Association in their annual survey.

First Up: Fish

Freshwater fish are amazingly popular. In America, 14.2 million homes have freshwater fish.[18] In fact, behind dogs and cats, they are the most popular acquisition. The top three freshwater fish are neon tetras, angelfish, and bettas. Also on the list are guppies, oscars, mollies, and goldfish. Fish are sometimes the first animal a parent will allow a child to have, assessing their child's commitment to responsible care and considering any fish deaths negligible. Fish are also the animal of choice if either space or time are a consideration or housing restrictions will not permit a cat or dog.

I found fish keeping a lot of work and an incredible responsibility. Properly maintaining an entire life-support system for another sentient being was too much for me. Once some of my neons jumped out of the tank while I was at work, and I had to coax a friend to drive thirty miles to my house to help me gather them up. Many years later, feeling better prepared, I *rescued* three feeder-goldfish from a pet store in Providence, Rhode Island. I happened in to buy a dog brush just when a strapping young man was eagerly buying goldfish by the bucket to watch some other animal devour them. That day I spent thirty cents on the fish and $300 on equipment. Once I stabilized the tank, I enjoyed having them, but never lost that overwhelming sense of responsibility. I regretted the fish that died while I learned the science of adjusting the water in the tank. When one became listless, I scoured the Internet, determined to learn how to euthanize fish[19] so it would not suffer because of my ignorance. Luckily, when my husband and I moved from Rhode Island to Virginia, a neighbor adopted the survivors and placed them in her pond. They thrived and were having a great life at last report.

After my experience, I do not understand the minimal-care angle that so many people attribute to keeping fish. With all due respect to people who adore and care for them, I also have a little trouble considering fish as companion animals. Experts agree that companion status is precarious because "you cannot take them out of their water habitat, hold them, touch them, or take them places as you can with cats, dogs, and birds."[20] Keeping fish, especially small ones such as the tetras, is more of a hobby. When you have thirty to forty tiny fish swimming in a tank, how can you name them and relate to them? Yes, they swim to the corner of the tank when you enter the room, but that barely meets any of the requirements for a relationship. Animals that lack a limbic brain are not capable of having an emotional life, and it takes a special person to keep an animal that provides no emotional or social feedback. "You get no flicker of recognition, nothing. The vacuity behind the glances sends a chill down the mammalian spine."[21] Despite their appearance, we are learning that fish may not be the dim-witted creatures most suspect. Thanks to the increased number of research papers published in the past decade, we realize that fish can learn and use tools, and they have memory. It is going to take a lot of convincing, but some scientists say that the cognitive powers of fish "match or exceed those of 'higher' vertebrates, including non-human primates."[22]

Your Heart under Their Wings

Birds are companions in 6.4 million American homes,[23] and are the third most common companion animal after dogs and cats.[24] As popular as they are, few studies focus on the human-avian relationship, but data is emerging. For example, one study showed that bonds formed with birds are just as strong as those formed with cats and dogs, and that birds most frequently are acquired to fill social needs. This is no surprise because birds are also social creatures, capable of extending "love, affection, friendship, and companionship." Other reasons, beyond social factors, for acquiring birds as companions include aesthetic appeal (i.e., "like how the feathers feel") and cognitive attributes (i.e., "they are smart").[25] Yes, birds are smart, and scientists say that birds' behavior suggest that avian intelligence compares favorably to that of chimpanzees.[26]

One need look no further than Alex, a world renowned African grey parrot for proof. Before his sudden and unexplained death at the age of 31 in September 2007, Alex was made famous by the groundbreaking cognition and communication research conducted by Dr. Irene Pepperberg. Together, they revolutionized notions of how birds think—over the course of thirty years of landmark research in modern comparative psychology at various prestigious academic centers, most recently at Harvard and Brandeis Universities. Alex learned elements of English speech to identify fifty different objects, seven colors, five shapes, and quantities up to and including six, including a "zero-like concept." He used phrases such as "I want X" and "Wanna go Y," where X and Y were appropriate object and location labels. He acquired concepts of categories, bigger and smaller, same–different, and absence. Alex combined his labels to identify, request, refuse, and categorize more than 100 different items demonstrating a level and scope of cognitive abilities never expected in an avian species. Research with Alex shattered the generally held notion that parrots are only capable of mindless vocal mimicry. A shop owner randomly selected the bird for Pepperberg's research, for which Alex was named (**A**vian **L**earning **EX**periment), but he became an integral part of her life, as well as her research. His death was a profound personal loss for Pepperberg, but she can take comfort in the knowledge that together they forged a significant scientific legacy—forever changing our perception of the term "bird brain."[27]

Parrots are the most popular avian companions. Finches, in fact, are the only non-parrot in the top five most desirable birds. Each of the most prevalent 350 species of parrots have a series of complicated Latin names that identify their taxonomic order, family, species, and sub-species. We are likely more familiar with their common or casual names, especially for the birds most often found in American homes, which includes cockatiels, parakeets, love birds, African greys, and macaws. Parrot species range widely in behavior, appearance, basic requirements, and cost. For example, parakeets cost between $5 and $25, while other parrots cost between $800 and $2,500.

Parrots are endangered in the wild and, with the exception of cockatiels and parakeets, are protected by the Convention on International Trade in Endangered Species (CITES), which must approve all legal imports and exports. Parrots arrive legally in the United States by one of four methods: (1) imported as wild birds before Congress strengthened the CITES legislation with the Wild Bird Conservation Act in 1992; (2) imported by special permit after 1992; (3) descended from birds caught wild and raised here; or (4) exempted from regulations (i.e., parakeets). Poaching is rampant and deadly, and imported birds suffer miserably in transit, possibly introducing diseases to captive populations.[28]

Parrots are not suitable companions for everyone. They require solid commitments of time, money, and other resources. First of all, routine maintenance for one bird can cost nearly $3,000 a year. Further, parrots live in flocks, do not like being alone, thrive best when given hours of attention each day, and do not like sitting in a cage—they want to be out with you. They are highly intelligent, but great patience is needed to coax them to talk. These magnificent birds are high-maintenance; knowledge of their specific dietary needs and many environmental sensitivities is crucial. This is definitely not the companion for cigarette smokers because secondhand smoke can be lethal. Air fresheners and scented candles can also kill parrots. Their cages need regular and frequent cleaning, as do the areas around the cage because they will throw seeds and scatter debris. Parrots chew constantly and are not picky about what. All that aside, particularly appealing is their enviably long lifespans, which is between fifteen and sixty years, depending on breed. In spite of the obvious attraction, simply walking into a store and falling for their beauty without appropriate preparation could be disastrous for both of you.

Despite the challenges, those who are fortunate enough to live with parrots are dazzled and amazed by their antics, playfulness, and keen desire to interact with their "human flock mates." In The Parrot Who Owns Me, Dr. Joanna Burger describes her relationship with Tiko, who, among other things, eats food from her plate, wakes her in the morning, takes showers with her, trims HER nails, and slides down the banister for fun.[29] This is not emotional, anthropomorphic drivel; Burger is an ornithologist and a Rutgers University biology professor.

A recent study showed that birds, like other companions, are considered family members, "Feathered Kids," or "Fids." People who live with them find parrots as "devoted and loving a pet as a dog or cat."[30] Dr. Piet Drent of the Netherlands Institute of Ecology conducted a study of birds that demonstrated they have "consistent personalities that remain stable for years."[31] To accommodate his unique study participants, Drent used methods similar to those used in psychological studies with children, employing objects and activities.

Parrots enjoy being near their humans and talking using not just words, but also their characteristic sounds and body movements, head bobbing a familiar one. Suzy Collins probably thinks that parrots talk too much. You see, she lived with Chris Taylor, but was having an affair with a man named Gary. When Taylor's parrot, Ziggy, began to make kissing sounds when the name Gary was said on television and saying "Hiya Gary" when he heard Collins's cell phone ring, Taylor knew trouble was brewing. After they broke up, Ziggy refused to stop his banter, and used Collins's voice, so Taylor let her take Ziggy. "I wasn't sorry to see her [leave] after what she did, but it really broke my heart to let Ziggy go," he said.[32]

Parrots delight and amaze us with their humanlike qualities, especially their ability to talk. As I said earlier it takes patience, and not all parrots can or will demonstrate the ability. But one particular bird, a captive bred African grey named N'kisi, is the top "language using" animal in the world. Aimee Morgana, a production designer from Manhattan, hand-raised N'kisi and taught him to speak, beginning when he was six months old, the way you would teach a child, by explaining things to him in context. As a result, N'kisi uses words in context, with past, present, and future tenses, and he creates words and phrases. With a vocabulary of 950 words (it only takes one hundred words to read half of what's written in English) and a demonstrated sense of humor, N'kisi initiates conversations with questions about what people are doing, feeling, looking at, or thinking (e.g., "What c'ha doing on the phone?" "Can you see that?" and "Ya hear that?") When N'kisi first met the famous primate expert, Dr. Jane Goodall, after seeing a picture of her with an ape, he asked, "Got a chimp?" N'kisi's unparalleled ability to communicate has many in the scientific community speechless. He has been featured in *BBC Wildlife Magazine* and is the focus of a project led by Dr. Rupert Sheldrake (whose work in morphic fields I mentioned earlier) because of N'kisi's apparent ability to know what Morgana is thinking or doing when she is not in the room with him.[33]

Parrots are no different from other companion animals in that they sometimes enter our lives in unexpected, almost mystical ways. Dr. Gerald Koocher (a past president of the American Psychological Association, a former Harvard professor, and now professor and dean of the School for Health Studies at Simmons College in Boston), whose care of and relationships with parrots spans decades, shared a moving story with me, the paraphrase of which follows, about one of his birds— Rags, a blue and gold macaw. Rags had joined the family about twenty-three years before the telling of this story, after a divorcing couple surrendered him, but he had recently died from what was diagnosed on autopsy as liver cancer. The remaining birds in the family were Omar and Goeth, both African grey parrots, and Joey an orange wing Amazon. Rags had been like a "lap dog" to Koocher's wife, Robin, who was grief-stricken when Rags died, and she vowed not to have another macaw. But destiny had other plans. Robin stopped by the pet store that had provided a healthy macaw to Rag's veterinarian for blood transfusions, and while there spotted a pair of baby blue and gold macaws, who were only nine-weeks-old. One had been purchased, but she phoned a soon-to-be-surprised Dr. Koocher for him to endorse the purchase on the remaining bird. The chicks would not be ready to leave the store until they could eat solid food, which occurs when they are about five months of age. In the meantime, they had to be hand-fed with liquid nutrients around-the-clock, four to six times a day. While she waited, Robin drove twenty miles three to four times a week to visit the baby, and Dr. Koocher joined her on weekends. They had been toying with "elaborate" Spanish names to recognize the bird's heritage. For no reason of which he is aware, Dr. Koocher suggested that Robin name the bird Sylvia after her beloved mother, who had died suddenly of a brain aneurysm fifteen years earlier. They agreed, not knowing the gender of the bird, which is not obvious from coloration and had to be confirmed by genetic testing. When the test results arrived they confirmed that Sylvia was a divinely providential name, indeed. The bird was female, and her hatch date was May 29, 2005. Robin's mother's birthday was May 29th.[34]

Chickens may not be as talented or beautiful as parrots, but they are surprisingly good avian companions. As is true with other companion animals, when chicks are raised with patience and kindness they respond early with trust and affection. It may surprise you that chickens enjoy human contact and frequently respond to their given names. In fact, chickens have a lot going for them as companions: They can be tamed easily, have an array of colors and sizes (between one and ten pounds), live about fifteen years, and eat table craps, which should be supplemented with feed for nutritional balance. Depending on city regulations, chickens can be kept indoors, but by all accounts are impossible to housetrain.

Sylvia, one of three parrots in the family of Gerald and Robin Koocher, delights in paper from Chico's, a store reportedly named for a parrot. Photo courtesy of Gerald Koocher.

People gravitate towards chickens as companion animals for the same reasons associated with other animals: They grew up with chickens; their parents instilled a respect for chickens as companions; or they grew fond of chickens as companions after becoming adults.

Scholarly papers on companion chickens are scarce as—well, as scarce as—hen's teeth, but anecdotal evidence is readily available. For instance, New York attorney, Barbara Moore thought it was "amazing" how her leghorn rooster adapted to city life. "He sits in a car like a person or on a sofa watching TV with the family." Jennifer Raymond of California says that chickens have "intelligence [that is] rarely nurtured by humans. When it is, the results are often surprising." Finally, Diane English said, "One day my bantam cochin hen, Gwen, came clear across the grass fussing and fussing 'till I asked her if she wanted to go in the house. Together we set out. She hurried ahead of me and hurried in when I opened the door. She needed that door opened for her to get to her cage where she could lay her eggs properly, and she knew I could and would do that for her. That is not stupid." People with companion chickens say they are not cowards, either. Hens and rooster are known to be aggressive and a rooster will sacrifice his life to save his mate, not backing down even to a cat. Cindy Pollock of Arizona said, "We have to remember that they are small birds, and survival instincts tell them to run most of the time when faced with danger. Wouldn't you, if you were eighteen inches high, with no arms, and surrounded by a bunch of giant predators?"[35]

No matter which bird flock calls to you, chances are you will be in good company because most recent research indicates that "Human-avian interaction is no less rewarding for humans than interaction with cats and dogs, and for some individuals, may be even more so."[36]

Slither, Scales, and Tails

Reptiles and amphibians are the most unlikely companions, but 13.4 million of reptiles live in nearly 5 million American homes as just that.[37] People who keep cold-blooded animals are often considered hobbyists, and I see the point. If I were to call any animal a *pet*, rather than a companion, it would be an amphibian because frogs, toads, newts, or salamanders do not meet important qualifications for a companion animal. A traditional human-companion animal relationship simply does not seem possible, but there is no denying that amphibians are popular, too. Many young children are awed when they learn that amphibians lead double lives—they are distinguished in the animal kingdom by having both a gill-breathing stage and a lung-breathing stage. Their lives begin in the water, where they are hatched, but they move to land as they mature and grow legs. Collecting tadpoles and watching them morph into frogs is a popular activity for children who live near ponds and lakes. Worldwide, amphibians comprise more than 6,000 species, many of them threatened with extinction because of habitat loss and exploitation.[38,39] Amphibians range in size—from the size of a dime to the size of a small cat, and cost—from a few dollars to thousands of dollars.[40] Sociological or psychological data on amphibians as companions or pets is essentially nonexistent, but available indicators suggest that the most popular amphibians are frogs.

Reptiles surpass amphibians in popularity, and increased consumer demand over the past decade has had tragic environmental and ethical consequences, both in the United States, and in the reptiles' various countries of origin. The notion of lizards as pets or companions is easier for me to accept than other animals in the class *Repitilia*, which also includes snakes, turtles, and crocodiles.

Snakes, well-known reptiles, are best categorized as exotic animals (or exotics), and their keepers are similar to hobbyists or enthusiasts. People who choose to keep most reptiles are not seeking much in the way of companionship, obviously. Good thing; because with a snake, that is impossible. Snake keepers are not looking for an animal to share experiences or social contact. Snakes are not social animals and do not really like being handled. Snake keepers need no recognition or communication—there is no light behind snakes' eyes. Many snake species can be deadly to humans, and injury and death are frequently reported. Tame is not a word that will ever apply to a snake even after years of captivity. A person is nothing to them because snakes are pure instinct, which compels them to eat, procreate, and survive. People who advocate snakes as pets point out that they are perfect for people with allergies because they have no hair or dander, do not require daily feeding, and are self-contained. True, but this does not qualify them as companions and certainly does not offset either the danger or difficulty involved in having them in the home. The person and the snake are at grave risk. Captive snakes suffer and die easily from inadequate care from uninformed people, same as with other captive reptiles. I cannot help but suspect that people who keep snakes, especially large ones, are thrill-seekers who like to stay a bit on edge. Think about it. A person who keeps a snake (such as pythons that become ten feet long), could be accidentally killed by the snake if it got out of its cage and was hungry, while the person slept. You have heard the stories. A snake cannot distinguish between you and food, and it is programmed to take down wriggling warm bodies. You know how a companion dog will release a bite once he or she realizes that your finger is wrapped around the ball, too. That is not going to happen with a snake. A loss of concentration or an unguarded moment can spell death for snake keepers.

Speaking of food: feeding a snake takes a person who can feed one animal to another, and when needed, kill one animal to feed to another. You see, if snake keepers cannot find a pet store that will humanely kill prey, most likely mice, they will have to find a humane way to do it themselves.

I am squeamish, and this is reprehensible to me, but there are people who enjoy the company of snakes so much that they are willing to care for them in spite of the risks and absence of recompense.

Snakes may not be good companions, but many snake keepers enjoy the companionship of each other during local nonprofit herpetological associations, whose stated missions often include educating of the public to the value of keeping snakes and ensuring that people interested in snakes are alert to the rigors of responsible, proper care. Some associations also offer adoption services, in addition to buying opportunities. Many associations lobby for laws and ordinances that favor their interests. Further, many local, state, and federal laws govern reptile-keeping, especially for dangerous and rare species, and licenses are often required.

If the threat of being crushed or consumed is not enough, recent research indicates that reptiles, in general, expose humans to *salmonella*. Diseases that spread from humans to animals are defined as zoonotic illnesses.[41] Of the nearly 1.4 million annual human *salmonella* infections—600 that end in death—74,000 are associated with exposure to reptiles and amphibians.[42,43] Consequently, the Centers for Disease Control and Prevention (CDC) recommends that children under age five and people with weak immune systems avoid contact with reptiles.

Dangers aside for a moment, reptiles have two characteristics that make them unusual and appealing companion animals. First, scales or hard shells cover their bodies, and they have long lifespans. Turtles, for instance, can live for more than thirty years, pythons for more than fifteen years, and lizards for more than twenty years. You will not have a tough time finding a reptile because more than 8,000 species exist. Lizards, the most popular reptile by far, comprise nearly 4,000 subspecies.

Simply put, lizards are four-legged reptiles with a tail. The most popular lizard is the one that most experts agree do not make good associates for humans: the green iguana. Melissa Kaplan, who has written extensively on iguana, says, "Iguanas are difficult, frustrating, complicated, complex—and potentially dangerous." As if that were not enough of a discouragement, she adds, "They are very complex to care for, environmentally, psychosocially, and nutritionally."[44] Iguanas do not thrive in captivity and, according to Kaplan, are the number one dumped reptile in America, and perhaps the world.

Iguanas are high-maintenance and few people can meet the challenge of caring for them successfully, resulting in abbreviated lifespans for the animals. People who care *properly* for iguanas need special characteristics. They must be resourceful and tenacious to create the very specific environmental and dietary needs iguanas require. Basically, they must be willing to turn some part of their own residence into a tropical rainforest or build a proper enclosure because commercials enclosures are rarely large enough. To make the matter more demanding, iguanas grow fast. In just two years their length increases from a few inches to two or three feet, with an ultimate length of five to six feet.

The person wanting to care for an iguana must be capable of sustaining interest in the face of challenges because they will face many to keep the animal healthy, not the least of which is finding a suitable veterinarian. The person should have the economic means to maintain the animal over their possible long lifespans, including basic supplies, food, and utilities to maintain a tropical climate year-round.

Adult iguanas are herbivores, but that does not mean they can survive on take-out salad from Whole Foods. Kaplan says that iguanas require a variety of healthy greens and fruits prepared in a way to make them digestible. She says that it takes one to two hours a week to prepare their meals, this after trolling stores for the right ingredients. Commercially prepared foods for herbivores are not sufficient replacements for "properly constructed fresh food."

I hope that I have said enough to discourage anyone from acquiring an amphibian or a reptile as a companion. It is a very poor arrangement, one that often puts the human inhabitants at risk, and is always risky for the animal. However, I am not naïve enough to think that anything I say will put an end to the practice of keeping reptiles.

So in the interest of full disclosure, let me include that people report great joy and pleasure from living with one reptile in particular, the iguana. Unfortunately, this is a shame because iguanas are reptiles most unsuited for living in captivity. (Okay, alligators and crocodiles, too, but you are strictly food to them, making them less likely adoptees, thereby not requiring my warnings.)

As things happen, when you hold strong opinions about something, as I do about iguanas as pets, the world often provides you with contradictory information to expand your thinking. Turns out that my editor for this book, Debora Carvalko, lives with and loves an iguana, a female named Ziggy. When she told me that Ziggy fell asleep on her chest as she whispered to him, I had to know more. Carvalko is not insensitive, unsocial, or reclusive—characteristics typically attributed to lizard lovers. Quite the contrary, she has a highly social career and is the mother of active children, with all the action that entails. I was fascinated that she refers to her care of Ziggy as "mothering." Her comments about Ziggy are reminiscent of any cat or dog lover. Carvalko has two cats, so technically, I guess I could refer to her as a cat person with an iguana, but that would demean her relationship with Ziggy.

Carvalko acknowledges, "It is amazing that a reptile can seemingly be so at peace and comfortable with a human," but Ziggy's favorite activity is to catch a nap on Carvalko's chest while she is napping. Sometimes Carvalko awakes to find Ziggy's head on her chin, and she can feel Ziggy's breath on her cheek. Ziggy is currently four feet long, "exceptionally alert and agile, and fast," Carvalko says. She has a leash for Ziggy and takes her on walks, which sometimes turn into runs if Ziggy spots a tree she is interested in climbing. In spite of Carvalko's diligent custodianship, Ziggy became ill, after eating an improper food that a pet store employee recommended. Without proper nutrition, Ziggy developed a form of osteoporosis that caused her lower jaw to thicken, and she was unable to chew. A conscientious caretaker, Carvalko fed Ziggy with an eyedropper and was prepared to do so for the rest of Ziggy's life.

With less dedicated care, Ziggy would surely have died, but Carvalko searched the Internet to find a palatable, powered diet with the balanced nutrients that an iguana required, which could be licked rather than chewed. Miraculously, Ziggy's condition reversed. Now, Ziggy eats what Carvalko calls a "real" diet that includes collard greens, dandelion greens, sprouts, snow peas, green peppers, mushrooms, carrots, and apples.

Ziggy's close call may have created what Carvalko describes as the "unexpected and strong bond" between them, and she jokes that she and Ziggy will be together long after her children are on their own. She envisions that she will grab her cane, get out of her rocking chair, and say, "Time to feed my iguana."[45]

Ziggy seems to recognize Carvalko's efforts and props herself up when Carvalko enters a room, slapping the front of the cage repeatedly in excitement at seeing her. It is not a great leap to think that Ziggy is trying to communicate with Carvalko.

A little science backs up some of Carvalko's observations. Scott McRobert, a biology professor at Saint Joseph's University in Philadelphia, and his colleagues noticed that the laboratory's iguana, Fido, would bob his head when McRobert approached, but ignored everyone else. They designed a brief study to determine if Fido could distinguish McRobert (who handled him the most) from strangers, and from a student who had cared for him four years earlier. The twelve-year-old iguana ignored the strangers, but responded to McRobert and the student equally when he could see them, but not hear them. However, when they read out loud, Fido bobbed his head three times as often for McRobert as he did the student. The response indicates that Fido recognized both McRobert's voice and his face. This was probably the first time a lizard's recognition of a human was evaluated scientifically. McRobert plans to evaluate Fido's response to incongruent visual and audio cues, using recorded voices.[46] Stay tuned.

Another study revealed that lizards have personalities, and differences therein. Some were found to be naturally gregarious, while others displayed a preference for being alone.[47] Mellow may not be a recognized personality type, but iguanas on the Galapagos Islands are in danger because they are too relaxed and mellow. With no natural predators on the island, the iguanas have lost the ability to respond appropriately to stress, according to a new study. The iguanas allowed humans to get within six feet of them before they took off. Even when they fled, they did so well below speeds at which they were capable, about six miles per hour. Scientists knew the iguanas were not stressed because they easily caught them, after trailing them for about fifteen minutes, and found low levels of corticosteroids, a stress hormone, in their blood. To prove their point, the researchers briefly bagged the animals after catching them and the iguanas' stress levels quadrupled. You could say that the iguanas are slow learners because once released they still gave the scientists other chances to catch them. I say that they are too trusting: they did not let the scientists get as close, but still did not run fast enough to get away. I am not sure what to say about this study. Allow me to digress for a moment to say that the study demonstrates the beauty of science and the investigational process. Who would think of such a thing? Chasing an iguana? Nonetheless, results from this study contribute to the pool of animal knowledge and serve a purpose. For one thing, researchers say their results explain why conservation methods that reintroduce a tame species with an aggressive predator do not work—the tamer species never learns an appropriate level of fear. I see that point, but we know that animals pass down information to offspring. So I bet sooner or later, those iguanas would learn what many wild animals know: Stay away from people! More seriously, the study results allow me to report the natural docility of these creatures, which likely contributes to their appeal as companions.

Empirical data on the iguana is hard to come by, but Melissa Kaplan has collected an enviable amount of data about iguana behavior, from decades of living with them. Unfortunately her data is anecdotal, but that is one way scientific theories are born.

When I contacted her, she said that her latest iguana, Mike, was "glued" to her chest, "with his tail hanging down, soaking up the rubs and baby-talk cooing." Who would think that these creatures like whispers of baby talk? She says that when Mike is stressed, he likes to soak in the bathtub. The cost of a long bath and a heated room are a bit high, so Kaplan said she had a little talk with him after chasing him back into his room from the tub about six times. She assured me that she does not really think he understands her, but she is adamant that iguanas "DO" learn words. Like dogs, they learn the basics: "Wanna bath?" "Go for ride?" and "Go poopy/potty?" She said that iguanas, "but not all iguanas, and not all the time," can also learn the names of other iguanas, other pets, and humans. She says that observant, experienced owners pick up on behavior that is more than "mere instinct or dominance." Mike clearly likes to spend time with Kaplan and makes his wishes undeniable by plopping on her and staying for nearly an hour or by traversing the house, long after his bedtime, to find her for a snuggle before being tucked in. Take a deep breath for this next bit of information: Mike likes to sleep in the bed, with his snout touching Kaplan.[48] Too cute.

Obviously, iguanas can become pretty docile from frequent handling and some enjoy being rubbed. However, many reptile experts urge caution during breeding season and discourage all facial contact, going so far as to suggest minimal handling because of zoonotic diseases. The CDC suggests a hygienic protocol when handling iguanas to reduce risk.[49]

Equine Fantasies Sometimes Come True

When I was a child, all of my friends dreamed of having a pony or a horse. We either wanted Prince Charming to ride in on one, run away to the circus on one, or become a cowboy on one. A pony at a birthday party was the ultimate fantasy, as they say, "back in the day." My personal wish was for a *baby horse*. I understood that horses were big and hard to manage, and I presumed that if I got one as a baby, we could grow up together. The horse would then know me, and not trample me. Later, I went through a clueless stage during which I thought horses were large, dumb creatures—so big that their heads rarely knew what their bodies were doing. Too many people get stuck in that phase, where they continue in perverse thinking that horses are only good for commercial ventures and sport. They never realize, as I finally did, that horses are complex, majestic creatures with an impressive social life and profound emotional reactions. Some very fortunate enlightened people, about four percent of the population, get to live the fantasy of actually having a horse. Most people with horses have children and large families of five or more and have the high incomes required to properly maintain horses.

People who select horses as companion animals do so for the same reasons that people want a dog, a cat, or any other animal: for the social interaction with the animal and other people who love them. In spite of the fact that horses do not live in the house with us, we still consider them family. A survey of pony clubs revealed that 80 percent of the adolescent members considered their horse a family member, frequently a brother or sister. Most riders think of their horses as children.[50] Unlike other companion animals, horses usually serve another function, typically that of mount. Many people acquire horses simply because they like to ride and do not see the horse as a companion at all. I have to think they are really missing out on a great opportunity. I must say that the sad majority of horses will never be more than livestock.

Before I leave a large animal category, I want to slip in someone special. Well, three special someones: Elvis and his crew. I have purposefully excluded discussing farm animals as companions, but I must make this one notable exception because the animal is remarkable and so is the man who calls him friend. Award-winning author Jon Katz delves into the lives of animals with precision, courage, and conviction. He typically reveals profoundly wise insights about the relationships between people and dogs. Consequently, the fact that he has taken up with a 1,800-pound cow, renamed Elvis, is a stunner. The cow had belonged to a friend of Katz, a dairy farmer named Peter Hanks, who lived near Katz in rural New Jersey. Katz describes Peter as a man "unsentimental about livestock." They are his livelihood and he doesn't get "emotionally attached" to them. This cow was different, as Hanks explained to Katz when he showed up with the cow, trying to get Katz interested in taking him on. Brownie, Hanks's name for the cow,

Author Jon Katz and Elvis, the cow who Katz taught to respond to commands. Photo courtesy of Peter Hanks.

followed him around, put his head on Hanks's shoulder, and even "licked him." (I will take the liberty of calling that a kiss.) Katz and Hanks struck a bargain, and Brownie became Elvis—Katz's new companion. Elvis continued to demonstrate his affinity for people, and his ability to learn conventions not typically associated with a cow. For instance, Katz taught Elvis to "come when called and stay when asked," and Elvis taught Katz, and the rest of us, that cows—when allowed—are smart, social animals, who love to play and show and receive affection.[51]

Size Matters Not

The last category of "pets" in the APPMA survey each year is for the "small animal." I guarantee that every animal small enough for a child to carry or coax home has been auditioned as a companion. Consequently, it is impossible to discuss each one, so I will focus on the ones who have remained popular as companions over the years.

First, a rodent companion may be a hard sell, especially a rat or mouse, but popular they are. Rats are said to be intelligent, affectionate, curious, and very social. Debbie Ducommun, better known as the Rat Lady, goes beyond the initial reaction most of us have to rats to appreciate the characteristics that make them perfect companions. She had rats as a child, and her love for all animals matured as she did. A long career in the animal care industry led to a job in the psychology department of California State University, where she was responsible for the rats. She took the job with mixed emotions, but accepted because she felt that the rats deserved to have a person who loved them to care for them. Her expertise with rats became renown, and she formed the Rat Fan Club in 1992. Membership growth has been steady, with 600 members in twelve countries. Satisfied that she has increased the popularity of rats, Ducommun has created the Rat Assistance and Teaching Society, a nonprofit organization to educate the animal professionals, especially shelters and veterinarians, about proper care for rats.

One of the reasons that rats make good companions is that they are trainable to the limit of your imagination, capable of responding to their names and learning tricks. Their abilities differ, as is true with all living beings. "[Rats] all have different personalities. Some are outgoing and social, some are quieter," said Jewel Waldrip of the Humane Society of Southern Arizona. "They really are individuals."[52] Rats are very responsive to handling and easily become affectionate. Scientists have recently discovered that rats even laugh.

Believe it or not, a rat is not just a rat. There are "Fancy Rats," with their own organization to establish and maintain standards of color and facilitate breeding for certain personality characteristics. Fancy rats carry prestigious names that match their appearance, such as Russian Blue Point and Himalayan, and they must meet rigid criteria to earn the name, just like dogs in the American Kennel Club. For example, to be considered a "Rex," the rat must have curly hair and whiskers. The "Berkshire Dumbo" has ears slightly larger than normally seen on a rat, and they flank the head rather than sit atop it. "Hooded" rats must have a different forefront color, and sometimes only one other color is allowed on the rest of the body. Another breed, the "Variegated," has the coloring of an English springer spaniel.

Other animals from the rodent family are not nearly as organized, but are equally popular, especially the gerbil, the hamster, and the guinea pig. All rodents have one thing in common; they take care and individual attention, and despite their size, are not disposable. These little creatures have big hearts and are able to gnaw their way into yours. They can provide as much pleasure, company, and entertainment as any dog and more than some cats. The only disadvantage people who love rats express is their short lifespans, which range from one to three years. People with cats and dogs lament having just ten to twenty years with their beloved companions, but that is an enviable long time to people who love rats.

Contrary to popular belief, another small animal that has found favor as a companion is NOT a rodent. Exactly what it is has been debatable, but one name most people agree on is "Bunny." I am referring, of course, to the rabbit, whose phylogenesis has been compared to animals from cats and rodents to primates and horses. Yes, rabbits may resemble rodents, but they do not belong to the order *Rodentia*, but to the order *Lagomorpha*.

Rabbits become particularly popular around Easter, when many people buy them impulsively thinking that they are low maintenance, but that is far from the truth. Actually, I hope you are getting the accurate notion that there is no such thing as a low-maintenance companion animal. A low-maintenance companion animal is as possible as a low-maintenance child. Both require long-term commitments and dedicated resources.

Rabbits need exercise, regular grooming, including nail trims. Rabbits are victims of their cuteness. People see them and respond to their beautiful eyes, long eyelashes, soft fur, and cute hopping. As a companion, rabbits can be quiet and smart with a good nature. They can learn to play with toys, recognize their names, and use a litter box. However, even rabbit enthusiasts admit that rabbits are primarily grouchy, can be little pellet machines (one type of pellet goes in, and another comes out), can gnaw you out of house and home, and really do not like being held and petted. "Babies are cute, but soon [at about five months of age] turn into a raging pile of hormones," says March Schaaf, founder of a California rescue group, called Save a Bunny. Intact rabbits "may spray urine to mark their territory," "hump anything from the family cat to a guest's leg," and "can become aggressive about their cage and supplies." When these things happen, many people abandon their rabbit to an animal shelter or release it to live with the wild rabbits. The latter is a sure death sentence because a domesticated rabbit—especially one bred in designer colors, such as the French angora—is a predator's dream. Rabbits are associated with speed, but fast when getting away from a human is not fast enough when trying to get away from an unleashed dog, a prowling cat, or a hungry hawk.

Because of the lack of accurate information on rabbits, people form many misconceptions about them, which results in many homeless hares. Save a Bunny rescues nearly 300 rabbits annually. This is a very sad, unfortunate situation. Schaaf says, "For the right family, rabbits are wonderful. People just need to first be educated."[53] Organizations, such as the House Rabbit Society, strive for improved care and better understanding of rabbits through education. The society has chapters across the country and is involved in advocacy and protection.

4

Roles That Animals Play in Our Lives and How We Influence Each Other

The heart has its reasons where reason knows nothing.
—Blaise Pascal, French mathematician

Much of the *why* and *who* as relates to companion animals is debatable, but one fact is indisputable: they have been and continue to be indispensable, irreplaceable members of human culture and society. Companion animals are asked to fulfill an array of roles for us, and for the most part, they execute their roles with contagious fervor and indefatigable perfection.

Most of the roles that animals play in our lives are a function of their sociability. Animals with highly social natures have demonstrated a more diverse range of possibilities as companions, and we capitalize on their tendencies, creating what we believe are opportunities that enhance and benefit their lives, as well as our own.

I cannot possibly mention each role, so I will focus on the more prevalent and successful roles, with a discussion of their occupational and therapeutic activities in Chapter 6. Once again, I must say that most of the data here pertains to dogs and cats, but I believe that other companion animals can perform many of the same roles.

WE ARE FAMILY

First and foremost, companion animals are family, particularly those who live in our homes.

Overall, 75 percent of people with companion animals consider them a member of their family, and the reasons for this continue to emerge. One author makes a convincing statement with which no data could argue: "Family members are devoted to each other; we rescue our [animals] and we believe that our [animals] are capable of rescuing us." He adds that when the animal greets you at the door after work, sits with you on the couch to watch TV after supper, perhaps sleeps next to or near you, and is taken into consideration when you plan your vacations, grocery shopping, and daily routine, that animal is family.[1]

The three most popular companion animals (i.e., dogs, cats, and birds) usually hold a specific role within the family—that of an infant or a young child.[2]

Companion animals are perfectly suited to be treated as a child because, for the most part, they are eternal babies, who require food, protection, grooming, and healthcare their entire lives. We coo and coddle them the way most people do with a child. Part of the their appeal is that they can satisfy our biological need to nurture. Unquestionably, this is why we bred miniature and toy animals, who can mimic infantile behavior for their entire lives.

I could provide an abundance of evidence to prove that we treat companion animals more like children than any other role. However, I think this one quote nails it: "The act that critically defines a pet as a child is our willingness to put up with the excrement—to handle it, to permit it in the house, to accept it in the street."[3]

Furthermore, we very often tolerate behavior from our animals that we do not from our children, and we extend privileges to them that we do not offer to our own offspring. What does the animal do to garner such favor? Primarily, companion animals have the edge over children in one important area: constancy. Your dog or cat, and especially your bird, is going to be there when the human children have left home or are mad and not talking to you. Your animal "child" is not going to grow up, become independent, and leave home. This child will never barter with or withdraw affection. You will always be the center of this child's world, and this child will pretty much do what you want forever.

Since the number of companion animals in the United States exceeds the number of children, some speculate that people are substituting animals, especially dogs, for children. Yet, the data do not support this theory. For instance, 30 percent of all families live with dogs, but 56 percent of families with children have at least one dog.[4] That hardly suggests people are replacing the children. Dogs, in particular, are often incorporated into a family to renew activities with the children and to foster a sense of family. Interestingly, it is not unusual for a child, especially those without siblings, to consider their cat or dog a sibling. Many children share the sentiments of Tre Walker of Branchburg, New Jersey, who said, "My dog, Ashton, a Jack Russell, is my best and only brother." The fact that we consider our dogs and cats as our children may explain some of the ways we spoil and pamper them.[5]

SOCIAL CONNECTORS

A dog's ability to be a friend to the friendless is legendary and unparalleled. Being a friend and providing social support are the most important functions that any companion animal fulfills. An animal can be the most significant companion in a person's life; this is especially true for children and the elderly.

An extensive body of research, dating back to the late 1970s, documents the importance of social support, and for many people, an animal either is that support or supplements other social relationships. Countless scientific and popular press publications expound on the importance of social support.

Recently, a specific kind of social connection emerged as especially important: a confidante. In the book, *Emotional Longevity* (which I had the pleasure of coauthoring), clinical psychologist Dr. Norman Anderson, CEO of the American Psychological Association, devotes an entire chapter to the critical nature of emotional disclosure, which can boost the immune system, improve mood, decrease doctor visits, and improve grade-point averages.[6]

Much of the research in this field, pioneered by Dr. James Pennebaker and furthered by Dr. Joshua Smythe, focuses on written disclosure, but giving *voice* to traumas by expressing them to someone else who will keep your confidence is also showing benefits.

What better confidante than one who cannot read, write, or talk? And we are making the best use of this unique quality: 98 percent of clients at a veterinary clinic at the University of Pennsylvania reported that they talk to their companion animals, and 80 percent said they spoke to them as if they were human. An important 30 percent of them said they confided in their animal.[7] Obviously, the potential for a companion animal to be a confidante enhances the benefits of the social relationships they provide. Companion animals listen without judgment, happy simply to be in your presence, enjoying your attention.

MATCHMAKERS

Must Love Dogs is more than the title of a movie; it's practically a new mantra. "Dogs are so important ... that they can ... make or break a relationship," says Gail Miller, spokesperson for the American Kennel Club (AKC). Sixty-six percent of respondents to a 2005 AKC survey said they would not date someone who disliked their dog. Of the 91 million single people in the United States, about 30 percent are self-described "pet lovers," according to another survey.[8] Being in a relationship with someone who is receptive to your companion animals can avert relationship tensions associated with issues such as allergies and shared animal responsibilities.

Not getting along with your intended's companion animals or the blended animals not getting along can be a "deal breaker." Consequently, dating services that cater to animal lovers are cropping up, and questions about animals is included in most surveys of all dating services. People like Cherie Wilson find comfort in that because she would like to add a boyfriend to the other four guys in her life—a Rhodesian ridgeback, an Australian cattle dog, and two cats—so she registered at www.AnimalAttraction.com. Dan Cohen conceived the site (where people post photos of themselves and/or their animals and wait for responses) after happening upon a "doggy happy hour," and noticing how easily the people interacted. "The whole vibe of the place was different than if you'd had the exact same bar without the dogs," he said.

His observation was in keeping with anecdotal and scientific data that people with dogs are more approachable, and are considered more social. This all makes perfectly good sense to Brian McGlynn, an engineer who shares his life with Kona, a black Labrador. He is interested in people with companion animals because he feels they are a "little more stable" and "responsible." "They're in charge of keeping at least one person alive," he says. McGlynn ended up finding an animal-loving steady the old-fashioned way: friends introduced them. Fortunately, their combined animals got along, because he said, "If they hadn't, it would have ended it, for both of us."[9]

Most of the online animal lovers post about cats and dogs, but people are also seeking other people who might like more unusual animals, such as ferrets, reptiles, and arachnids. Even a snake can facilitate social interaction said Andrea Miller, of *Tango* magazine, "A pet snake, for instance, forces you to go places where other people with pet snakes might be." Laura Hinson Miller, author of *The Dog Dialogues*, agrees, adding that exotic animals are "great personality indicators." She feels exotic animals demonstrate that people are "maybe more adventurous, a little left of center. Pets telegraph who you really are. It's a wonderful way to connect."[10]

Some singles find dog parks and doggy yappy hours preferable to singles bars. Cherie Wilson said that her dogs are excellent judges of character and on more than one occasion have growled at unsuitable suitors.

Some companion animals, especially dogs, are not only matchmakers, but also establish hard criteria to match as well. Ninety percent of respondents to a survey conducted by the AKC said that their dog had at least one quality they would like to see in their significant other. The 1,000 adult respondents were evenly divided as to having or not having dogs, and 34 percent of the women agreed with this statement, "If my dog was a man, he'd be my boyfriend."[11]

Obviously, not all companion animals model good relationship behavior, but dogs sure hit the mark as evidenced by a recent AKC poll. Women listed the following attributes, found in their dogs that they wish the men in their lives shared:

1. Always in a good mood,
2. Always willing to spend time together,
3. Always ready for a couch cuddle,
4. Likes to exercise, and
5. Not picky about what's on for dinner.

Men had wishes of their own, identifying the following desirable characteristics in women that they appreciated in their dogs:

1. Satisfied not going out and just hanging around the house,
2. Very affectionate when he comes home from work,
3. Unconcerned about how much sports are on the television,
4. Not a fashion critic, and
5. Unconcerned about what he's thinking.

Both men and women found that not talking back was an attractive behavior modeled by their dogs. All good advice, maybe, but primarily just good tongue-in-cheek fun.

TEACHER

Historically, we have viewed ourselves as the teacher or trainer where our companion animals are concerned. Nonetheless, many people suggest that we are often the beneficiaries of *their* training and innate knowledge. From a practical perspective we know that dogs and cats can train us to do things they want us to do. How often have you heard a dog or a cat person lament, "I'm not sure who's training whom?" We know that animals can inspire us, as children do, to operate outside of our established comfort zones and engage in activities we might otherwise avoid.

An increasing number of people believe that animals teach us profound lessons about life, love, and the all-important "living in the moment." Admittedly an esoteric viewpoint, but some go so far as saying that animals impart spiritual lessons about inner peace and a connection to God or nature. They believe that cats and dogs teach us by modeling behavior that we translate into a value system that includes forgiveness, loyalty, openness, and trust. For example, one animal guardian, who lives with a twelve-year-old female Manchester rat terrier, said that the dog "doesn't differentiate among those who come to the door. It is of no consequence to her whether the visitor is Catholic or Jew or Buddhist or atheist. Whether banker or beggar, light or dark skinned, straight or gay. Her heart is open to all who come. She hones my spiritual awareness through such behavior."[12]

This is a sentiment that psychologist, spiritual seeker, and animal activist Dr. Mary Lou Randour, author of *Animal Grace*, understands. Her book explains how our deep kinship with and responsibilities to animals can manifest into profound spiritual understanding. From her unique vantage, she can assert (among other principles) that "animals have a wisdom, that is, as yet, largely undiscovered by some, and unexplored by others. In many ways their sensory world is vastly different from ours. In that difference, animals have access to levels of reality that might remain hidden to us without their help." She reminds us that a quest for more spiritual connectedness through our companion animals does not require us to do anything special. "It is in ordinary events that we find extraordinary spiritual possibilities," she says.[13]

COWORKER

In the next chapter, you will read about animals with real jobs, but what I refer to now are animals who accompany their people to work, as an extension of their primary role as companion. They go to work simply to be with their guardians. Their purpose is to make the human employees feel better about having to work. By some counts, one in five American companies allow companion animals at work because they believe that having them around can lower absenteeism and encourage employees to get along.[14]

A survey by www.SimplyHired.com indicates that 66 percent of people with dogs would work longer hours if they could bring their dogs to work and 32 percent said they would take a pay cut for the privilege.

Amazon and Google were among the recognized names listed in the survey of dog-friendly workplaces. A surprising dog-friendly place is Replacements Ltd., which specializes in china, and they have 11 million pieces of it, according to their Web site. The North Carolina company has irreplaceables and breakables, but according to their president, Scott Fleming, the dozens of dogs who come to work each day "have not broken a single piece." He cannot say that about the human employees.[15]

When A2L Technologies, a Florida environmental engineering consulting firm, bought its headquarters building, the first order of business was to fence in the backyard and install a doggie door because all of the employees bring their dogs to work. A2L CEO and president Larry Schmaltz believes that employee retention is enhanced because the staff appreciates the perk. He said, the dogs "give a calming sense in the office and sometimes even entertain us. When someone is frustrated with a problem or dilemma, petting one of the dogs takes their mind off the problem and relaxes them."[16]

Pets are said to boost employee morale, increase productivity, and reduce stress, but not everyone loves dogs, and companies must consider allergies and phobias of other employees. Consequently, workplaces establish policies as they do with dress codes and other potential allergens, such as perfume, to insure that everyone has an appropriate work environment.

Inviting dogs into the workplace is not a passing fancy because each June 10,000 businesses participate in Take Your Dog to Work Day, which is sponsored by Pet Sitter's International.

The American Pet Products Manufacturers Association (APPMA) 2000 survey said that 20 percent of companies that allow pets at work show a decrease in employee absenteeism, 96 percent of companies say pets create positive work relations, and 58 percent of employees stay later at work.[17]

Obviously, many work environments are unsuitable for animals, places where their presence could be unsanitary, impede workflow, or otherwise create havoc. However, when appropriate, dogs in the workplace often improve the mood of employees and clients.

CHILD'S PLAYMATE

A child's personality, age, and development should be taken into account before a companion animal is acquired. Although children mature at different rates, many animal welfare organizations discourage animals for children under the age of four or five. Children younger can mishandle and harm an animal, especially baby or small animals. Young children are not developed enough themselves to understand animal behavior and may unknowingly stress an animal until it bites. For instance, as cute as they may look together, a puppy and a toddler are not a good combination. Children learn gentleness and responsibility at different rates, and a companion animal should fit the child's current developmental level. A companion animal is not something that a child should "grow into." Parents must always be prepared to either take over care or oversee a child's interaction with companion animals for the safety of all concerned. I do not support animals being brought into the home to help teach children empathy or responsibility. Children should have demonstrated these characteristics before the care of an animal is turned over to them. Animals do not exist to be teaching tools, and all animals deserve to have their basic care provided and social needs satisfied. A common mistake is for parents to incorporate an animal in the family to entertain, distract, or teach lessons that can come at the expense of the animal. Care must be taken to match the child's emerging personality with an appropriate animal. For example, children who are active and impulsive may have greater success with sturdy and calm companions, which is probably why retrievers are so overwhelmingly popular. A special caveat: most children are not fastidious enough to care for a reptile, which I do not recommend as companions anyway. I am also not a proponent of "starter pets," which fish are often considered. Freshwater fish are easier to manage than saltwater fish, but neither should be considered disposable—collateral damage on the child's way to bigger and better animals.

SOURCES OF FUEL

A bit of trivia is always fun, and I imagine you did not know that among companion animals, dogs and cats alone produce 10 million tons of waste each year. Most of it ends up in landfills "mummified for generations in plastic bags" or seeps into human water supplies. San Francisco is exploring a creative, progressive way to deal with companion animal feces, which makes up 4 percent of its residential waste—almost as much as disposable diapers. The Bay City is the first in the United States to investigate transforming companion animal waste into methane, which can be used in any equipment powered by natural gas. The company responsible for the city's waste removal is conducting a feasibility project to determine if collected matter can be processed through a "methane digester" to create methane fuel. This may seem preposterous, but several European cities and a few American dairy farms already convert animal waste into energy.[18]

THEIR INFLUENCE ON US

I had planned to say that companion animals *exert* influence on us, but frankly, the influence happens without any exertion on their part. They simply just do it. Influence, as defined by the *Oxford American Dictionary*, is "the capacity or power to have an effect on the character, development, or behavior of someone or something."[19] Given that, you cannot dispute it; they influence us one-on-one and are also responsible for widespread cultural and social changes in American culture.

Overstating the importance and the impact of companion animals on our lives is nearly impossible. The sky is too conservative a limit when considering the potential benefits and meaning of these relationships, and their influence is too vast to describe fully in this text. What follows is a representation of their impact.

Those of us who live with animals have known for decades what research is catching up to: companion animals are critical to human culture and sustain humans in innumerable ways, whether you are referring to highly trained animals who provide a service or a small furry someone, who waits at home for a person to return from work or school. Each animal is special to us for reasons unique to the animal, the person, and the situation, but each fills a role that would otherwise go wanting, or they fill it in a way nothing else can.

Animals can transform us. They make us feel protected and help us cope with inner turmoil. Sometimes having an animal is the only aspect of our lives that makes us feel human. You remember the homeless couple in Chapter 1 who expressed that sentiment.

"Overall, pet owners have fewer minor health problems, better psychological well-being, and decreased feelings of loneliness and isolation," said Dr. Stephanie LaFarge, Senior Director, Counseling Services, American Society for the Prevention of Cruelty to Animals (ASPCA). The influence on health is so great that Chapter 6 is devoted completely to the impact of companion animals on human health and medicine.

Animals also influence the body of knowledge that pertains to human behavior and development. Scientists gain great insights when they study animals. I am not speaking here of animal research that is conducted at the expense of animals with the primary goal of improving human health or beauty. I am referring to noninvasive observation and evaluation of animals for the sake of understanding them better or research to effect improvements in the health of a specific breed or species.

Consider world-renowned audiologist Brenda Ryals and her colleague Robert Dooling, who are learning how birds hear and learn songs. Their internationally acclaimed research advances the understanding of human hearing loss and associated speech patterns. They are examining the mechanisms by which birds regenerate damaged hair cells in the inner ear, which essentially reverses hearing loss and restores song.[20]

Another research project, the unprecedented and dynamic genome mapping of the domestic dog—*Canine familiaris*—will not only advance veterinary medicine, but also contribute to scientific understanding of what causes human genes to express. We can then learn how to modify our behavior and environment to establish and maintain good human health. These common benefits will be possible because all but a few of the 19,300 genes in dogs are close copies of human genes.

Since our genes and environments are so similar, it is no surprise that we share similar illnesses.[21]

Human advances from animal study are not restricted to the fields of health and medicine. For instance, one study provided information that may help us win more Olympic medals. Analyses of the speed and footfalls of forty greyhounds running around a track revealed that they maintain their legendary speed while banking hairpin turns because they support their weight with their forelegs and use their hip and back muscles for power. Think about how cyclists use their legs, back, and hip muscles to power a bicycle. It's the same principle: in dogs, the muscles used for power are as separate from the part of the body that supports the weight as cyclists are separate from the structure that supports their weight, the bicycle. For running, four legs are simply better than two; not much we can do about that. However, the information gleaned from this study will help scientists understand motor function, which can benefit sports medicine and the development of robotics.[22]

In spite of competing electronic media, television and movies remain extremely popular forms of entertainment and education. Television programming and movie topics reflect the interests and obsessions of the culture, so quite naturally companion animals are often featured. Some might say their influence on movies and television is widespread. For instance, since 1996 Animal Planet has been a television channel dedicated exclusively to the relationship between people and animals, and it has become extremely popular. Animal Planet reaches more than 81 million homes in America, and is available in seventy countries around the world.[23] I doubt there is a religious channel with such reach.

The fanatical popularity of reality shows spread to companion animals, as evidenced by *Off the Leash*, a reality show on Lifetime television that showcased seven dogs, all vying for a contract with a Hollywood pet talent agency.

Hollywood has long known that movies with animals are successful. From the little dog in *The Wizard of Oz* to the whale in *Free Willy*, animals of almost every stripe have starred or been featured in movies. Again dogs are the most frequent actors when it comes to companion animals, included in forty-four movies since 1974, followed by horses, featured in twenty films. I am one of those persons who avoids movies with animals because I worry the entire time that the animal character will be harmed or killed, and I cannot cope with even the on-screen tragedy. An industry that will script an actor to cook a rabbit for revenge cannot be trusted with my heart.[24] Regardless of how precarious a scene looks, I know that thanks to the American Humane Association (AHA), when I see "No Animals Were Harmed" in the credits, the animals were safe, and have been, for more than sixty-five years because AHA's Film and Television Unit has protected the interests and welfare of animal actors that long.

When you influence automobile design, you are a force with which to reckon, and dogs did just that when Honda Japan designed a dog-friendly car, with a special crate under the dash that allows the dog to have visual contact with the owner. A larger crate also pops up from under the back seat when needed.

Adding to these safety features is a special seat belt for larger dogs. The car is equipped with removable, washable, rollout flooring, and has wide sliding doors.[25]

Much of the influence that companion animals have on us is evidenced by the ways we incorporate them into our daily lives, which will be discussed in detail in the next chapter. Their influence is so pervasive that we find creative ways to keep close contact at all times.

Infrequently, the contact comes with a price. Significantly, zoonotic diseases are those acquired first by animals and then transmitted to people. They are caused either by direct contact with the animal, its bite, or excrements; or transmitted by a vector, such as a tick or mite. You are familiar with some zoonotic diseases such as the Avian Influenza, West Nile virus, and Rocky Mountain Spotted fever, but may not be aware that dogs, cats, and birds can harbor dangerous parasites and bacteria with zoonotic potential. For instance, dogs expose us to leptospirosis, a bacterial disease that can pose sudden and serious health problems. Other zoonotic conditions include streptococcosis, dermatophysis, leishmaniasis, rabies, certain fevers, mange, roundworms, and hookworms. We rarely contract zoonotic diseases from our companion animals, but care is warranted with certain species as I have said or with animals who are sick.[26]

DO WE INFLUENCE THEM?

We live—sometimes in the same house; we eat—sometimes the same food; and we sleep—sometimes in the same bed—with our companion animals. So, of course we influence them! This is true especially for dogs, and cats too, to an extent. Again, much of what follows is about them.

Our lives have been so intertwined for so long that isolated observation of one species separate from another is nearly impossible. We have been too much to each other for too long to have any idea what one would have been without the other.

Dogs are the product of thousands of years of evolution in a very specific environment—our homes.[27] The dog will never be what it was or might have been without our influence, or *interference*, depending on your vantage. We created an entirely new animal—one that still has the DNA of its wild ancestors, but is more like us than it is like any other animal, including its own ancestors. Moreover, dogs are more like us than are our closest DNA cousins, other primates. Dogs adapted so well to living among humans that the human environment is its new natural habitat. The adaptations have led to marked changes in their communication, social, cooperative, and attachment behavior.[28]

The question of whether or not our influence is essentially interference depends on whom you ask. Dr. Patricia B. McConnell, author of *The Other End of the Leash*, says, "Look what we've done for dogs; the domestic dog is now one of the most successful mammals on earth."[29] She has a point. The dog is the most celebrated, pampered animal in the world. Any individual animal or species embraced as a companion has certainly won the universe's lottery. The next chapter focuses on all the apparent benefits we bestow on our companion animals.

But is it all good? Well, of course not. Our relationships, which often border on obsessions, with animals often have negative effects on them. We say that we care for them, but our actions are not always in their best interests, and we rarely allow them to be themselves. We bestow them with our bad habits, such as a tendency towards laziness. The consequence of this inactivity contributes to life-threatening obesity, affecting 9 percent of dogs and 14 percent of cats, according to APPMA's 2007–2008 survey.

"Who dogs are and how they behave are partly defined by who we humans are and how we ourselves behave," Dr. McConnell said. Loosely translated, if we have problems, we can make dogs have problems. Dr. James Serpell presented cases in *The Domestic Dog* that demonstrate a connection between owner personality and dog behavior. One woman was agoraphobic and so was her dog. Another woman was overly fastidious and smoothering with her small dog, causing him to become irritable, demanding, and aggressive. The woman faulted herself for "spoiling" the dog, but took great pleasure in doing so.[30]

I remember *teaching* my dog to be afraid of thunderstorms, a tradition in my family. I had learned to get away from the windows, stay away from the phone, and turn off the lights. So, when a storm threatened, I scooped up my puppy, Muffin, and ran around the house, battening down the hatches. Months later, I noticed Muffin would scurry into a dark room when a storm loomed. When I realized what I had done, I stopped. Muffin would begin her neurotic behaviors, and I would simply ignore her, moving around the house as usual. Eventually, she joined me and stopped her learned fear-based reactions. Parents of human children are familiar with this phenomenon, and often overcome their own fears, as I did, to resist passing them on to their children.

Similar anecdotal evidence abounds, but reliable scientific evidence of a connection between their behavior and ours is scarce.

Some human personalities are associated with problem behaviors in dogs, but not in every instance. The association could simply be "correlation without causation," a term my psychologist husband loves to remind me of. It means that simply because two things happen at the same time, one does not cause the other.

Yet, there is no dearth of tales to suggest that animal behavior is, indeed, influenced by the human with whom they live. We know that people are drawn to dogs who resemble them, but whether our personalities actually affect theirs is a question that goes beyond appearance. For example, if a timid/nervous man has a timid/nervous dog, how can we know whether the man chose a breed or individual dog coincidentally prone to nervousness and then contributed to the dog's tendency by his own nervous behavior? (Environment helping heredity along, as it is wont to do.) Could this man have caused another dog, without a predisposition, to exhibit timid/nervous behaviors? Conversely, maybe the dog would have been timid/nervous no matter the temperament of the guardian. Few studies have been done to address these question.

Dr. Serpell finds the question of particular interest, and although he has an abundance of anecdotal evidence from clinical practice, he is the first to acknowledge that the absence of objective, reliable data makes a scientific conclusion impossible. An accomplished researcher, Serpell set about to change that by sampling clients to gather information about their dog's behavior, which he compared to results from a personality inventory each custodian completed. He regards his results as only suggestive, but found that "owner attitudes and personality" and a dog's behavior are related. For example, he found an "element of truth" to the stereotype that "indulgent" custodians have small, snappy dogs. In this case, clinical experience agreed with popular stereotypes.[31] More evidence will follow because as knowledge of the many health benefits of living with companion animals has increased, so has personality research on people and their companion animals. Scientists want to know not only how the animal influences the person, but also how the human personality might affect the animals, particularly as relates to the animal's potential success as a companion or service animal. Cross-species comparative personality research is also being done to determine whether humans contribute to behavior problems in their companion animals, problems that may result in abandonment or surrender—a problem discussed in the last chapter.

The behavior and personality of dogs is difficult to study because as Serpell points out, "It seems unlikely that the social systems of the domestic dog ever operate in an entirely unrestricted way for long enough to exhibit all of the complexity of which the animals are capable, so it is necessary to piece together the whole picture from studies that are aimed at particular aspects of behavior."[32] Most dogs live their entire lives in a world that we have created for them. Even if we allow them to live with other dogs, the dogs are of our choosing. We even select their mates, except in the cases of escaped or unrestrained animals.

We know that we have altered some natural tendencies of dogs and taught them to tolerate human behavior. For instance, as primates we want to greet each other upright, chest to chest. For our own benefit, we have taught dogs to accept "ventral-ventral" contact. Primates love to hug, but dogs (although highly social) do not hug. In fact, dogs will often interpret a hug as aggressive, responding with a bark or growl.[33]

Surprisingly, we cannot extrapolate what a dog might have been by looking at wolves because of the distinctions between them. One I find of particular interest: male dogs rarely take care of puppies, but male wolves provide a "high-level" of care for their pups.

Dogs are not "wolf-lite" or are they? The possibility exists when it comes to intelligence and cognitive abilities. One study suggests that we actually created a dumbed-down version of the wolf. The domestic dog is certainly dependent on us, but have we made them stupid?

Hungarian investigator Dr. Vilmos Csányi demonstrated that the relationships we have with dogs has a negative effect on their problem solving skills. He found that companion dogs, especially those in strong relationships (one indicator was that the dogs were viewed more anthropomorphically by their guardians), continually looked at their custodian for permission or help when presented with a problem. He says that decreased problem-solving ability in the domestic dog is not due to their domestication, but to their strong attachment to humans.

Dogs identified in working relationships were the best problem solvers. However, once the companion animals were given permission to respond, the difference between the two groups disappeared.[34] Regardless, it is not fair to pit the behavior and intelligence of dogs against that of wolves. Each has evolved to suit the specific needs of their environments. They are equally smart, but certainly in different ways. This doesn't necessarily mean that dogs have suffered and been made stupid. If you consider responding to humans a mark of intelligence, then wolves would not fare well. Several studies have demonstrated that dogs pick up on human cues much quicker than wolves. To demonstrate, investigators hid food and indicated its location by touching it, pointing to it, or looking at it. The wolves ignored all of the cues.[35] Maybe we have made dogs smarter, but only as it involves the ability to live with humans.[36]

Breeding

We have certainly changed the appearance of dogs, just one of the outcomes of breeding dogs to suit our preferences. Temple Grandin, author of *Animals in Translation*, asserts that breeding for fashion can have awful emotional and behavioral consequences. She points out that 74 percent of fatal dog bites are from purebred dogs.[37] The negative consequences of breeding are well documented from hip dysplasia in German shepherds to joint and teeth problems in miniature breeds. In our effort to create dogs with pleasing, perpetual infantile features we often create problems. One striking example is evident in dogs such as bulldogs and pugs, who have abnormally short facial bones, a condition considered a severe disability in humans (called brachycephaly). As a result of the deformity, the dog cannot breathe properly, which among other problems, interferes with maintaining the brain at an optimal temperature. Some dogs have such short muzzles that their nasal passages cannot function properly, and their jaw is so small it can barely fit all of their teeth. Tears constantly run from the eyes of my Maltese because her muzzle is short that her tear ducts are malformed. This is a common malady in small breeds such as Maltese and poodles.

The selection process that has given dogs such appealing, humanlike behaviors has also given many breeds humanlike genetic diseases. Early ancestors of golden retrievers, for example, were chosen for the color of their fur and their patient personalities, but with those desired traits came an unfortunate side effect: a genetic predisposition to cancer, which claims up to 63 percent of these wonderful dogs, according to one study.[38] Our desire for perfection can result in exaggerated characteristics with adverse effects. For example, dogs with drooping ears may not hear well, and dogs with docked tails are unable to signal other dogs as they would with their natural tails. More than 800 breeds exist around the world and physical defects from breeding are common. If satisfactory results cannot be obtained by breeding, we are not reluctant to employ unnecessary surgery to get what we want. Included in these types of procedures are declawing, devoicing, ear cropping, tail nicking, and teeth cutting.[39] Yes, dogs are living the life—what could beat being engineered to suit human whims.

I was all set to lambaste breeding and vilify breeders in this book, but then I met Seattle psychologist Dr. Douglas Haldeman. A more intelligent, compassionate, and spirited man is difficult to find. I discovered immediately that he is my kind of person, one who unabashedly talks about how he loves his dogs and who carries their photos in his wallet. I was bewildered to discover that he is a dog breeder, a practice of which I am not a fan. I had learned to value and respect his opinions, so I often plied him with questions about breeding. Consequently when I needed information to present a balanced view of breeding for this book, I asked Dr. Haldeman for an interview. We talked for more than an hour, finding a lot of common ground, and he helped me understand that dog breeding is not all bad. I already knew from being around him that dog breeders themselves were not all bad.

I learned first that breeders, *responsible* breeders specifically, are more accurately referred to as "dog fanciers." The term applies to breeders who actively promote purebred dogs and adhere to ethical codes of conduct that include participating in breed rescue. "If you don't rescue, you don't breed," is among other important tenets, Haldeman explained.

Based on what he told me, I can now confidently separate breeders into two categories: "for profit" and "not-for-the-profit." The latter are the dog fanciers, who according to Dr. Haldeman, are people like him, who value the unique contributions of a particular breed, Samoyeds in his case. Dog fanciers' goal is to support the continuance of a breed as an emotionally and physically healthy component of the canine species. He said, "This is really about love [for a breed] at its root." His hobby kennel (a term that signifies the goal is not money) breeds infrequently, rarely over successive years, and never more than two litters a year— important distinctions from "for profit" breeders. Dr. Haldeman is an example of what is referred to as a responsible breeder, one who breeds with "thought, care, and concern because they care about the breed, not because they care about profit." Responsible breeders provide the best prenatal and postpartum care, whelp carefully, and screen for known breed diseases. They ensure that affected puppies are adopted and spayed or neutered to prevent passing on disease. Puppies in these types of kennels are raised as part of the family with lots of human contact to facilitate social and intellectual development, and new homes are carefully screened. His expectation is that dogs purchased as companions will be spayed or neutered. Dr. Haldeman's kennel stays in touch with new homes and will accept return of any dog, at any time, and for any reason; responsible breeders are committed to their dogs for life. Dog fanciers have what might be considered a noble cause—preservation of existing breeds.

The "for profit" category has two types of participants: the puppy mill breeders (discussed in Chapter 9), who have no redeeming qualities, as I see it, and backyard breeders. The latter are sometimes simply opportunists, who happen to have a dog they think will produce cute puppies to sell, so they find another cute dog, through friends or family, and mate them. Other backyard breeders breed as a primary source of income or as a consistent supplemental income, and run a small business out of their homes. Regardless of how it begins, Dr. Haldeman explained that backyard breeders are "people who are trying to make money." Established backyard breeders promote themselves in ways similar to dog fanciers, and are often indistinguishable to the uninitiated from dog fanciers. Dr. Haldeman gave me what might be a controversial distinction between the two, but I like it: backyard breeders advertise puppies in the newspaper. "Anybody who needs to advertise their puppies in a newspaper. . . ." he said, and paused thoughtfully. "That is a puppy to be avoided. You're better off going to a shelter, and there are countless anecdotes to support that."[40]

I am still a bit unsure how I feel about dog fanciers, but I am less ambivalent about backyard breeders, and completely decided about puppy mills. As Dr. Haldeman said, "It's not like we need to produce companion animals for people because there are enough dogs on the planet, and they are available through rescues and shelters." Until I understand this complex issue better, I will tread lightly. Prior to my enlightening conversation with Dr. Haldeman, I posted a criticism of breeding on a small dog listserv to which I subscribe. I made what I thought was an innocent comment related to a slogan from an old Humane Society of the United States (HSUS) bumper sticker: "Until there are none, adopt one." I was flamed, as they say in Internet language; one woman told me that she never wanted to read my book if that is how I felt. I am still puzzled about that comment, but I was bombarded with e-mails from people explaining why they *had to buy* a purebred puppy. That experience taught me that people take their cognitive dissonance[41] very seriously and that people feel strongly that they *need* to have a specific breed to ensure the success and longevity of the relationship. Moreover, they believe that the best dog possible starts with the purebred puppy. They ignore the following important facts: (1) many, many purebred dogs are available in animals shelters around the country; (2) many purebred dogs suffer emotionally and physically on their way to pet shops; (3) most breeding is a business; and (4) purebred dogs account for a high percentage of abandoned shelter animals. I was amazed at the visceral responses to my comment, but my eyes were opened to the enormous challenge facing those of us who want to reduce the suffering caused by inappropriate, irresponsible breeding of dogs.

IT IS WHAT IT IS

I learned the above phrase during my first (and last) visit to Block Island, Rhode Island, when the proprietor of a bed and breakfast spoke it to my husband and me after placing us in a room overlooking a parking lot. We had made our reservations far in advance of the Labor Day weekend during which we arrived, and our room preferences (none of which included a parking lot) were communicated and accepted. Because of the blunder, we wanted our money back before the next ferry left the island, and she wanted a guest in that room. We apologized for demanding that she reconsider her refund policy, but we held our position. She refused to apologize, and summed up our impasse with the phrase, "It is what it is." And this aptly describes the situation between us and our companion animals, dogs especially: It is what it is. We cannot go back and change the evolution that brings us here, and we will never know what would have been. Our world is now their world. In the next chapter you will see just what it means for them to be embedded with humans.

5

Embedded with Humans–Animals in the Human World

I've seen a look in dogs' eyes . . . and I am convinced that basically dogs think humans are nuts.

—Jon Steinbeck

GOLDEN

This is the Golden Age for companion animals—a time of prosperity, good fortune, and ideal living. Many live in circumstances luxurious enough to make some *people* envious. Companion animals, especially those in the care of people who have a certain generous sensibility toward them and expendable resources to match, are frequently the recipients of everything humans find good about the world. Dogs, in particular, have been embedded into our world so completely that they have no other place to call home. "The human world is the dog's natural environment," says Dr. Vilmos Csányi, the international expert in animal behavior and member of the Hungarian Academy of Sciences whom I mentioned earlier.[1]

It is not only the money we spend on them, but also what we buy. We shower our companion animals with gourmet and organic foods, spa treatments, state-of-the-art medical care, luxurious vacations, and financial security. It is all part of the package that comes with being a member of the family, which is how 75 percent of people with dogs feel about their dogs and 50 percent of people with cats feel about their cats, according to an American Animal Hospital Association poll in 2003. This is a new position, nestled somewhere in the upper realm of child status.

Reflecting their new status, 39 percent of companion animals have human names, according to the same poll. You do not see many "Spots" or "Rovers" anymore. Now, you are more likely to be introduced to Cody, Ginger, Grace, Sam, or Madison.

According to the 2005 survey by the American Pet Products Manufacturing Association (APPMA), 80 percent of dog people buy them gifts, and 63 percent of cat people do the same. Gifts are not only given on special occasions such as Valentine's Day, Chanukah, Christmas, Easter, and Halloween, but gifts are also bestowed for no special reason. I am not talking about cheap gifts, either: the average price is $17.

We take our cats and dogs to spas, celebrate their birthdays, bring them along on vacation, and grieve deeply when they die. Coping with the death of our faithful animal companions is a topic covered in Chapter 8.

Earlier, we examined the question of why we are so devoted to our companion animals. The question I pose now is this: *why now?* Why have our companion animals now moved from possession to family member, or as someone clever said, from the backyard to the bankbook? Could it be more than happenstance that the indulgent treatment of companion animals comes when baby boomers—with all their famous boomer money and infamous reputation for self- (and extended self) indulgence and excess—are increasingly becoming empty nesters. Boomer's largesse is not the only reason because you can take a slice from almost any segment of society and find people who indulge their companion animals. For instance, people without children or who postpone parenting seem to be redirect-ing their energy and income to their animals, dogs in particular, spending money on all kinds of things to keep their companion animals satisfied inside and out. In general, guardians simply want the best of every thing for their companion animals. Boomers are an easy target because they have a well-earned reputation for setting cultural and social trends, and this may be another example. Propo-nents of the trend to indulge and pamper our companion animals insist that the animals, dogs in particular, are simply getting their due. They say it is high time we gave our companions the respect and privileges they have earned by being our constant companions and in recognition of the increasing demands that we are placing on them. Ten-year-old Brenda Martinez confirms the adage that children speak the truth when she says, "We should take care of our animals, as we take care of ourselves."[2]

Everyone is not convinced that our motives are altruistic, and they suggest that it is we who are really benefiting from all of the pampering, and that ours are the needs really being satisfied. That makes a lot of sense. After all, animals are simple creatures who, without our intervention, would exist just fine with only provisions from the lower levels of Maslow's Hierarchy.[3] They do not *need* pink sweaters or aromatherapy. And *who* enjoys buying the gifts? *Who* is always seen laughing at the dog park? *Who* is that enjoying the drop off at the doggy day care so much? *Who* gets so much satisfaction from the little precious having the very best of everything? When you look at it that way, it is easy to see the strength behind the argument that we are projecting our needs onto our companion animals and that what we do has more to do with us than them.

Author Jon Katz, in *The New Work of Dogs*,[4] is just one person warning us (like a proverbial canary in the cave) that we may be crossing a line that ultimately puts too much pressure on our companion animals to fill our emotional needs and that we are damaging them by not allowing them to be who and what they really are. Many experts agree with him and fear that we are depending too much on our animals to be the *people* we treat them as.

In this chapter, you will read profiles of many people who demonstrate that this Golden Age is upon us. For example, people such as the Shumakers and the Settlemyres. First the Shumakers, who indulge their dogs, Heidi, Sable, and Hobbes with toys, expensive food, and private obedience classes. Sherry Shumaker said that she and her husband organize their lives around the dogs and factored them in when deciding what kind of car to buy—opting for a roomy Subaru Outback, and the kind of home—opting for one with a large yard. She confesses that she spends ridiculous amounts of money on things such as acupuncture therapy and organic food. "I just wish I could use them as a tax deduction every year," she said laughing. "They're worth every penny."

Second, MaryAnn and Michael Settlemyre, after adopting their dog Bailey from an abusive home, discovered that he was so phobic about water that a puddle would terrify him and a bath was nearly impossible. In spite of the teasing, they enrolled him in canine swimming lessons so he could enjoy his vacations at the beach or lake, and they beamed like any proud parent when Bailey took his first swim.[5]

With all of our gifts, gadgets, and toys we may be making the same error in judgment that some parents make with their children—we think stuff communicates love. Maybe we are trying to bridge the gap between our worlds by sharing our things. We cannot be sure that they understand our words when we say we love them; maybe they will understand from all the stuff just how much we care about them.

GIVING ANIMALS THE BUSINESS

A formidable industry has grown up around our devotion to our companion animals, and established businesses and those interested in the "pet products industry"[6] rely on the APPMA to monitor consumer habits and predict the direction of the spending wave that shows no signs of cresting. Since 1988, APPMA has been collecting and publishing the industry's most comprehensive consumer data, including detailed demographics, buying habits and other traits of people with dogs, cats, fish, birds, reptiles, small animals, and recently horses.

The eagerly awaited data is compiled every other year into *The APPMA National Pet Owners Survey*, and is the most respected, reliable source of its kind. It not only reveals how much we spend, but also the kind of people we are. For instance it reported that "pet owners are health conscious, like to look our best, and like to exercise with our pet. We are also happy and maintain a well-organized home."[7] It reveals whether we buy caskets or urns and what design of combs and brushes we like to buy. Unless otherwise stated, the data in this chapter are taken from this impressive survey.

You are not likely surprised that the amount of money we spend to comfort our creatures is increasing. Sales of pet products doubled between 1994 and 2004—from $17 billion to $34.4 billion.[8] The APPMA predicts that by the end of the decade approximately $50 billion will be spent annually on these products. Most of the money goes for food, $15.4 billion in 2006, along with more than $9 billion each for veterinarian care, supplies, and over-the-counter medications. Pet services such as grooming and boarding came in at a mere $2.9 billion. The biggest pet spenders are 34–54 year olds.[9]

More pet products than toys or candy are sold in America, and not by small margins. In 2004, 60 percent more pet products were sold than candy. That year people spent $34.4 billion on pet products, but only $24 billion worth of candy was sold.

Some companies, known for their people products, are adding pet products to their offerings. OPI, a manufacturer of premier nail products, has a line of nail polish for dogs. Habro, an international leader in the design and manufacture of games and toys for the pleasure and recreation of people, is now making toys for dogs. Harley-Davidson, synonymous for motorcycles, offers a "little leather jacket" for dogs, and John Paul Mitchell Systems, one of the fastest growing privately owned haircare firms in the country, has launched a line of pet grooming products.[10]

Dogs are getting everything from organic food to frequent-flyer miles. Things that once seemed foolish are becoming commonplace. Okay, some things really are foolish, but that is beside the point, which is: Saying that someone is being treated like a dog no longer has a pejorative connotation.

Dogs have consumer power. It is indirect power, as is the case with young children, but it is strong, and marketers are not missing a beat. Businesses are creating ads that target the emotional connection we have to our companion animals rather than the nutritional or economic value of their products. Dog food advertising, for instance, used to be "all about science and the rational benefits of the food," said Chris Adams, copywriter for Pedigree's "Dog Rule" advertising. That strategy changed, he said, because "people love dogs like their own children, and no pet food company was really nailing that." An art director associated with the campaign said, "[marketers] talk about target audiences. This might be the greatest target audience we've ever had." Vicky Lynn Morgan, president of Pet Market Consultants said that what people spend is a reflection of the lengths people are willing to go for their loved ones and she believes, "It's almost a recession-proof industry."[11]

Clever businesses help us find solutions to problems with our companion animals, and make us aware of problems that we did not know we had. Some businesses that do not sell pet products tap the market by using the *pet* imagery to push everything from banking to lawn equipment. Advertisers have said that sex sells, now *pets* sell. "If you want to move it, put a puppy on it," seems to be the new marketing mantra.

National chain stores that sell pet products are capitalizing on the trend. For example, services for companion animals is one of the fastest growing segments of business for PetSmart, Inc. (previously known as PetsMart), which had third-quarter revenues jump 24 percent from 2004 to 2005, and they expect similar growth through 2007. Not to be left out, small and local entrepreneurs are holding their ground and see the wisdom of catering to this burgeoning niche. For example, Peter Perretta transformed his grooming business into a "pet resort," moving it to a fancy building with a granite floor—a building that is larger than the child day care center next door.[12]

I cannot possibly discuss every type of business that has emerged as a function of our love affair with our newest family member, who happens to be a furry, feathered, or finned animal. This section is not intended to be a compendium of the pet industry, but a sampling of some of the more unusual offerings. *Unusual* being in the eye of the beholder, because what was once unusual can quickly become compulsory in the pet industry, if you strike the right vein in the goldmine.

Someone to Watch over Me

When doggy day care—a type of sitting service—entered the market, it was dismissed as a foolish notion, embarked on by and for overachieving yuppies with overdeveloped guilt complexes, who wanted luxuries not only for themselves, but also for their companion animals.

It may have started out as an oddity, but it is now an industry staple, and not just the rich or famous are looking for doggy day care anymore. Pet sitting in its various forms, which includes scheduled daily walks, transportation to veterinary appointments, overnight boarding, in-home care, and camps, is one of the most popular businesses in the pet industry. Clients love it, and business owners can reap sustained economic rewards, if they stay in touch with what guardians want. What most of us want are "premium" services from day care and boarding. This includes valet or pickup service to accommodate our busy lifestyles, playgroups that are based on our companion animal's size or temperament, and assurance of adherence to the companion animal's specific needs and personality.

Finding the best sitter to tend your animal companion while you are at work or on vacation is harder, in some respects, than finding a sitter for your children. For one thing, childcare facilities are regulated, and your children can tell you if they are being mistreated, but your animals are stuck with whomever you select. Many people are reluctant to put their dogs or cats in a traditional kennel because of the possibility of stress or maltreatment, which could be as much as abuse to as little as not pandering to their every need. Some facilities respond to high-maintenance animals, and their demanding guardians, by providing accommodations similar to a luxury hotel or country club, including pools; webcam surveillance so you can see your animal from anywhere in the world from your computer, PDA, or cell phone; custom diets; human roommates; solo or supervised playtime; specialized toys; tuck-in service; and suites with windows and television. Private rooms with telephone access so you can call your dog or cat is not unusual; some of them reportedly talk back. With some encouragement, my schnauzer would bark into the phone. I could put the receiver to her ear, and she would actually listen. My

Maltese acts deaf when I do that. Maybe listening to a phone is some kind of dog intelligence test.

Even the more pedestrian facilities offer heated runs for dogs and rooms with windows for cats, and cage free environments are almost a staple. And you can be sure that none of this comes cheaply. As with a luxury hotel, you get what you pay for. At the more opulent places, a walk could cost $20, and fees for overnight stays with human companionship rival a modest hotel. For example, you can easily pay $100 a day or more, depending on the services you request. You often need to make reservations months in advance, especially during holidays. Some facilities also care for companions beyond the usual cat or dog. Potbellied pigs, ferrets, rabbits, goldfish, beta fish, and hermit crabs have been guests at Larkin's Run in Durham, Connecticut, for example. Many facilities, such as Larkin's, distinguish themselves by becoming members of the American Boarding Kennels Association (ABKA), a trade organization with more than 3,000 members, who adhere to certain ethics and care. ABKA offers comprehensive, in-depth training and certification for kennel personnel and facilities.

Many of the posh places for companion animals are on the West Coast. Consequently, as an East Coast denizen, I am pleased to report that we have places like Seneca Hill Animal Hospital, Resort & Spa, which exemplifies what is expected in day care and extended stay. It is difficult not to sound like an advertising agent in this part of the book, but I have to explain the services in a way that conveys the luxuriousness of the accommodations. For instance, Seneca Hill was designed with optimum comfort and superior care in mind. Seneca Hill can accommodate 150 animals, and you will never hear barking or smell "poop or pee." Owner, Marty Veron says they do not use the words board, boarder, or kennel here. Animals in their care are *guests of the resort*. The fully enclosed building has 27,000 square feet with seven outdoor exercise areas. Twenty-two heating and air conditioning units ensure consistent temperature and are secured by an emergency backup generator.

The resort was designed with no gutters to collect bacteria and contribute to odor. There is one *host* for every ten guests, and a thorough admission check-in procedure ensures a parasite-free environment—take that Ritz-Carlton. Surveillance cameras provide around-the-clock security, indoors and out, and all exits have double or triple doors. An agility course, training room, and swimming pool are available for guests. What I have described are just the common areas. Luxurious individual accommodations are available for cats and dogs. Cats can stay in one of twenty-eight "Cat-O-Miniums" with an enclosed 90 square foot living room, color television, easy chairs, a bay window, and cat trees—all to simulate home. Dogs can stay in two-room "Estate Suites" of 105 square feet each, with an outside window, color television, toddler bed with linens, and piped-in soothing music. Smaller accommodations include a "Club Suite" with 68 square feet, or a cottage with 49 square feet. Suites and cottage have similar amenities, but guests in the cottages have to slum with fleece bedding, rather than bed linens. With all of this luxury, it is easy to see why Veron says that Seneca Hill's day care is

A client of Seneca Hill Animal Hospital, Resort & Spa in Great Falls, VA, enjoys the luxurious accommodations. Photo courtesy of: Seneca Hill. Used with permission.

harder to get into than Montessori. After talking to him, I was ready to make reservations for my own stay.

Sometimes even the most posh environment is unacceptable to you or your companion. Trouble may brew because the animal is afraid of strange environments and exhibits emotional distress by refusing to eat or developing physical problems. Consequently, you may prefer not to put your friend through that stress, or you have other concerns, such as exposure to disease. Then, an in-home pet sitter may be a better choice. In-home services range from a noonday walk to overnight stays. These sitters either live in your home while you are away or visit several times a day and night to tend your companion. Advantages beyond animal care are that your home will not be vacant and the sitter typically will also take care of your mail and plants. The advantage of in-home care, of course, is that the companion animal gets to stay home and miss just you. The possible disadvantage with any sitter is they do not have to be certified, but to establish credibility and ease the minds of clients, many belong to organizations that promote a certain level of care. One of these is the National Association of Professional Pet Sitters, which boasts 7,350 members across the United States and is self-monitored and self-regulated. Pet sitting can be a lucrative business, with average national rates in 2003 of $14.36 for half an hour, plus an extra $1 to $3 for each additional animal. Finding someone who will take proper care of your companion animal—either in your home, their home, or a designated facility—and treat them like a privileged member of the family is truly priceless, and we go to great lengths to find proper absentee care for our animals. I know from personal experience that great caution is warranted. Out of complete desperation, I left my beloved Grace with a sitter unknown to me before I interviewed her. Grace was getting old and I had refused for more than two years to leave her because I had not found satisfactory care after relocating. Regrettably, a family obligation made travel imperative, and I was compelled to leave her. Now, with the benefit of perfect hindsight, I wish I had stayed home because Grace was returned to me with respiratory symptoms that began an unfortunate chain of events culminating in her death.

Although, it is great fun to talk about the excessive pampering we bestow on our companion animals, when something unfortunate happens to them, especially one who has high status in the family unit, everyone wishes they had been more demanding, and more careful—thoughts of cost disappear. Suddenly what we do does not seem so extravagant.

Pretty Is as Pretty Gets

Grooming is another staple in the pet products industry. Although a bath and a haircut are hard to change, you can change where they are given and by whom—that is what has happened with grooming. We no longer simply put our dogs in the tin tub in the backyard and spray them with the garden hose; we take them to spas for their bath where an attendant uses aromatherapy oils, clips and buffs their nails, cleans their teeth, gives them a body massage, and adorns them with a seasonal bow or scarf. The biggest change to hit grooming is mobile grooming, and one of the first places in the country to have it was Los Angeles. Mobile grooming, where the groomer and the shop come to you in a state-of-the-art, equipped, air-conditioned van is a great service for busy guardians or nervous or elderly animals who do not fare well in strange environments for grooming. I tried to get an appointment for my dog with a mobile groomer for a firsthand report, but the waiting list for an appointment was more than a year.

Our obsession with looking and smelling good is driving a large segment of the pet industry related to pet grooming products. In 2004 we spent $165 million on items such as skin care for our pets. These include shampoos, therapeutic skin care, brushes, and spa products. Most products are sold in specialty stores, but traditional retailers such as PETCO, PetSmart, and Wal-Mart, with its own product line, are maintaining or increasing market share.[13]

You and Me Babe

One of the biggest developments in the relationships between people and their dogs and cats involves travel. We structure our lives to accommodate our companion animals and often feel guilty when we leave them home alone for a few hours to go to work, a necessary separation. Consequently we definitely do not want to leave them for weeks. How are we supposed to enjoy ourselves with all the guilt and worry? Besides, they are part of the family; you cannot just leave them behind. According to the APPMA, in 2005, more than 15 million people took their companion animals on a trip; 29 million Americans traveled 50 miles or more with their companion animals, 80 percent with dogs and 15 percent with cats. The rest vacationed with birds, ferrets, rabbits, or fish.

Savvy business owners are coming up with all kinds of ventures in response because they realize that the majority of guardians are like Jody Henderson, who says of her thirteen-year-old Bichon Frise, "Basically, she is our third child. She's like our 'youngest,' as we laughingly call her. She goes everywhere with us, everywhere except restaurants, churches, and movies. When we visit family, she flies in the airplane with us."[14]

In 1967, a forward-thinking airline worker and entrepreneur named Frank Hasenauer started JetPets, after watching animals sit for hours in tiny crates while awaiting transfers or pickups between flights. He was so successful that later the government asked his assistance in quarantining animals involved in international travel. The company still provides a rest stop for animals going through the Los Angeles International Airport and arranges the domestic shipment of a cadre of animals, including horses.[15]

Some people, and I am one of them, prefer small animals because they are easier travel mates. My Grace was the most gracious of guests—she never barked or whined on the plane, never soiled a hotel room, and never had a flea. My husband and I would travel with her under the seat and check her crate as luggage. Once at the hotel, she would rest comfortably and quietly in the crate while we were out sightseeing and be the snuggly bunny when we returned. I could enjoy myself completely because I was not worried about her. Máni, our Maltese, on the other hand, has not made the road team. She is unpredictable and very prone to yapping it up. Until that changes, I have to focus on finding reliable, trustworthy sitters, so I can at least leave the worry behind at home, if not the guilt.

People with animals often leave with great anxiety as I have mentioned, and prefer to have their furry family members along so they can really relax. Fortunately, several venues understand the motivation and accommodate animals that meet certain size and species restrictions. The challenge is to find a place you would like to stay that will accommodate your animal companion.

One of those is the Ritz-Carlton Hotel. In New York, the hotel near Central Park has a Very Important Pooch program for dogs up to sixty pounds. Not only can they stay with you, but they can also get aromatherapy spritzes, hand painted ceramic dinnerware, 22-karat gold-plated identification badges, quilted travel mats, and Burberry raincoats on loan to protect them from the elements.[16] Teddy, who had accompanied his human from Detroit, spent his afternoons by the pool at the Ritz-Carlton in Miami, where a uniformed attendant kept him plied with water. In the evening, Teddy was eligible for special turndown service, which often includes a special bone and a bottle of water.[17]

Lowes includes the "Lowe's Loves Pets" program in their signature family benefits package. Your companion animal's stay begins with a special note from the manager that includes routes for walks, location of veterinarians, pet shopping, and groomers. While in the hotel, your companion has access to all kinds of amenities including leashes, bones, catnip, scratching posts, special videos, litterboxes, and pooper-scoopers.[18]

Teddy enjoys time by the Ritz-Carlton pool, while on vacation with his guardian. © 2006, *The Washington Post*. Photo by Valerie Strauss. Reprinted with permission.

Some entire cities seem to be desirable destinations for people with dogs. Miami is one, with a tradition of welcoming dogs to its trendy restaurants and posh beach hotels. Visitors to Miami's famous Lincoln Road are treated to a veritable dog walk, where dogs are welcomed dinner companions. Miami is also home to a 24-hour specialty store for pet products, The Dog Bar, which describes itself as the most unique luxury full-service store of its kind in the country. Everyone is not completely happy about the intermingling of dogs and dinner, so common in Miami, but the practice has pretty much become common law and trumps a few curmudgeons.[19]

Luxurious vacations are not the only option because the pet industry has spawned travel services that help you find the vacation theme perfectly suited for you and your companion animal. I have never been on a "pet-centered" vacation, where the programs are designed to provide quality fun time with my dog. Most seem to involve the great outdoors, which is not high either on my list or that of the little dogs I favor. We tend more toward the reading, shopping, and lying around kind of vacations. No matter your pleasure many resources are now available to you, such as www.PetFriendly.com and www.Petswelcome.com, two of the most comprehensive businesses devoted to finding that perfect venue. Others, like Europeds and Breakaway Adventures, specialize by geographic locale or activity.[20]

If a cruise is your preference and you happen to want to travel between South Hampton (London) and New York with your furry companion, you are in luck because the Cunard Lines Queen Mary 2 trans-Atlantic can take you both. Your precious will have to stay in the kennel, under the care of a full-time kennel master, but you see each other for three hours, three times daily. Your companion gets fresh-baked biscuits, a choice of bedding, fleece blankets, toys, premium food, a souvenir sweater with the QM2 logo, and a personal cruise card. You get a complimentary portrait to share the memories of your trip when you get home. You are both in good hands, as it was Cunard's Carpathia that came to the rescue of Titanic's passengers.[21]

School Days

Dogs' ever-present status requires the very best behavior. Consequently, professional training is very popular. Since November 1975, Sandy and Carlos Mejias have operated the Olde Towne School for Dogs, in Alexandria Virginia, where they have transformed thousands of dogs into model citizens.[22] These serious and experienced trainers have one of the most respected dog schools in the country. The idea of a school that dogs could attend just as children would, with a school bus, lunch, recess, and P.T.A. meetings, was a humorous idea to many people in 1975, but no one is laughing now. Guardians wait several weeks for private lessons and several months for the three-week day school.[23]

What Crate Ideas

Custom furniture for companion animals in not new. From specialized bedding for rodents to Tempur-Pedic and pedestal beds for aging cats and dogs, our homes are filled with their furniture. One product—designer crates—stands out as an example of how clever, talented entrepreneurs identify unique goods or services that solve common problems, while promoting harmonious relationships between people and their companion animals. Crate training has long been a popular, successful way to housetrain and control dogs, capitalizing on their proclivity for cave dwelling, making nests, and keeping their living quarters clean. Crate training involves temporary confinement in a space large enough for even big dogs to turn around, stand, and sit in comfort. Many dogs love the crates and use them to have private time in a personal space. I crate-trained my first dog, Muffin. When the crate was moved to the attic, Muffin would lie where the crate once stood. Crates can be useful training tools and respites. However, they are ugly, obstructive boxes made of plastic or wire. That is until Cratehaven developed crates concealed in beautiful hardwoods in an array of finishes that would make any interior designer smile. The crate, from size mini to extra large, can be hidden in a nightstand, side table, or an armoire, with costs ranging between $429 and $650, depending on size and finish.[24]

Travel crates have not changed much in the past—well—ever! They are plastic boxes with cage doors. We put our dogs and cats in them, turn them over to airlines, and pray they will arrive safely. The biggest danger is that temperatures in baggage storage are a crapshoot, no matter what the airlines tell you. Now, if you absolutely must put your dog in a carrier for a trip or any other reason, you can control the temperature in a climate-controlled carrier that uses "conduction/convention" technology to turn on cooling when the temperature reaches 72 degrees Fahrenheit and warms up when the temperature drops below 65 degrees. These crates can be real lifesavers, in unheated garages and on long car trips, too. Now you can run in and grab a quick burger and not leave your four-legged travel companion sweltering or freezing in the car. Small carriers sell for around $400, and larger versions are planned.[25]

The Dirty Work

Like the poor Thanksgiving turkey, entrepreneurs let no part of the pet industry go unused. Animal Waste Specialists (do not laugh; they have a trade association) have turned dog waste into a lucrative business. For upwards of $15 a yard, companies with clever names such as Doody Calls and Poop Masters will rid your lawn of the end product of all that gourmet food and treats.

One of the intrepid entrepreneurs of the pet industry found a way to deal with the most distasteful aspect of having a cat—the litter box. It needs cleaning, changing, and an out-of-the-way location to please you and your cats. Fragrant cat litter, special rakes, and flip-top boxes crowd the market, but the most innovative product does everything but use the litter box for the cat. CatGenie removes the waste, disposes of it through your sewer system, cleans and dries itself, and resets for the next visit.[26]

Not nearly as high-tech, but perfect nonetheless, PetáPotty is targeted for city dogs whose guardians need to skip a walk now and then. I use mine when it is raining and my dog refuses to go outside or late at night when walking a Maltese is not the safest thing to do. PetáPotty is a box with sod or an AstroTurf material on top and a collection tray at the bottom. One size is small enough to fit a high-rise balcony or in-town deck, but another is big enough for more than one dog.

If you have a city dog, you know that you have to pick up the droppings for proper disposal. Thanks to yet another clever entrepreneur you can make the dog carry them in a little sack designed to go around the dog's neck.[27]

If the sack idea does not appeal, and neither does a warm poop bag, thanks to another clever businessperson, you can just spray the droppings with "Poop-Freeze," which comes in a canister similar to the products sold to unfreeze car locks. It freezes the matter instantly for clean, smell-free transport home.[28] As someone famously said, "I can't make this stuff up."

Mother Invents out of Necessity

Dana Brewington was mom to her beloved Mr. Chips, a Pomeranian with impeccable indoor training, for ten years before he was diagnosed with diabetes and began voiding in the house. Brewington was extraordinarily dedicated to Mr. Chips and prepared herself for everything the veterinary said to expect: rigid dietary changes, increased veterinary expenses, and daily insulin injections.

Lucy models the Fourth of July design of Do-Rite Dog Diapers. Photo courtesy of The Do-Rite Holding Co., LLC., used with permission.

She was not deterred when the veterinarian also told her to expect frequent accidents in the house because she presumed she would simply buy Mr. Chips some disposable dog diapers at the nearest pet shop. Little did she know that no such thing existed. Brewington discovered, in the worse possible way, a hole in the pet products niche. She found one company that offered a blue denim cloth diaper, but it had to be washed, and that would not do. "We don't even wash baby diapers anymore," she said.

Brewington began altering baby diapers for Mr. Chips, but learned quickly that they would not stay on his little bottom or trap waste properly. The road to a successful design was long, but she says that finally she found a way "to keep the diaper on the dog and the dog in the diaper." Another human product was transferred to pet use, and Do-Rite Disposable Dog Diapers were born. As is the case with many entrepreneurs, Brewington was encouraged by the response of people who saw Mr. Chips in his diaper, and she was smart enough to patent her design. Good thing because one of the companies she talked to about manufacturing her product "was so impressed with my idea that they took it to China and started producing the diaper," she said. She was disheartened by the theft of her idea but has some patent protection in place pertaining to special features of her design.[29] In addition to demonstrating the great emotionalism behind many innovative products, Brewington's story exposes the competitiveness of the market. Seasoned business people are savvy enough to know how ripe the market is and some are ruthless enough to take advantage. The pet industry is big business and the stakes are high.

Mr. Chips, who inspired the Do-Rite Diapers. Photo courtesy of The Do-Rite Holding Co., LLC., used with permission.

NOTHING'S TOO GOOD FOR MY BABY

The lightening rod issue when we talk about companion animals is all the pampering—the special food, the parties, the clothes, the vacations, the funerals—the special treatment and activities typically reserved for humans. We created the pet industry with our insatiable desires to please and pamper our companion animals. Critics say the treatment is excessive because the recipients are, after all, animals. But those of us who extend the pampering do not consider the treatment special, perhaps because we do not consider them animals. Therein lies the reason for our behavior, and critics say, therein also lies the problem. I am not going to solve that debate, but I will explain why we do what we do.

Giving human characteristics to animals is referred to as anthropomorphism. The word has roots in Greek, with the first part "anthropo," meaning human. The second part of the word comes from "morphe," which means having a particular form or character. You are probably more familiar with the last part of the word, "ism," recognizing it from words such as racism and sexism, and know that it means to exhibit or maintain a certain philosophy.[30] We are accused of being anthropomorphic when we assign human thoughts, feelings, and emotions to our animals. But we cannot help it because the tendency to do so is part of our evolutionary heritage. What we are doing is using knowledge of ourselves to understand the behavior of others. This ability distinguishes us as *Homo sapiens* from Neanderthals, who had no such capacity, and could be part of the reason why homo sapiens were better hunters who could plan attacks, rather than wait for food to happen by. We watched and used the "specialized weapon for penetrating and exposing the minds of prey." Our ancestors' ability to attribute human thoughts, feelings, and beliefs to other species also allowed them to incorporate other animals into the "human social milieu."[31] This helped open the door to domestication of animals and all its benefits. We are evolutionarily disposed to anthropomorphizing, but we seem to blur the lines more and more as time passes. Sometimes animals seem to suffer as a result, but most of what I describe next is about excessive pampering, not doing harm. Keep an open mind because one person's pampering is another person's necessity or as one indulger said, "I don't think it's pampering. It's what you do."[32]

A Sound Mind

First things first: mental health. I take seriously the treatment of emotional problems and mental illnesses so I thought carefully about whether to include animal therapy here—in a section focused on excessive pampering—or in the chapter on protecting our animals. I decided to begin the topic here because the interest in therapy for our animals is a function of an increased appreciation of treatment for our own mental illnesses and emotional problems. We go to therapists; so we send our animals to therapists. Similarly, we want to share the bounty of psychotropic medications, such as Prozac, which are enormously popular. Make no mistake; I am not ridiculing either the application of therapy or medication to treat medical conditions in animals or people. Our animals can suffer as much as we from chemical imbalances in the brain or can develop emotional problems that require behavioral intervention. I must point out that we cause many of the emotional problems from which our pets suffer. The primary reasons that companion animals require therapy are related to improper care, training, or handling.

Animals with emotional problems see professionals like Dr. Petra Mertens, who is one of just a hundred veterinary animal behaviorists in the world. She treats animals for problems such as excessive aggression, phobias, obsessive disorders, and separation anxiety. She is one of two animal behaviorists in the Animal Behavior Service at the College of Veterinary Medicine at the University of Minnesota in St. Paul, which sees about 500 new patients a year, making it one of the busiest behavior services in the nation.

Mertens says that 80 percent of her patients are dogs, followed by cats. She also treats the occasional bird, horse, rabbit, ferret, and various small animal. Mertens says that her dog patients are usually brought in because they bark all day, chase shadows, hunt invisible bugs, jump out of windows, or cannot stop licking a spot on their leg. Cats are often seen for aggression, problems with housetraining, or urine marking. Bird problems include compulsive feather plucking and constant screaming. Each patient receives about five hours of treatment, which includes some combination of behavior management or modification (for both animal and human, I suspect) and medication. Cost is similar to treatment for humans, about $190 per hour. Mertens says that her caseload is increasing, but adds, "I don't think it's because there's more behavior problems, but because of a higher awareness of people, awareness that these services are available."

Applying what we know about psychology to dogs makes sense because they have acclimated themselves to our world and we share so many of the same experiences. One man—Cesar Milan—has single-handedly brought what he calls dog psychology into our homes, thanks to his flash burn popular television program, *The Dog Whisperer*, which appears on the National Geographic channel. Milan, a handsome, young, exceptionally charismatic immigrant who grew up surrounded by animals on a farm in Mexico, opened the Dog Psychology Center in Los Angeles, where he uses what he refers to as the real mind of a dog to "rehabilitate" them while "training" their people. "Humans tend to treat dogs like they are a human. But a dog is an animal. A dog needs calm, assertive energy from its owner, then exercise, discipline and affection—in that order," says Milan. Rather than trying to get the dog to see the world from our point of view, Milan, understands how dogs interact socially, and suggests we see the world from the dog's point of view. "Many trainers strive to have the animal fulfill the need of the human first. With my method, I first connect with the mind of the dog, and then I connect with it on a physical level. This process allows me to communicate with the dog and rehabilitate the dog's behavior."[33]

Anyone as popular as Milan is bound to have detractors, especially in a country filled with other professionals who have devoted their lives to training. For instance, Nicholas Dobman, director of the Animal Behavior Clinic at Tufts University's Cummings School of Veterinary Medicine said, "To call his operation a psychology center is a total paradox." He refers to Milan's tactics as going to war with the dogs. He says that Milan uses "positive punishment" and "flooding," two techniques that were in vogue with military dog trainers. Positive punishment involves use of an aversive action to stop a behavior and the other involves exposure to extinguish a behavior. Some well-known animal behaviorists have gone on record criticizing Milan, saying that he has regressed dog training twenty years.

Milan's defender's give as good as he gets. "You don't have to have degree in psychology, human or otherwise, to see what's behind the Milan bashing," says Marc Goldberg of the Chicagoland Boarding School for Dogs in Chicago. "There's an enormous envy factor at play here." Goldberg says that Milan has given us a "new world view" of dogs and credits him with tackling tough cases and saving dogs from euthanization.[34]

A Sound Spirit

Whether humans have a soul is up for debate in some circles, so to pose the question about animals is to join a fool on an errand. Regardless, many people who believe that humans are spiritual beings with souls, created by God, expect and look forward to seeing their companion animals again in whatever they envision the afterlife to be. Consequently, they want to make sure the animal gets there. But does the animal need to go to church? Or is the inclusion of animals in our spiritual and religious lives simply a vivid demonstration that our actions are for us, not for them?

Remember, this chapter is about companion animals as a part of *our* world, and if church is a part of our world, we bring them there, too. This is nothing new. For example, when human culture was primarily agrarian, animals were cherished and blessed with other aspects of nature, and early theologians often referred to animals. Typically, when people embrace spirituality or religion, they include animals in their beliefs, especially animals who are considered family. As a result, the practice of including animals, especially dogs, in church services is increasing. What follows in this section are delightful examples. In response to parishioners' requests, many denominations have annual services to bless animals, with many Christians patterning their services after Catholic feasts to honor St. Francis of Assisi, the patron saint of animals.

One of those is the St. Francis Episcopal Church in Stamford, Connecticut, where Lillian Kraemer started it off by bringing her King Charles spaniel, Grantham, to an early service. Kraemer says that Grantham has impeccable church manners, so much so that when she wants him to be quiet outside of church, she uses the command, "Church," and he pipes down.

The Rev. Molly McGreevy, an avowed dog lover, feels that incorporating animals in the service is fitting, given the name of the church, and was the catalyst behind formalizing the services beyond the "once a year splash." So many animals started coming to church that a special separate service was created to accommodate allergic communicants or those with small children who became too excited in the midst of the animals, which so far has included, among the dogs and cats, a parrot, gerbil, and fish—in attendance. "It's the most fabulous thing we've ever done," she said. McGreevy is particularly attuned to parishioners who live alone with their animals and who are pleased to be able to bring their animals to church. Importantly, these communicants, once isolated, get to know others who live alone with their animals, and friendships develop. Rev. Mark Lingle,

Reverend Molly McGreevy blesses her dog, Petey, during the regular companion animals service at St. Francis Episcopal Church in Stamford, CT. Photo courtesy Helen Neafsey.

who co-directs the special service, says that the animals are well trained, but reportedly admits to keeping the "Nature's Miracle" (a liquid enzyme to remove stains) not far from the holy water. While the guardians receive Communion at the altar, the animals get a blessing. Regardless of which end of the animal eventually gets presented, McGreevy bestows a blessing such as, "And may you live a long and happy life in the care of those who love you. Amen." For what more could any creature ask?[35]

Although some people feel that a companion animal has no place in church, others return to church because they *can* bring their animals. Rev. Lingle said that there is no denying the importance of this phenomenon. He has had communicants tell him that they have not been to church in ten years and now that their *pet* can come, they are taking Communion and saying prayers.[36] Whatever brings people back to church is good according to a study published in the *Annals of Behavioral Medicine*, which found that seniors who regularly attended religious services have healthier lung function than those who do not.[37]

The Rev. Jane Heenan, rector of Holy Trinity Episcopal Church in Lincoln, Nebraska said that when she prays, her adopted Persian cat, Beeker, purrs. Heenan believes that "our pets are gifts of God." She adds that there is deep spirituality in the relationship between an animal, the pet guardian, and God. She calls it a "three-way relationship of trust." The Rev. Bob Schlismann, an ordained Presbyterian minister, conducts services for companion animals upon request, keeping the programs "as broad and nondenominational as I can." He agrees that "prayers and blessings for pets seems perfectly natural because animals are part of God's creation." Consequently, he was taken aback when he was rebuked by the church board for requesting prayer for his dog, Hazel, a cocker-mix suffering from cancer. "It's just a dog," was the remark. Schlismann believes that companion animals deserve more. "Pets can teach us much by modeling values. They can express love and teach us how to love. They love us even when we don't deserve to be loved," he said.[38]

Pastor Hans B. Hallundbaek of Croton Falls Presbyterian Church believes that animals have an intuitive connection to the infinite and the sacred. "They're not religious in our sense . . . but I think they are connected to a universal spirit." He adds jokingly that they are also too smart to divide themselves into different denominations. Parishioners at the church's first animal blessing in 2005 reported an unusual calm, even in their normally hyperactive animals. One of the animals being blessed that day, Faith, a pit bull rescued from the cruel waters of Hurricane Katrina, was a living testament to salvation on earth. A fire fighter had rescued her from the cruel waters of New Orleans where she had been tied to her guardian, who had been dead for at least ten days.[39]

One little Lhasa Apso found his way from a Wal-Mart parking lot into the arms of Lama Zopa Rinpoche, a prominent disciple of His Holiness the Dalai Lama and the spiritual director of one of the largest Buddhist organizations in the West. The revered Buddhist monk, an animal lover, who encourages followers to bless and care for animals daily, named the foundling Jangsem, which means mind

Lama Zopa Rinpoche, a disciple of His Holiness, the Dalai Lama, and spiritual director of one of the largest Buddhist organizations in the West, blesses a lost Lhasa apso with a stupa containing relics of Buddha. Photo courtesy of Roger Kunsang, used with permission.

of enlightenment. The dog was quite afraid, but ran straight for the Rinpoche when he saw him, and received Lama Zopa's personal fleece blanket, which was quite a blessing in its own right. Jangsem spent a week with the joyful Rinpoche, running and hiking, before being turned over to his original guardians, but not before receiving a special blessing with a stupa, a type of crown that holds relics of Buddha himself.

Sir Roudy Bushreid of Winterset, a six-year-old Golden retriever proved himself to be a bit rowdy when he attended the annual blessing of the animals at the National Cathedral in Washington, DC. His behavior was understandable because it was a hot, humid day in the nation's capital, and Roudy was mighty thirsty. Consequently, when the priest came near to sprinkle some holy water, Roudy commandeered the special chalice and helped himself. His enthusiasm was well received and Roudy was blessed inside and out.

My husband and I have friends whose dog takes *himself* to church: Meet Leonardo DaVinci, a six-year-old basset and beagle mix. For the first three years of his life, "Leo" would sneak away on Sunday mornings from the home he shares with Dr. Neil and Ellie Schneiderman (he a prominent psychology researcher and she a doyen of the arts), when a visitor would inadvertently leave their door ajar. (I can attest that the Schneiderman's house is a buzz of vibrant social activity on Sunday mornings with basketball games and stimulating conversations on the arts.) The combination of being free and the sound of the church choirs was apparently too much for Leo, and he would be seen, tail wagging joyfully, heading for one of two churches in his quiet neighborhood: one Catholic, the

Roudy makes friends with a priest at the National Cathedral in Washington, DC, after taking a slurp of the holy water during the blessing of the animals. Photo courtesy of Paul S. Garrard.

other Episcopal. (As a former Episcopalian, I am entitled to say that I find it hard to believe he was drawn to the choir.) Well, the doors to the church were open, as they say, and Leo would go straight to the altar and sit down quietly next to the priest, ostensibly attending to the service. Initially, someone in the congregation would call the number on Leo's collar, but after several visits, they just waited for Ellie to retrieve Leo, who was apparently too much of a distraction for the churchgoers. Dr. Schneiderman says, "Nowadays Leo is less likely to get out of the house, but it is not entirely clear whether the people we know have grown more careful or Leo has lost some of his early interest in religious services."[40]

Companion Animals and Us includes several remarkable accounts of religious ceremonies held in honor of companion animals, including a "bark mitzvah" for a "thirteen-year-old Labrador retriever whose twenty guests received monogrammed hats to wear at a barbeque reception." Most notably, a special education teacher in Long Island, New York, sponsored a *bar mitzvah* for her horse, Sonny, because she wanted to show "gratitude and love" for him. She got the idea from one of her students, who was studying for his *bar mitzvah*. The teacher created a special version of the traditional candle-lighting ceremony, and Sonny wore a yarmulke and a tzitzit, and received gifts, as is the custom. She said that she had "planned the event as a joke," but was emotionally "overwhelmed by what had transpired."

A California couple gave a cat *mitzvah* for their thirteen-month-old cat, whom they named "Fifi Katz." Only one of the ninety invited guests refused to attend, and those who came brought gifts, feasted on Greek food and danced. Fifi's "dad," a "former Jesuit priest explained that the "event was for fun," but had a "serious side" because he "deeply respected tradition." He said he wanted to "celebrate the beauty of creation as manifested in a particular little animal."[41]

A Sound Body

We all know how popular day spa treatments have become, and many lucky cats, dogs, and horses get to enjoy them, too. Tails of Olde Towne in Alexandria,

VA, is one of those places where dogs get treatments, massage in this case, typically reserved for humans. Certified canine massage therapist Joyce Tischer, who is also a child psychologist, started the company in 2000 that provides therapeutic massage to help alleviate and prevent a host of conditions. As is the case with massage for humans, animal massages have medical benefits that go beyond relaxation. Canine massage improves circulation, promotes lymphatic drainage, increases range of motion, and shortens rehabilitation time after injury or surgery. Yeah. Yeah. But it feels soooo good. Canine massage costs in the range of $40 to $70 per session, depending on the size of the dog, and The International Association of Animal Massage and Bodywork provides a list of practitioners by state.[42]

The Zen Den at L.A. Dogworks is a bit more about the pampering with its aromatherapy infused massages and personal shopper. Most indulgent humans do not frequent spas with 24-hour security and valet service. Even when I can squeak out time and resources for a massage, no one drops me off and picks me up as they do for clients at Zen Den. Zen Den is designed like an eastern retreat with natural elements of slate and bamboo that promote a soothing and tranquil experience for dogs.[43]

My favorite yoga asana (pose) is known as downward facing dog. Anyone who lives with a dog has seen it and its counterpose, upward facing dog. Dogs do it every morning to stretch and it is part of their solicitation maneuver when you come home from work.

Many asanas have informal animal names, such as cow, fish, and pigeon, but none mimic a posture characteristic of the animal as do "down dog," "up dog," and the "cat back."

This, and our insatiable desire to do everything with them, was a cue for some to incorporate dogs into yoga classes, one called Doga. One instructor says that yoga is calming for dogs and can help with their range of motion. I accept that possibility because dogs live in this crazy world we have created and can benefit from quiet time with their person and enjoying stretches. Regardless, dogs and certainly cats, do not *need* yoga. They *are* yoga. One instructor was quoted as saying, "It's hard for a dog to be mindful, and because they do not understand English you can't lead them through a guided mediation."[44] Please. Dogs and cats, as is true about most animals, embody the principles of mindfulness, living in the moment, and being in the body. Any dog or cat who appears to enjoy yoga or *need* meditation would probably benefit just as much from being left alone for a while. Yoga for dogs seems like one of those human-driven endeavors without much real purpose for the dog.

You Have a Lawyer

We have a reputation for being a highly litigious culture, so it is no surprise that we want our companion animals to have the benefit of legal representation when we feel they have been aggrieved. In Chapter 7, I will discuss using the law to protect our companion animals, but here I refer to lawsuits that seek legal remedies.

Animal law is a new specialty that includes not only companion animals, but also farm animals, research animals, and wildlife in civil and criminal cases. It is emerging as an important discipline being taught at prestigious law schools, including those at Duke and Harvard universities. Sixty-seven animal classes are taught in the United States, and twelve state bar associations have animal-law sections. Unfortunately, companion animals are viewed as property in most states, which restricts opportunities for monetary compensation and remuneration.[45]

Stephen Wells of the Animal Legal Defense Fund, an organization devoted to representing animal interests in the legal system, says that gone are much of the "scoffing" and raised eyebrows that he encountered when he began animal law.

Many believe it is high time. "Our laws ought to honor the bonds that human caregivers have" with animals, said Leana Stormont, a People for the Ethical Treatment of Animals (PETA) attorney. "There's a real difference between property and the animals we share our homes and hearts with . . . People who grieve for their animals shouldn't have to accept market value as a measure of damages." In contrast, veterinarians are concerned that an established system of animal law will result in more malpractice suits and increased malpractice insurance.

Steven Wise, an attorney and director of the Center for the Expansion of Fundamental Rights, and author of *Drawing the Line: Science and the Case for Animal Rights*, says that veterinarians benefit financially from the attachment they promote between people and the companion animals. He believes it is hypocrisy to say on the one hand, "spend more money on animals because they are worth more," but then on the other hand want the animal to have little value in malpractice cases.[46]

When my Grace died unexplainably at the veterinarian's office, it never occurred to me to sue. I was hurt beyond repair and mad as hell, but suing would not bring my dog back. As it turned out, I got what I would have wanted from a lawsuit anyway, a lasting memory for my dog and a way for her death to have meaning. The veterinarian established a memorial fund in her honor, and we collect money to treat homeless and at-risk animals. The photo of Grace on the dedication page is of the plaque the doctor designed to hang in the lobby of the office. Other veterinarians are not so compassionate, and if a death is unequivocally the result of malpractice, I think it is good for people to have the option to pursue legal remedies as much as with any loved one. Wrong is wrong, but each situation should be evaluated on its own merit, not just as a knee-jerk reaction for financial gain.

One of the biggest legal battlegrounds involves divorce custody cases, and they are spilling over into animal law. The *Los Angeles Times* has reported a hundred-fold increase in the frequency of custody cases in the past fifteen years. Another report estimates that companion animal issues come up in one of every twenty divorces. Most courts do not look beyond making the determination on the animals as property, just another asset to be divided. You know that if people use their children as bargaining tools during divorce, they will do the same with their companion animals. Tucson divorce attorney Deborah Pratte explains, "It's not unheard of that one party might use the other party's affection for the animal against the other party." For example, as with children, one party will use the custody of the animal to gain leverage with other issues, such as support payments.[47] In contentious divorces, people find out what the other spouse wants and want it more. Then, they try to take it. When children are also involved, pets are frequently better off going with the children. *Pet* prenuptial agreements are becoming more popular in Britain, and it probably will not be long before the practice catches on here. Animals suffer when their value as a bargaining chip is placed ahead of their well-being. Typically, the animals will have demonstrated a preference for one person or the other, and judges will base the decision on that, but sometimes that is not feasible. Manhattan divorce attorney Barnard Clair said, "As animals become recognized as sentient beings with the right to enjoy their time on their planet, the law will continue to evolve."

Not all cases involve divorce, and one with a different issue threatened the nature of the pet adoption process when two parties entered into a custody battle over a cat, Oliver, who left home while his first guardian was away and was adopted as a homeless animal by a second woman, who refused to give him up when his original guardian surfaced. Known only as Jane Doe, the second woman contended that the cat had not been cared for properly, as evidenced by his escape, that the cat was "thrilled with her," and that the two had bonded. Doe, who happens to be an attorney, in her bid to keep the cat, cited an old law on the New York books that an owner's right to reclaim a lost pet is terminated if the animal is not claimed within forty-eight hours. Oliver had been missing longer than that after the original guardian's blind roommate inadvertently let him out while she was away, and she did not get to the shelter in time. It took more than a year to resolve this issue, but days before the trial, Doe agreed to return the cat within ten days, and they settled out of court. In the private settlement Jane Doe requested only that the original guardian put a collar on the cat.[48]

Although most judges do not look forward to custody cases involving companion animals, the courts are taking them more seriously, awarding damages beyond what would be expected just with property. For instance, since 1997, courts in Kentucky and California have awarded damages to pet owners for loss of companionship, emotional distress, and other factors beyond market value. One of the largest judgments ($39,000) was awarded to Marc Blueston in California in 2004 after his dog Shane (a mixed breed) died of liver failure after being misdiagnosed. Only one-third of the award was for veterinary bills, with the rest for the dog's "unique value." In 1997, a Kentucky jury awarded $15,000 in the case of a German shepherd who bled to death after surgery, when the judge instructed the jury to consider that the dog had intrinsic value, like an heirloom. Another jury awarded $28,000 for a botched dental surgery on a Rottweiler.

Richard Cupp, a law professor at Pepperdine University, fears the trend toward higher damages will lead to increased veterinary costs, making care cost-prohibitive and opening the floodgates to lawsuits not based on our emotional attachments to pets, but to our increased expectations for longer lifespans resulting from improvements in veterinary care.[49]

That may be a danger, but worth the risk, according to people like Adam Karp, who believe that the injustices in the way we treat animals are serious, and that the law is a "ripe tool for affecting change." Karp, a law professor founded the animal-law section of the Washington State Bar Association—he won the largest case on record at the time ($45,480) involving a cat who was mauled and killed by a dog. Another case became the largest on record when the U.S. Supreme Court declined to reverse a California court's decision that required Santa Clara County to pay nearly $1 million to local members of Hells Angels after police shot and killed three of their dogs during a raid.[50]

Paw-T Down

Many of us love a good party, and we are throwing shindigs that give new meaning to the phrase "party animal." Following are a few examples.

When Tonka turned one-year-old, he sported a white "birthday boy" T-shirt at the party given by his proud "mom," Amanda Reif, a Washington DC, contracts negotiator, who refers to her boxer as "my child with fur." Reif spent $500 on the party that included all kinds of toys and attractions for her dog and his dog pals, including a piñata filled with Puppy Chow and covered in bacon grease, a doggie tunnel, a kiddie pool, and a homemade birthday cake made with strained baby food in beef stew and carrot flavors, and dog food: all shaped like a bone. The party was held at Seneca Hill Resort & Spa, and guests were primarily neighbors (some of whom brought their children), and friends that Reif made at a dog park (none of whom had children). The people munched on "store-bought platters of chicken and veggies," but the dogs got all homemade food and gift bags with treats. The *Washington Post* covered Tonka's party.[51]

Parents of human children have long known the value of play dates to provide their children with social activities and to catch a break themselves. With our ever-increasing desire to ensure that our companions have full and happy lives, we carry over the practice of supervised play for them. In fact, unsupervised play is often considered unwise, especially for small dogs, for whom dog parks can be unfriendly and downright deadly. I remember the first (and last) time I took my Maltese to a dog park. Two hyped-up Dalmatians rolled her around like a ball and could have easily killed her before my husband could wrench her from their jaws, had they not been just playing. Not my idea of fun. Animal behaviorist Peter Borchelt agrees with me. He says, "individualized play dates have a place—if a dog is shy, easily frightened or has been 'mugged' by another dog."

The pressure is on with play dates. As is the case with play dates for children, part of the attraction is to meet like-minded people, but the dogs have to be compatible because *parents* of poorly behaved dogs are ostracized along with their unruly pooch—and you just cannot show up without your dog. Then what is

During the "Bark Ball," in Washington, DC, Roudy presents famous bipartisan couple Mary Maitlin and James Carville with a bottle of his specially labeled California Merlot, "Roudy's Reserve." Photo courtesy of Paul S. Garrard.

your excuse? People looking for play groups use sites such as www.meetup.com and www.craigslist.com. Another site, www.DateMyPet.com, began as a dating service, but evolved when the founder noticed that people just wanted to get their pets together to play. "People will bring pets to a date and they might not get along, but the dogs get along so the owners stay friends," Borchelt said. This is a totally new phenomenon.[52]

Stacy Cruikshank, owner of Bark Avenue Pet Boutique in Fernandina Beach, Florida, throws "puppy showers." She says that when you have a baby or get married, you need things, and when you get a new puppy, you need things. Cruikshank promotes the parties she throws, which are complete with an online gift registry, personalized invitations, customized party ware, and party supplies.[53] Shure Pets specializes in direct sales of pet products, promoting in-home parties where hosts earn points and prizes, while sharing the love of companion animals with friends and family.[54]

Paul Garrard of Arlington, VA, makes sure that Roudy (of the holy water fame mentioned earlier) arrives in style when he parties. Each year the duo attends "Bark Ball," the annual fundraiser of the Washington Humane Society, and the only dog-friendly formal event in the nation's capital. Several hundred people and their dogs break out in their finery for what Mary Maitlin (who with husband James Carville forms the most famous bi-partisan couple in the United States) says is the most social and fun event in the city. Even among these powerful and prestigious guests, Roudy is the only dog seen bounding out of his own limousine. He was definitely the only dog to present a bottle of his specially labeled 2003 California Merlot, "Roudy's Reserve," to the power couple.

It is easy to see that the common theme in all the *pet* partying is people: people laughing, people fraternizing, people socializing, and people having fun. As we negotiate the social lives of our animals, we get to go along. This is one of the ways in which having a companion animal enriches our lives, by not only providing direct social support, but also providing opportunities for us to interact with others. From being the catalyst to an active social life to simply being the topic of brief conversations that you have with a colleague or a person you pass in the street, having a companion animal becomes part of your system of social support.

Looking Good

People love to dress their companion animal, and go to extremes with dogs. Cats, birds, and reptiles are also candidates for outfits. Our obsession with clothes is an anthropomorphic function of our seeing the dog as a child, a child who must be dressed.

Clothes for creatures are almost out of hand and unless you live in an extreme climate, they do not make much sense. Forget your dog bringing your slippers; he has too many of his own to carry. Clothes for animals are clearly an example of our trying too hard to make our animals human. They do not *need* clothes. Most dogs, for instance, would prefer to remain naked, bereft of collar or leash. Notice how puppies and kittens make a project out of releasing themselves from their first collar, no matter how thin and light it is. A ferret does not need a snappy sweater and a French beret. Dressing animals in clothes is a stark example of the trend toward humanization of companion animals. Even people who are not into clothes for their dogs will put a bandana around their necks. Every conceivable item of clothing is available, with every possible adornment—a dog coat with a fur collar goes beyond cognitive dissonance. Apparel and accessories for dogs and cats are sold everywhere from convenience stores and super stores, to stores on Rodeo Drive.

By some accounts, New York, followed by Los Angeles, is the driving force behind canine fashions. They say you can even tell where dogs live by the clothes they wear. For instance, on the Upper East Side, known for historic wealth, the dogs wear tweed, real fur, and diamond accessories. Conversely, grunge and urban chic attire is visible in the Village and Soho neighborhoods of New York.

Marketers know who is doing the buying. That is why many canine fashions follow human fashion trends. They also know that the purchases are not about the dog, but about looking cute *with* the dog or responding to the expectations of other people. Kerri Cowing says that she dresses her Australian shepherd, Sierra, because "there's kind of a peer pressure when you're walking around. People say, 'You don't have a coat on that dog?'"[55]

My Máni is a Maltese, one of the breeds that guardians are prone to dress, but she HATES clothes. She would rather go outside with what God gave her to face a foot of snow, which is twice her height, than put on a coat. But to me, a coat for her is a necessity; it is not as if she were a Malamute. Having now experienced Máni, and earlier Grace—who in direct contrast, really *liked* to wear clothes, appreciated wearing sweaters in New England winters, and beamed (really) in the little black formal coat that my friend Mary gave her—I know that dogs can exhibit preferences about clothes and that certain animals benefit from clothing to protect them from the elements. However, a closet full of designer togs, I do not understand. People like Kathleen Hilllman mystify me. She buys jackets, hats, sunglasses, and outfits for her Chihuahua, Bug, one of her five dogs. She admits that she spends more on Bug's clothes than on her own.[56] Why do we do it? Family psychologist Dr. Alan Entin, who focuses on the role of companion animals in the family, explains, "I think of it in the same way as people who dress

Psychologists say that people dress their companion animals for the reflected glory. This handsome Golden retriever, Cody, is happy to accommodate in a costume that signifies his special status as a super companion. Photo courtesy of author.

up their young children for Halloween. The children don't know what Halloween is, and yet parents will dress the kids up and take them around, because it makes them feel good. It's a reflected glory."[57]

Gifts and Gadgets

A discussion of the gifts we bestow on our companion animals could take up an entire book that would need updating by the minute. You can get everything under the sun for companion animals now, from special horse blankets to booties for pigs. I will mention just a few of the most unusual items and then invite you to let your imagination run wild.

For instance, in keeping with the "*pet*-as-child theme," one of the most popular gadgets is a "pet stroller." Hammacher Schlemmer in New York has one for cats or dogs for less than $150. Animal guardians who run can keep up with those stylish human parents and their jogging strollers, by buying a stroller designed just for their little ones, too. Jeep even makes a rugged stroller for dogs up to 70 pounds. Cyclists, too, can get a stroller that hitches to their bike.[58] Then, there is the water bowl that lights up when it needs changing, called "Thirst Alert." I am not making this up! Finally, voice mail so you can record a message to play at set times to comfort your latchkey companion animal.[59] Suffice it to say, if it is available for you, some entrepreneur has created a version for your companion animal.

ANIMALS AT WORK

Not all companion animals have lives of constant pampering. Many animals—dogs in particular—work, which the *New Oxford American Dictionary* defines as "activity involving mental or physical effort done in order to achieve a purpose or result." Dogs are active creatures who get great satisfaction from having a purpose and successfully executing tasks, and the work our companions do is diverse and complicated, as you will see.

I cannot include every possible type of work here. Consequently, I will focus on a sampling of the most common and a few of the most unusual. Working side by side with a dog is the best way to celebrate the relationship and establish a deep connection. Dogs are workers by design, not layabouts, and they usually perform better than humans or machines in their skill sets. For instance, nothing on earth can herd sheep better than a Border collie or sniff out drugs better than a—well, any dog. Dogs' keen senses of sight, smell, and hearing are perfectly complemented by their instincts to make them perfect for many tasks. Foremost, as a pack animal, dogs have a stronger desire to please, obey, and be with the boss (whom they see as the alpha dog) than any other creature on earth. And we have reinforced those natural tendencies through association and breeding. Dogs also love to chase, hunt, and kill (typically only their toys)—instincts capitalized on in rescue and police work. Dogs are naturally territorial and prone to defend what is theirs or identified as theirs, which is also advantageous. Actually, dogs can excel at almost any work they are asked to do because they want only to please you; they love to keep busy; and they have the intelligence and skills to adapt to almost anything. Following are a few of the familiar and a couple of not so familiar types of work we ask dogs to perform.

Dogs in Blue

Protection is the first work that dogs performed for their humans, beginning with standing guard at the cave. Consequently, police work, as part of a canine-handler team, is still the most prominent work they do.

Referred to as K-9 officers since the 1940s, thousands of dogs work with handlers across the United States, having been established here with help from England. The exact number of teams serving is unavailable, but two of the three main professional organizations for K-9 units report more than 3,000 active teams. The United States Police Canine Association, one of the three national membership organizations for K-9 teams, is the oldest and largest of the associations devoted to assisting law enforcement by providing continuing education and informing the public about K-9's important mission. The North American Police Work Dog Association and the National Police Canine Association are the other two, and all support the various local and regional associations that rely on them for guidance and support.[60]

Midge, on duty in the Geauga
County sheriff's office in Muscon Township, Ohio. She
is the smallest K-9 officer.
Reprinted with permission
from WKYC-TV.

Space will allow me to profile just a couple of unique situations involving
K-9 police officers. First, let me introduce you to Midge, who weighed just two
pounds when she auditioned for her job with the Geauga County sheriff's office
in Muscon Township, Ohio. The little Chihuahua rat-terrier mix was the runt of
her litter, but she is the perfect size to police nooks and crannies where the bad
guys can hide drugs. Her specialty is marijuana because a cache of cocaine could
be too potent for her petite nervous system. On her first birthday, Midge became
a certified "marijuana sniffer," a dog who looks for drugs in high school lockers,
car interiors, and other tight places. She is believed to be the smallest K-9 police
officer in America.[61]

Dogs are not the only companion animals suited for police work, as demonstrated by Fred, an alley cat who actually went undercover to expose a fake
veterinarian who was placing animals in harm's way with his unorthodox, dangerous treatments. Top investigators, working for the New York District Attorney,
Charles J. Hynes, involved Fred in a six-month investigation that included a
sting. Thanks to Fred's work, the bogus doctor was charged with "operating an
unauthorized veterinary practice, criminal mischief, injuring animals, and petty
larceny." No longer undercover, Fred wore his badge for the press conference,
where reporters were told by DA Hynes that Fred was the city's "first undercover
cat."[62]

Dogs are the most prominent species in the police ranks, and the work takes
an enormous toll on dogs, as it does on people. Police dogs have a shorter life
expectancy than most dogs because of on-the-job injuries, according to Dr. Greg
Herbert, a veterinarian who treats canine officers in Brooklyn. He mentioned that
German shepherds generally live to be about twelve years of age, but that he is
aware of police dogs being euthanized as young as eight because of injury or illness.
Many K-9s are companions before they join their guardians on patrol. Those who
did not originally live to the handler typically become part of their handler's
family.

Handlers who lose their canine partners have a particularly hard time because
the dog is their family, friend, and trusted backup, and the mutual bond and

commitment are intense. This is one of the most gut-wrenching kinds of losses, and the handlers speak of their canine partners with the utmost reverence and respect. For example, Officer Rick Rodden talked about his partner, Jari (pronounced Ya-dee) who was euthanized because of a debilitating degenerative back condition, using words like "dad" and "son," when he described their relationship. Jari was an national award winning canine, who began his training at the age of four months in the Netherlands, where he was born. He was certified by the United States Police Canine Association and trained to locate bombs, search suspicious packages, apprehend subjects, and search for missing persons and items. Jari was a stellar and seasoned canine officer when his career ended. The department paid $8,500 for Jari, but he was truly priceless to Rodden—at work and at home. Rodden described Jari's playfulness at home around his human son, "He was like a light switch. He would be on when he needed to be on and off when he needed to be off. I have countless pictures of him being mobbed by kindergarteners."[63]

Canine police officers are not always easy to recruit. In fact, the Gross Pointe police force had to get their first canine officer, Raleigh, from an academy in the Czech Republic, but he proved his worth before his official badge was delivered. Raleigh is a crime fighting, public relations machine who ferrets out illegal drugs, forces the bad guys to give it up rather than face his wrath, and schmoozes with teens at the local Starbucks. Raleigh lives with handler Michael Almeranti and his family, which includes a nine-year-old son, who loves Raleigh. "That's the nice thing about him," Almeranti said, echoing the sentiments of other handlers. "The dog is your family pet after work is done. He's like my best friend already." Sounds like the canine officers have a much easier time than their handlers at leaving work behind and focusing on fun. Just goes to show you how important it is to live in the moment.[64] Subspecialties of canine police work includes accelerant dogs who locate evidence of ignitable liquids, and "Ag" dogs who identify agricultural quarantine items, and narcotic and bomb dogs.

The Federal government employs some of the special canine-handler teams in at least three agencies—the Transportation Security Administration (TSA); the Bureau of Alcohol, Tobacco, Firearms, and Explosives; and the U.S. Customs and Border Protection agency. Thirty dogs across the country supplement antiterrorism efforts in the nation's commuter rail and bus system, and the nation's capital is one of ten U.S. cities that recently received three explosive-sniffing dogs from the TSA for its rail transit system. The TSA also has 345 of the dogs deployed at 66 of the nation's airports.[65]

Dogs in Red

One of the most welcome sites you could ever see if you are lost or the victim of a disaster, is the red harness of a search and rescue dog (SAR). The practice of employing dogs in SAR reportedly dates back to the year 980 when a monk at the monastery of The Great Saint Bernard Pass, which provides a route between

Switzerland and Italy, employed dogs (now known as St. Bernards) to locate stranded travelers of the Pass. In America, SAR dogs were first used in World War I by the Red Cross to locate injured soldiers. After the war, the Swiss Alpine Club discovered that working with dogs was a more effective way to find avalanche survivors than probing the snow, and now more than ninety teams of qualified dogs are on call around the clock.[66] The American Rescue Dog Association, founded in 1972, is our nation's oldest organization for "air-scenting" dogs. They set the standard for training and evaluation of units across the country, such as the Virginia Search and Research Dog Association, which also employs air-scenting dogs, rather than those trained in traditional "tracking." Air scenting has an advantage because the dogs can work behind other searchers if necessary, in any kind of weather, and after extended time has passed. The dogs are trained to seek the unique scent produced by bacterial activity on human skin cells, which is released into the environment. The dogs follow the scent along the air currents and can detect a human scent within 500 yards, in good conditions. In fact, during good conditions, air-scenting dogs are equivalent to about twenty human searchers. In poor conditions, dogs are even more valuable because they can work equally well in dark or light.[67,68]

Lately, we have become well acquainted with the Federal Emergency Management Agency (FEMA) because they were news fodder after Hurricane Katrina hit New Orleans. In spite of daily news tutorials, I still associate the agency with disaster cleanup, not *rescue*. Yet, they are heavily involved in both. For example, after the terrorist attacks on the World Trade Center in New York on September 11th, FEMA deployed twenty K-9 rescue teams to the towers and four teams to the Pentagon, where sixteen dogs worked in twelve-hour shifts to keep dogs on the site around the clock. Eighty-five percent of dogs certified to work on FEMA's Urban Search-and-Rescue task forces work with civilian volunteer handlers from across the country, and both dog and handler must pass rigorous national certification to serve and must recertify every two years to stay in the program. Dogs must demonstrate command control, agility skills, and barking alert skills, and overcome innate fears of tunnels and unsteady surfaces. Dogs work off lead during a rescue and are taught what is called a "soft walk," where they spread their toes for maximum traction and safety. Dogs with advanced training, which takes years, work without supervision or guidance from their handler.[69]

Potential rescue dogs are typically identified as puppies or adolescents by their love of fun and play, particularly tugging games. As serious as the work is, it is taught as a game. For instance, a dog with a strong desire to play can be taught to recognize his target and bark when he finds it to get a reward. That is a very simple description of an extremely complex training.

Rescue dogs certainly can become depressed in massive disasters where survivor rates are low, but one handler explains that if the dogs are taught and handled properly, they work for the game and the reward. The comment suggests that the dogs do not get upset because of the loss of human life, but because they simply cannot successfully find what the handler wants them to find. That is a nice thought, but anyone who lives with a dog knows that they understand death and experience grief. For that reason, even if the dogs are not affected by the deaths, I believe they can pick up on their handler's mood and experience depression as a result.

One of the handler's primary responsibilities is to maintain the interest and mood of the dogs. Consequently, if a rescue dog goes a sustained time without recovering victims—the reward—handlers will construct a situation with a human volunteer, usually another handler, so the dog can experience a success. Given how smart we know dogs are, I have to believe that they know the decoy was not the person they were actually supposed to find, but still revel in the discovery because the handler seems pleased.

These very special dogs work hard and save lives, and they are constantly training to maintain their skills. Rescue dogs usually live with their trainers and learn to ride in helicopters, boats, and airplanes to get to their jobs quickly because moments matter in rescue work. To succeed, some dogs have to overcome an inherent fear of heights and learn to walk lightly on collapsed structures for their own safety and that of their finds. They work with such diligence that they must be encouraged to eat and get proper rest. They are real heroes, who happen to be canine!

When Closure Is All That Is Left—Cadaver Dogs

Disaster rescue requires that some dogs receive specific training to find the dead. Chief, a member of Illinois Search Dogs, Inc., is one of those trained to find cadavers—a dog who works with a volunteer handler to search for victims lost too long in brutal conditions, buried, or drowned. Chief's expertise is water search, and he has been trained to alert his handler when he detects human odor under the water. Chief is also trained to search through avalanches and had to learn to ride a chairlift to gain access to rugged environments. When Chief is called in, he helps narrow the search coordinates to give the human searchers a better chance of providing grieving families the only thing they have left—an opportunity to bring their dead home for proper burial. Chief himself was rescued—from an animal shelter.[70]

Dogs of War: Military Working Dogs (MWD)

This was the most difficult section of the book for me to research and write, which I found odd because pacifist is not a word that jumps to mind to describe me, but obviously I am. Living in the United States during two of the country's declared wars has certainly taught me that I value peace, and I have become especially repulsed lately by the horrors of war. Yet, anger is an emotion with which I am intimately familiar, and I am not shy about speaking up in the face of injustice. I do not mind a good fight for a good cause, but I fight my own battles, and if someone takes on my fight, I do not leave them hanging. Perhaps that is what upset me the most about animals (again primarily dogs) used as weaponry.

Kwinto, a military working dog
(MWD) trained to detect explosives
at vehicle checkpoints, on security
patrols, and during weapon cache
sweeps, with the 24th Marine Expedi-
tionary Unit, shown with his issued
protective gear in the northern Babil
province of Iraq, November 5, 2004.
MWD gear includes a flak jacket,
safety goggles and protective booties
made for canines. Official USMC
photo by Cpl. Sarah A. Beavers.

They fight for us in *our* wars, never knowing how expendable they are. You see,
the military has a history of considering a dog as "equipment," a *thing* that can
be written off as collateral damage when convenient, and that offends my sense
of justice. I have strong (remember that anger) views about the sacrifices men
and women of the military make, particularly during a war. It tears my soul to
know they are in harm's way. Nonetheless, in recent history, our country has not
had a draft, and the men and women who constitute our courageous armed forces
decide, for reasons of their own, to enter the military. Dogs have no such option.
They are all drafted and serve with their hearts, never knowing they are tools.
When I learned how egregiously dogs of war have been treated, I was stunned. In
spite of their contributions, "success in battle is seldom shared with the animals
involved."

From the beginning, dogs joined forces with humans and fought to defend
common interests, mainly food and territory. The earliest use of dogs in battle is
attributed to a type of Mastiff in Tibet during the Stone Age. Later, practically
all the famous—and infamous—military leaders around the world used dogs. In
America, Benjamin Franklin is accepted as the first person to suggest using dogs
in a war—fought against indigenous Americans. Dogs were later used during
the Civil War as messengers, regimental mascots, and sentries. The Spanish-
American War found dogs primarily in the role of scout. The British were the first
to use dogs in World War I and shared their expertise with America for World
War II and the Vietnam War.

The Red Cross taught dogs to find wounded soldiers and ignore the dead ones.
They were taught not to bark and carried supplies to the wounded, bringing back
helmets to alert rescuers of survivors.

After the attack on Pearl Harbor, two "dog fanciers" convened and established
Dogs for Defense, as a network of volunteers and their dogs. In 1942, the Secretary
of War directed the Army Quartermaster Corp (QMC) to train dogs for duties
other than sentry, such as search and rescue, patrol, and messenger. The QMC
established War Dog Centers across the United States and by 1945 had trained
nearly 10,000 war dogs for the Army, Navy, Marines, and Coast Guard. The first
combat dog was Chips, a German shepherd-husky-collie cross who earned during

World War II the Distinguished Service Cross, the Purple Heart, and the Silver Star, all of which were revoked because he was a dog. Chip was discharged after serving three years in the Army, but as is the case with police work, war takes its toll on dogs, and he died after only fours months as a civilian. According to the Web site of the Army Quartermaster Foundation Web site, dog training was transferred to the Army Field Forces in 1948 and given to the Military Police Corps in 1951. Dogs continued to serve, with 1,500 in Korea and 4,000 in Vietnam.

Dogs were in Vietnam before the involvement of American fighting troops, serving as guards or sentries for the Army of the Republic of Vietnam as early as 1960, without benefit of veterinarians or capable handlers in the Republic.

As the war continued, the dogs suffered from accidents, injuries, and contaminated food. In 1967, eighty-nine dogs from fifteen platoons died from an "idiopathic hemorrhagic syndrome," which was officially termed "tropical canine pancytopenia" (TCP). The epidemic spread through military and civilian dogs "like a scythe," and was eventually traced to ticks on British dogs in Malaysia. Veterinary care improved dramatically afterward, but "the Veterinary Corp was handcuffed by shifting priorities, primitive laboratory and surgical facilities, infighting, lack of medicine, and the constant stress of . . . war."

As the United States began to withdraw from the Vietnam War, a decision was made to leave the dogs behind and "most American dogs were condemned to permanent exile and eventual death in a foreign land." Unlike earlier wars,

Corporal Christopher Bello, a twenty-three-year-old Marine dog handler from Queens, NY, shown in 2005 with his dog, Kastor, during a quiet moment. They supported Operation Iraqi Freedom by finding explosives, explosive-making materials and weapons on daily missions alongside infantrymen. Official USMC photo by Cpl. Tom Sloan.

after which dogs were "demilitarized" and returned to U.S. shores, the military made what was a cost-effective decision to minimize logistical concerns for the handling of *equipment*, which dogs were considered—you do not need it, leave it behind. Amidst the protests of soldiers and the whining confusion of the dogs, thousands of dogs were abandoned, left to fend for themselves, or turned over to the Vietnamese for disposition.[71] "These dogs saved about 10,000 American lives; They deserve better than what they got," said Ron Aiello, a former Vietnam veteran and military dog handler and the president and co-founder of the United States War Dog Association. "For most every handler who had to leave their dog in Vietnam, it was a traumatic experience." Dogs and handlers were together around the clock. Aielo said they ate, slept, and even went to the bathroom together. "The bond was so strong because you were never separated and you depended on each other to stay alive," he said. Dogs are still classified as equipment, according to Aiello. That policy was not changed, but Aiello said, "They don't leave them behind; That they don't do."[72]

David Keeton, a handler and member of the Vietnam Dog Handler's Association, self-published a book to honor his dogs. In his second book, *King "Moo"–War Dog*, which is a frank and heartfelt account of his eighteen-month partnership with a K-9 soldier (whose serial number was M00), Keeton talked about how the dog was saved from the fate of abandonment, but after being dipped in malathion and surviving quarantine to make enter the States, Moo succumbed to cancer two years after returning home. King Moo had been stationed in areas subjected to Agent Orange.[73]

Dogs have continued to serve: in Desert Storm, Afghanistan, and Iraq. In 2005, Major Jennifer Damko was responsible for approximately ten dogs in Mosul, Iraq, where temperatures can exceed 100 degrees. While keeping her troops alive, she also nurtured the camp's war dogs, which were there to sniff out bombs and find enemy forces. The men and women, and the dogs, are all soldiers, but Damko admitted, "There is nothing better than forgetting for a moment that I'm in a war zone and just 'hang' with the dogs."[74]

The United States War Dog Association is a nonprofit military organization that trumpets the accomplishments of canines and their handlers. Founder, Aiello said, "We focus on the dogs. We [the handlers] are here because the dogs saved our lives. We owe it to them to do whatever we can. They are the world." Among other activities, USWDA supports active duty canine/handler teams with care packages and assists in adoptions of retired dogs. The Association has been working on a commemorative postal stamp and a national war dog memorial for the dogs and handler to get the widespread recognition they deserve. While awaiting for Congressional authorization for the national memorial, the Association dedicated the first official State War Dog Memorial on June 10, 2006 at the Vietnam Veterans' Memorial in Holmdel, NJ.[75]

It costs nearly $20,000 to train a dog, and the military wants to recoup its investment by having the dog serve as long as possible. So when Air Force Tech. Sgt. Jamie Dana asked the military to release her dog, Rex, they responded

Kastor and Bello quickly run down a sidewalk after taking small arms fire from insurgents during a mission in Iraq on June 25, 2005, with Company A Marines. Official USMC photo by Cpl. Tom Sloan.

that it would not be "a legal or advisable use of Air Force assets in spite of the sentimental value and potential healing affects it might produce."[76] Dana had a right to be sentimental. She and Rex had trained for three years before being deployed to Iraq where they scoured villages for hidden bombs. Just three weeks into her tour, a roadside bomb exploded under the Humvee in which she and Rex were riding. Dana nearly died from her injuries, including a collapsed lung, spinal fractures, and a broken pelvis. Before she lapsed into a coma that lasted a month, she asked about Rex and was told he had died. While recovering at Walter Reed Army Medical Center she discovered that Rex was alive and began asking about adopting him. She explained that she never wanted to be separated from him again saying, "He's my best friend. I thought he was dead, and that made the feeling to be with him a lot stronger." A swell of support garnered national attention and resulted in a Congressional measure that allowed special exceptions to the military's rules. The efforts were not without opposition from factions who thought Rex should remain in the military where he could save the lives of other soldiers. Ultimately, Rex was formally discharged and officially given to Dana in a small adoption ceremony.[77] Dana and Rex were guests of the First Lady for the State of the Union Address in January 2006.

Reading Tutor

A match made in heaven is a child who needs a nonjudgmental audience to practice reading skills and a dog, both of whom love one-on-one attention. In the Reading Education Assistance Dogs (R.E.A.D.) program, dogs are registered through the Delta Society as Pet Partners, who then act as "literacy mentors."

Dogs specifically trained for this important work and their human handlers form hundreds of teams across the United States and Canada to help children enhance their reading and communication skills. The teacher remains involved, encouraging the students not only to read to the dog, but to explain what they read, which has the added bonus of helping students develop important comprehension skills. R.E.A.D. targets young children, middle and high schoolers, and children learning English as a second language. The children acquire important skills for continued growth and development and develop respect and appreciation for animals. Forty-five states have more than 750 dog reading teams in local schools and libraries. Quite an increase from 2004 when there were only 100 registered teams.[78]

Never Sniff at a Job Opportunity

Man has not been able to create an instrument to rival a dog's natural sense of smell. Dogs' super evolved olfactory equipment is opening up all kinds of job opportunities. Some of the new opportunities have medical applications, which will be discussed later, and the most common ones involve law enforcement, but others are a bit surprising. For instance, the Motion Picture Association of America employs dogs to detect the smell of DVDs (the polycarbonate fumes gives them away) to thwart video pirates trying to transport their stolen wares through London's Heathrow Airport. Farmers are using dogs to detect whether cows are in heat; thereby increasing the likelihood of successful artificial insemination. (Remember you heard it here.) On a more serious note, dogs have also been taught to detect the smell of cell phones to catch terrorists who might use the device to detonate bombs. Posh hotels and expensive New York co-ops are employing dogs to sniff out bedbugs. The best part of this arrangement is that many of these newly minted careers go to dogs who were rescued from shelters.

Overall, dogs are born with the perfect complement of psychology and biology to excel at any task. They have what it takes: the nose, the enthusiasm, and the *joie de vivre*. A good trainer can insure that these lucky dogs have something fun to do that will occupy their minds and give them a sense of accomplishment. It's the least we can do, if we are going to ask them to wear clothes.

6

Pets As Medicine

In the beginning, God created man, but seeing him so feeble, he gave him a dog.
                    —Alphonse Toussenel (1803–1885), French writer and journalist

Yes, companion animals get lots of pampering, some of it expensive, but in return for our apparent generosity we get much more than we could ever give. The icing on the cake is that our companion animals may be good *medicine*, with a proven ability and an uncharted potential to cure what ails us. You see, establishing and maintaining optimum health requires a harmonious balance between the mind and the body, and companion animals excel in enriching our lives and encouraging balance. Interacting with animals also has an effect on our physiological processes.

Historically, physicians have had a dualistic approach to medicine, treating the body as everything from the neck down and the mind as something only in the head. Now, body-mind medicine is a respected, evidence-based approach in modern medicine, and a widely accepted fact is that psychosocial factors can influence the function of the mind and thereby the body. Medicine has moved from a pure biomedical model of care, which considered only the biology associated with an illness, to a biopsychosocial model that also considers psychological disposition, environment, and social interactions.

For instance, a person complaining of chest pains visiting a cardiologist, who operates out of the biomedical model, might find that the cardiologist is interested only in the functioning of the heart, the biological pathology of the heart that might be causing the pain. A cardiologist operating out of the biopsychosocial model would have those same concerns, but would also have concerns about the person's state of mind and other contributing factors in the environment. A biological intervention might be nitroglycerin tablets, whereas a biopsychosocial intervention might add cognitive behavioral therapy, biofeedback, or relaxation techniques. These kinds of interventions, once considered alternative therapies, are part of mainstream medicine from pediatrics to geriatrics and in fields as diverse as dermatology and neurology.

AAT AND AAA

As mainstream, traditional medicine becomes more inclusive, Animal Assisted Therapy (AAT) and Animal Assisted Activities (AAA) have gained wider acceptance. Distinctions between the two are best described in the Delta Society's *Standards of Practice for Animal-Assisted Activities and Therapy* (excerpted below). The Delta Society was founded in 1977 as an international clearinghouse for human-animal bond research and has become the most recognized, respected name in animal therapy. The organization's primary mission is to improve human health by understanding the relationships between companion animals and humans, and the role of service and therapy animals in human health.

> AAT, a goal-directed intervention in which an animal that meets specific criteria, is an integral part of the treatment process. AAT is directed and/or delivered by a health/human service professional with specialized expertise, and within the scope of practice of his/her profession. AAT is designed to promote improvement in human physical, social, emotional, and/or cognitive functioning. AAT is provided in a variety of settings and may be group or individual in nature. This process is documented and evaluated.
>
> AAA provides opportunities for motivational, education, recreational and/or therapeutic benefits to enhance quality of life. AAA are delivered in a variety of environments by specially trained professionals, paraprofessionals, and/or volunteers, in association with animals that meet specific criteria.

AAA and AAT appear similar, but AAT is more formal, has established goals, is delivered by a trained medical professional or paraprofessional, and AAT activities must be documented. Ironically, the therapy animals used in AAT do not themselves have a legal definition, but service animals, such as guide dogs, are defined under the American with Disabilities Act of 1990. Federal law mandates that service animals have free and full access to accompany their human charges in all public places. No such provisions are in place for therapy animals. In 2003, the Department of Transportation attempted to establish criteria that included therapy animals, but much confusion has resulted, as you will read.

How It All Began

Involving animals in therapeutic environments is more widespread and accepted than ever, but the custom is not a novelty, and has several historical documentations. For instance, in 1792, animals were used in a British psychiatric hospital (known then as lunatic asylums) in a progressive move to encourage patient independence by caring for the animals.[1] Florence Nightingale, whose name is synonymous with compassionate care, noted that "a small pet is often an excellent companion for the sick," and she suggested birds specifically for patients with chronic disabilities.[2]

In 1919, the Secretary of the Interior wrote a letter to the head of St. Elizabeth's Hospital, a psychiatric hospital in Washington, DC, suggesting companion dogs for inpatients.[3] Later, in the 1940s, a convalescing Army Air Corpsman reportedly requested a dog to keep him company as he healed, and other patients later made similar requests.[4] The convalescent center in this report was located on a farm where patients were "encouraged to interact with various farm and pet animals."[5] The next documented involvement of animal assisted therapy was accidental: Psychiatrist Boris Levison happened to have his dog, Jingles, in his office during a scheduled session with an eight-year-old boy, who was characterized as withdrawn and uncommunicative, but he opened up to the dog. Levison made breakthroughs with this patient, and Jingles became an important component of his treatment with other children in his practice.[6]

Therapeutic riding has been prescribed since the seventeenth century, and was made famous by Liz Hartel, who despite being in a wheelchair, represented Denmark in the 1952 Olympics and won the first of two silver medals for dressage, a specialized riding technique. She showed the world that people with disabilities could benefit from horseback riding. When horseback riding is used to effect specific changes in the rider's posture, balance, and mobility, it is referred to as hippotherapy, from the Greek word for horses: hippos.

EVOLUTION OF AAT RESEARCH

Animals are involved in the treatment of many human maladies. Many of the animals are strictly companions, and the results are neither observed nor recorded, but testimonies abound. Furthermore, investigative research is providing compelling, if only sporadic, evidence that contact with animals can improve health and prevent illness. Positive results have been demonstrated with children and the elderly; in mental and physical diseases; and treating unique populations such as juveniles with behavioral problems and the incarcerated. Animal interactions have been shown in research to reduce blood pressure, lower cholesterol, improve recovery from cardiovascular disease, increase exercise, forestall symptoms of Alzheimer's disease, and prevent acute health crises, such as seizures and panic attacks.

Study designs are often criticized either for not having sufficient sample sizes, not being randomized, and being difficult to replicate, or issuing conflicting results. Investigators frequently and openly discuss the problems inherent in this kind of research, and acknowledge the need for more studies. They realize that we need conclusive, consistent results to confirm the excellent indicators that our companion animals can comfort us when we are ill and motivate us to achieve higher levels of health and well-being.

It has been twenty years since the National Institutes of Health (NIH), the arbiter of all things scientific in America, convened a working group to explore the health benefits of companion animals. Then, the experts did not seem comfortable drawing strong conclusions from evidence they described simply as "persuasive."

Times have changed, and as the NIH admits on the Web site devoted to this report that their previous statements and conclusions are outdated and quite possibly wrong. The view may be clearer now for more definitive statements, which would be well received.[7]

Current research continues to build on the classic and oft-cited studies by pioneering investigators such as Erika Friedmann and Alan Katcher, who in 1980 published critical research demonstrating health benefits of living or having interactions with a dog.[8] In this chapter, I will present findings from some of the more recent compelling research and discuss remarkable demonstrations of therapy and service animals.

Many species of animals are involved in therapeutic activities, but most are mammals, and the dog is the most well suited and popular for this work. Dogs have an innate desire to please and their herding and nurturing inclinations are of immense value in therapy work. Those advantages aside, any other animal capable of providing unconditional affection, reliable responses to training, and nonjudgmental interactions has great potential. Horses, monkeys, and snakes have also been involved in therapeutic activities, with horses being of keen interest because of their lack of allergenicity and their long lifespans.

While research is done on a variety of species, dogs' therapeutic value is frequently evidenced. A recent overview of the relationship between dogs and human health revealed that dogs can have both a "prophylactic and therapeutic value for people," helping us recover from acute illnesses and cope with chronic illness, as well as warning us of impending illness.[9] Dr. James Serpell found a significant, sustained reduction in minor health problems over the course of a ten-month prospective study.[10]

Involving dogs in therapeutic activities is not without human risk, but proper selection, training, and care eliminates potential problems, such as dog bites. Some risks, such as zoonotic diseases and allergic reactions can become insurmountable barriers to involving dogs in health care.

Despite early reservations about (and resistance to) including animals in therapeutic environments, success over the years insures that involvement will increase as research continues to reveal and document the powerful healing benefits of interacting with companion animals.

Clearly, the benefits to us are becoming more evident, but what about the risks to them? Investigators have begun to question and examine the risks to animals involved in therapy and service work. Previously, all research considered only the value of the animal to achieving therapeutic goals, but as we become enlightened to the emotional lives of animals, we must take into account quality-of-life issues for them. Animals in certain therapeutic environments are at risk for injury from equipment, such as wheelchairs, canes, and crutches. They can suffer from the stress of overuse and extended work hours. Patients to whom the animals are assigned can be unstable and volatile, capable of causing harm. We know that animals can read our emotions, but research is just beginning to reveal the toll being involved in our care takes on them. I remain haunted by the demeanor of a guide dog I once saw, who had the saddest face and eyes that I had ever seen. The dog looked miserable and depressed. On another occasion I saw an old and clearly arthritic dog trying to help a blind man, who had other physical disabilities, maneuver a busy intersection—they both needed help.

We know that dogs live to serve and please, but when does enough become enough and who is monitoring that? Several programs pride themselves on *saving* dogs from euthanasia by adopting dogs and puppies from shelters who are then trained for therapy or service work and placed with human clients. Similarly, many shelters pair adorable puppies and complacent dogs with volunteers and send them out to nursing homes and schools. At first blush, these seem like good ideas, but are they? Alison Hatch reviews these and other disturbing aspects of dogs, especially shelter dogs, being dispatched for this kind of work in, The View from All Fours: A Look at an Animal Assisted Activity Program from the Animals' Perspective, which was published in *Anthrozoös*.[11]

ANIMAL ASSISTED THERAPY

AAT is used in various therapeutic environments across the country where goal-directed interventions with specific recorded outcomes are required. The animals, usually dogs or horses, are thoroughly trained to achieve the desired goals and to work with human facilitators, who are equally trained and often possess professional medical backgrounds.

The DOGtor Is In

Several national organizations train and help place dog-therapy teams to achieve both physiological and psychosocial outcomes.

A common application is as an adjunct to physical therapy programs where the therapy animal can initiate or encourage movement and facilitate range-of-motion activities. I had a chance to see this in action as a reporter, when I was invited to observe a trained therapy dog, who regularly visited a day care facility for adults with learning disabilities. The dog's task was simply to allow himself to be brushed, while the staff recorded the progress that participants made in their ability to master their use of the comb and brush on the dog's hair. Improvements in language skills associated with the activity were also tracked. A wide variety of such programs can be designed and implemented with a dog purposefully trained to enhance the physical capabilities of target populations.

Dogs have demonstrated repeatedly that interacting with them can boost psychological well-being, which can contribute significantly to physiological well-being. Stroking or talking to a dog has been shown to decrease blood pressure and heart rate, and the mere presence of a dog can lower autonomic responses to stress. Perhaps this explains a dog's remarkable ability to facilitate recovery from heart attack. Replicating earlier published work, Friedmann confirmed that people with dogs were more likely to survive the first year after a heart attack than those who did not have a dog.[12]

The first randomized trial to examine AAT as an adjunctive treatment in critically ill patients demonstrated that a twelve-minute visit from a dog is more therapeutic for patients with heart failure than a visit from a human volunteer. In the study, specially trained dogs entered the ward and lay where the patient could pet or talk to them. Researchers found that self-reported anxiety scores decreased 24 percent for patients receiving a visit from the dog, compared to 10 percent after a visit from the human volunteer. Blood levels of the stress hormone epinephrine fell 17 percent in patients who had a visit from a dog, compared to 2 percent in those who had a human visit. A control group with no visitors actually had a 7 percent increase in epinephrine levels. Atrial blood pressure (a measure of pressure in the atrium of the heart) dropped 10 percent in the dog-visit group, but increased 3 percent in the human-visitor group, and 5 percent in those with no visitor. Remarkably, systolic pulmonary artery pressure (a measure of pressure in the lungs) dropped in the dog-visit group 5 percent during therapy and 5 percent after therapy. However, this value increased during and after the visit time in those with no visitor or a human visitor. Lead investigator, Kathie Cole, an advanced clinical nurse, said, "This study demonstrates that even a short-term exposure to dogs has beneficial physiological and psychosocial effects on patients." She added that the therapy warrants serious consideration as an adjunct in this critically ill patient population. "Dogs are a great comfort. They make people feel happier, calmer and more loved," she said. "That is huge when you are scared and not feeling well."[13]

Achieving positive psychological outcomes in therapy seems almost too easy for dogs. These naturally social animals can bolster human psychological well-being with one paw tied behind their backs. Research has shown that a "simple snuggle" can reduce stress, by suppressing stress hormones and releasing oxytocin,[14] and who gives better snuggles than a dog? For years, considerable research on human-animal interactions (HAI) has shown that animals, dogs in particular, can ameliorate the effects of potentially stressful life events, such as divorce and grief; reduce levels of anxiety, loneliness, and depression; and enhance feelings of autonomy, competence, and self-esteem. They are naturally affectionate, display unbridled joy when greeting you, and possess unrivaled loyalty—all of which collaborate to promote feelings of self-worth and increase self-esteem.[15]

Companion animals are also of enormous psychological benefit to people, who because of illness or disability have limited social contact or are rejected or isolated. The literature substantiates that the unconditional acceptance therapy animals offer is crucial to improved psychological well-being.

A Horse? Well, of Course!

The extended lifespan of horses and their unlikely potential to cause allergic reactions are almost enough to make them prime candidates as therapy animals, but they have other advantages, particularly with certain patient populations, which may surprise you.

Persons with physical disabilities are obvious candidates for riding therapy (hippotherapy) because a horse's gait almost mimics the motion of human walking. It "provides the person who has a disability a normal sensorimotor experience" that "stimulates the rider's balance mechanism" because the rider must make constant adjustments to the horse's varied movements. Bareback riding is particularly useful because it provides increased stimulation and requires more intense effort to establish and maintain balance and equilibrium. Horseback riding is used in various movement disorders to help people with balance exercises. Conversely, therapeutic horseback riding is inappropriate in patients with unhealed pressure sores, fragile bones, hemophilia, and uncontrolled epilepsy. When used appropriately, therapeutic outcomes can also include improved muscle strength, better posture, increased muscle control, and a wider range of motion. Several remarkable cases have been reported. One involves a "seven-year-old unable to hold up her head or walk alone before hippotherapy." After six months, she was "independent on crutches" with improved head and neck balance. Another child of the same age who could only "walk four steps with crutches" was walking four blocks using one crutch after the same time frame.[16]

At Fort Myer's Army Base in Arlington, Virginia, horses are helping a few of the multitude of military amputees returning from Iraq and Afghanistan to regain feelings of freedom in a remarkable therapeutic riding program that employs the horses normally used for military funerals at Arlington National Cemetery. The trainers in the program report that the horses are noticeably "tender" with the amputees. After an injured soldier is placed on the horse, three other soldiers surround the horse to secure the rider, walking with the horse to ensure the rider's safety, but the amputees report that the extra help does not interfere with the therapeutic or emotional value of the experience. Army Specialist Nick Paupore, who lost his right leg to a roadside bomb and works with a horse named Arabi, said, "Even though you have three guys helping you, it seems like they're part of the horse. Once you start riding, you realize the horse works with you, and that if you relax, it will relax and you will become one with horse." The horses help the amputees exercise unused muscles, improve their balance, and recreate the motion of walking. "I definitely started walking on my own a lot more since I've been riding the horse," said Capt. Michael Blair of the United States Marine Corps, who was injured in Iraq and works with a horse named Mickey. Army Specialist Natasha McKinnon who also lost a leg in Iraq said, "When I get up on the horse, I feel like I have two legs. I don't think about the injury. I feel that I can do what I normally do. I think good thoughts, you know, like I'm free."[17] After she finishes rehabilitation, McKinnon intends to pick up the dream that was the catalyst for enlisting, becoming a veterinarian, and now she is interested in equine veterinary care.[18]

Horses are very social creatures with distinct attitudes, moods, and personalities that can be matched with particular clients to achieve other specific types of health-related goals. Moreover, as prey animals, horses have heightened sensitivities and intuition, and are capable of facilitating self-awareness in a deep and profound way. They are big, powerful animals who can help clients learn to overcome fear and quickly develop confidence.

For example, young women and girls suffering from eating disorders gain greater self-acceptance and learn to feel at ease through equine-assisted therapy at the Remuda Ranch in Arizona as part of their intensive inpatient program. "Horses readily perceive our fear, feelings of inadequacy, and sorrow," says Edward Cumella, Ph.D., director of research at Remuda Ranch.[19]

"The beauty of working with horses is that you can't fool them," says Dianne Kennedy, a psychotherapist, registered riding instructor, and founder of Medicine Horse in Boulder, CO. Something transcendental takes over when people get close to a horse. We are captivated by their majesty. They perceive us in a pure way, undistracted by words, appearances, or social standing. The Medicine Horse Program complements psychotherapy with equine-assisted therapy for adults and children in four distinct programs. For example, Healing with Horses, teaches grieving children to express their pain and demonstrates ways to reduce stress and isolation. Working with hospice-trained staff and professional therapists, in conjunction with the horses, they learn to achieve goals and deepen connections with others.[20]

ANIMAL ASSISTED ACTIVITIES

The majority of animals used in AAA are also trained before they enter a therapeutic or service environment, with the defining difference here that goals are more self-directed and spontaneous. Although progress is not charted, the outcomes can be significant. I am including in this section service (or assistance) animals because their contributions also are not charted, and a patient's progress is not measured by a medical professional or paraprofessional.

Service animals are trained to assist people who have physical disabilities. These animals learn to perform a myriad of physical tasks, such as opening doors and picking up things, and they can even help people dress. Assistance animals include dogs who alert to medical conditions, such as seizures. In these cases, they may be referred to as medical response dogs, seizure alert dogs, or simply alert dogs.

In this section, I am also including what I call accidental animal therapists and assistants. These are the untrained animals who happen to be in the right place at the right time and contribute to a positive emotional or physical outcome. You will see that some people are taking questionable steps to ensure that their untrained companions are around just in case, and controversy is stirring.

Horses to the Rescue

I will start this section where I ended the previous one, with horses, miniature horses to be specific, who are trained as service animals to guide the blind.

Miniature horses make remarkable guide animals for the visually impaired because as prey animals they have a heightened sense of awareness of their environment and remain vigilant for danger. Horses are naturally docile and have a natural guide instinct, which is valuable in guide work. Reportedly, sighted horses in a herd will help the blind ones. Horses have incredible vision and because their eyes are on either side of their head, have a wide range of vision of nearly 350 degrees. They are capable of independent eye movement and can see clearly in darkened conditions. Miniature guide horses do not get fleas and are often granted easy access to public places because they are not confused with being a *pet*. The overwhelming factor is their long lifespan, which is an average of thirty to forty years, compared to that of a dog, which is between eight to twelve years.

Since 1999, the Guide Horse Foundation has been involved in a program to determine the suitability of miniature horses, which has met with outstanding success.[21] For example, Panda, who stands just twenty-nine inches tall with a weight of 120 pounds, is a trained protective, alert, and housebroken miniature guide horse who has been helping fifty-eight-year-old Ann Edie since 2003.[22] According to the Guide Horse Program's Web site, 27 percent of respondents to an international poll by the Discovery Channel indicated they would prefer a guide horse if they needed a guide animal.

Petie the Pony, courtesy of Victory Gallop, is the only horse in the country allowed to visit children at the hospital. Richard Miller, Petie's handler at Victory Gallop, a therapeutic riding center in Bath, OH, makes sure that all 400 pounds of little Petie are scrubbed surgically clean before every visit. Petie, who stands just three feet tall, must also be shaved and spritzed with Listerine, and his tail and hoofs are wrapped in surgical tape, which is removed before he enters the ward. Petie, a thirteen-year-old horse-and-pony mix, makes bedside visits during his rounds everywhere in the hospital, from the burn center to the cancer ward. "At first the kids are shocked," says Victory Gallop cofounder Sue Miller. "He just seems to know when people need him." Parents often report that their children smile for the first time following a visit from "Dr. Petie."[23]

Eleven-year-old Ben Gibbs, who has cerebral palsy, has made such progress with his regular horseback riding that for the past five years he has not required injections to stop muscle spasms. Because his goals and progress are not charted or medically supervised, his riding is not considered AAT, but his mother is quite satisfied with his improvements, saying, "The experience of him continuing to gain confidence is the goal."[24]

Just Say Whoa is an AAA that targets teenagers with problems such as truancy, substance abuse, anger management, depression, and low self-esteem. The program employs equine-assisted learning activities to develop communication skills and strategies for setting boundaries. In the program, students are encouraged to identify their feelings and explore positive expressions of emotions and needs, and develop leadership skills, a sense of appreciation, and empathy for themselves and others.

Petie the Pony, from Victory Gallop, makes the rounds at a children's
hospital. © 2007 William S. Henry,
used with permission.

The Equus Integration Project is another program, but it focuses on diversity issues with the goal of breaking down barriers and easing conflict that result from differences in language and culture.

Finally, the HopeFoal Project addresses issues of low self-esteem, depression, and suicidal ideation in young girls. In a unique partnership, the girls are paired with Premarin foals,[25] who are newly separated from their mothers. The girls have the responsibility of gently caring for the foals, who have had a rough start in life and need great amounts of love and kindness. This is something with which the girls can identify, and the relationship provides both the foal and the child an unusual opportunity for personal growth. The girls learn to embrace life once again, while the foals flourish from their newfound trust in humans.

When the Dog Knows Best

We are most familiar with service dogs who provide guidance for the blind, dogs made famous by the Seeing Eye organization, which was founded by Dorothy Harrison Eustis. She is credited with being the first person to recognize the widespread freedom dogs could give to people who had lost their sight. She became acquainted with the concept while living in Switzerland, where she bred and trained German shepherds for police work and observed the dogs guiding veterans of World War I. Thanks to her efforts, countless visually impaired and blind people from all walks of life have independence and enhanced companionship, courtesy of their guide dog.

The original repertoire of therapeutic activities has expanded, and dogs provide assistance to people who have a wide variety of medical concerns. Canine Partners for Life (CPL) is one of several national organizations that provides several types of assistance dogs, including medical response dogs and companions for private homes and residential facilities.

Since 1989, CPL has matched dogs with about 300 people in forty states, according to founder Darlene Sullivan. As is customary, dogs are trained for at least two years before being matched. Training begins with volunteers who teach basic commands, before the clients, who must be at least twelve-years-old, receive one-on-one training at the CPL school in Pennsylvania.[26] The nonprofit organization is able to charge recipients a fraction of the $22,000 it costs to train the dogs, thanks to generous donations. The waiting list is between six months to two years.

Candice Hernandez knew about the long wait when she requested her dog, and prepared herself for a long wait, especially since she needed a seizure-alert dog because only six out of twenty-five dogs have the talent for this unique service. To her surprise, CPL called her within weeks and invited her to a three-week orientation. Her designated canine partner, Chiper, was just finishing her two-year training, and Hernandez was asked to ship a package of clothes so that Chiper could become familiar with her scent. When they met, Hernandez said that she fell in love immediately, "She was the cutest, most beautiful dog ever." However, Hernandez was a bit stubborn, and did not like heeding Chiper's warnings, because she was accustomed to being an independent, active young woman whose seizures began in high school. She has a family history of epilepsy, but doctors believe that her seizures were triggered by a car accident, and within a month of her first seizure, she was having up to four a day. When medications failed to block the seizures, doctors inserted a vagus nerve stimulator (VNS), which acts like a pacemaker for the brain. When Hernandez feels the sensations that initiate a seizure, she passes a magnet over the VNS to diminish the seizure's effect. Chiper now senses the seizures and barks, paws, or nudges Hernandez to activate the device. She tended to ignore Chiper in the beginning, but the dog would become insistent, emitting piercing barks, until she complied. Chiper and Hernandez are inseparable, and Chiper does not like sharing, which made things a bit interesting when Hernandez became attracted to her neighbor, Tim Escandons. Now, Chiper had to learn to be less stubborn, but was reluctant to let romance bloom. She would block kisses and literally stick her nose in-between them. Chiper came around, and she was stunning in her own wedding attire when Hernandez became Mrs. Escandons. One happy family—husband, wife, and therapy dog.[27]

Canine Partners also placed a yellow Labrador named Jinks with Gina Goldblatt, a twenty-three-year-old who has cerebral palsy and uses a wheelchair. Jinks' skills are so keen that he can pick up a dime—literally. Goldblatt says that the yellow Labrador is everything to her and gives her function that she no longer has from her arms and legs. Jinks accompanies Goldblatt everywhere, including

Chiper, a service dog for Candice Hernandez, is part of the wedding party when
Hernandez marries Tim Escandons. Photo
courtesy of Len Pepe, used with permission.

school, and is trained to remain focused on Goldblatt when she needs him. But
he knows that when his harness comes off, he can be all dog. Goldblatt says that
he romps around and loves the water.[28]

Shea Megale, a ten-year-old from Centreville, Virginia, who uses a wheelchair
and has limited motor skills, has the constant attention and assistance of her dog
Mercer, who helps Shea in all the traditional ways. More importantly Mercer
increases Shea's self-esteem. "I'm not known as the kid in the wheelchair," Shea
says. "I'm known as the kid with the dog. That changes a lot for me." Mercer has
absolutely changed Shea's world according to her mother, even making doctor's
appointments less anxiety producing. The dog is such a fixture in Shea's life
that he earned a photo in the school's yearbook. Next to the headshot of Shea
is one of "Mercer Megale." Shea received Mercer from Canine Companions
for Independence (CCI), which provides dogs without cost to carefully selected
applicants, who pay only $100 for a two-week training session. CCI has more
than 1,000 placements across the United States. Nearly 60 percent of puppies are
released from the program because of health, behavior, or temperament problems,
and are typically adopted by their volunteer trainer or are placed in carefully
selected homes.[29]

Asta is an example of a dog trained to assist with disabilities beyond the realm
of the physical. The seven-year-old Rottweiler is trained to help Carey Ivey, who
has a panic disorder severe enough to qualify for federal disability benefits. Asta
braces Ivey when she feels dizzy and has an astonishing ability to sense Ivey's
panic attacks, allowing the young woman to leave the threatening situation or
take medication.[30]

Monkey Can Do

Many breeds of animals can be trained to perform varying types of service work. The breed with whom we share most of our DNA and whose body is most like ours seems a natural assistant for people with mobility issues. Case in point is Minnie, a five-pound, fifteen-inch tall capuchin monkey, who became the arms and legs for Craig Cook, after a car accident that left him a quadriplegic. The design engineer lost his job, his affluent lifestyle, his fiancée and her son— and all hope. Cook was in the throes of deep depression when a friend found Helping Hands, an organization that trains and places capuchin monkeys with the disabled. The extremely dexterous animals, familiar for working with street musicians, have humanlike hands, are very strong, and can learn an array of tasks. Minnie prepares meals for Cook using the refrigerator and microwave, and operates a CD player, and a television. She can also feed Cook. Minnie is also a mini mood reader, who strokes Cook's eyebrows, face, and head when she senses he is feeling down.

Helping Hands began at Tufts University in 1979, with monkeys rescued from animal laboratories in an experimental project that combines "rehabilitation engineering, occupational therapy, and behavioral psychology." The program now breeds monkeys, who live with nondisabled foster families for the first five years of their lives "so they can enjoy a childhood complete with toys and tummy kisses, and interact socially with humans and household pets." The training and lifetime care for the monkeys costs $35,000, but they are provided free to qualified recipients. Helping Hands has made one-hundred-and-sixteen placements to individuals with conditions such as Lou Gehrig's disease, muscular dystrophy, multiple sclerosis, and stroke. When Cook applied for a monkey, only dogs for the visually impaired were legal service animals in California, but Helping Hands worked to change the laws, and in 2004, Cook became the first person in the state to have a monkey as a service animal.[31]

Dognosticians

Dogs can be trained to identify people with various illnesses, such as bladder cancer. As far-fetched as it seems at first, the notion makes perfectly good sense. Dogs have twenty-five times more smell receptors than humans. Their noses are infinitely more sensitive than ours, with an ability to distinguish odors as dilute as parts-per-billion. Remember, they locate explosives and drugs by smell, so why not disease?

For years, researchers have known that the chemicals associated with cancer, such as alkanes and benzene, exude a distinctive odor, and since 1989 research has been ongoing to determine if dogs had the ability to detect it. The answer is yes. Researchers in Britain developed a seven-month training program to familiarized dogs with urine samples from people with bladder cancer. Then, the dogs were taught to distinguish normal urine from the cancerous samples, and to lie down next to a sample they thought was suspect. The dogs successfully identified the specimens with bladder cancer 41 percent of the time, compared to 14 percent that is possible by chance alone. The most startling outcome of the study is that the dogs selected a control specimen with such consistent conviction that the patient was retested and found positive for kidney cancer.[32]

Another extraordinary study demonstrated that dogs can also distinguish people with both early and late stage lung and breast cancer from people who are cancer free. Five "ordinary household dogs" were trained for more than three weeks to detect lung or breast cancer by sniffing the breath of cancer participants, who had been diagnosed with cancer using conventional methods. The breath samples were captured in plastic tubes filled with polypropylene wool and presented to the dogs, who were trained to sit or lie down in front of the test station with the cancerous sample. The dogs detected all "four stages of cancer with sensitivity of 88 percent and specificity of 98 percent." Both studies were well designed, rigorously conducted, and have withstood criticism and suspicions.[33]

With the kind of tenacity and determination known only to mothers, Michele Reinkemeyer took it upon herself to teach three dogs to detect low blood sugar, to protect her son and daughter from life-threatening Type I diabetic seizures. Reinkemeyer's son, Joseph, was having so many seizures that she set alarm clocks to check his blood sugar hourly throughout the night, but nothing worked. Her heart broke, watching him endure the seizures and becoming afraid to leave the house to play with friends. She describes herself as a "horse and cattle" person to whom a dog was a "questionable pet" that chased rabbits in the yard. Yet, she read of a woman who had a service dog for a physical disability that spontaneously alerted to low blood sugar. Reinkemeyer figured that if a dog could do that naturally, a dog could be trained to do it, and she set out to learn how. She read everything she could find on dog training and devised a plan. She took a leap of faith and used a credit card to buy an expensive puppy, recommended by a service organization, and went to work. She was almost startled by her quick success. The pup, a German shepherd whom she named Delta, woke them up one night barking and fussing, but Reinkeymer presumed the young pup simply had to go outside. When Delta continued to whine, Joseph got on the floor to calm him, and Reinkeymer noticed Joseph was shaking. She tested him, discovered low blood sugar, and realized that Delta was alerting. Reinkemeyer trained Delta completely in four months, using clothes that Joseph wore when he had seized. After Delta joined the family, Joseph had only one seizure—a night that Delta spent at the veterinarian. Reinkemeyer trained two other dogs for her daughter, Alice. One died from a brain tumor, but Lance survived and is equally skilled at detecting low blood sugar for Alice. Other people asked Reinkemeyer to train dogs for them, and she did, eventually creating Heaven Scent Paws in St. Elizabeth, MO, which saves the lives of shelter puppies by training them for this unique work. The puppies are socialized early to improve their mental and social development and facilitate training. The organization has a four-year waiting list for a dog, but do-it-yourself classes are held regularly. Reinkemeyer learned how, and she passes the knowledge on—a beautiful manifestation of the adage, "Each one, teach one."[34] Cleo is one of the lovely dogs that Reinkemeyer rescued and trained. In fact, were it not for Reinkemeyer, Cleo would never have been born; she would have died when the shelter euthanized her pregnant mother, Mitsy. You see, Reinkemeyer rescued Cleo's mother from a shelter that immediately euthanizes incoming pregnant dogs to avoid dealing with the puppies. Thanks to Reinkemeyer, Mitsy gave birth to seven healthy puppies. She was spayed and trained to be a therapy dog in a nursing home. Six of her seven puppies became service dogs with successful placements, and one is a search and rescue dog. The lovely Cleo became a medical alert dog for a little girl in Georgia. Kudos to Reinkeymer for saving and enhancing so many lives.

This section is on animals *trained* to execute their duties. Yet, I must include examples of companion dogs who are demonstrating astounding abilities to perform diagnostic behaviors spontaneously without training.

The attention of Debbie Marvit-McGlothin's dog, Autumn, was drawn to a tiny mole on the back of the woman's left leg. Autumn licked the mole and tried to bite or scratch it. The dog was so persistent that Marvit-McGlothin told her doctor, who removed the mole and biopsied it, finding melanoma, the severest of cancers that kills 80,000 Americans annually. Doctors later confirmed that the cancer had not spread to her lymph nodes. Autumn agreed; the dog paid no further attention to Marvit-McGlothin's leg.[35]

Steven Werner had seen the segment on *60 Minutes* about dogs detecting cancer, so when his surviving golden retriever, Wrigley, persistently sniffed at his right ear as they consoled each other over the death of the Wrigley's aged litter mate, Werner paid attention and contacted a doctor. An MRI showed a small benign tumor that doctors said might have caused a stroke within a year.[36]

Cleo, at eight-weeks-old, after her pregnant mother was rescued from a shelter by HeavenScent Paws, an organization that trains and provides service animals. Photo courtesy of Heaven Scent Paws, Inc., used with permission, http://www.heavenscentpaws.com/.

The Accidental Therapists

Companion animals can be little miracle workers without even trying, and the effects are so profound that they attract attention and become noteworthy.

One study showed that just being around dogs may boost the immune system sufficiently to ward off bouts of gastroenteritis, at least in children. Researchers observed nearly 1,000 children between the ages of four and six years and found that children with a cat or dog in the home were 30 percent less likely to suffer from nausea, vomiting, and diarrhea than children in homes without those companions. Another study showed that the germs to which cats and dogs expose children may actually serve as a buffer to illness. Further, children living with at least two animals were up to 77 percent less likely to develop allergies.[37]

Contrary to logic, early exposure to dogs and cats reduces, rather than increases, asthma in children. In this case, the more diversity in the number of animals is the better. Examining children from birth to age seven, researchers found that children in homes with *combined* dogs and cats had close to a 70 percent reduction in sensitivity compared to homes with either (a) no animal; (b) a cat *or* a dog; or (c) two cats or two dogs.[38]

In another study, researchers collected blood from infants immediately after birth and one year later and discovered similar responses. After taking into account parental history of dog and cat allergies, researchers found that babies are less likely to develop allergies and asthma when exposed to cats and dogs in the home (19 percent compared to 33 percent). The mechanism of action is that the early exposure increases levels of endotoxin (a type of bacteria), and increased exposure is linked to a reduced incidence of allergic dermatitis, hay fever, and asthma. The dog or cat likely licks the child, conferring the bacteria that enhance the immune system.[39]

The first study to determine if living with a companion animal conferred the same health benefits to men with AIDS as it does in children, people with disabilities, and the elderly showed promising results. Those men with AIDS who had a close attachment to a companion animal were shown to suffer less from depression than men without pets. "Pet ownership among men who have AIDS provides a certain level of companionship that helps them cope better with the stresses of their lives," said researcher Judith Siegel.[40]

Organizations such as Pets-DC are formed so that people with HIV/AIDS can maintain close attachments to their companion animals. These organizations understand the powerful unique love that companion animals provide, and they ensure that people with failing health and financial hardships secondary to HIV/AIDS do not lose their cherished animal companions. "In the early days of the epidemic, people [with HIV/AIDS] had their pets taken away from them," said volunteer Christine McCann. "Now, people recognize the benefits of having pets for companionship." Since 1990, hundreds of volunteers have walked dogs; changed cat litter boxes; cleaned fish tanks; negotiated discount veterinary care, grooming, and food; and arranged foster care and adoptions for beloved animals left behind. Veterinarian Chip Wells, cofounder and director of Pets-DC says of the organization's clients, "They tell us their pets are keeping them alive and making living worthwhile."[41]

As Florence Nightingale reasoned in 1860, birds can help alleviate depression. A study of thirty eight elderly men, with a mean age of seventy-six years, who participated in an adult day care program responded very favorably when a bird was introduced into the environment. Researchers attributed the reduced depression symptoms they observed to increased social interaction instigated by the bird.[42]

Cardiologist Stephen Sinatra, a nationally recognized expert on cardiovascular disease and founder of the New England Heart and Longevity Center in Manchester, CT, brings his dogs to his office so they can help heal the healer. He said that he wants to be at his best when treating his patients all day, and he knows that he needs to remain calm and energized with his patients. "It's not their fault, but some patients can be cruel at times. A lot of them are suffering and it is definitely understandable, but it can drain you as a physician," he said. "I don't want to bring toxic energy from one patient to another." To reduce that possibility he explained, "I'll visit and pet my dog. I make loving contact with her eyes, and I'll be renewed for the next patient. I practice much better medicine when the dogs are in the office," he said.[43]

You read earlier that untrained dogs can spontaneously detect cancer, so it should not surprise you that untrained dogs exhibit medical alert behaviors. Meet Squirt, a Chihuahua who awakened his guardian, Jimmy Webb, by acting like the proverbial Mexican jumping bean. Squirt pulled Webb's pants from a chair and dragged them over to Webb. Then, he pulled Webb's shoes to him by the strings. Webb thought Squirt was making such a fuss because he had to go outside, but when he began having chest pains, he knew Squirt had awakened him for something more urgent. Webb's pains quickly worsened, but he had time to get a glycerin tablet and drive himself to the hospital where he remained for a week after suffering a heart attack.[44]

Untrained dogs have demonstrated such success at alerting their guardians to epileptic seizures that, in 2004, a group of Canadian investigators conducted a telephone survey to confirm that this remarkable ability, which seems to develop spontaneously in dogs belonging to adults with epilepsy, was also evident in dogs who lived in families with epileptic children. Of the forty-five families surveyed, 40 percent reported seizure-alert behavior in their dogs. Typically, the behavior developed after approximately a month in the family, usually not long after the dog first witnessed a seizure. Parents reported that the dogs were rarely wrong and the alert behavior began within a few seconds to five hours of the seizure. Parents reported that the dogs exhibited behavior such as sitting on a toddler or pushing a child away from stairs before a seizure. Dogs are apparently sensitive to subtle, early symptoms of epileptic seizures, and their recognition is reinforced when the seizures occur. Families with dogs who gave warnings reported a higher quality of life as a result.[45]

One of the most logical health benefits of having a dog is that you get an automatic partner for running, jogging, or walking, who will encourage you to have consistent workouts that are fun. A dog is an ideal running partner who will never compete with you, meet you late, cancel workout sessions, or debate which trail to run. Your job is not to be a foolish trainer; dogs must gradually build strength, stamina, and distances, and veterinarians suggest that dogs are fully grown before they are allowed to run, especially on hard surfaces. Small dogs and toy breeds might not be suited to this role at all, but all dogs love a good, long, walk.[46] An Australian study showed that dog owners are seven times more likely to achieve the recommended level of exercise a week than non-owners, fifty-five more minutes a week on exercise than people without a canine companion.[47]

A snake is not an animal associated with health benefits, certainly not *reducing* anxiety, but the concept makes sense when you get over the initial shock. Nonetheless, when given the choice of a "friendly dog, a rabbit, or a snake," 25 to 47 percent of children with disabilities chose to hold, touch, or pet a snake—a "placid and nonpoisonous species of snake." A part of the study examined seniors' reactions to snakes and by the third encounter, almost 10 percent of the elderly agreed to interact with the snake. The study concluded that the "affinity" for snakes in the populations studied was strong and outweighed "cultural stereotypes, widespread fears, and negative attitudes," about snakes.[48]

Some people are making a bit too much effort to ensure that their untrained companion animals are with them to offer succor in self-identified times of need, and critics say they are taking advantage of laws established to protect the disabled. No one will admit to taking advantage, but the guidelines released by the Department of Transportation in 2003 threaten to make a mockery of the 1990 Americans with Disabilities Act (ADA). Without a doubt, the guidelines certainly leave a very tempting loophole. You see, ADA mandates that service animals must be allowed full access to all public businesses without question or confrontation, which means that a business owner cannot ask either about the nature of the disability or the training of the animal. However, ADA clearly defines a service animal as follows:

> Any guide dog, signal dog, or other animal individually trained to provide assistance to an individual with a disability. If they meet this definition, animals are considered service animals under the ADA regardless of whether they have been licensed or certified by a state or local government.

The last sentence and the privacy required in implementation of the Act are where the unscrupulous and the opportunistic are taking advantage. Because no licensing is required and no one can challenge a declaration that an animal is a service animal, the ADA operates on the honor system. However, the letter and spirit of the ADA, as it stands, is that "service animals are working animals, not pets." Animals providing emotional support are not service animals as defined by the ADA because they have not been trained to perform tasks that mitigate a physical disability.

The Department of Transportation muddied the waters in 2003 when they issued a "clarification" of earlier guidelines to expand the definition of service animal to include "emotional support animals." Carriers are advised to accept as evidence various identifications including, "presence of a harness" or "credible verbal assurances." Professionals in AAA and AAT found the directives outrageous, but stories of people successfully carrying their *pets* onboard (some had letters cajoled from doctors) spread on the Internet like a flash fire. The situation is complicated by the financial incentive that the ADA requires airlines to transport service animals for free. Unfortunately, the jackets, vests, and patches to identify any animal as a therapy, support, or service animal can be purchased on the Internet.

The ADA does not pertain to housing (which is under the auspices of the Fair Housing Act, and does not define service animals), but it protects the rights of people with disabilities to avail themselves of service animals without housing prejudice. The Fair Housing Act would require accommodations for service animals to afford a person with disabilities fair use and enjoyment of the home.

Manipulation of the ADA for personal gain by individuals without conditions for which the act was established is morally and ethically wrong and represents a disservice to people with disabilities. They are selfish acts that jeopardize the rights of those for whom the law is intended.

SPECIAL POPULATIONS

In addition to the near spectacular health benefits across the board that are supported by science and testimonials, animals seem to have significant beneficial effects in certain unique populations.

The Elderly

People in this segment of our population are at grave risk for loneliness and its secondary illnesses, such as depression and high blood pressure. Lonely people tend to withdraw and are reluctant to seek medical care or support in stressful situations.[49]

A study conducted at Saint Louis University revealed that nursing home residents felt much less lonely after spending one-on-one time with a dog than they did after spending time with a dog accompanied by other people. The results contradict the notion that we benefit from companion animals because they enhance our social interactions with other people and demonstrates that companion animals reduce loneliness simply by being with us. This study also showed that the loneliest individuals benefited the most from the visits with the dogs.[50]

In the elderly, companion animals can also rekindle an interest in life, giving them someone else to care for, and remind them to care for themselves. Pets can improve the quality of life for older people and have a positive impact on life.[51]

I would be remiss not to mention that some studies with the elderly report marginal or nonexistent benefits.[52]

In spite of occasional negative results (not what the researcher expected) of some studies, I can safely say that the majority of studies about the health benefits of companion animals for the elderly, confirm that having a companion animal confers health benefits. For instance, studies show that people with companion animals adapt more quickly to the stress of bereavement and other adverse life events than people without them.[53] These people also schedule fewer doctor visits.[54]

Often researchers are not able to explain why a treatment work. Even package inserts for approved medications will often include the following statement: "Mechanism of action is unknown." However, Japanese investigators have demonstrated an avenue by which elderly people benefit from walking a dog. They evaluated a small group of healthy volunteers, who walked either with or without a dog, and found that "walking a dog provides potentially greater health benefits than walking without a dog." Walking with the dog led to changes in the activity of the autonomic nervous system that, in turn, benefited parasympathetic activity. The mechanism of action begins with the autonomic nervous system,, which controls functions of the body related to the cardiovascular system, such as heart rate, blood pressure, and breathing rate. The autonomic nervous system is influenced by a balance between two other systems: the parasympathetic and the sympathetic systems. An increase in activity of the sympathetic nervous system leads to increases in heart rate, blood pressure, and rate of breathing, which may increase risk for cardiovascular disease. Conversely, an increase in parasympathetic activity (which happened when people walked with dogs) leads to a decrease in those values—decreases that are associated with better health.[55]

Nursing homes across the United States include animals, either in official (AAT) or unofficial (AAA) capacities to enrich the lives of their clients. "I have people who are so arthritic that they can barely open their hands, but they get their hands open to pet the dog," said Derek Tuntland, director of nursing at Good Samaritan Center. The dog of whom he speaks is Gunner, a 108-pound black Labrador, who roams the halls of Good Samaritan, which is home to fifty-five other residents, outside of Sioux Falls, SD.[56]

Paul Klaassen, Founder and CEO of Sunrise Senior Living, Inc., the largest global provider of senior living services, feels so strongly about the health benefits of companion animals that he requires them in each of Sunrise's 440 facilities. Each location allows residents to bring their companion animal, but also provides animal-free areas to accommodate allergies, and people not interested in living around animals. He also provides a resident cat and dog.[57]

Living arrangements that allow companion animals are extremely beneficial because older people are fiercely devoted to their animals and will put themselves

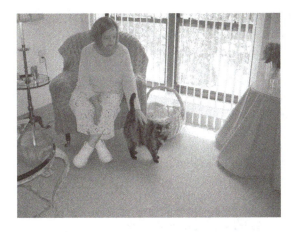

Vera Persons and Isabella share one of their precious moments. Photo courtesy of the author.

at risk to keep them, overcoming enormous challenges and going against family wishes if they have to. In return they get unconditional love, crucial social interaction, and sometimes a reason to keep going. Vera Persons is a tough Texan, delicately in her 80s, and a beautiful steel magnolia if there ever was one. A lady of culture, sophisticated manners, and disarming charm, but you had better not mess with her cat, Isabella, whom Persons adopted, after the cat's family abandoned her and moved to Europe. Persons nearly died a few years ago and suffers from considerable breathing problems, which Isabella likely aggravates. Nonetheless, Person's family knows to remain mum about that because the ten-pound calico is staying put. No matter that the terms of the relationship are set by Isabella, who likes to scratch the furniture and wake Persons up in the middle of the night for food. Isabella also wants Persons to stay in the kitchen with her while she eats. Later as Persons gets back to bed and drifts off to sleep, Isabella creates a fuss when the newspaper is delivered, until Persons gets up and brings it in. Isabella is worth her weight in gold to Persons who says that her feelings for Isabella remind her of feelings she had for her children when they were little and defenseless. Despite her nocturnal demands, Isabella rousts Persons if she lingers in bed in the morning. They spend the day together, time which Person feels no one else really needs to understand. They read the paper every day, enjoy television, and beautiful views from the window. "She calms me down," Persons said. "We have our own little thoughts."[58]

Children and Animals

Nothing less than alchemy is involved when animals and children get together, and the resulting magic has healing properties that work well. For example, a dog in a classroom of children with emotional disorders prevented emotional crises and improved how the students felt about being in school, and helped the children learn responsibility, respect, and empathy.[59] In another study, nearly

90 percent of the *entire* families with a child under the age of eighteen, who had a service dog gained "overwhelming" social and cognitive benefits, while the child received additional physical and medical benefits. The study also revealed that family dynamics must be considered when a service animal is placed with a child, including the possible financial and logistical hardships of animal care.[60]

A five-day therapeutic riding camp reduced anger significantly in a group of "able-bodied" youngsters with no history of taking psychotropic medication or having known psychological disabilities. Investigators of the study surmise that the positive impact may have been related to one or more of the following: interacting with the horse or the other children, getting to ride the horse, or being in the camp itself.[61]

Numerous studies have demonstrated that school counselors can successfully involve animals such as gerbils, hamsters, and guinea pigs in sessions to help children cope with grief, express their feelings, or build rapport.[62]

School administrators have been so impressed with the benefits of having a dog around that many are adopting trained therapy dogs for their schools. Take Allie, who found a new home in Bryan Middle School in Bryan, NJ, when her original charge died from a stroke. Allie really lives with the school counselor, Jackie Boyd, but spends her days walking the halls, stopping to listen to stressed students or to deliver attendance slips to the office. Allie is a helper, a healer, a counselor, an inspiration, and a trusted friend. She is also a conference presenter who traveled cross-country, sitting in the plane's cabin with her human colleagues, to the annual convention of the California Association of School Counselors. Because of the success of "The Allie Program," other schools in the city are applying for therapy dogs. Counselor Nancy Baxter sums up the effect of having a dog in school, "The climate just becomes more positive when a dog is there."[63]

The Incarcerated

Pairing forsaken animals with imprisoned people seems to be just what each needs. Despite opposition, prisons in at least fifteen states have operated animal therapy programs with impressive results. Early evidence indicates that the inmates benefit by learning new skills that promote better self-esteem and provide job skills. The animals benefit because they are frequently saved from euthanasia and trained to work as service animals.

The first successful prison animal therapy program in the country began after a psychiatrist noticed how the behavior of men in an Ohio prison changed after they found an injured sparrow on the prison grounds. The inmates protected and cared for the bird, working, for the first time as a group and relating better to the staff. The prison hospital conducted a one-year randomized study and found that inmates in a ward with pets required less medication, had less violence, and had no suicide attempts. The other ward with no pets had eight suicide attempts during the year.

The biggest complaint about the programs is that prisons should focus on punishment not rehabilitation, but the programs can reduce prison costs, which may offset criticism. Costs are reduced because inmates in the programs are least likely to become repeat offenders, it seems. Recidivism is one of the biggest problems facing the prison systems, with two-thirds of state and federal prisons affected. However, in one program alone, not one of the released inmates who was part of an animal program returned to prison.[64]

Many of the animals used in prisons are saved from death row themselves, in shelters across the country. The Lansing Correctional Facility turns unwanted dogs into "cherished pets." Toby Young, who started the Safe Harbor Prison Dog Program, adopts dogs from high-kill shelters across the Midwest and pairs them with inmates trained to be handlers. "Every dog we brought in here was going to be put to sleep," he said. In one year, Safe Harbor was able to send 600 dogs to new homes through an association with PetSmart in Shawnee, KS.[65]

KNOWS NO BOUNDS

The therapeutic value of the powerful bond that we have with our companion animals is as boundless as every other aspect of the relationship. The onus is on us not to abuse the privilege of being recipients of their special healing powers, and to ensure that their own health and safety are preserved.

7

Protecting Our Companion Animals

Life is as dear to a mute creature as it is to man. Just as one wants happiness
and fears pain, just as one wants to live and not die, so do other creatures.
—His Holiness The Dalai Lama

An inherent part of a healthy bond between humans and companion animals is
our desire to keep them well and safe. Having brought them into our world, it is
our responsibility to help them navigate it without incident.

Not all companion animals are treated equally, but those in the types of
relationships described in this chapter are the beneficiaries of the best care and
protection that guardians can access and afford. These guardians use their power
to wield the best medicine, public policy, and circumstances to protect their
companion animals from all kinds of harm, from early death to a loss of assets.

Humans are the safest when we have good health, proper medical treatment
when needed, and the law on our side. This holds true for animals, and companion
animals are afforded these protections more than any nonhuman animal on earth.
This section presumes basic responsible care and focuses on what might seem to
an outsider as extraordinary measures to assure that companion animals are safe
and protected.

MOVING MOUNTAINS WITH MEDICAL TREATMENTS

Veterinary medicine in the twenty-first century is vastly different from anything the field has experienced and goes a long way toward establishing and
maintaining a high quality of life for our companion animals. Advances happen
so rapidly that veterinarians must work hard to stay abreast of developments
and are almost forced to specialize. The field has more doctors, more specialists,
more patients, and greater expectations than ever. Veterinary medicine is highly
focused on treating companion animals, with more than one half of the 85,000
doctors practicing in 2006 devoting themselves either exclusively or predomi-
nately to companion animals.[1]

Veterinarians have at their disposal sophisticated diagnostic tools and treatments such as MRIs (magnetic resonance imaging), radiology, organ transplants,

pacemakers, and chemotherapy. Guardians demand these state-of-the-art treatments and more. For example, one survey showed that more than half of companion animal guardians also use treatments categorized as complementary and alternative therapies to treat their cats and dogs, such as herbs, chiropractic, acupuncture, massage therapy, and nutritional therapy.[2]

The life of one little Jack Russell Terrier, aptly named Miracle, is a testament to many of the recent advances in veterinary science. First of all, she would not exist without a veterinarian who specialized in reproductive medicine because Miracle was born more than a year after her father died, using sperm that had been stored for nearly a decade. It will remain a mystery to me how a dog who was wanted enough to garner a $2,000 artificial insemination fee was left unguarded long enough to be hit by a car, but that is what happened to Miracle. Consequently, she moved further along the continuum of modern veterinary medicine when the accident fractured her neck and caused internal bleeding and shock. Barely breathing when taken to the veterinary hospital, Miracle had surgery (and all of the accompanying diagnostic marvels) to repair a fracture of her spinal cord at a cost of $5,000.[3]

The Neuse River Golden Rescue in Raleigh, NC, had to activate a cadre of medical treatments to save Phoenix, a dog who was found injured on an interstate highway, where he had apparently laid for days. However, this is not a story about rescue, but about the medical treatments bestowed on Phoenix that saved his life. Phoenix was taken to Veterinary Specialty Hospital in Cary, NC, where he was "diagnosed with a broken front and back leg, dislocated hip, mange, skin mites, ligament tears, and severe muscle atrophy." After his hospital stay, he was transferred to a rehabilitation facility, called VetHab, where he stayed for four weeks. Initially, Phoenix could not stand unassisted and needed slings to support his front and the back body. His treatments included massage therapy and walks on an underwater treadmill, before he graduated to walking unassisted on a regular treadmill. He feasted on a high-calorie diet to gain eight much-needed pounds. Phoenix's amazing recovery cost nearly $12,000.[4]

George Bailey became the first animal to receive a surgically fitted prosthesis when North Carolinians Kathy Vincent, a nurse, and Al Simmons, a pharmacist, spent $1,500 for him to get one in March 2005. The cat was born without rear paws and his guardians had made accommodations such as putting a "handicap ramp on the litterbox." Even though the first prosthesis worked for only a month (another may follow), Vincent says it was money well spent and completely justified. She said that the expense was no more than she would have spent to have a child's tonsils removed, and the return on the investment was well worth it. She could easily justify the cost because she is not facing long-term parenting expenses, "We don't have to buy him $200 sneakers and video games and stuff. We don't have to send him to college."[5]

When Carol Kalinoski's fifteen-year-old cat, Henry, began dragging his legs and steroids did not help, her veterinarian suggested an MRI of Henry's lower spine at a cost of $1,200. The result was inconclusive and he suggested a second

MRI of Henry's entire spine, doubling the cost. Having spent $2,400, Kalinoski was told that Henry had a tumor and that surgery, with only a 50 percent success rate, would cost $3,200. "He was so close to being put down," Kalinoski admits. Contrary to her initial reaction, she spent the $5,600, and Henry is jumping off the furniture like a younger cat. Kalinoski said she would do it again.[6]

Enhanced survival following trauma or surgery means enhanced needs for rehabilitation, as was the case with Phoenix, and today's veterinarians also oversee or conduct extensive rehabilitation regimens using state-of-the-art equipment similar to that available for people. Standard treatments include stretching, massage therapy, and electrostimulation, followed by treadmill workouts or weights to increase strength. Some centers have "wobble boards" to facilitate balance (if you have ever had knee surgery, you know all too well what that is) and laser surgery to facilitate wound healing. Pablo, a poodle who was burned with chemicals before being abandoned, is an example of a dog protected from euthanasia because of treatments unavailable a generation ago, such as ultrasound and physical therapy. Little Pablo became aggressive because he was in so much pain, from scar tissue and inflammation from his burns, but he healed at a rehabilitation clinic and became eligible for adoption, not euthanasia. The kind of physical therapy and rehabilitation he had cost about $30 per quarter hour, after an initial examination and evaluation, which runs about $100.[7]

Most dog guardians do not have the financial resources of Lance Armstrong, but they share his desire to do whatever it takes to keep their dogs alive. His family dog, Rex (a gift from Sheryl Crow) was born with a terminal leaky heart valve that made the dog listless. Armstrong had Rex flown to Colorado State University (CSU) for open-heart surgery, a four-and-a-half hour procedure that cost more than $10,000. Pricey, but more than the likes of Lance Armstrong are taking advantage of this lifesaving procedure because CSU performs about twenty-five of the operations a year.[8]

Dr. Michael Buenau, an optician from Delmar, NY, had to protect his Bichon Frise, Lucky, from blindness after he was diagnosed with bilateral congenital cataracts at the age of two. After veterinarians at Cornell University tried unsuccessfully to remove them, Buenau had to take action to preserve Lucky's vision. "He's like a family member, and if you had a family member who could see better with glasses, you would not think twice about it," said Buenau. He added that it seemed unfair for Lucky's vision to be taken while he was so young. He did not want the little dog walking around afraid, unable to identify things in his environment. Consequently, Buenau prescribed Lucky's glasses using a procedure similar to that used for children, where a light is shone into the eye with a retina scope, to observe how Lucky's eyes responded to various lenses. Lucky adjusted to the glasses well and is enjoying himself again. His frames and prescriptions cost $75. (Such a reasonable amount probably reflects the family discount.)[9]

Cancer remains one of the scariest words to leave a doctor's lips, and when uttered by a veterinarian, the situation used to be hopeless. Today there are a variety of options, from pain management to the most aggressive surgical, chemical,

Optician Michael Buenau plays with Lucky, who is wearing the special glasses that Buenau made for him after the dog was diagnosed with bilateral cataracts. Photo courtesy of Michael P. Buenau.

and radiation therapies, including investigational drugs and hospice. Treatments can be expensive but guardians appreciate knowing that cancer is not the death sentence for their companion animals that it once was. Veterinary oncology is a relatively new field, established in 1989, with only 160 oncologists across the country to treat the millions of dogs and cats with cancer. By some estimates, 50 percent of all dogs beyond the age of ten will die from some form of cancer. When Laurie Kaplan's Siberian husky, Bullet, was diagnosed with cancer, she became so frustrated with the dearth of general information on veterinary oncology that she resigned her position as editor-in-chief of *Catnip* magazine and self-published a guide, *Help Your Dog Fight Cancer*. The 118-page manual is a culmination of the knowledge she acquired during years of helping Bullet battle cancer and gives guardians help in protecting their companion animals as they wage war against the disease.[10]

In 2005, Tequila, an adopted fourteen-year-old basset hound, was the beneficiary of current veterinary oncology treatments, becoming just one of 455 animals treated in the oncology program at Michigan State University that year. At the end of the year, he joined other recipients of medical miracles at the "Celebration of Life" party, held for companion animal survivors of serious illnesses or accidents who were treated at the university.[11]

In 2005, a two-year $30 million project to map the dogs' genetic code, known as the Dog Genome, was completed. This kind of time and money was obviously not invested to enhance our understanding of the dog, but to further knowledge about humans and human health.[12] Nonetheless, understanding the DNA sequencing that makes a dog a dog will certainly result in advanced care for this companion animal, and the cat genome with similar advantages cannot be far away. For example, using information from the dog genome, veterinarians will be able to develop individualized preventative care and treatment plans for dogs. They will also be able to understand why certain breeds are susceptible to certain diseases and gain insight into temperament and related behavior issues.

One of the biggest behavioral issues behind numerous dogs being relinquished to shelters, and perhaps euthanized, is getting some treatment now: separation anxiety. Dogs who suffer can become so stressed when left alone that they go berserk and destroy things in the house, hurt themselves with nervous biting, or cause problems with constant barking. A chewable, flavored, canine version of fluoxetine (marketed for humans as Prozac) seems to be protecting dogs from that fate. I am not suggesting that we drug dogs to solve a problem that many canine experts say we create by making dogs pathologically dependent on us. The point here is that because of the increased value we place on the relationships we have with our companion animals, pharmaceutical companies, which are reluctant to conduct clinical trials for veterinary products because of the costs involved, now see marketing potential in drugs for companion animals. Consequently, unique medications are becoming available by one of three ways. Companies are either conducting animal-specific tests, reformulating products successfully used in humans for animals, or reviving abandoned products that may have applications in animals. In spite of the pharmaceutical companies' self-serving motives, the outcome can be better medications for our companion animals.[13]

Cutting-edge medical treatments are not cheap as you have seen, and guardians are turning to health insurance—another new feature of the *pet* industry—to mitigate costs. As is the case with human health insurance, everything is not covered and sometimes nothing is covered, but insurance can come in handy. The average lifetime veterinary costs for a medium-size dog are about $10,400. Small dogs cost slightly less, large dogs slightly more, and cat care costs are around $10,600.[14] In a medical landscape that can include $1,200 MRIs, $12,000 dialysis, and $40,000 cancer treatments, insurance for companion animals has appeal and is growing, but is more popular in Europe than in the United States. In the United Kingdom, for example, sixty insurers offer hundreds of plans that cover 14 percent of dogs and 5 percent of cats. Conversely, in the United States, fewer than ten insurers cover only 1 percent of companion animals.[15] Premiums vary with coverage and change as animals age or have pre-existing conditions.

PREVENTION IS THE BEST PROTECTION

I believe that the best way to avoid harm is to prevent it. I am one of those guardians who does everything possible to circumvent problems. For example, my animals never travel as cargo on airplanes. Moreover, to the chagrin of a neighbor, one of my biggest peeves is people who let their cats go outside unsupervised. A bit overprotective you might say, but experts agree that roaming outside increases an animal's chances of getting hurt, sick, or killed. According to the Humane Society of the United States, a free-roaming cat lives less than three years, compared to fifteen to eighteen years for the average indoor-only cat.[16]

Rep. Tom Stevenson, a member of Pennsylvania's general assembly, took a particularly bold step to protect companion animals when he introduced a bill that required them to be "buckled up or battened down in seat belts or in crates." The bill tried to make a connection to human safety by saying that animals can distract drivers and cause accidents. He made no friends among people who thought he should either focus on human safety or not impinge on dogs' joy of open car windows, but he made his point, which was to get people to think about safety issues when transporting their companion animals.[17] The truth is we take a risk with our animals whenever we transport them unrestrained in a car. For example, unsecured cats and dogs become projectiles in the car during an accident and can be seriously harmed by a deployed air bag. Dogs who hang out of car windows can fall out if the car makes an odd turn or a quick stop or get debris in their eyes. All great consequences for brief fun.

Companion animals are unquestionably safer inside, but staying home can also turn to tragedy. More than 40,000 companion animals died in house fires in 2005, with most deaths due to smoke inhalation. Unfortunately, firefighters are not outfitted with proper gear for our companion animals. As a result, they try to use adult or pediatric masks, which are too big and do not fit around a muzzle. In 1999, a North Carolina newspaper photographer captured the remarkable image of a pregnant red Doberman, Cinnamon, expressing her sentiments (and mine) to firefighter Jeff Clark for what firefighters do: put their lives on the line to save us and all of our loved ones. Clark was amazed at the letters he received in response to the photograph. "To me it wasn't any big deal, nothing out of the ordinary. A lot of people were surprised that we go in looking for anything alive," said Clark. "In the same fire, we brought out a snake and a parrot, but neither lived." Rumors spread on the internet that Clark had saved Cinnamon, earning himself a "kiss," but she was already outside and approached Clark with such affection for reasons all of her own. I am sad to report that Cinnamon died in January 2005 of uterine

Cinnamon, a red Doberman, surprises Charlotte fire fighter Jeff Clark with a "kiss" of appreciation. *The Charotte Observer*, photo by Patrick Schneider. Reprinted with permission.

cancer, but she had her puppies and gained fame and spread good will around the globe. Cinnamon's guardian, Jane Cook, said, "She was the smartest dog I ever had in my life."[18] And a darned good judge of character, I might add.

Lately, many firefighters across the country are being equipped with specially designed oxygen masks for cats and dogs. They are available in three sizes: one to fit a small-to-medium dog, another for a large dog, and a third for a cat. The smaller masks can also fit birds, reptiles, and other small animals. Masks cost approximately $50 each, which is often donated by the public or contributed by the firefighters themselves.[19]

Psychologists tell you that one of the best ways to cope with tragedy is to find meaning in it or transform tragedy into triumph. That is exactly what Dr. Janet Olson, a veterinarian, and her husband, Brian, a Minnesota firefighter, did with the tragedy of being helpless to save the beloved dog of fellow firefighter (retired), Mark Clark. His housefire was quickly dispatched and Clark begged the firefighters to find and save his beloved thirteen-year-old German shorthaired pointer, Bart. At the time, the firefighters had neither the equipment nor the training to save Bart, who was found unresponsive, suffering from extensive smoke inhalation. Bart died that day, but the Basic Animal Rescue Training Program (BART) was born soon after, and now countless animal lives can be saved. In response to the tragedy, Dr. Olson designed the first, and still only, course that teaches firefighters how to safely restrain and handle animals, assess their injuries, and perform basic first aid and CPR. Since December 2004, BART has trained more than 1,500 first responders, primarily firefighters, and in early 2005 the program expanded beyond residential companion animals to include equine and livestock training. Upon completion of the course, the trainees receive a specially designed kit that includes gloves strong enough to withstand cat scratches, a stethoscope, animal tags, treats, and oxygen masks for dogs. BART operates entirely with volunteers and charitable donations, receiving the largest amount yet from the American Veterinary Medical Foundation in the form of a $50,000 challenge grant to "jump-start [BART] chapters in five additional states."[20] Dr. Olson told me that BART is also in the process of becoming the model course through the Federal Emergency Management Agency (FEMA) to prepare first responders to

BART, whose tragic death led to the creation of the Basic Animal Rescue Training Program, which trains fire fighters to rescue companion animals. Photo courtesy of the Basic Animal Rescue Training Program, used with permission.

deal with the pets that they encounter in emergency situations on a local, state, and national level.

NO MOUNTAIN TOO HIGH

Science and technology give us amazing ways to protect our animals and extend our time together, but sometimes guardians have to take matters into their own hands and put old-fashioned ingenuity to work to protect the animals who mean so much to them.

Notably, Ciccy Lacks fought a coyote to protect her four-year-old poodle, Annie. The sixty-year-old retired Chicago high school English teacher reported engaging in a tug-of-war over Annie, holding on to the dog's front body as the coyote tried to prevail by clamping its jaws around the dog's hind legs. The fight seemed to last forever, but Lacks said that probably after a few seconds the coyote gave up because she yelled, kicked, and threw a package at it. The twenty-pound poodle survived with only a gash and several teeth marks. Coyotes are a growing presence in Chicago and, as they adapt to encroaching suburbia, they attack companion animals with disturbing frequency, but this was the first report of a coyote attacking a dog in the vicinity of a human.[21]

Jon Silver had a particularly daunting challenge to protect his fiancée's German shepherd puppy from the predators that roam—and own—the foothills of Boulder, CO, or his fiancée, Diana, would not become Mrs. Silver. However, Silver, a resourceful man of many talents, was not intimidated. "I'm a problem solver, and

Jon Silver standing near the tunnel he constructed for MeToo. Photo courtesy of Jon and Diana Silver.

there was a problem," he said. "Diana would not move in with me unless her dog, MeToo. was safe in the mountains, period!" Silver rented a backhoe and drove it to his yard. There he dug a deep trench, forty-feet in length, and installed four, ten-foot sections (bolted together with special collars) of thirty-two-inch diameter culvert (which the highway department uses under roads to carry water) to create a safe passage for the dog. They married, and refer to the tunnel as the "Love Tunnel" because it was a labor of love, initiated by love. MeToo enters the tunnel in the garage, using a doggie-door in the kitchen. At the end of the tunnel is a forty-foot dog kennel that is strong enough to support the weight of a bear. (I can only guess how they know that.) Jon modified a motion sensor to detect MeToo's movement as he enters the tunnel and turn on rope lighting that stays on for ten minutes. Jon later rigged a trap door in the garage for the tunnel opening that closes when the garage door opens, so they can use the garage in the winter. Also, if MeToo happens to be in the tunnel, the door keeps him safely there until the car is stationary. The Love Tunnel allows the family to live together safely in their idyllic mountain environment.[22]

Faith, a Chow-mix, was one of a litter of deformed puppies born near Christmas 2002 in Oklahoma City. The runt of this unfortunate litter, Faith was unable to compete for food, even with the other weak littermates. Death was closing in on Faith when the son of a nearby family became aware of the situation and removed her from the litter of dead or dying puppies, who were being actively neglected or smothered by the mother dog.

The three-week-old puppy became a member of the Stringfellow family, headed by mom Jude and three children, all recovering from a divorce. When Faith joined the family, she had three legs, but her front left leg was badly deformed, eventually

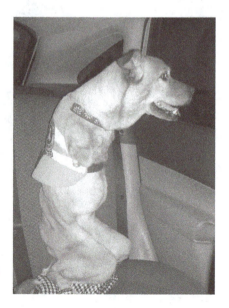

Faith Stringfellow, born in a litter of deformed puppies, was rescued and learned to walk upright like a human. Photo by Jude Stringfellow, © Faith Stringfellow, used with permission.

atrophied, and had to be removed when she was seven-months-old. Stringfellow said that the family intended to teach Faith to hop so she would not damage her body trying to push herself along the ground. To that end, they used treats to encourage her to stand on two legs, but walking was Faith's idea. Having learned to stand, Faith put one paw in front of the other at about three-months-old. She now walks upright like a human, earning her name, Faith, from the scripture in the Bible that suggests Christians "walk by faith, not by sight." Stringfellow said, "Faith has been a great dog, and we forget she's handicapped. You'll turn around and she's chasing the geese at the park, running, jumping, skipping, and acting like any other dog...well, any other dog with a nose reach of 40-feet from the ground!"[23] Stringfellow's family preserved Faith's life, and their success encourages others to let dogs with similar deformities live, as well. As recently as June 2007, the North Shore Animal League reported three Chihuahua puppies born without front legs for whom prosthetics were being investigated.[24]

My friend Jaye Ruth Efland is the consummate, tenderhearted animal lover. So, she was the perfect person to care for her sister's dog, Rocco, who had lost his leg when he was three-years-old. The German shepherd jumped a fence, probably got his leg caught in a trap, and was missing for three days before being found in a pool of blood. After circuitous events, Rocco moved in permanently with "Aunt Jaye," and she became mom to a big, aging, special needs dog. She first fenced in her backyard and then bought a ramp for her deck. Her challenge increased just a few weeks later, when Rocco was diagnosed with a slipped disc. The veterinarian decided to treat Rocco with steroids rather than surgery because a postsurgical rehabilitation would be too difficult with only three legs. Rocco returned home from the hospital after a week, and Jaye found a special harness to support his back without putting too much pressure on his bladder. She put extra water bowls around the house for his comfort and convenience. In spite of all the attention, Rocco became depressed after the veterinarian insisted she restrict Rocco's movement further by blocking him in the kitchen. Consequently, she blocked off her deck instead so he could go outside and put a gazebo over the

Rocco, who lost a leg in an accident, has learned to walk in spite of his disability. Look closely and see that he is actually balancing on one leg. Photo courtesy of Jaye R. Efland.

deck to protect him from the sun. She also put two beds on the deck for Rocco to have a choice and added a runner between them so he would not drag himself on the wooden planks of the deck. Jaye echoes what many guardians of special needs animals say, "Rocco has this uncanny ability to take things as they come. His will to live and to please is enormous, and he has taught me many lessons during the short time he has lived with me." Rocco now gets around on his own and receives daily medication for pain and arthritis. Jaye's dedication to Rocco has extended his life; the veterinarians are amazed at his progress.

Russell Schmidt and Mary C. Roberts are doing more to protect the health of their cat than they are willing to do for themselves. You see, the couple, both of whom smoke, never smoke inside their home because of the dangers of secondhand smoke on their young cat, Q.T. They know that secondhand smoke is dangerous for humans and presume the same is true for cats. Their intuition is correct because "studies have linked secondhand smoke with higher rates of cancer and respiratory illness in cats and dogs," according to Dr. Helen Ross, codirector of the Providence Cancer Center in Portland, OR. Obviously, it would be best for the entire family if they both stopped smoking, but Roberts said, "I know it sounds crazy, but I have always considered her like a daughter. I wouldn't smoke in front of a child. Heck, if I had my own, I'd probably quit. We love this cat and would never want to harm her, so we smoke outside."[25]

A scraggly, flea-bitten, malnourished, but precocious Iraqi puppy captured the hearts of U.S. Marines from Kaneohe, Hawaii, who kept the five-week-old dog safe by feeding him military rations and hiding him in their duffle bags, after discovering him during the battle for Fallujah, part of the Iraq War. They named him Lava to honor their battalion name, Lava Dogs—a tribute to the ground on which these rugged Marines train—and they turned him over to Lt. Col. Jay Kopelman, a Marine Corps reservist on duty in Iraq. Kopelman promised the battalion he would take care of Lava, and he kept his word in spite of the challenges he faced because of military regulations banning troops from adopting pets. With the help of other Marines, journalists from National Public Radio, an anonymous Iraqi citizen, representatives from the Iams Company, and a lot of good fortune, Lava made it to the Green Zone and was reunited with Kopelman in the United States just a few days after Kopelman left Iraq. He says that Lava "has issues, as would most people who've been through what he has been through," but that Lava has a "sense of happiness" and "gives us a sense of hope."[26]

Earlier, I mentioned Jamie Dana and her military dog, Rex, in another context, but I want to reiterate the story here to focus on what the then Air Force Sergeant did to protect her trained military dog. She went up against military tradition, the law of the land, and the U.S. Congress, to protect her K-9 partner from further military duty after the Humvee they were riding in exploded from an enemy device during the Iraq War, nearly killing her. She depended on him for her very life, and she was determined to protect his. She successfully brought Rex home after Air Force officials and lawmakers collaborated on a measure to grant her an exception that became part of a defense bill signed by the President in 2005.[27]

Protection comes in many forms and addresses various dangers, but we must do whatever it takes to keep our companion animals safe. We must do no harm; we must permit no harm.

ACTIVISM

Frequently to protect companion animals, we have to not only take things into our own hands, but also join hands with others to get things done. Animal protection as a social movement is a modern construct that began in England during the eighteenth century.

Most modern protection activities that focus on companion animals try to avoid a controversy that stems from the differences between animal "rights" and animal "welfare." Traditionally, people involved in animal rights maintain that *any* use of a nonhuman animal is "wrong in principle and should be abolished in practice," and that whatever gain humans achieve from that usage is "ill gotten." The animal rights movement emerged in the 1900s with protests against the use of animals in research, and reemerged in the 1960s. Animal welfare proponents focus on the way animals are treated rather than what rights they should enjoy. Their goal is to improve the treatment and well being of animals by asking that all animals, even those used in research and food production, are treated humanely, without pain and suffering.[28]

Activists for companion animals are primarily involved in preventing suffering and cruelty, providing proper care, and finding good homes, while educating the public about the importance of spay and neuter. Some people may find those activities extreme, but hopefully they are not the kind of activities that the Federal Bureau of Investigation had in mind, when they accused animal rights activists of extreme behavior and named them a top terrorist threat.[29] You can understand why the distinction between and activist and a welfarist could be so important. For now, I believe activists who focus on companion animals are best served safely tucked in the realm of welfarists. In terms of identification, I frequently hear, and have accepted for personal use, the simple term "animal movement," which eliminates any divisions and focuses on what needs to be done to improve the quality of life for all animals.

One of the most widespread grassroots activities focused on companion animals involves animal rescue, for which countless numbers of people open their homes and hearts to animals who might otherwise end up in shelters, facing almost certain death. Some rescue organizations specialize in finding homes for specific breeds, but the majority are equally active and successful at finding homes for the endless numbers of homeless mixed-breed animals. Often a local organization will develop around a few individuals who are inspired to perform rescue work in honor of a beloved companion animal or in response to an experience that spurred them to action. Most rescue organizations focus on protecting animals in their immediate communities and perform a critical service, usually with meager funds and tireless, dedicated volunteers. I tried my hand at rescue, but this work is for the courageous of spirit, not for the tenderhearted. During my brief experience,

I made a lifetime friend, Leslie Grenick, whose rescue odyssey began in the early 1990s, and typifies that of so many selfless, tireless people, who take on the overwhelming and unending task of finding loving, permanent homes for abandoned animals. Leslie, a former human resources analyst for Durham County, NC, began volunteering with a local rescue organization called Independent Animal Rescue (IAR). She had previously volunteered at the local animal shelter and had a short stint as the temporary Director of Animal Control, while the county recruited a new director. She had seen the animals at the, then new, county shelter struggle a bit under the management of a private animal protection group, but the animals received reasonable care. The environment in which the animals lived was stressful, and they usually survived for only days before they were killed to make room for more. The specter of euthanasia loomed constantly. "Only the most 'perfect' would be adopted," she said. As a shelter volunteer, she had walked the dogs on weekends and said of her experience, "I remember never asking about the dogs I had taken care of the week before because I didn't want to hear they didn't make it. I wanted to hope they had been adopted." At the time, the shelter was killing, "as a matter of policy," Chows, pitbulls, and some Rottweilers (pure and mixes). Very few exceptions were made, and even rescue organizations had difficulty getting those particular dogs from the shelter. Aware of the unnecessary slaughter of so many animals with great companion potential, Leslie was anxious to work for an organization such as IAR, which, working on the foster-home model, was one of the few organizations nearby that took in sick and injured animals and others unlikely to survive the shelter. Working with IAR, she was able to work with the "questionable" animals, assuaging their fears as much as possible and finding them homes. There were never enough homes, in spite of the fact that according to Leslie, "Most animals had been neglected and needed only some basic care and love to blossom." She admits that some were never adopted out and remained in the homes of volunteers. Nevertheless, hundreds were placed, including some tough placements to specially screened families, who could care for special needs animals she said. She kept a rescue kit in her car and would not hesitate to pick up an injured or roaming dog from the highway. IAR may have had more lenient policies for accepting animals, but they had necessarily strict guidelines for adoption. They required adopters to sign contracts obligating a lifetime commitment, spay and neuter, no chaining, and return of any animals if care became impossible. As is the case with most rescue volunteers, Leslie's work with IAR involved much more than rescue, care, and placement. She was involved in the trap/neuter/release (TNR) of feral cat colonies, including a huge colony of hundreds of cats at a rural hospital; providing emergency financial assistance to guardians so they could keep their animals; collaborating with other organizations to place other animals such as horses and potbellied pigs; coordinating donated supplies; running a hotline for citizens; and distributing food. She recounted for me a rainy night that turned wonderful when IAR volunteers unloaded a semi-trailer full of food from IAMS (before Proctor and Gamble bought them) into waiting vans from about ten local groups. Leslie remembered how rewarding it was to watch the vans leave, full of food for needy animals. The Internet had not yet become a primary means of communication, so Leslie's other tasks involved telephone counseling and responding to queries. Tired at the end of her regular workday, she triaged calls for two or three hours from people wanting to find a place "other than the shelter" to relinquish their animals. Talking to desperate, emotional people about the uncertain fates of their animals was draining. The enormous challenges notwithstanding, Leslie had been considering forming a new organization of her own, and decided to take the helm at IAR when the founder relocated. She led IAR for three years, resigning with "heavy burnout," which was diagnosed by her doctor. As is true with most rescue volunteers, Leslie will never really stop. Case in point: When authorities recently raided a North Carolina puppy mill, she organized and managed a "laundry train" for six months to provide truckloads of clean sheets, towels, and bedding to frontline volunteers who were two hours away. They had their hands full dealing with 300 untrained puppies and dogs they could not take outside because of the legal ramifications of losing one. In spite of the toll of her rescue work, Leslie tears up talking about the rewards. "Huge. I have so many tremendous memories of rescuing animals, caring for them, watching them develop, and finding responsible, loving homes for them," she said. "And the people you work with are so outstanding and special. They take unknown animals into their homes, accept and love them unconditionally, and give them attention and structure. Then they have the strength to give this animal, who has taken their love, to someone else." Rescue workers are indeed a breed apart. Leslie should know; she is one of them—an outstanding, special person.

Any basic Internet search, community bulletin board perusal, or classified advertising review will reveal groups and individuals in your neighborhood who are working diligently, against great odds, to protect the at-risk animals near you. Join them; they can use your help.

Sometimes just one individual, in one small place, can take on a cause with such vigor that shock waves are felt across the country, creating change and improving the quality of life for many animals, now and in the future.

Tammy Sneath Grimes, of Tipton, PA, a small rural town in the middle of the state, is a perfect example. For years she drove by chained dogs in Tipton, sensing their pain and feeling helpless to stop it. One dog in particular, an aged "simple black dog, the kind all too easily ignored," spurred her to action. In August of 2002, she created Dogs Deserve Better (DDB), an organization devoted to helping dogs live unshackled lives. Chaining a dog, a highly social animal, is abysmally cruel. Significantly, they lead lives of futile desperation and become depressed, feeling essentially rejected by their pack. They are usually exposed to the elements and can become easy targets for abuse. Moreover, they can become tangled in their chains, or are choked by outgrown, embedded chains. Grimes drove by the black dog, named Worthless, for six years, silently promising him a better life. In October, she saved the desolate, aged dog, transformed his life, renamed him Bo, and made him the face of an international campaign to eliminate chaining.

Grimes and Bo had only six months together before he died, but she had kept her promise to him, and she extended the promise to other dogs, who are saved in his memory.

Keeping the promise has not been without strife. As this book goes to press, Grimes is facing a trial, after being arrested for helping a dying chained dog. A woman, who had tried unsuccessfully to get help from the local humane society, brought the dog to Grimes' attention. When she saw the dog, named Doogie, she thought he was dead because he was not moving and had reportedly been lying on the cold wet ground for three days. No one was home, so after documenting Doogie's condition on video, Grimes took him to the veterinarian. He also documented his findings, which included low weight, sores, missing fur, and painful back spurs that contributed to his inability to walk. Grimes refused to turn Doogie over to the police, and she was charged with "theft, receiving stolen property, criminal mischief, and criminal trespass," and released on a $50,000 unsecured bond. Doogie lived for nearly six months in a foster home before dying "peacefully on his own terms." In spite of the legal battles ahead, Grimes has no regrets and said that she could not have lived with herself had she left Doogie to die alone in chains. The video Grimes took suggests that the criminal activity was perpetrated long before she arrived on the scene. Whether justice will prevail remains to be seen, but I have no doubt that Grimes will keep her promise to protect dogs from chains.[30]

Ten years ago, Betsy and Jared Saul started Petfinder.com after making a New Year's resolution to help homeless companion animals, and boy did they ever. Five million people visit the site each month and stay twenty minutes longer than they do on Amazon.com. The site started out small, and Betsy wrote the animal profiles herself. Now, nearly 9,000 shelter and rescue groups post information for almost every kind of animal you can imagine, all with one sad commonality—they all need forever homes.[31]

One group of friends—best friends actually—coalesced to form the largest animal sanctuary in the world. The group of seventeen people had been friends for fifteen years and were active in social issues since the 1970s, when a few pooled resources to buy a farm in Arizona. Here they pursued their passion to rescue and care for homeless animals. From the beginning, they rejected the notion that overcrowded animal shelters had to euthanize animals who were deemed unadoptable. These friends adopted hundreds of "cast-offs" from shelters, rehabilitated them, and found them permanent homes. Their deepest desire was to find a large place where forsaken animals "could be safe, loved and allowed to live out their natural lives." Their dreams began to manifest in the summer of 1982, when they located an "oasis" in the desert near the Grand Canyon— 3,000 acres, about the size of Manhattan. They pooled their money again and established the Best Friends Animal Sanctuary, which became the "flagship of the rapidly growing no-kill movement throughout the 1990s." Their goal of "No More Homeless Pets," contributed to a reduction in the number of animals killed in shelters from 15 million in 1990 to a number more recently near 4 million. Best Friends continues to operate the largest sanctuary for homeless animals in the country and works with shelters, rescue groups, and individual members across the nation to provide adoption, spay/neuter, and educational programs. Of the 1,500 animals who live at the sanctuary, nearly 1,200 are cats and dogs, joined by an assortment of others, including horses, burros, wild birds, rabbits, goats, and farm animals. Best Friends also publishes the "largest general-interest animal magazine" in America.[32]

People interested in improving the quality of life for companion animals gravitate toward and depend upon organizations such as Best Friends for information on the critical issues and guidance about how to help. Other recognized, powerful organizations with programs that benefit companion animals are the Animal Society for the Prevention of Cruelty to Animals (ASPCA), the Humane Society of the United States (HSUS), and People for the Ethical Treatment of Animals (PETA). Each is different in important ways, but each is devoted to the overarching goal of saving animals. Specifically, the ASPCA was founded in 1866 and is considered the first humane organization in the western hemisphere. As their name implies, the ASPCA focuses on battling cruelty. The HSUS is well known for its work devoted to companion animals, but included in its expansive reach are international programs that encompass wildlife, farm animals, and laboratory animals.

PETA was founded in 1980 and is considered the largest animal rights organization in the world to focus on ending animal exploitation, particularly as it relates to farm animals, laboratory animals, and animals used for clothing and entertainment.

Frequently, individual activists or local organizations will galvanize around a particular issue that affects companion animals—usually after being informed and educated by one of the aforementioned organizations. Not in recent memory has an issue caused as much consternation as the illegal trading of dog and cat fur.

You may be surprised to know that dog and cat fur was sold legally in the United States, as garment trim and decoration, until Congress banned the practice in 2000. Unfortunately, a loophole in the law exists such that goods valued at less than $150 do not require labeling. The consequence is that fur continues to be imported, either inappropriately without any labeling or with labels that misrepresent the origin and species of the fur. Guardians of companion cats and dogs were outraged to discover that animals just like those they loved at home were being skinned alive elsewhere for their fur, which was sold in America. They were further incensed to learn that the United States imports half of its fur garments from China, where millions of cats and dogs are killed in heinous ways for their fur. I am confounded by the many people who profess to love their cats and dogs, but who wear fur regularly. This type of behavior seems the ultimate in cognitive dissonance. Most would not extend an interview or could explain no further than saying, "It's different." I presume that kind of sentiment is why this situation was like a lightening rod for so many dog and cat lovers: There is no difference. The fur on these garments comes from animals just like the beloved cats and dogs with whom we share our lives.

Animal advocates and activists continue to educate the public about this and other abuses of companion animals, some of which are explored in the final chapter.

THE WILL OF THE PEOPLE

More and more people involved in improving the quality of life for companion animals realize that the only way to insure protection is to get the law on their side. One of the biggest stumbling blocks to ensuring protection for our companion animals is that they are considered mere *property* in most states, but change is taking hold as court decisions across the country are beginning to permit damages for emotional distress. This is a troubling trend for some people, including noted author Jon Katz, who warns that granting human-like legal status could create unconsidered consequences, including higher malpractice insurance and higher liability awards. Curiously, Bob Vetere, president of the APPMA, was quoted as calling the "pets-as-people trend 'nonsense.'" Not that he needs me to defend him, but he may have been referring specifically to the controversy related to *guardianship* of companion animals.[33]

When public policy is not in line with how people feel, changes are required in laws that pertain to companion animals. Unfortunately, the political process moves slowly, and animal advocates seem to be the slowest of learners, according to Julie E. Lewin, president of The National Institute for Animal Advocacy. "Every other issue group functions politically and the animals desperately need us to identify, recruit, and endorse candidates. Candidates have been able to ignore us without threat. We are so apolitical," she said. She makes a convincing argument, and is adamant that "voting blocs for animals can achieve laws and ordinances that are now mere fantasies."[34]

Increasingly, thanks to organizations such as Humane USA, the first national political action committee devoted to animal causes, voters can measure candidates by their stance on important animal issues. Humane USA was formed in 1999 to raise money, donate to state and national campaigns, and to lobby for crucial animal protection legislation. It keeps a keen focus on animal protection, keeps the heat on the candidates, and keeps voters informed. Also, the HSUS has a political arm, The Humane Society Legislative Fund (HSLF), which actively works for the election or defeat of candidates based on issues key to the animal movement. HSLF issues a periodic "Legislative Lineup," to keep constituents current on bills before the U.S. Congress, so they can encourage their representatives to focus on animal issues. HSFL's results are impressive, but win or lose, their influence is growing, and lawmakers realize they can pay a price for their stance on animal issues.

Lawmakers also realize that informed voters, who are committed to animal causes, are forces with which to be reckoned. For example, the majority of Americans are against the slaughter of horses for consumption, and they refuse to remain silent as the majestic creatures are butchered for consumption in other countries. Although all horse slaughterhouses are banned in the United States, horses are brutally transported to Canada and Mexico for consumption there or in elsewhere. The horses endure long, grueling transport and are often stabbed to death, or worse. In April 2007, the State Commerce Committee approved the American Horse Slaughter Prevention Act, but it afforded only temporary protection.[35] As this book was being completed, a bipartisan group of lawmakers was being besieged to permanently ban the brutal slaughter of the more than 100,000 healthy horses who die each year.

California Governor, Arnold Schwarzenegger, found out how quickly activists could mobilize when animals' lives are at stake. The governor, in an effort to shave some dollars from his 2004–2005 budget, proposed to shorten the length of time dogs and cats would be kept alive in shelters and permit immediate killing of hamsters, rabbits, turtles, and potbellied pigs. The measure would undo the protection imposed by the previous governor (Gray Davis) in 1998, which had doubled the days animals must be kept alive in California shelters from three to six. It did not take that long for people tracking animal issues to see the slashed days tucked in the Governor's plans, and within a few hours, he reinstated the six-day waiting period and admitted his mistake.[36]

In the wake of the disturbing images of people who died in the aftermath of Hurricane Katrina for refusing to forsake their animal companions, animal advocates across the United States pressured politicians to pass a federal law that requires local and state disaster agencies to include companion animals in disaster plans, and make arrangements for evacuees to have emergency shelter that allows companion animals.

Victims of violence depend on the laws to protect them, and now that a connection is emerging between domestic violence and animal cruelty, animals can also receive protection under the law. The connection between abuse of animals and violence against humans is well documented, with profiles of many criminals whose violent behavior began with animals. We also know that domestic batterers use violence against family animals to control and manipulate their human victims. In the cases of violence against women without children, who are often especially attached to their animals, the scenario can play out in heinous ways. Karen Days, president of an organization against family violence in Columbus, OH, recounted that one of her clients told her: "When I left him before, he started mailing me pieces of my cat to tell me, 'if you don't come back this is what I'm going to continue to do.'" Whether the victim is alone or also trying to protect children, the most important issue is for the victim to feel secure enough to leave the dangerous environment before it explodes. If staying behind to protect an animal is a barrier to safety, the animal must be secured, not just for its own sake, but also for the sake of the victimized family members.

Susan Walsh testified for legislators in Maine that she was afraid to take her two children and leave her husband because she was terrified for the welfare of her animals. He had run over her blind and deaf Border collie, shot two sheep, and strangled two prized turkeys on the thirty-two acre farm they shared. Thanks in part to Walsh's testimony, Maine became the first state to enact a law that allows inclusion of animals in protection orders associated with domestic violence cases.[37] Several other states are following suit to protect the companion animals who are caught in the web of domestic violence. "Its a very short line from harming somebody's animal to harming that person or that person's child," said Rep. John Fritchey (D-IL), who introduced a "pet protection measure" in his state.[38]

The first protection order in New York to include a companion animal was issued, not because the human partner was the victim, but because only the dog, Bebe, a Bichon Frise, was victimized. The violence was instigated by an argument between Derek Lopez and his partner, Frederick Fontanez, one morning before Lopez left for work. Upon his return, Lopez noticed that Bebe was in pain. A veterinarian visit confirmed that Bebe had injuries consistent with abuse, and a neighbor's report of sounds from the apartment consistent with Bebe being beaten were sufficient evidence for a protection order. Consequently, under legislation signed by Gov. Pataki just months before, a judge signed the first-ever restraining order for a pet, against Fontanez, who was later arrested and charged with torturing and injuring an animal. The offense is punishable by $1,000 and/or a year in jail.[39]

HOW TO PROTECT THEM WHEN YOU CANNOT BE THERE

Many people worry what will happen if they outlive their companion animals or they become too ill to care for them, but the animal is too old to be adopted and there is no family to take over. The last thing we want is for our beloved animals to be turned over to a shelter if we become sick or die.

Many guardians are turning to trust funds and wills to insure that their companions are protected under the aforementioned circumstances, and new legislation makes these documents legally binding.

Real estate maven, Leona Helmsley, who died in August 2007, famously bequeathed $12 million to her beloved eight-year-old Maltese, Trouble. That is a lot of money in an absolute sense, but when you consider that her estate was $8 billion, the amount is not so unreasonable.[40] What she did is the equivalent of a person with an estate of $60,000 leaving $90 for the care of their companion animal, essentially 0.15 percent of the total. You will get no argument from me that $12 million is a lot of money to care for a Maltese (I have one; I know), and the money could have been put to a lot of other uses.

Fellow New Yorkers Richard and Patti Brotman, who live near the site of the terrorist attacks, were compelled to established a $200,000 trust agreement for their two dogs and six cats, which specifies a caretaker and a trustee to provide expenses. "We thought it was important to plan for an unfortunate eventuality. We saw what happened right across the street," they said.

Thirty-nine states allow people to establish legally binding trusts for their companion animals. Rep. Earl Blumenauer (D-OR) introduced a bill in 2007 that will permit federally deductible trust funds. As a member of the Ways and Means Committee, which oversees tax policy, Blumenauer said that he wanted to improve the federal tax code to give "peace of mind to the many Americans who consider their pets as family."[41]

The Bide-A-Wee Golden Years Retirement Home in Westhampton, NY, is not an option for everyone, but $15,000 guarantees a space at Bide-A-Wee, with complete reassurance that your devoted companion will be cared for forever. The complex has cage-free living spaces, indoor playrooms, outdoor exercise areas, high-quality meals, and onsite veterinarian care. Cats are grouped by temperament and get to select their own sleeping quarters from the dormitory-style accommodations that permit both privacy and socialization. Dogs live in large cubicles outfitted with plush bedding. A veterinarian who specializes in the care of aging animals administers a complete examination prior to admission, and checkups follow every six months, with surgical and emergency facilities on site. Animals suffering from incurable diseases are evaluated by a panel of outside veterinarians to ensure objectivity in case reviews that consider euthanasia. When residents die, they are interred in the Bide-a-Wee Memorial Park with a marker inscribed as directed by the original guardian.[42]

SAFETY GIZMOS AND GADGETS

We are a high-tech society, so it stands to reason that we would turn to technology to extend protection to our companion animals. Here are just a couple of examples.

The Pet Cell is a wireless device that hangs around your dog's neck allowing two-way communication. Each *phone* has a "call owner" button and a GPS function, compatible with existing cellular and satellite technology, to allow guardians to used the web to map coordinates of the animal. PetMobility, which developed PetCell also plans to have options for a small wireless camera, a temperature sensor, and an alert if the dog wanders beyond preset parameters. The company is working on miniaturization to make a device suitable for cats.[43]

Two million cats and dogs are walking around with microchips inserted under their skin that carry an identification number to link them to their guardians. The system is not perfect but increases the possibility that a lost dog is protected from long-term homelessness or euthanasia at an animal shelter. Unfortunately, devices to read the chips are not standard and the databases where the information is stored are not universal. As things stand, the life-saving information could be in the national database of the chipmaker, in the office of the veterinarian who inserted it, or at the shelter where the animal was adopted. Not a perfect system for sure, but it increases the chances of a reunion. Two organizations are working to establish universal standards for identification and develop a uniform chip. Even the best technology can be thwarted, and if someone finds your dog or cat and prefers to keep it, there is not much the chip can do.[44]

From digging a ditch to employing wireless technology, most of us take seriously our obligation to protect our companion animals. We use everything at our disposal to ensure their safety and protection.

8

When Love Hurts

We who choose to surround ourselves with lives even more temporary than our own live within a fragile circle, easily and often breached. Unable to accept its awful gaps, we still would live no other way.

—Irving Townsend

Sometimes there is nothing we can do; their body wears out, or they run off, fly away, get hurt, or are kidnapped. We ourselves may get old, sick, or disabled. We outlive most of the companion animals who grace our lives. Consequently, at some point, for some reason, we must face an inevitable reality and figure out how to cope with the loss of a beloved companion animal, whose relationship has meant so much.

Our society is not comfortable with death. We avoid talking or thinking about it, as if that avoidance will bestow immunity. Until death is forced upon us, we try to pretend that it is not a part of life, ignoring the fact that none of us gets out alive. Authors John James and Frank Cherry, in their book *The Grief Recovery Handbook*[1] discuss the irony that we are taught first aid as early as grade school, and everyone knows to dial 911 in case of an emergency, but we are never taught how to grieve or support those left behind by the more than 2 million people who die each year.[2]

Experts from various pertinent fields now realize that people experience the same symptoms of grief when their companion animal dies as they do when a close family member or friend dies—sometimes even more. And why not? Companion animals are considered family members with distinct roles, most of which are related to emotional and social support. Consequently, they are sorely missed when they die or disappear, and their deaths cause great grief.

The depth of the grief is directly related to the meaning the animal had in our life. Grief reactions may vary widely, even within a family, depending on the animal's age, the magnitude of the relationship, and how the animal died or disappeared. "The death or loss of a beloved pet can be a life-changing event. Because of the immense contribution [of the relationships], the death, loss or theft of a beloved animal results in the end of a special relationship and can be one of the most difficult times in a person's life. The impact will vary . . . across a wide continuum of response patterns."[3]

This is the time when the critical nature of the relationships we have with companion animals becomes most salient because the grief and the associated emotions are real, and we suffer deeply. Yet, this is the time when people with companion animals are most alone. Although the grief is "legitimate and justified,"[4] our culture provides no acceptable way to grieve on these occasions. Our feelings are frequently trivialized by our friends, our extended family, and therapists. Everyone understands how difficult it is to cope when a person you love dies, but when an animal you love dies, few people understand. Even veterinarians, to whom we might naturally turn, often underestimate the enormity of the grief. Consequently, we are reluctant to share our grief for fear of being criticized or rejected.

Those of us who choose to share our lives with companion animals are likely to experience this grief several times, but that does not make it easier. As an adult, I have twice endured the death of a dog, and the circumstances were so different that I cannot draw any conclusions about what I will experience the next time. The experience for the loss of each animal was different, based on the particulars of the relationship and the quality of my life at the time. I *can* say that coping with the grief is easier when you are surrounded by people who genuinely understand how you feel and allow you to experience the grief as fully as you require without ridicule or embarrassment. People who do not give that permission risk disrupting the balance of their relationships with the bereaved, positioning everyone for damage that exacerbates the grief and could create tension in future social interactions.

As a society, we are beginning to comprehend the significance of companion animals in human lives. Now, we must realize the impact of that significance when the animal dies or the relationship is terminated for other reasons, and we must give people our consent to grieve openly and completely, in order to effectively circumvent widespread emotional problems and to promote healing.

TYPES OF LOSS

We may *lose* our companion animals in a mind-numbing variety of ways, with death being the most prevalent. In this chapter, I avoid using the word "lose" as a euphemism for death. Rather, I use the words "lose" or "loss" to refer to the collective possibilities that result in death or other separation. For example, our companion animals may run away, mysteriously disappear, or get abducted. Death, itself, typically is caused by old age, illness, or accident. We may experience symptoms of loss when we relinquish our companion animals to a shelter or foster care, especially if we do so because we feel overwhelmed by personal or financial instability. We may also lose rights to keep our companion animals in a custody battle or become infirmed from either an acute or chronic illness and become unable to care for them. The point is anything *can* happen. As is the case with the humans we love, there is no end to the types of tragedies that can take our companion animals away from us. There is, however, a significant type of death from which we are spared with our human loved ones—euthanasia, which is such an agonizing aspect of our relationships with companion animals that I discuss it separately.

Grief experts have classified loss into four categories: primary, secondary, ambiguous, and symbolic. Death, of course, is a primary loss. Where companion animals are concerned, an example of a secondary loss is when a working dog, who is also a companion, dies. In that kind of situation, beyond the primary loss of the animal's death, the work the animal was performing is considered a secondary loss. Ambiguous losses leave unanswered questions or unfinished business in the minds of the survivors. Companion animals who are lost, stolen, run away, or die from unknown causes are examples of ambiguous losses. Symbolic losses are losses that are compounded by being linked to other aspects of a person's life, such as when a dog is shared with a deceased spouse.[5]

Euthanasia

Most of us hope that we and those we love will die peacefully during sleep. The American judicial system does not allow us to choose euthanasia for human family members who are suffering, but we are not so fortunate when it comes to our companion animals. Euthanasia is probably the most common and agonizing decision that animal guardians have to make, and it is a decision that guardians know likely awaits them. As our animals become frail or their bodies fail because of accidents or trauma, we are frequently put in a position of having to choose life or death for them—it is a gut-wrenching decision. Although the decision is always traumatic, it is "demanded by humanitarian obligation, when it provides necessary relief by ending terminal suffering and poor quality of life."[6] Euthanasia is a complicated issue, which leaves most guardians with some level of guilt and doubt. I have faced the decision once in my life, so far, and I still feel guilty that I gave up too soon. After nearly twenty years, I realize the guilt, which will surely influence future similar decisions, is something I may carry forever. Because choosing death for an animal for whom we have cared and protected is contrary to our beliefs and behaviors, we try to distance ourselves from feeling complicit in the death by using euphemisms such as "putting the animal to sleep." The cognitive dissonance that we experience is often mediated by knowing that we have often committed an act of love, actually protecting them to the end of the relationship. Our final act is to protect them from a painful, prolonged death.

Undoubtedly, some people elect euthanasia as a convenient, "hasty dispatch of a sick or injured animal." Perhaps, they cannot cope with the excruciating pain of watching the animal die, or parents may want to spare their children the experience of witnessing the death. Parents may be imparting the wrong lesson in the latter case because euthanasia under certain circumstances can teach children that animals are expendable, "especially when [maintaining the animal] becomes expensive or difficult."[7]

A decision to euthanize, especially in response to a chronic or terminal illness, must be carefully considered and discussed with a trusted veterinarian who is familiar with you, your companion animal, and your history together. Typically, the way a veterinary communicates a prognosis will give the guardian an indication whether or not to consider euthanasia. Bond-centered veterinarians are sensitive to the profound nature of the decision and prepare the guardians as much as possible. There are no real guidelines about when *enough is enough* because no one knows your companion animal better than you. Deb Acord, a reporter for the *Colorado Gazette*, who wrote a poignant account of the final days of her dog Waldo, was given the following advice for when to consider euthanasia: "When he quits being Waldo, doing all the things that make him Waldo, you'll know it's time."[8]

Clinically oriented suggestions include the following "red flags" for unrelenting pain, which is often a deciding factor in euthanasia:

- Refusal to eat for more than twelve hours
- Reluctance to move
- Crying
- Whining or whimpering
- Inability to achieve a comfortable position
- Behavioral changes
- Aggression
- Panting while at rest
- Shaking or shivering.[9]

The traditional operating procedure for veterinarians where euthanasia was concerned was to minimize their human clients' exposure to the procedure. There was not much discussion or explanation; the guardian typically turned the animal over to the veterinarian and returned later for the remains or cremains (remains after a cremation). Things have changed, and veterinarians typically discuss the procedure in detail and invite guardians to be present if they choose.

Large animals, such as horses, can present an exception. Veterinarian Julia Brannan made a statement that succinctly described the poignant difference between euthanizing a large companion animal rather than a small one: "A horse is a large magnificent animal and it is going to drop to the ground."[10] Barbaro immediately came to mind. He was not a companion horse, but he stole the heart of America as we watched in hopeful anticipation that he would overcome the shattered leg he suffered during the Preakness Stakes in May 2006. As we witnessed this horse's unfortunate course end in euthanasia, we gained a better understanding of what it is to love and lose one of these majestic creatures. The emotional impact of losing a large beloved animal may be magnified by the loss of their large physical presence in your life. Witnessing the end of a life force of that magnitude may be too excruciating for the guardian, and best reserved for the veterinarian.

Whether a large or small animal is involved, if veterinarians are concerned that the guardian cannot cope well with being present during the euthanasia, potentially increasing the anxiety of the animal or interfering with the procedure, they will discourage involvement.

I have never witnessed euthanasia, but from all I have read, it is not pretty. Death occurs in a matter of seconds after the lethal injection is given, but the body may twitch and excrete fluids. The procedure is not easy for anyone, including the veterinarian, some of whom are concerned about becoming emotional in the presence of their clients. I dare say that, most guardians will understand and welcome a show of emotion from their veterinarian, who is a part of a veterinary health care team that has cared for a companion animal in a bond-centered practice. Professional veterinary organizations such as the American Animal Hospital Association now counsel veterinarians on how to prepare themselves, their team, and their human and animal clients for the procedure, including care and support for all parties when it is over. Veterinarians are encouraged to provide information on grief itself, the need for grief counseling, the importance of creating memorials, and the warning signs for symptoms of post-traumatic stress disorder.

In small ways each day over the course of our relationships with companion animals, we decide whether they will live or die by how we care for them. Consequently, we are obligated to them to accept responsibility for this ultimate life and death decision. The obligation then turns to ourselves, to insure that we understand grief and bereavement—no matter which kind of loss caused it.

GRIEF AND ITS COMPONENTS DEFINED

According to the *Encyclopedia of Psychology*, grief is "an emotional response to the loss of a loved or otherwise significant person, usually following a death." The said that a debate exists in scientific literature about the kinds of situations to which grief can be applied. Nonetheless, I was surprised that the death of companion animals was not included until I read further in the entry that the loss of siblings was only "more recently" considered an acceptable "occasion" for grief. This is a tough crowd. The encyclopedia also did not include companion animals in a list of situations that might cause "grief-like reactions," such as the loss of "homeland, livelihood, or job, loss of physical function through illness or accident."[11] I located other references, more to my liking, which state for example: "the loss or death of a cherished pet creates a grief reaction that is in many ways comparable to that of the loss of a [human] family member."[12] Better yet, another author asserts that "loss of a companion animal . . . is an unqualified occasion for bereavement."[13]

Bereavement was described in the psychology dictionary as a condition applied to those who have lost a "loved one through death." I have established sufficiently that our companion animals are our loved ones, and I agree with the author who writes the following: "It is clear that the behavior of pet owners at the time of their animals' death appears to mimic in many ways the stages or phases that have been described as characteristic of bereavement after human death."[14]

Mourning was distinguished as the "social expressions of grief during bereavement," and includes funerals and other ceremonies, with the caveat that some people consider them synonymous.[15] I agree. Consequently, I will consider a person in grief as bereaved or in mourning, and will use the terms interchangeably. Remember, I am not using the term *loss* as a euphemism for death, but I will use the word *missing* when talking about an animal who has been kidnapped, stolen, or run away. I maintain that regardless of how it happens, the feeling is the same because an absence is an absence. Some types of loss have added potential for guilt as you will read, but I submit that all bereaved guardians experience some guilt as a component of grief.

Much of the literature tends to marginalize or assign pathology to the grief associated with companion animals, assuming that the relationships are inferior and that the grief is insignificant.[16] Yet, what is happening to people is not insignificant, and this is not new knowledge. For instance, a retrospective data analysis of bereaved guardians whom veterinarians had referred to a social worker in 1980, showed that 93 percent of participants reported that the animal's death disrupted their daily routine, including causing problems with sleep and appetite. Fifty-one percent said they chose to avoid social activities, preferring to spend time alone at home, talking very little with anyone. Forty-one percent missed between one and three days of work, took sick or vacation days, and experienced problems at work. Only one person in the entire data analysis did not experience any problems.[17] Other studies concur, providing reports of emotional problems following a loss, such as decreased motivation, stress, intense depression, thoughts of self-harm, anxiety, and worry.[18]

Grief is as inevitable as death, but even the guardian is often caught unawares. Scientific literature and the popular press are filled with reports and examples of people who had no idea that their companion animal's death would have such an impact. In some cases, they report that the veterinarian had provided details about the animal's illness, the euthanasia procedure, and options for disposing of the body, but had not said a word about the grief and bereavement that would follow.

Death and the resulting grief are the most common of all human experiences—"normal and spontaneous responses to loss." Grief is a process that is "necessary for healing the emotional wounds caused by a loss."[19] Because it is a process, not an event, it is not always clear when it begins and when, if ever, it ends. Unfortunately, given how our society operates, people have to find their own way. In the absence of education about the process, the least we can do is allow the process to unfold naturally for others and ourselves. Suppressed feelings are simply that—suppressed—poised for inevitable eruptions or leaking out in unaccepted, psychologically damaging ways.

Before I close this section, I want to point out that surviving animals in multi-animal homes may also experience grief, though not as will be described in the next sections. However, animals who live together become attached to each other, recognize when one is missing or dead, and may respond. They may become restless or depressed and experience changes in eating and sleeping behaviors. Give them time to heal, too, but if the problems persist talk to your veterinarian. Do not establish unhealthy dependence or attachment behavior in an attempt to soothe their grief, and try to keep a regular schedule for the surviving animals. Immediately after a death or loss is not the time to incorporate a new companion into the house. The surviving animals will not be fooled by attempts at replacing their friends, and you may be postponing your own grief response.

Disenfranchised Grief

Experts distinguish grief based on severity of symptoms over certain time-frames. I have chosen three types of grief that bereaved guardians of companion animals experience most often: Disenfranchised grief, Anticipatory grief, and Complicated grief. One universal fact I discovered is that following the death of a companion animal, most people suffer in silence, alienated from friends and family and reluctant to seek help. This is described as *disenfranchised grief* because the bereaved are *deprived* of the understanding and compassion of other people. Women who experience miscarriages, especially early in their pregnancies, frequently experience this type of grief. Many times their friends and family were not aware of the pregnancy, and the women grieve their unborn children in silence; frequently not able to share their feelings of profound loss even with their husbands. This example is meant not to equate the losses by any means, but to give an example of disenfranchised grief that is easy to comprehend. The term was introduced by Kenneth J. Doka as grief that is "not openly acknowledged, publicly mourned, or socially supported." He also said that disenfranchised grief has three possible triggers: (1) The relationship with the deceased is not recognized; (2) the loss is not recognized; or (3) the griever is not recognized. I believe that all grief associated with the loss of a companion animal is compounded by an element of disenfranchised grief.[20]

Why Is It So Hard to Help?

Death is a paralyzing enigma. Most of us are afraid of death completely; we are uncomfortable around the dying and people who have had recent death in their family. We do not know what to say, and we feel awkward and stupid. We realize that nothing short of bringing back the dead will offer any solace. So we tend to avoid the grief-stricken and let them work it out until their pain is not so palpable, because we cannot bear to witness the suffering. Our society has established customs of acceptable behavior when a human dies and we get through them because we know what is expected of us, and the consequences of not participating in those customs. However, our society has no accepted way to grieve for the death of a companion animal.

Betty Carmack, a registered nurse and counselor, who has facilitated a monthly pet loss support group at the San Franciso Society for the Prevention of Companion Animals, spoke of a client whose eleven-year-old shepherd-collie mix, Chloe, died after a long illness. She counseled the guardian, suggesting many ways to deal with the immediate grief. In particular, she encouraged her to leave home and stay with friends when the grief was overwhelming. "If this was an eleven-year-old child, no one would expect you to be alone, she explained. They would come over to your house or invite you to theirs."[21]

When companion animals die, people really do not know what to do. The deaths are "not recognized consistently by friends, acquaintances, or colleagues as a significant or authentic occasion for bereavement."[22] Companion animal guardians suffer what can be one of the most traumatic experiences of their lives, and often cope with little compassion and understanding from others. People who grieve the death of their companion animal are frequently subjected to ridicule, disbelief, curt statements, and rude behavior from people who are supposed to be their primary support system, as well as from those in their extended social circles. People make callous remarks either directly to or about the grief-stricken, such as "It's just a cat" or "It's been two weeks, isn't she over it?" Faced with this kind of insensitivity, bereaved guardians keep to themselves.

Carmack reasons that the people who diminish the grief after the death of companion animals likely never had a companion animal. I find that hard to accept, given the number of animal lovers in the world. I suspect the callous behavior has more to do with our generalized discomfort with death and a widespread absence of appropriate sensibilities about animals.

Whatever is the cause of the callous treatment, the result can be damaging to the bereaved because the "lack of social and professional sanction for the bereavement of a pet's loss can complicate or derail grief and adaptive coping." Unexpressed grief of any kind can manifest into chronic headaches, anxiety, fear, sleep disorders, digestive disturbances, dysfunctional relationships, loss of communication, and inability to focus.[23]

Anticipatory Grief

Scholars are not in agreement about how to identify or classify anticipatory grief or whether it even exists, but I believe it is a phenomena—one that applies to relationships between humans and their companion animals.

According to the National Cancer Institute's Web site, anticipatory grief occurs in anticipation of an impending loss. Where human relationships are concerned, anticipatory grief can provide family members with time to gradually absorb the reality of the approaching death and complete unfinished business. Nonetheless, anticipating a death and experiencing anticipatory grief does not necessarily reduce the amount of grief suffered when the death actually happens, but there is an element of being able to prepare. Where human–human relationships are concerned, *both* the dying and in those close to them can experience anticipatory grief. Although anticipatory grief is typically applied after a terminal illness is diagnosed, I maintain that people with companion animals stay, because of the animals' short lifespans, in a state of anticipation and wariness that the death is looming, and the pain is forthcoming. How could we not? Many popular companion animals have lifespans of ten years or less. Guardians are aware that a comparatively early death is inevitable, but the sadness and depression associated with anticipatory grief do not manifest until and unless the animal receives a terminal diagnosis or becomes aged. The reality of their short lifespans always hovers in the background. How we cope with that reality depends on our coping strategies in general, I presume. Some people refuse to get companion animals because they cannot cope with the inevitable *premature* loss. Others, after one shocking experience, simply never put themselves in that position again by never having another companion animal. Still others, take the bitter with the sweet, if you will, forging ahead, one animal after another, not deterred by the pain, as the quote at the beginning of the chapter suggests. The latter are the majority. We are compelled by the benefits and privileges of the relationships to face the grief. Yet, I have never talked to a person who did not, if even for a moment, agonize over what was to come.

Complicated Grief

As the name implies, the nature of this grief is often complicated by circumstances surrounding the grief. As a consequence, the immediate response to the loss is exceptionally devastating and the passage of time does not moderate the emotional pain or restore competent functioning.[24] Symptoms of complicated grief resemble those of post-traumatic stress disorder.[25] This is especially true for people who have witnessed the traumatic death of a companion animal. People with service animals who die and for whom the death may represent a loss of freedom, mobility, security, and self-esteem are also at risk for complicated grief. "Many report the brutalizing experience of becoming deaf, blind, or handicapped all over again!"[26] In fact, where service animals are concerned, all aspects of the death seem primary because death or loss of the animal can cause complete upheaval under these complicated circumstances. Another typical person at risk for complicated grief is one whose animal was the final link to a deceased loved one, especially a spouse or deceased child. Consider that 75 percent of 900 dog and cat guardians reported that their companion animal's death "revived memories of past bereavements, both human and animal," and they expressed a need for professional bereavement support.[27]

Several other situations, as shown below, can contribute to complicated grief:

- No previous experience with significant loss, death, or grief
- Recent losses

- A history of losses
- Little or no support from friends
- Poor personal coping skills
- An unexplained disappearance
- Deaths that occur in conjunction with other significant life events
- Sudden, untimely, or mysterious deaths
- Feelings of guilt or responsibility for death[28]

Scholars believe that "most people in Western society carry some remnants of" complicated grief, manifested as unresolved grief, a specific form of complicated grief that occurs when people never actively process the emotional fallout of grief, letting it build with subsequent events. People with this type of complicated grief may make "elaborate arrangements" to avoid reminders of the death, such as driving out of their way not to pass a park, veterinarian's office, or room in their house that reminds them of their dead companion animal. When grief goes unattended, pathological grief may result where the most tragic outcome is suicide. Veterinarians are not expected to be equipped to deal with these intense manifestations of grief, but they can remain vigilant and proactive in making referrals to mental health professionals. Complicated or not, grief will not go away on its own. It must be confronted and normalized to enable the bereaved to function in spite of the loss.

Our society could benefit from accepted approaches to death, the dying, and the bereaved that are more frank. Bereaved animal guardians, in particular, would benefit from more societal acceptance, support, and compassion.

Occasionally, the death of a companion animal is felt so profoundly by a community that its residents seem to coalesce around the bereaved to offer support, creating unique memorials or employing established human traditions to memorialize the fallen. This is what happened in the following two examples. First, I am honored to introduce you to Foxy, a ten-year-old white American pit bull terrier whose relationship with her homeless guardian Ralph Vargas of Hoboken, New Jersey, "was a testimony to the companionship between man and dog." The inseparable pair were fixtures on Hudson Street, where passersby gladly gave donations toward their care. Vargas, who had rescued Foxy from an abusive situation, was a devoted guardian for many years, who dressed Foxy in layers to keep her warm on the streets during inclement weather. "It wasn't the perfect situation for a dog, but it was for her because she had him," said an animal rescue volunteer familiar with the pair. One Monday morning the community was stunned and saddened to learn that Foxy had been killed by a hit-and-run driver of a pickup truck as she ran, uncharacteristically, across the street ahead of Vargas to greet a friend. Vargas carried her three blocks to the Hoboken Animal Medical Hospital, but Foxy's internal injuries were too severe, and her heart stopped beating. The community realized the impact of Foxy's loss on Vargas and rallied around him during his time of intense grief. They knew Foxy as a gentle, sweet dog who was completely devoted to a man who worried about her more than he did himself.

Foxy, the belle of Hoboken, NJ, and the companion of a homeless man, Ralph Vargas, was killed by a hit-and-run driver. © 2007 Diana Pappas, used with permission.

A freelance photographer had happened to take a photograph of Foxy just days before the accident that allowed "one of Hoboken's most well-liked dogs," to be remembered in the local paper. Companion Animal Placement, a local rescue organization, had routinely paid for Foxy's shots, medicines, city licenses, and her board fee at the animal hospital on especially bitter winter nights. They also collected funds to pay for her cremation and created a pendant with a few of Foxy's ashes that Vargas can wear around his neck.[29]

K-9 Sirius, a member of the Port Authority Police Department, was the only dog who died at the World Trade Center attack on September 11, 2001, in New York City. Sirius, whose primary duty was checking trucks and unattended bags for bombs, had lived with his partner, David Lim. He had left her behind in a kennel, thinking she would be safer there while he responded to what he thought was a bomb explosion in the building. He remembers telling her, "One must have gotten by us. I'll be back to get you." Lim guided hundreds of people to safety and was trapped himself for five hours, but the collapse of the towers made it impossible to keep his vow to Sirius. When the dog's remains were found four months after the attacks, all work ceased at ground zero for Sirius' body to be brought out in ceremonial fashion, just like the other fallen heroes. Later, two-hundred-and-fifty officers from Port Authority, the New York Police Department, and as far away as Chicago, attended a memorial ceremony to honor Sirius. One at a time, one-hundred handlers with their dogs stepped up to the dais to salute a portrait of Sirius and honor her cremains. Each officer knew what Lim was going through. One said, "It's the same kind of loss as when you lose a [human] partner." An FBI agent presented Lim with Sirius' water bowl, which had been later recovered from the debris. Lim said, "To many people, this would be just a water bowl, but this is something I'll cherish for the rest of my life."[30]

PROCESSING GRIEF

Although we process our grief in very individualized ways, several theories provide insight into what is happening during grief and suggest ways to cope with the pain. The most widely known and accepted theory was introduced by Elizabeth Kübler-Ross, who identified the following fives stages of grief:

- Denial
- Anger
- Bargaining
- Depression
- Acceptance.

In this model, people must go through four stages of grief before reaching the fifth, normalized stage of acceptance. The stages are not necessarily sequential, may not all occur, and are open ended.

I find the task-based models more appealing because they are proactive and give the bereaved some element of control over events rather than waiting for stages or phases to pass. For example, J. W. Worden refers to four tasks of mourning that *must be dealt with*, which are easily applied to grieving guardians of companion animals. The first task requires that the bereaved *accept the reality of the loss*. This may be particularly difficult in cases of accident or sudden death from illness, as the guardian must come to grips with the fact that the animal is gone, and routines associated with the relationship are terminated abruptly. The second task in Worden's model is to *experience the pain*—a primary component of grief that cannot be avoided, no matter how overwhelming it may feel. Continuous attempts to deny the pain or distract from it will cause unresolved or complicated grief. The third task requires the bereaved to *adjust to an environment without the object of grief*. For example, this task might require the bereaved to become accustomed to coming home to an empty house, not hiking in the woods with a dog on weekends, or no longer participating in agility trials or cat shows. Adjusting to the loss of tangible and intangible roles fulfilled by the companion animal can be the most emotionally difficult task, but also perhaps the most pivotal, preparing you for the fourth and final task: *invest emotional energy into a new life*. Many guardians feel that success in this final step is a betrayal to the memory of the animal for which they grieve because they are basically being asked to "move on" emotionally. They fear they will forget the beloved animal. However, in this model, the bereaved are urged to keep pictures and other keepsakes that will sustain memories.[31]

This is not a self-help book, and I urge anyone experiencing grief from the death or disappearance of a beloved companion animal to seek help from a mental health professional, one who specializes in grief, and *pet grief* specifically, if possible. A myriad of resources are available on the Internet or from your veterinarian, and membership organizations for mental health professionals may be helpful.

Many bereaved guardians turn to specialized support groups and hotlines where they know they will find like-minded people who know what they are going through and are aware of appropriate professional resources in their vicinity. Thanks to pioneers like Enid Traisman, support groups for bereaved animal guardians are plentiful. In 1986, she founded the second support group in the country for bereaved guardians—to the ridicule of her friends and family, and veterinarians who refused to participate. "People weren't sensitive about the issue," she said. To get started, Traisman, a social worker with experience in neonatology, offered to lead a free support group at Dove Lewis Emergency Animal Hospital in Portland, Oregon. After twelve years as a volunteer, she became director for pet-loss support services at the hospital and is now a recognized national expert, who gives workshops and lectures across the United States. People attend her meetings distraught over a variety of animals. For example, one lady was "an absolute wreck" over a deceased bearded dragon that had been so much a part of her life that she included the reptile in her wedding. Traisman says that sometimes people are reluctant to admit how broken up they are, and some are taken by surprise. "Our dog died on Sunday," a participant explained to Traisman. "I am at a very intense stage of grief. If someone had told me that I'd feel such pain, I wouldn't have believed it." Other people reported being unable to work and feeling ostracized. "Although it's getting better, there is still less permission in society to grieve over a pet," Traisman said. Her groups are an oasis of comfort and understanding. "You can come here and cry. You can come here and people will love to hear every detail about your companion animal," she reminds her group.[32]

Companion Animal Related Emotions (CARE), is an example of a confidential telephone helpline. It is staffed by veterinary students from the University of Illinois College of Veterinary Medicine, who have been trained by professional grief counselors and are supervised by a licensed clinical social worker.[33]

The following suggestions from Kübler-Ross's official Web site (www. elisabethkublerross.com) can be helpful for guardians awaiting triage to appropriate resources:

- Attend support groups in your area
- Obtain therapy with a psychologist or a qualified mental health professional
- Try Journaling (writing is a catharsis for many)
- Eat well
- Exercise
- Get enough rest

- Read and learn about death-related grief responses
- Seek comforting rituals or solace in the faith community
- Allow emotions (tears can be healing)
- Avoid major changes in residence, jobs, or marital status.

No amount of knowledge can really prepare us for the personalized, intense, and persistent pain of grief. However, the above theories of grief, and others, can inform us that our experiences are normal. They help guide us through the treacherous terrain that we must navigate on our own terms and in our own time, commensurate with our needs and the depth of the loss.

BURIALS, CEREMONIES, AND MEMORIALS

When a companion animal dies we frequently want to acknowledge their lives, and we do so with the only kinds of ceremonies and rituals we know. My favorite example is of Jill Schaffer, a Christian, who *sat shiva*—a gathering, in the Jewish tradition, of family and friends to mourn a loved one and comfort the survivors—when her cat Della died. She invited friends to her home the night she returned from the crematorium, and they ate pizza and shared stories about her "big, wonderful cat."[34]

We also typically want a permanent, visual reminder that symbolizes the relationship, but the most immediate need is to arrange for disposition of the body in a respectful manner. Schaffer is not rare in her desire for a ceremony based on a religious tradition. Many people with spiritual and religious orientations often choose religious rites of passage for their animals that include a leader from their faith, presiding over a funeral. Glenn Lane, director of Noah's Ark Pet Cemetery in Falls Church, Virginia (near Washington, DC), said that he has seen every type of clergy represented except a Buddhist monk. He recalls a Muslim family that included an Imam and "wanted to make sure the pet was facing east when he buried it." Harold White, Jewish chaplain at Georgetown University in Washington, DC, says that he "wings it" with prayers that he creates, because Judaism, as is the case with other religions, has no set ceremony for animal burials. "The most important thing is to bring solace to people who have suffered a loss. I believe an animal who lived with dignity in the home should be buried with dignity."[35]

Guardians planning secular ceremonies seek the services of people such as India Cooke, a jazz violinist and composer with an international resume that includes performances with other artists such as Ray Charles, Frank Sinatra, and Diana Ross. She founded Angel Airs, "transitional music and ceremony" provided by caring, professional musicians. Cooke currently has four cats and is no stranger to the impact of the grief associated with a companion animal's death. She decided to blend her love of music with the love and devotion she has for her own companions, and to celebrate with ceremony the lives of animals lost.[36]

Burials and Cemeteries

Graveside services are the most common ceremony for deceased companion animals, with at least seventy-five companies in the United States offering bereavement or cremation-related products and services.[37] Many offer a complete line of urns and caskets, vaults, memorials, mausoleums, prepayment plans, and/or a furnished stateroom for viewing. They are part of the multifaceted *pet loss industry*, which includes cemeteries, crematories, grief counselors, hotlines, books, tapes, and chat rooms.

Pet cemeteries have become increasingly popular because some cities prohibit burial of animals in private yards or public property. A recent article in the *New York Times* reported that "there are more than 1,000 pet cemeteries across the United States and many provide most everything from funeral services and customized burial sites to cremation and bereavement counseling." The article said that "the sky is the limit when it comes to options" for guardians who want to give their companions a "proper send off." This is the case with A. R. LaMura, who has made prearrangements in the six-figure range for his dog Sandy, "a mixed-breed terrier" he found on a loading dock fifteen years prior to her being diagnosed with cancer. He has cared for the dog "as if she were his own child," and he has created a "granite mausoleum," a replica of his family mausoleum in a Bronx cemetery that awaits his beloved Sandy with a "copper coffin as nice as any child's."[38]

Guardians choose cemeteries for companion animals for a sense of dignity and permanence, but permanence is elusive. Stories of cemeteries turned over to developers or left in disrepair are a concern to guardians. Cemeteries are unregulated in most states, leaving remains vulnerable to be moved without notice to make room for development, regardless of their historical significance or the famous animals interred. Take the case of Rosa Bonheur Memorial Park outside of Washington, DC, one of the first cemeteries in the country to allow burial of people next to their companion animals. "The problem is that the property is worth too darn much," said Robin L. Lauver, president of the National Association of Pet Funeral Directors. "Now you have hundreds of pet cemeteries that can be sold off as building lots. And there are no laws to stop it." The graves of 22,000 animals and about twenty people who are buried in Rosa Bonheur are at risk, and volunteers are struggling to keep the cemetery clean, while mapping and documenting the headstones and lobbying for legislation in the Maryland Assembly to preserve it. In the region of the cemetery, Virginia is the only state—and one of few nationally—with restrictions on pet cemeteries, requiring landowners to put $12,000 in a fund to insure perpetual care. Maryland, where Rosa Bonheur is located, and the District of Columbia, have no such laws.[39] Guardians often find themselves embroiled in protracted and costly lawsuits to protect what they consider sacred burial grounds of their animals. For example, as of January 2005, Dorothy M. Shapiro of Potomac, Maryland had spent more than $500,000 to protect Aspen Hill Memorial Park, an eight-acre cemetery in Silver Spring, MD, where 40,000 animals are reportedly buried, including a Cairn terrier belonging to J. Edgar Hoover, a World War II mascot named Rags, and a dog from the popular television show of the 1930s and 1940s, *The Little Rascals*. Shapiro gave ownership to People for the Ethical Treatment of Animals (PETA) in the 1990s for a promise that they would maintain and preserve it. When the organization relocated from Maryland to Virginia, they helped Shapiro find another party to take over, but that arrangement has not worked out. The fate of what is considered the second-oldest pet cemetery in the country is still unknown.[40]

These types of problems do not stop people from assessing the need for animal burial grounds and opening other cemeteries. For instance, Jerry Groome, a retired Air Force fighter pilot with service in Vietnam, opened the St. Francis Pet Funeral and Cemetery in 1999 after working in the funeral business for more than thirty years and noticing that there were many requests from people who wanted funeral services for their companion animals, including embalming, obituaries in the paper, and visitation hours. Groome's cemetery is the only facility in North Carolina that provides "full-service funerals" for companions, and clients hail from across North Carolina, Virginia, South Carolina, and Georgia. Animal cemeteries require hard work, and he has tried to train apprentices, but they have not lasted long. One of the apprentices was overwhelmed by the grieving families, and left after three days. Another could not meet the physical demands of the job—dead animals are heavy, smell bad, and can be disfigured—and quit after four months. Groome perseveres, taking his responsibilities very seriously. "It's not something we should be judgmental about," he says. "If it's tragic to [guardians] and emotional to them, then it's our job as funeral directors to take care of their needs." The cemetery has nearly 5,000 grave sites, and 300 animals, primarily dogs with a smattering of ferrets, rabbits, and one horse, have been buried at a cost of between $500 for a basic service and $5,000 for a package that included a casket, a 100-year vault, and a graveside service.[41]

To meet the burgeoning need, some human cemeteries are becoming *pet friendly*, setting aside space in existing cemeteries for people's companion animals. For example, a cemetery in suburban Chicago has set aside a couple of its forty acres for guardians who want to be buried with their companion dog, cat, fish, or bird, and people inquire about two or three times a month. Since animals typically die first, they are buried about seven-and-a-half-feet deep. Then, the guardian can be buried one foot or so above them and still maintain the traditional depth for human burial. The cost of the dual plots exceeds those for humans only, which cost about $300.[42]

While burials are becoming more elaborate and common, cremations are really on the increase, mirroring a similar trend in human cremation. According to the Cremation Association of North America, 32 percent of people chose cremation for themselves or their family in 2005, compared with 17 percent in 1990. Comparable figures are not available for companion animal cremations, but directors of companion animal funeral homes estimate that cremations account for

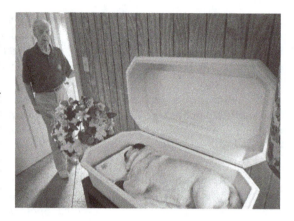

Clifford Neal, proprietor of Sugarloaf Pet Gardens, in Barnesville, MD, checks arrangements for Chuckie, a six-year-old pug he will bury. © 2005, *The Washington Post*. Photo by Bill O'Leary. Reprinted with permission.

80–90 percent of arrangements.[43] Cremations do not eliminate burials because cremains are typically buried, if not kept at home.

When my Grace died at the veterinarian's, they offered to have her cremated, and I accepted. Grief and guilt were searing my very being, and I was desperate to find a container to house Grace's ashes. The Internet is filled with shysters and frauds who will prey on bereaved animal guardians, but I had the great fortune to stumble across Ann Cheers and her husband, Jon Terry, artisans who not only provided a remarkable product, but also sincere and heartfelt emotional and spiritual support for my early, raw grief. They allowed me to participate in the design of the container for Grace's ashes, which ended up being a customized ceramic box. Jon poured his heart into making the container for Grace. In fact, it was so labor intensive that he no longer makes them. I am fortunate that he gave me a permanent and splendid manifestation of the love I shared with a completely unique creature, and he gave me a way to honor and memorialize our relationship forever. Through Cheers Pottery in Colorado, Ann and Jon provide the kind of urns and memorials that we all want to find for our animals—one-of-a-kind, handcrafted masterpieces perfectly suited to their lives.

Not everyone's idea is so well received and some seem designed to capitalize on the bereaved. Consider J. Hall, a taxidermist, who received hate e-mails after advertising what she called "pet pillows," cushions that "featured the skin of the animal on one side" and fabric on the other. People who ordered the pillows were required to freeze their animals in a double bag to prevent freezer burn and "hair slippage," and ship the corpse by overnight delivery to prevent further deterioration.[44] Not exactly the way most people want to treat the bodies of their beloved companion animals.

Modern technology sparks some creative ideas for memorials, such as LifeGem, diamonds created from the carbon of the cremains of any loved one, including a companion animal. Dean Vanden Biesen, LifeGem's cofounder reports, "Thirty-five percent of our business comes from people wanting to memorialize their pet." Diamonds range in size from less than a quarter of a carat to almost a full carat,

Potter Ann Cheers, of Cheers Pottery in Pagosa Springs, CO, works on a customized urn. Photo courtesy of Jonathan B. Terry. Used with permission.

in prices between $2,600 and $12,999. Other unique ideas include VIP Fibers, which will create a throw, scarf, or other keepsake from yarn spun from your dog's fur. Then, there are companies such as Perpetual Pet, which specialize in "freeze-drying" animals, as an alternative to conventional taxidermy. This is considered gruesome to many guardians, but the company dries up to one hundred animals a year at a cost of nearly $600 for an animal weighing up to twenty pounds.[45]

WHAT CAN WE DO TO MAKE THINGS BETTER?

The first and the most important action we can take is to create a foundation of acceptance, care, and support for bereaved guardians of companion animals, so they can process their grief as the natural human experience that it is. We must recognize the emotional significance of the bond they shared and give them permission to mourn and cope with what may be one of the most profound and traumatic experiences of their lives. Because the death of a companion animal is not fully recognized as a significant loss and the bereaved are exposed to disparaging, insensitive remarks, their trauma is exacerbated. We must begin to view the relationships, not as inferior, but as having value in and of themselves and understand that the bereaved may always have some level of sadness about the loss.

The grief response is so individual that it creates a challenge to researchers and mental health professionals alike. Yet, we need more research related to the grief experienced following the death or disappearance of a companion animal, especially the latter. "The grief surrounding a missing companion animal or one found dead is significant and affects people severely. It is one area in which health care and counseling professionals will be challenged to provide comprehensive assessment and intervention."[46] From research to practice, we need the experts in the field to guide right actions and appropriate thought. Veterinarians can take the lead by developing sensitive, bond-centered practices that attend to the medical needs of their patients (the animals) while showing compassion for the emotional needs of their clients (the human guardians). Veterinarians are in a position to recognize the valuable roles that animals play and to model behavior that demonstrates care and understanding. They can participate in and enable clinical and psychological research that feeds their own knowledge and can make their practices repositories of information for scientists and the public.

While you and I wait for breakthroughs from research and guidance from practitioners, we can take thoughtful steps, born of our humanity, to embrace those who grieve. We can use examples from our lives to guide us. For instance, as a member of a Greek social organization, I am encouraged to "lean on the shield." That means if I need help with a personal challenge, I can count on a sorority member to honor the oath we took in front of our sorority's shield, by offering help. Whether she understands my problem or not, she will support me in my time of need. She knows I will do the same for her. That is what we need to do for animal guardians; lean on the shield of love and compassion. We can understand grief as a manifestation of the human condition and reach out to help another person who is hurting. Each of us has lost someone or something dear to us, and we know what that kind of hollowness feels like. Whether we have a companion animal or not, we can take some of the following steps to help the bereaved:

- Offer empathy and genuine feelings
- Talk and ask openly about the current loss
- Encourage the griever to talk and engage in emotional catharsis
- Encourage the grievers to slow their lives and take time to grieve
- Be there for grievers; offer help with everyday tasks
- Lend support and simple companionship
- Acknowledge and validate grievers
- Listen; be silent
- Offer therapeutic hugs.

Things that are not helpful are offering sympathy in the form of clichés; giving advice or reinterpreting the bereaved's beliefs; shifting conversations to yourself; scolding, lecturing, or giving pep talks; discounting the bereaved's thoughts and feelings; or encouraging them to get another pet or medicate their pain.[47]

9

Love Gone Bad

The worst sin towards our fellow creatures is not to hate them, but to be indifferent to them. That's the essence of inhumanity.

—George Bernard Shaw

Mercy to animals means mercy to mankind.

—Henry Bergh

As a society, we profess to care deeply for our companion animals, and most of our behaviors suggest that we love them and have their best interests at heart. Yet, other behaviors betray the relationships and violate the trust, loyalty, and devotion our animals give us. Cats and dogs are the primary victims of our betrayal, as evidenced by activities such as cruelty, overpopulation, puppy mills, cloning, and hoarding. Where is the love in those circumstances? We love them, I firmly believe that, but as the saying goes, we have a funny way of showing it. We feel the emotion, but the way we express it is the problem. "An act of love is not just telling a dog every morning that you love them," says Cesar Milan. "This is simply loving yourself. You are fulfilling your need to tell someone you love them. That is fulfilling a human need." Milan insists that the kind of love we give nurtures instability,[1] and he may be right given the number of failed relationships that end with dogs and cats relinquished to shelters across the country. Love, at least the way we demonstrate it to our companion animals, is not working well for them. One reason for bad outcomes, as Milan suggests, is that we care more about our needs than theirs. We try to turn our companion animals into little people who must look and behave as we wish. Then, when they cannot become the little people we want them to be, the love goes bad in many ways. I explained earlier that our inclination to anthropomorphize animals gave early humans an advantage over animals. It made us better hunters, who could "penetrate the mind of prey."[2] Our efforts to anthropomorphize our cats and dogs may have again turned them into a kind of prey, but instead of killing with weapons, we are loving them to death.

That is a strong statement, the first of many in this chapter, and a departure from previous chapters in which I took great care to strike a balance and maintain journalistic distance. I do not see much balance in the activities I discuss in this chapter; the scales are tipped against the animals, and I find no value in treading lightly. I am not interested in excusing what I consider bad human behavior. I want to bring these issues to your attention for what they are: irresponsible behaviors that in some cases border on evil. There is no delicate way to discuss the many perverse ways we lord over our companion animals, creating no end to their misery.

PUPPY MILLS–COMMERCIAL BREEDING

Evil: I cannot think of a more perfect description for a puppy mill, a hellish place where literally thousands of dogs are reared on a bastardized agricultural model. In spite of the shameful numbers of dogs and cats who are abandoned and homeless, we want more and more and more. Unscrupulous breeders, who care not about the future or integrity of a breed, but only their own financial futures, use ruthless, deplorable methods to mass-produce dogs. (Cats have been spared the horrors of commercial breeding imposed on dogs.) The exact number of puppy mills is not known because their owners often fail to register their operations, as is required by law. Estimates of more than 4,000 have been attributed to the Humane Society of the United States (HSUS), but the exact number will never be known.[3]

We may not know how many there are, but we know what they do, and Puppy Haven Kennel, which is north of Madison, WI, is typical of their sorry operations. It is a 1,600 "dog compound" that sells 3,000 puppies a year. Nearly 1,000 dogs at a time are housed in a series of long buildings, cordoned off by chain link fencing. One whelping house has 4,300 square feet filled with 400 dogs, most of them puppies, in 120 elevated cages. Fourteen employees, some part-time and family members, care for the animals. That means one person to care for around 115 puppies each day, if you *only* count the puppies. "I feel all dogs should be bred in a kennel just like mine," said the mill's owner, Wallace Haven. The man who speaks these words so proudly was suspended by the American Kennel Club for ten years for refusing kennel inspections. In fact, the U.S. Department of Agriculture (USDA) has repeatedly cited him for inadequate care. Despite these sanctions, his, like other puppy mills similarly cited, remains licensed—spewing out puppies despite the recurrent violations of the Animal Welfare Act—granted an impotent law that is further weakened by poor enforcement.[4] For example, Puppy Love Kennels in Lancaster County, PA, which is home to more commercial dog breeders than any other county in the United States, had so many consumer complaints (200) that it was the focus of a *20/20* investigation. Their cruelty is no secret. Yet, in spite of fines, they continue to breed: 1,968 puppies during a twelve-month period, ending February 2006.[5]

National and local organizations are working independently and collaboratively to strengthen or create laws that protect puppy mill puppies, but changing laws is a long and arduous process. Existing laws are typically weak, such as "lemon laws," that allow purchasers to return a puppy to a pet shop (where most puppy mill puppies are sold), but do nothing to protect the puppy. Sellers covered by a lemon law will simply offer you another puppy as a replacement. And, of course, you know what typically happens to the returned puppy. Nothing currently exists that either spares the puppy the suffering or spares the guardian the heartbreak and expense of trying to care for a sick puppy. Purveyors of commercially bred puppies rather replace the puppy because they know they would go broke trying to provide veterinary care. Their puppies are some of the sickest puppies you will encounter, the innocent victims of many illnesses and diseases, some of which do not manifest for years. Reports from undercover investigations and raids reveal a disturbing picture. A senior investigative reporter at a Wisconsin television station reported that dogs purchased from Puppy Haven had conditions such as canine herpes, kennel cough, parasites, and bacterial infections. The report included a pug-beagle mix puppy whose foot had been chewed off by his mother. "That comes from having puppies in a stressful situation, and they don't know what they are doing, and they will just gnaw," explained a rescuer.[6] As this book was going to press, a Tennessee puppy mill had been raided for the second time, freeing nearly 140 puppies, all small breeds (such as Yorkshire and Boston terriers, Maltese, and poodles), who were all in varying stages of medical decline, according to a report by the Best Friends Network. Nancy Green, the assistant director of the local humane society that took possession of the hapless puppies, said, "We're seeing skin infections, urine burns on newborn puppies, dental problems, and sore feet from standing on wire."[7] Adding insult to injury, puppies rescued from puppy mills remain the "property" of the owners, pending resolution of legal issues. This hampers anyone hoping to provide care or find them new homes, but local rescue organizations, bolstered by community volunteers and contributions, take responsibility for care and foster of the puppies.

Pennsylvania has the dubious distinction of being the "Puppy Mill Capital of the East Coast," because of the number of puppy mills in Lancaster County, PA. But the state's former Senator, Rick Santorum, tried to stem the tide, by introducing a bill, the Pet Animal Welfare Statute (PAWS), which called for persons who sell more than twenty-five dogs a year to submit to federal inspections or face stiff suspensions. The bill divided breeders and faced stiff opposition and ridicule.

In spite of the challenge, the only way to save puppies from the endless torture of commercial breeding it seems is to put the breeders out of business by curbing their profits with hefty fines. We have the power to curb their profits by not buying the puppies, but we refuse to admit the horrors of puppy mills. Worse yet, puppy mills have found another outlet for their puppies with the Internet.

It is not enough that dogs have to endure mass production, but now rabbits (as if they needed help reproducing) and birds are also the victims of mills. The avian equivalent of puppy mills provides most of the birds sold in large pet stores. As is the case with puppies in puppy mills, breeder birds are kept in small cages and are never handled or given any mental stimulation, which leads to neurotic behavior. Most bird mills wean chicks on cheap seed-only diets to save money, which can cause serious health problems and makes transitioning to a nutritious diet difficult. The birds can also develop behavioral problems, which puts them at risk for being surrendered by owners. Consequently, their presence in shelters and rescue organizations is increasing. Another practice in bird mills is the prophylactic use of antibiotics as a substitute for good sanitation. This can have terrible short-term and long-term effects on the birds. Critically, broad-spectrum antibiotics destroy the beneficial flora and fauna residing in birds, leaving them even more susceptible. The unnecessary use of the drugs can cause birds to develop resistance to antibiotics, making the drugs useless when the birds really need them.[8]

DESIGNER DOGS

The name suggests the problem: dogs who are designed. This practice is about control and manipulation to suit human whims and desires. Designer dogs are first-generation hybrids of two purebred species, blended to yield specific characteristics that are regarded as desirable. Labradoodles were the first popular hybrid, created to give other breeds the advantages of poodles' nonshedding, hypoallergenic coats. In the late 1980s, an Australian dog breeder, trying to make a guide dog for the blind crossed a poodle with a Labrador retriever. In 1998, he began exporting them to the United States for $2,500 each.

A canine geneticist, quoted in the *New York Times*, said that designer dogs were "a phenomenally good idea" because they are a way to eliminate some of the nearly 400 diseases and disorders to which dogs are prone. He added the caveat of IF—"if the breeding is done conscientiously." I do not see much chance of that happening. Regardless, there are more than enough dogs looking for homes now without adding to their numbers. Besides, high-priced designer dogs are not immune to abandonment. They end up in the shelter, looking just like every other homeless *mutt* that is there.

Wallace Haven is considered the person who created the puggle, more than twenty years ago. I am not sure why he chose the pug and beagle as his first hybridization, but he has since created thirty-five other hybrid breeds. He now gives the dogs what he considers clever names to disguise their combinations and discourage others from copying his combinations. Too late, the evil secret is out. In fact, the American Canine Hybrid Club is about to recognize its 400th purebred-to-purebred cross. Hybrid breeds are about to surpass the established 400 pure breeds of dogs now known. The American Kennel Club is not likely to be impressed with any of them any time soon, given they have only recognized 155 breeds of dogs during their 123-year history.

Hybrids do not breed true and designer dogs must be bred from "scratch to keep from getting a hodgepodge of characteristics."[9] Bob Vetere of the American Pet Products Manufacturers Association (APPMA) is quoted as saying that purists consider what these breeders do as "voodoo science." What little I remember from college zoology tells me that not each of the hybrid puppies in a litter will display the desired characteristics, and I wonder what happens to the *rejects*. Whenever

I read about hybrid, designer dogs, I am reminded of Dr. Moreau, a fictional character who wrecked havoc trying to convert animals into something they were not intended to be. He is introduced in H. G. Wells' 1896 novel, *The Island of Dr. Moreau,* and vividly portrayed in at least two modern film adaptations. Moreau got what he deserved for messing with Mother Nature.

The *New York Times* article posed a profound question: "To what extent are these new mutts a remedy for what's wrong with our old dogs and to what extent are they a symptom of what's wrong with us?"[10] You can probably guess that answer. Another question, taken from the Steven Spielberg movie *Jurassic Park,* sums up my thoughts on designer dogs: "Just because we can do something, should we?"

DESIGNER CATS

Allerca, a small biotech company in San Diego, CA, proudly announced in 2006 that it was ready to deliver a hypoallergenic cat, which it calls "lifestyle pets." Eager American customers would have to wait twelve to fifteen months, (longer in Europe) and pass a "finicky screening test" before paying $4,000 for one of the cats. Company CEO, Megan Young, said, "You're not buying a cat; it's a medical device that replaces shots and pills." She was quick to add, "At the same time, this is a living animal, so the well-being of our product comes before our customers." Each kitten is neutered at between ten to twelve weeks of age to prevent feline overpopulation, according to Allerca. The motive behind the sterilizations may not be completely altruistic because "each kitten carries the dominant hypoallergenic gene, and in theory could produce other hypoallergenic kittens."[11]

CLONING

Cloning is another variation on the theme of control and manipulation, and seems particularly foolish when we have too many companion animals now to care for properly. The South Koreans were the first to clone a dog, and they named him Snuppy for "Seoul National University Puppy." It took 123 dogs to clone one puppy, who started life as an embryo in a Petri dish after scientists took a cell from the donor (the animal to be duplicated), an Afghan, and fused it with a surgically acquired egg from which they had removed the original DNA. The cell was then transplanted into dogs who acted as surrogates. Three of the 123 surrogates became pregnant, but one miscarried, and one delivered a newborn who died of pneumonia, which is considered an "inexplicable fate of young cloned mammals." Mary Beth Sweetland, a vice president of People for the Ethical Treatment of Animals (PETA), made a profound point when she said, "The cruelty and body count outweighs any benefit that can be gained from this."[12]

Scientists outside of Milan, Italy cloned a foal, Prometea, from the "skin cell of an adult mare that was fused with an empty equine egg." Cesare Galli, Prometea's creator, is quoted as saying he is delighted with his achievement and believes it could have major implications for horse racing. He said, "You could have a race full of clones of the greatest racehorses competing against each other." He adds it could also perpetuate "the sporting success of male show and jump horses," who are castrated at an early age.[13] All I can say is that these are lofty scientific goals.

A business venture, Genetic Savings & Clone, has emerged to sell cloned animals to people who want to replace deceased companion animals. In 2004, five customers paid $50,000 each for a copy of their cat. The company intends to make cloning more accessible with projected costs reduced to $10,000 for a cat and $20,000 for a dog, and anticipates cloning thousands of companion animals a year. Lou Hawthrone, company CEO, admits that the company produces newborn animals, not full-grown exact replicas: "In terms of genetics you are getting the same animal back, but not in terms of consciousness. Personality-wise there are differences."[14] So, buyer beware! I suggest you become familiar with "nature-nurture" theories from high school science before you consider cloning a beloved animal.

HOARDERS

Collecting, as hoarding was once known, is "cruelty masquerading as compassion." People who have more animals than they can realistically care for—such that they and the animals end up living in unsanitary, unsafe conditions—are considered hoarders. Although animal hoarding does not appear in diagnostic manuals for mental illnesses, it may, in fact, be associated with obsessive compulsive disorders (also referred to as OCD).[15] The first comprehensive study of hoarding found many similarities among the 2,000 cases of animal hoarding reported annually. "The interaction between an animal and a person just adds a level of intensity that doesn't exist with a pile of newspapers," said Dr. Gary Petronek.[16] Most of the subjects in the study also met criteria for self-neglect. Moreover, if family were in the home, they were usually neglected, too, if not abused. Study results do not accurately capture the "extreme lack of sanitation and toxic atmosphere" that is found in the homes of hoarders. Following is a description from a typical case: "Household interiors were coated, often several inches high, with human and animal urine and feces, sometimes to an extent that the floor buckled." The majority of hoarders in this study were women and most were single, widowed, or divorced, with a median age of fifty-five years, and nearly half were employed, some in professions such as teaching. Researchers found that cats were the most hoarded animal, followed by dogs, birds, reptiles, small mammals, and horses. Despite the obvious human health and safety issues, relevant health agencies had sometimes abandoned the cases because they could not establish mental incompetence. The first successful intervention was usually carried out either by animal control or a rescue group, to save the animals.[17]

People who hoard animals sometimes say they are trying to protect them. Unfortunately, they are unable to control their perverse desire to accumulate the animals. In the absence of even the most basic care, the animals usually suffer from neglect, and die. Hoarders seem unable to comprehend the dangerous conditions they create for the animals. Many states are grappling with establishing laws that make animal hoarding a crime, with stipulations that the convicted hoarders get psychological treatment. Regrettably, the repeat rate for animal hoarders is 100 percent by some calculations.[18]

OVERPOPULATION

Companion overpopulation, commonly referred to as "pet overpopulation," is a human-animal bond crisis—a shameful embarrassment of our own making that we ignore and perpetuate. This crisis and our response to it are sad commentaries on humanity, in general, and our American society specifically. The world does not need more companion animals, and our efforts to create more in so many bizarre ways are foolish. We do not take proper care of the ones who are alive now. In spite of our negligence, we continue to increase their numbers, knowing that the majority will suffer and die, or merely exist, deprived of basic needs. If this is how we treat the animals who live only to love us, we demonstrate our depravity. I cannot comprehend that we "pick one and kiss the others goodbye," an early slogan for a national pet overpopulation campaign. The truth is that countless millions of domesticated companion animals are homeless, abandoned, and living precariously in pounds and shelters. How did this happen to our best friends? For one thing, unchecked, cats and dogs can breed and multiply at staggering rates, producing thousands of new animals *daily*. For example, according to the Humane Society of the United States (HSUS), a single female cat can have three litters a year producing an average of five kittens per litter. In just seven years, she and her offspring can produce 420,000 cats. In just six years, one female dog and her offspring can produce 67,000 puppies.

Commercial breeders add to the problem, with 25 percent of puppy mill dogs ending up in shelters. Both purebred and mixes end up in the shelters, but the animal shelter is not where people look who are interested in particular breeds. Tragically, every animal purchased from a breeder represents one less home for a shelter animal. As long as the animals keep coming, we will never find homes for them all. That is a stark truth, which is often denied. Far more animals are being born every year than can be placed in homes. If everyone in America adopted just one dog, for example, a surplus would still exist. I read that each person would have to adopt seven dogs to take care of what we have now, and they keep coming. The only reasonable solution is to change people's attitudes, especially about spay, neuter, and surrender. Preventing surrender would take care of 30 percent of companion animals who are considered disposable and relinquished to shelters. We must stop thinking of companion animals as something easily left behind or dropped off when life gets tough. As you read, we treat our companion animals like children according to most experts, but not in this respect. I am not suggesting that we must treat them as children, but I believe we have a moral obligation to provide permanent homes for them.

Companion animals are profoundly helpless to help themselves. They are dependent upon us, and if we refuse to satisfy our moral obligation to them, then legal mandates seem appropriate. Given that many people in our society are also suffering, from issues such as inadequate health care, unemployment, and poverty—and we are slow to institute measures that can really help even other people—I doubt that *pets* will ever be a priority. Yet, we have the knowledge and ability to implement measures that could immediately curtail and eventually eliminate the suffering of animals. Yes, the measures would be considered drastic if we were talking about people, but we are not, and we are the source of the suffering. None of the measures are popular, and they will never get approval, but I see no other way out of this *pet* overpopulation crisis. First of all, a temporary ban on commercial breeders would go a long way to ending overpopulation. Second, obligatory spay and neuter for all companion animals (as opposed to show-dogs) would stem the tide. A portion of the funds from fines for abuse and breeding violations could be directed to low-cost programs for people in need. Third, if that does not suffice, then a moratorium on all breeding for a number of years, calculated by how long it would take to clear the shelters, should be considered. Until the population crisis is over, breeds in danger of becoming extinct during the moratorium could be bred by a few licensed breeders. Or, we could put some of the science to use to preserve cells and reproductive material for later use to ensure continuation of current, recognized breeds. I warned you that you would not like my proposal, but I have a right to dream. At the very least, a temporary federally mandated (and subsidized) spay and neuter program seems reasonable— and achievable, if we would face up to what we have done and take responsibility for ending the suffering caused by the crisis of too many companion animals.

SHELTERS

The companion animal crisis spills into our municipal and private shelters, both of which are supplemented by private, volunteer rescue organizations. Most stray and abandoned animals who end up in the shelters across the country are on borrowed time. Animal shelters are underfunded and staffed by weary and overworked, but primarily caring and compassionate people, who are doing society's dirty work: cleaning up behind our fickleness and irresponsibility. I have heard informed people scoff at the term "shelter" because the facilities are not harbors of safety for discarded companion animals, but killing factories. In fact "pound," the legal term in many municipalities, is becoming a frequently used term for public facilities that *impound* and house unwanted and abandoned companion animals because the word does not euphemize what is really happening in shelters. According to the *Oxford American Dictionary*, pound was originally used to refer to an enclosure for cattle, but an animal control officer told me years ago that the usage came about because early in our country's history, unscrupulous people who ran the facilities sold dogs by the pound for research. Pound-seizure is how we now refer to the sale or release of cats and dogs from a pound for research, and it is a dirty little secret about what happens to abandoned and lost companion animals. I was shocked to discover that "three states—Minnesota, Oklahoma, and Utah—still legally require that publicly funded shelters/pounds provide dogs and/or cats to institutions for experimental or educational purposes, and other states allow it. Several states have no law either way."[19]

The HSUS estimates that 6–8 million animals enter a shelter annually, but I have seen figures as high as 12 million. Every animal abandoned in the shelter "is the living embodiment of a broken bond of some sort . . . an emissary of some prior human entanglement."[20] Nothing and no one will ever convince me that the fault lies with the animal, no more so than child abuse is the fault of a child. We abandon animals because we fail them and do not know what else to do but get rid of our failures.

Facts back me up: studies suggest that about a third of people who relinquish dogs do so because of perceived behavioral problems. Problems which are frequently based on unrealistic expectations, particularly in young dogs under one year of age, who represent more than half of the surrenders. Puppies should not be expected to behave perfectly; they are babies. The most common behavioral problems reported are hyperactivity, housebreaking issues, biting, chewing when left alone, fearfulness, and barking. All pretty normal behavior for a puppy, except for the biting, which could be play biting interpreted as aggression. "People are attracted to young pets because they're so cute," said Dr. Sara Staats, professor of psychology at Ohio State University. "But young animals have a lot of energy and are rambunctious. Many people either don't have the skills or aren't willing to acquire the knowledge to give them proper training." Cats were most often (29 percent) relinquished because people move to a new house or apartment, often a place that will not accept the cat. Married people were found to relinquish more often than single people, which I found curious, but the theory is that the married people may have children and other responsibilities that conflict with responsibilities to the animal. Beyond behavioral problems, people in a study that Staats conducted[21] relinquished animals for the reasons given below and are consistent with other findings.[22] Her study included 130 people—56 with dogs and 73 with cats:

Dogs
- Dog takes too much time, work, or money (21 percent)
- Owner is moving (19 percent)
- Owner is ill or allergic to dogs (9 percent)
- Dog part of a new litter (5 percent)
- Dog is ill (4 percent)
- Other (12 percent)

Cats
- Owner is ill or allergic to cats (15 percent)
- Cat has behavior problems (14 percent)

- Cat part of new litter (13 percent)
- Cat takes too much time, work, or money (13 percent)
- Cat is ill (5 percent)
- Other (13 percent)

To compound problems, people are not completely honest about behavioral problems when they surrender their animals, probably fearing that the details will contribute to the animal being put to death.[23] Yet, an honest assessment of temperament can facilitate proper placement. It is not as if the animal is keeping a secret that will not be discovered. Honesty saves time in making assessments, gives shelter volunteers and staff insight into what is required for rehabilitation, and would enhance the adopter's comfort with using the shelters. A broad array of experts including psychologists, veterinarians, dog trainers, and experienced shelter staff and volunteers are trying to identify and implement strategies for increasing adoption rates at shelters. Studies show that animals, dogs in particular, form fast attachments[24] and can be easily integrated into new homes. They may be wounded souls, but they are not beyond needing and seeking companionship, even in that artificial environment. Some shelters employ behavior assessment tests with mixed results. The practice is well-meaning, but the conditions are so stressful that I believe it is impossible to predict suitability,[25] and some assessments are too subjective and restrictive. Innovative ideas to calm animals include piped music and pheromone diffusers.[26]

Kill Versus No-kill

Many people agonize over the millions of companion animals who are killed daily and believe as I do that every animal deserves a loving, permanent home. It has been suggested that shelters take on a no-kill philosophy, taking all comers and caring for them until that permanent home is found. The most widely accepted definition of a no-kill shelter is a place where all adoptable and treatable animals are saved and where only unadoptable, terminally ill, or severely injured animals are euthanized. The keyword in the previous sentence is "adoptable." Critics of no-kill shelters say they are a sham because they simply do not accept animals that cannot be easily rehomed. They have the luxury of being selective, whereas public facilities are obligated by law to accept any animal.

Most nonprofit no-kill shelters operate on funds from donations and fund-raising projects, work closely with rescue organizations, and are able to try innovative programs to reduce the number of stray animals in the community. Many no-kill shelters keep waiting lists so that needy animals can get in as soon as space is available. San Francisco took a bold step in 1994, becoming the first city to reject killing in the name of population control, when the city's Society for the Prevention of Cruelty to Animals (SPCA) and its Animal Care and Control Agency formed a partnership to stop killing cats and dogs, a practice that had prevailed for more than a century.[27] The debate over kill versus no-kill is ongoing with some surprising perspectives. For instance, PETA has come out against no-kill shelters saying the animals are basically being warehoused, which can lead to greater cruelty. Kim Intino of the HSUS expressed a similar sentiment, saying, "If they're not being adopted and they're not being euthanized, they're just sitting there. I've visited shelters where the animals have been there upwards of a year or more."[28] Yet, stories abound of animals who seemed to languish in shelters, but finally found permanent, loving homes. Some situations are worse than death, but I am not sure waiting for a permanent home is one of them. Sometimes it may just take patience and time.

All the rhetoric may be hiding the real issue: It is cheaper to kill animals than to save them. Some municipalities are willing to put their money where their hearts are—at least where they are supposed to be. For example, when the Richmond SPCA became no-kill, its budget jumped from $1 million to $3 million, with $500,000 going to spay/neuter alone. Besides money, other components of successful no-kill shelters are time, leadership, and collaboration. Julie Morris, senior vice president for National Shelter Outreach at the American Society for the Prevention of Cruelty to Animals (ASPCA) said, in 2003, that success is a "matter of dedicating to homeless animals the same respect and resources we devote to pets."[29]

Shelters that have a no-kill philosophy are often more successful than traditional shelters because people are attracted to them. For instance, volunteers often flock to no-kill shelters because it is easier to work with a dog if you know the end result is a chance at a good life, not euthanasia. And quite frankly potential adopters feel comfortable that they are not condemning to death the animals they consider, but cannot adopt. I believe people avoid traditional shelters sometimes because of the guilt associated with walking down "death row." The phrase that I mentioned earlier of "pick one and kiss the others goodbye," becomes very salient when you are in the shelter. No-kill shelters enjoy other benefits and advantages such as improved staff morale, greater community support, and wider funding sources.[30]

EUTHANASIA

With the exception of the states that allow pound seizure, once an animal goes in the shelter door, there are only three ways out: (1) adoption; (2) rescue; and (3) euthanasia. Death by euthanasia is the way most animals get out. The word "euthanasia" has Greek origins from *eu* for "well" and *thanatos* for "death," loosely translated as a good death or an easy and painless death. As much as we would like to believe it, death by euthanasia is not always good. An injection of sodium pentobarbital is the preferred agent of death because it is considered the most "humane, safest, least stressful," according to guidelines from HSUS.

Many years ago, as a young, naïve, idealistic shelter volunteer, I chose to work in the pre-euthanasia room, sure that I could console the animals, and give them a few moments of comfort before they were killed. Based on what I saw, I do not think an easy death is possible in the shelter. Anyone who thinks these animals do not know what is going to happen to them—that they cannot either sense their impending death, discern the death of those who have gone before them, smell the chemical agents of death, or *something portentous*—are deluding themselves. The animals I saw were beyond consoling, with pupils dilated and bodies stiff or trembling. A shelter worker's report, in a recent article, concurred with my experience. She said that animals would start to vomit or soil themselves the moment they enter the euthanasia room.[31] The shelter where I volunteered used the injection, but many shelters still use gas chambers, and I have heard stories of pounds in rural areas where dogs are shot; or worse is done. The sad fact is that most animals who are euthanized are very fine companions or could become so with very little time and effort.

Euthanasia is generally accepted as a means to end suffering, and some people think that suffering includes sitting in a cage for too long, waiting for a new home. Some people believe that euthanasia is better than some of the homes available to shelter animals, and that we delude ourselves that good homes can be found. They believe euthanasia is the best and most certain way to end suffering. A shelter supervisor told my friend Leslie (profiled in the previous chapter) that she did not worry about the animals she euthanized; she worried about the ones who were adopted. Now, that is delusional thinking.

Corinne Dowling devotes herself to easing the stress of dogs on death row, with Give a Dog a Bone, which she founded in 1999. She works with dogs in long-term custody, secondary to legal cases, and "on dark days her work requires her to escort an animal to its death." She believes they deserve a good day, even if it is their last, and she gives them toys, cradles them in her arms, and lathers her fingers with creme cheese as the needle goes in.[32]

The following example demonstrates what I suspected: that most people do not want to think about euthanasia and prefer remaining ignorant of what it involves. In September 2005, the *South Bend Tribune* ran a story that included a picture of a dog being euthanized and received so many letters from outraged readers that the paper issued a special section to print them. A sampling follows: "This is the most offensive and unnecessary article and accompanying pictures I have read. I am aware that some cats and dogs are euthanized, but I do not expect to read about it and see it in the paper!" "I did not need to know the details of how the cats are euthanized and what they go through before they actually die." "I cannot get the picture out of my mind. It is a shame that people treat their animals so poorly that this has to happen. In the future please don't show it being done."[33] Ignorance may be bliss for us, but not for the thousands of animals killed daily across the country.

Euthanasia statistics in some locales are mind-boggling. In California, for instance, 500,000 animals are killed each year. Animal control agencies in Greater Los Angeles killed more animals in 2005 than any metropolitan city in the United States—104,841 total: 35,000 dogs, 55,000 cats, plus other small animals such as rabbits, chickens, snakes, and guinea pigs.[34] In response, a California legislator has proposed a controversial mandatory sterilization bill, which would be the most comprehensive law of its kind in the country, if it passes. The bill would require guardians to spay or neuter their dogs and cats by the time they are four-months-old or face a $500 fine. Twenty-five states require spay or neuter for cats and dogs adopted from shelters, and in 2006, Rhode Island passed a law requiring sterilization of cats by the time they are six months of age.[35]

People deny the necessity of spay and neuter, but the procedures save lives and locales that offer low-cost procedures show impressive results, such as Asheville, NC, where the Humane Alliance performs 22,000 sterilizations annually, and is considered the "gold standard for low-cost, high-volume procedures." The euthanasia rate in the Asheville area has been reduced by 72 percent since the program began. Contraceptives, a low cost alternative to surgery, are in limited use in Europe and Australia, and could be available in the United States by 2008 for male dogs.[36] (This option should help men who cannot bear to have the procedures done on their male dogs, as if to do so damages their own virility.)

Studies show that shelter staff are part of the collateral damage associated with euthanasia because thousands of workers across the country, whose job is to kill animals, suffer immensely. These workers are often differentiated from the other shelter staff, and the welfare community at large. Their being involved in euthanasia essentially separates them from workers in other departments.[37] The stress and strain associated with performing euthanasia is prevalent, affecting even experienced staff, who never become accustomed to its psychological consequences. Results of a study show that the staff involved in euthanasia have increased job stress, work-to-family conflict, somatic complaints, and substance use, along with low job satisfaction. Euthanasia work affects the worker's overall well-being. Workers say they feel angry, sad, guilty, and disgusted. They also find it hard to detach from the animals and to conceal their negative feelings.[38]

Public scorn compounds the stress, contributing to compassion fatigue, a type of burnout that is secondary to traumatic stress. Euthanasia workers report having nightmares, as did April Primus, who dreamed that her own beloved animals were being killed by lethal injection. Others report "depression, suicidal thoughts and fears of going to hell." Steven Szot recounted a dog that licked his face as the needle was going in—an experience that haunted him for days. His supervisors removed him from euthanasia duties, observing that he cried afterward. He said his stress level plummeted when he moved to a "limited-admission or 'no-kill' shelter."[39]

ANIMAL CRUELTY

We commit the most heinous acts of violent cruelty on our companion animals, a form of social degeneracy.[40] Worse yet, in spite of the exalted position that companion animals hold in our society, our laws do not bring to justice those who perpetrate what can only be called crimes. Like children who are the victims of domestic violence, animals cannot effectively defend themselves (in most cases), cannot understand why they are being hurt or terrorized, and cannot seek outside help on their own behalf.[41] Animal cruelty is a complex crime requiring cross-disciplinary attention. For example, law enforcement and animal control officers need to (1) work together; (2) be aware of the signs of animal abuse; and (3) and educate prosecutors to the seriousness and implications of these crimes.[42] According to the ASPCA, our nation's historical expert on animal cruelty, abuse is nothing new. It has been documented as far back as the 1700s, when it was portrayed in a woodcut that showed a character who begins abusing dogs in the school yard, progresses to other crimes, and finally, is executed for murdering his lover. In the United States a concerted effort to protect animals was begun in 1866 when Henry Burgher founded the ASPCA.[43] Recently, correlations between animal cruelty and violence against humans are legendary.[44]

I do not recount graphic examples of cruelty in the following section to offend you. Yet, you may not be familiar with some of the macabre things people do to companion animals, their own animals and animals belonging to others. We cannot turn our faces; we must acknowledge that animal cruelty occurs and work to change the laws so that helpless creatures are protected and that people who perform these despicable acts get the treatment (medical and judicial) they deserve. I believe we should care about animal abuse for the sake of the animals alone, but research has shown that violence toward animals is associated with and is an indicator of violence toward people. If the violence is not happening simultaneously, it is just a matter of time before people who torture and maim animals will do the same against humans. In spite of this proven connection, we do little to save ourselves or the animals from these sociopaths. No breed of animal is safe, as you will see.

- Two teenagers (ages seventeen and nineteen) are accused of duct-tapping a puppy's snout and paws and cooking the animal alive in an oven. They showed the dead puppy to children, whom they also threatened to kill if they reported the crime.[45]
- A woman in Utah wired shut the mouth of her chocolate Labrador puppy to stop him from barking.[46]
- Armed bandits stole a Yorkshire terrier named Princess at gunpoint from a couple in the lobby of an apartment building and strangled the dog as they fled.[47]
- In a case that attracted attention from animal advocates from around the world, a Northern Virginia man stomped to death his girlfriend's declawed, fourteen-year-old arthritic cat, who he said was trying to bite his leg. He received a three-year suspended sentence and five years probation, during which he could not have an animal, had to "maintain steady employment and a stable living situation," and had to "undergo a mental health evaluation." His girlfriend expressed pleasure that the man did not receive jail time.[48]
- Demonstrating (as I said) that no animal is safe, police arrested an eighteen-year-old for stealing a family's twenty-five-year-old, forty-two-pound tortoise, Bob. He was accused of hacking Bob's shell, apparently trying to pry it open. The turtle's

hind legs were also badly cut, a toe was cut off, his neck was slashed, and his shell was punctured with a sharp object. The tortoise, who had encouraged the family's six-year-old autistic son, William, to speak, had roamed the backyard in peace. After the incident, he was moved to a turtle sanctuary following three days of intensive care that included tubal feeding.

- As this book was going to press, a federal grand jury indicted a prominent, popular National Football League (NFL) player, alleging that he actively participated in dogfighting, including executing dogs who did not perform well.[49]

This high profile case mentioned last may expose dog fighting for the insidious, underground organized crime that it is. The blood sport is completely illegal in the United States, and has reached epidemic proportions in all urban communities and is thriving in many rural areas, too. Dog fighting exposes children to an atrocious violence where puppies are frequently used as bait or to train the fighters. Dog fighting is often associated with gambling or drug trafficking.[50] Anyone confused about whether dog fighting is animal cruelty need only become familiar with the HSUS fact sheet on dogfighting, which says, "The injuries inflicted and sustained by dogs participating in dogfights are frequently severe, even fatal. Dogs used in these events often die of blood loss, shock, dehydration, exhaustion, or infection, hours or even days after the fight. Some owners train their dogs for fights using smaller animals such as cats, rabbits, or small dogs. These 'bait' animals are often stolen pets or animals obtained through 'free to good home' advertisements."[51]

Proper arrest, conviction, and punishment will go a long way in preventing animal cruelty—now, animal cruelty is just too easy to get away with. At the end of 2004, forty-one states and the District of Columbia had felony animal cruelty laws, an increase from only four in 1990. Despite this progress and a growing recognition of the gravity of animal cruelty, it is too often viewed as a secondary offense, and many cases never reach the courts. Overworked prosecutors are not able to give animal cruelty a priority in the face of heavy caseloads that include equally violent or more serious offenses against human victims. To make matters worse, when cases are prosecuted successfully, judges often do not impose sentences commensurate with the crime because they do not appreciate the significance of the crime and the risk to the community.[52]

EXOTICS–LOVE GONE WRONG

Exotic animals—certain birds, lions, tigers, wolves, bears, reptiles, and non-human primates—belong in their natural habitat and not in the hands of private individuals as *pets*. By their very nature, these animals are wild and potentially dangerous and, as such, do not adjust well to a captive environment.[53] "A wild animal is like a loaded gun—it can go off at any time," said Jack Hanna, the host of *Jack Hanna's Animal Adventure* and director emeritus of the Columbus (OH) Zoo. But, he added, it's not that the animals are inherently dangerous, but the way they may react around humans. "It's only using the defenses that God gave it," said Hanna.[54]

We also face the danger of zoonotic diseases because most wildlife arrive in the United States with no quarantine and minimal screening for disease. The government employs just 120 full-time inspectors to record and inspect incoming wildlife. There is no requirement that the inspectors be trained to detect diseases.[55]

The allure of exotic animals is strengthened by movies such as *Duma*, which chronicles the relationship between a young South African boy and an orphaned cheetah cub, whom he names Duma, Swahili for cheetah. The bond they share is romanticized as only Hollywood can, as the two travel hundreds of miles across South Africa to return the cheetah to his natural habitat. It is difficult to resist the compelling story and the beautiful panoramas of Africa, but the real message of the movie is one that we ignore: "Duma has to live the life he was born to—or he'll never be fully alive."

Animals caught in the wild to become companion animals begin to suffer from the moment the capture begins. Capture involves being torn from their families in violent, brutal ways, many die immediately—collateral damage—while others die en route to pet stores. Those that make it to stores, get the privilege of living abbreviated, unnatural lives, often dying from inappropriate care, given by humans ignorant of their needs.

I find the stories of exotic animal abuse particularly heartbreaking because we have no business bringing them into our environment. One morning I watched a news report of two young men in Michigan who brought their pet alligator to a PetSmart, MI. The newscasters made light of the story, bantering with questions about whether the police handcuffed the alligator before they took it or if the young men brought the alligator to the store to pick out a favorite toy. I was not amused watching the store personnel try to subdue the animal and close it in a Rubbermaid container. The young men were ignorant to the danger of having an alligator, as evidenced by a dismissive statement to the effect of, "A dog's teeth are bigger than his teeth."[56]

While researching this book, I read about poor little Cleo, described as a cute, cuddly cougar cub, whose *owners* had put a harness on her to walk. But Cleo grew, and they could not handle her enough to remove the tiny harness that became completely embedded in her skin, threatening to crush her ribs. When Big Cat Rescue founder, Carole Baskin, was called in, she found Cleo too malnourished to survive the anesthesia required to remove the harness. Baskin said the cat seemed to sense her predicament and would allow Baskin to cut away with a razor the harness and the skin that had grown around it. Cleo would growl and hiss in pain and walk away when she could take no more, but she never attacked the person trying to help her.[57]

In response to concern for exotic animals' welfare and the public health risks associated with keeping exotic animals as pets, citizens and animal protection organizations have made a concerted effort to seek support from legislators to make keeping exotics illegal or to regulate the practice heavily. As of 2005, fifteen states prohibited keeping dangerous exotic animals, and nine have partial bans on exotic animals. Unfortunately, thirteen states have no license or permit requirements, but an equal number requires a permit through a relevant state agency.[58]

WHAT ARE WE DOING AND WHERE ARE WE GOING

We domesticated the most popular companion animals to serve us. Lately, we ask that the service take the form of being, in essence, "little people, animated worry beads, and stress absorbers: to undertake jobs that engage their loyalty— sometimes to the point of exhaustion."[59] On the surface the relationships that we have with companion animals appear to benefit them, but they always serve at our pleasure. In the majority of relationships, our needs come first, and we are not above any form of manipulation to get the results we want. Consequently, we have an increasing number of animals, especially dogs—our best friends—who have behavioral problems that precipitate them getting put out and put down. Katherine Grier said, "The dogness of a dog has become problematic. We want an animal, that is, in some respects, not really an animal. You'd never have to take it out. It doesn't shed. It doesn't bark. It doesn't do a lot of stuff."[60]

When we cannot change them by breeding, we clone the ones we think are perfect. When that does not work, we create gadgets to deal with them. We can take care of our dogs with timed, refrigerated feeders and water fountains, monitor them with web cams and console them while we are away with telephones attached to their collars. The pet products industry has just about every conceivable tool to allow us to have our freedom and the dog, too.

I will ask again: Just because you can do something, does it mean you should? No. We must take responsibility for our role in these relationships and show some compassion and caring. Dr. Leo Bustad, a pioneer in human-animal bond theory and application, cofounder and first chair of the Delta Society, and dean emeritus of the Washington State University College of Veterinary Medicine, said, "We've ignored our inherent responsibilities. Responsibility has essentially faded from the contemporary scene." Bustad brings our attention to the quote of a fellow professor who said, "As things are now, it may well be that the survival of the species will depend on the ability to foster a boundless capacity for compassion." Bustad explained that "compassion is not merely a feeling or sentiment, but actively helping to relieve pain and suffering in others."[61] An awareness that all living beings are intertwined and dependent on each other fosters compassion and caring. The word "care" comes from the Gothic, *kara*, which means to lament, to grieve, to experience sorrow, or to cry out. The phrase "take care of" suggests "getting rid of a nuisance or removing a problem." Yet, caring, compassionate people touch hurt rather than offer solutions or advice.[62] There are no specialists in compassion, no Ph.D.s of compassion, Bustad says. These are not activities that can be delegated. "It is the responsibility of each of us," and "every human being possesses some measure of ability to care and to be compassionate."[63]

Can We Be "Fixed"?

Perhaps. More insight from research into the human-animal bond will foster enhanced appreciation, respect, and humane treatment of companion animals, while benefiting all nonhuman animals.

I made the point earlier (and demonstrated in the many studies I have discussed) that scientific investigations continue to provide the compelling evidence that we so often take for granted about animal behavior and our relationships with companion animals. Anthrozoology has a long and distinguished history, encompassing many fields of research, crossing various scientific boundaries, and drawing from a wide range of scientific disciplines. We can learn from our companion animals, if we would just pay attention. We need them as much, if not more, than they need us.

Anthrozoological research can enhance our appreciation for and understanding of the dazzling potential of our relationships with companion animals. Science is poised to reveal what some of us take for granted about our companion animals and what some of us have *known* for years—but more than any of us could have ever imagined.

Researchers will continue to prove that the human-companion animal bond has boundless power to improve our lives as humans, by improving our health, facilitating our interactions with one another, informing our self-knowledge, and making us better guardians—not just of the animals, but of the planet we all call home.

Assimilating this information is not going to be easy, and humans are slow to change their ways, even in the face of compelling evidence. Consider the stunning example that as recently as 1980, surgeons around the world performed surgery on human infants *without anesthesia*. You see, previously many babies had died from anesthesia overdoses, so "doctors gave babies large doses of muscle relaxants to paralyze them." No one believed that the babies were experiencing any kind of stress, according to K. J. S. Anand, a pediatrician who discovered that the post-surgery stress hormone levels for babies were triple that of adults, who had received anesthesia. He began a "quiet revolution" (proper use of anesthesia) that saved babies' lives. It is hard to fathom that we had a difficult time accepting that our own babies have real feelings based on their experiences. In fact, a sixteenth century authority is quoted as calling babies "a lower animal in human form." Imagine! Early medical communities thought the baby's brain was "too immature to comprehend" the pain.[64] If we are this blind, ignorant, and yes, stupid, when it comes to understanding and treating our own babies, I guess I should not be surprised at the slow progress in a better understanding and treatment of our companion animals. It has been long enough. Now is the time to remove the shroud from our consciousness. Biologist, Dr. Frans de Waal, coined the word "anthropodenial, to describe blindness to the human-like characteristics of other animals and to our own animal-like characteristics."[65] Somewhere between anthropodenial and anthropormophism the secrets may be discovered—there, I believe, the common ground is waiting to be discovered.

Domestication, for all its other aspects, is a story of domination. Our relationships with companion animals are born of submission and control.[66] The bond we have with them is powerful, but so is our dominion over the animals with whom we bond. Worse, we betray and break the bond constantly. The courageous and compassionate among us are striving to repair the fissures, to insure humane treatment and a full understanding and appreciation of our companion animals' lives, not for our sake, but for the sake of the animals.

The Rainbow Bridge is a term taken from an anonymous poem about a mythical place where companion animals who have died await their guardians. It is a place where the animals have plenty of "food, water, and sunshine," are "warm and comfortable," and are enjoying "health and vigor." Death should not be the prerequisite for those experiences; we owe them these things and more. We domesticated them to be our companions. They have upheld their part of the bargain; now is the time for us to uphold ours.

Series Afterword

As *Our Powerful Bond between People and Pets: Our Boundless Connection to Companion Animals* goes to print, one of the most high-profiled cases of animal abuse is making big headlines. The case reinforces the relevance of author Elizabeth Anderson's book for our contemporary times, as for all time. Popular football quarterback Michael Vick pled guilty in a federal case to illegal dogfighting, including executing dogs that did not perform well. The case evoked public outrage, and brought to light a long-held understanding of the soft place animals hold in a vast majority of people's hearts and loves.

In her book, Anderson explores every angle of this "human–animal bond" (HAB) in a way that both informs and fascinates. A journalist, Anderson provides a sound basis for her thesis about the role animals play in our lives—as rescuers, therapists, and matchmakers. She applies theories that professionals can appreciate, yet translates them in a reader-friendly style that everyone can understand and relate to. For example, she calls the powerful emotional bond as "oxygen for the psyche," and explains that the biological basis for animal interactions—known as "biophilia" and considered as part of an "evolutionary heritage"—really just means that "we are hard-wired for kinship with animals." Her explanation for HAB is appreciably multidimensional, including biological, social, and psychological levels, the latter based on attachment theories like that of Bowlby, and on theories of needs as defined by the field of self-psychology. The bond is even spiritual, based on what is called "cosmic destiny." At the bottom of it all, Anderson proposes, the bond is based on "love," which, as she says, is "hard to find and even harder to explain" despite the fact that we psychologists write about and research it.

Anderson's journalistic talent is even more evident in her story-telling, as she brings vividly to light stories like that of senior-citizen Craig Peel, who resisted evacuation during the Hurricane Katrina disaster rather than leave his eleven-year-old Lhasa apso, Sassy. Or we delight at the unselfish feats of animals like Bob, an eighty-pound Chow Lab dog who threw himself in front of an alligator to save a woman. Or we marvel at the uncanny talents of animals like Oscar, the cat with an ability to predict death by curling up to nursing home residents in their final hours, thereby alerting staff and family to their fate, or of Delta the dog who woke up barking and fussing to alert his owner of a diabetic seizure, thereby saving his owner's life. Dogs have also been found, Anderson tells us, to detect people with bladder cancer, as their keen sense of smell distinguishes normal urine from cancerous samples.

As a good journalist, Anderson also presents us with facts, like survey results—for example, that 75 percent of people with companion animals consider them a member of their family. Other surveys show that some people feel closer to their pets than people—something I was made keenly aware of when counseling couples on a Richard Bey TV show segment, where spouses were complaining that their mate cared more for their pet than for them. I especially recall a wife whose husband was so attached to his pet snake that she felt exceptionally ignored and jealous.

Readers of this book are also treated to fascinating research, like the findings of one study that 1,000 children four-to-six-years-old with a cat or dog at home were 30 percent less likely to suffer from headaches, nausea, vomiting, or diarrhea compared to children in homes without such companions. Studies on animal-assisted therapy have long shown that horseback riding is therapeutic for people with disabilities, helping them with posture, balance, and mobility. And new research keeps reinforcing the role of animals in health care, like that older people who stroke cats have lowered blood pressure.

What can explain the intense bond between pets and people? Cycle medalist Lance Armstrong spent $10,000 for his dog's open heart surgery. Even people who are not rich go to great lengths for their pet's health and well-being. The answer could lie in the brain, Anderson suggests, supporting her thesis about love as the basis for HAB by reporting research on the activity of the primitive (limbic) brain.

Readers cannot possibly resist being riveted by studies Anderson cites of matching pets to their owner's characteristics (for example, that women with long hair prefer dogs with floppy ears, likely because they match their self-image) or to their owner's personality. For example, investigators have found that male owners of horses were aggressive and dominant, while females were easy-going. Bird people were socially outgoing and expressive; turtle keepers were hardworking, religious, and upwardly mobile; while snake owners were unconventional. Cat people are not very extroverted and are more likely to live alone than dog lovers. With all that is said about how people and their dogs tend to look alike, I am fascinated as a researcher, that a version of the Interpersonal Adjective Scale—by the same designer who contributed to the development of the well-known Minnesota Multiphasic Personality Inventory—can indicate which dog is best for a person given his or her personality. For example, extroverted women are most compatible with dogs who are independent (Siberian Huskies and Samoyeds) or protective (Akitas and Rottweilers), and dominant men and women with steady and self-assured dogs (like Newfoundlands and Silky Terriers).

Research is even being conducted on the animal's traits, like about how lizards have different personalities. And cutting edge $30 million dollar research is mapping the genetic code of dogs, to identify the "Dog Genome" to understand DNA sequencing that makes a dog a dog.

Anderson's book is not only informative and compelling, but is also comprehensive. Chapters cover the history of the human-companion animal bond, treatment of pets in countries around the world (including the dire situation of street dogs in Greece), the role of pets in our lives (including as political image boosters, like terrier Bala was for President Franklin Roosevelt), the choice of pets, and animal rights movements and legal efforts. As the wife of a noted psychologist and CEO of the American Psychological Association, Anderson even offers wise advice about coping with the loss of a beloved pet. Such grief is personal, as Anderson describes her own devastation at the loss of her beloved dog Grace, and also her guilt about cremating another dear dog.

Anderson's serious approach to the human-companion animal bond is especially welcome in these days, not only when cases like NFL player Vick's animal abuse are uncovered and appropriately harshly treated, but when celebrities are using animals as a fashion statement. For example, the public is offended, not impressed, by starlet millionairess Paris Hilton who sports a new Chihuahua for her new outfits, and is photographed in magazines with the tiny pet under her arm, as if using it for a fashion accessory.

Anderson's credentials for writing this book are supported not just by her talent as a good story-teller or her scholarly exploration of the subject, but also as a social activist. As I write this, I am wearing the green t-shirt Anderson gave me, with a big black paw print on the front and the words "Psychology Volunteers4Animals.info (PV4A). The shirts were made as part of the effort to help animals victimized by Hurricanes Katrina and Rita—a project that took place at the annual convention of the American Psychological Association held in New Orleans as a deliberate assistance to the recovery. With similar social consciousness, Anderson points out the challenge of an Air Force Technical Sergeant, Jamie Deers, who was deployed to Iraq and who became very attached to her dog, trained to search for hidden bombs. Deers successfully contested laws refusing to allow dogs to be brought back to the home country.

Anderson makes a cogent case on behalf of animal welfare. It's a concern that my good friend, investigative journalist and animal rights activist Jane Velez-Mitchell continues to heighten my awareness about. A recent gift to me was nail polish made without any animal products. The issues have reached global concern, as evidenced by the fact that the World Society for the Protection of Animals hired a colleague of mine representing NGOs at the United Nations, to lobby governments, ministers, agencies, and even communities worldwide. Larry Roeder, a retired American diplomat, also cochairs a committee of experts from the Red Cross movement, the United Nations, and other international organizations trying to streamline animal welfare into disaster management plans. He told me that his job is particularly focused now on promoting and protecting the welfare of animals in developing countries, like Afghanistan, Argentina, Kenya, and Bangladesh, including horses and cattle as well as cats and dogs, who have been neglected either because of poverty or lack of education suffered by the people.

On reading Anderson's book, one cannot help but reflect on one's own connection to pets. In fact, the HAB is most evident in children, impacting their psychological growth, comfort, and education. My own memories evoked from reading Anderson's book include my aunt Maye's menagerie, including a monkey often perched on her shoulder. In my own family, our beloved Parakeet "Johnny Bird," who lived to a rare ripe old age of twelve (unusual for that species), amazingly enough learned to speak, as my mom painstakingly repeated to the bird, "Johnny bird, pretty girl," until much to our delight, the bird actually repeated the phrase. And I recall my fascination—and confusion—the occasion of waking up on the morning of an elementary school speech about hamsters, rushing downstairs to see our pet hamsters, only to find one stuffing what looked like worms into her mouth. They turned out to be not worms but babies who had been born during the night—a shock to us, considering that we thought we had bought two male hamsters. It was also a horror to my child mind and heart to hear someone suggest that she was actually eating them—the act intended to protect them in her pouch actually endangered their survival. Nor can I forget the trauma of everyone panicking at the blood pouring from my face when I was thrown from a horse at age eight, but how my insisting on getting back on the horse within a few days of recovering served as a powerful lesson about resilience (a popular concept addressed in psychology today, about "bouncing back").

My own childhood memories of our Johnny Bird's human-like phrase are supported by investigators who make a strong case for communication between animals and humans. When famed journalist Barbara Walters claimed that her dog clearly said "I love you," her report was championed by some and ridiculed by others. But Anderson presents some support for the real possibility—which I have long believed, given psychological research teaching gorillas to use human language. I was convinced early in my career as a radio talk show host, when I interviewed Penelope Smith, an expert in human–animal communication. As she explains in her books, *Animal Talk: Interspecies Telepathic Communication* and *Animals: Our Return to Wholeness*, people can learn to communicate mind-to-mind with animals, understand their animals' behavior better, and enhance their lives through such contact with other species. Smith's decades-long work and Anderson's book give credence to Walters' claim, and similar experiences of millions of pet owners and animal lovers. While the concept may seem New Age, or require expanded consciousness, science is gradually providing proof.

The HAB is not only part of my childhood but also my professional work. For example, in my many lectures about how singles can find love, and pointed out in my book, *The Complete Idiot's Guide to Dating*, I describe how one of the best ways to find love is to walk a dog! This is because strangers find it easier to talk to the dog than to a person who catches their eye. What you need to do, I advise, is to interpret anything that the person says to—or about—your dog ("Isn't your dog cute!") as really meant to apply to you. As another example, parents can use a pet's giving birth as a "teachable" moment to explain the facts of life and reproduction to their children, as kids often ask "how are babies born?" when their dog has puppies or a cat has kittens.

People often anthromorphize animals, bringing them to life, as if they were human. To prove this, we have only to look at the examples in popular culture where "Mister Ed" the horse talked. TV dogs Lassie and Rin Tin Tin were as real to us as people. It is also no mystery that the world mourned the tragic death of Australian "Crocodile Hunter" Steve Irvin and now adores his eight-year-old daughter Bindi carrying on his tradition. Nor is it surprising that millions of people have adored Geico's Gecko, the battery company's Energizer bunny, or Taco Bell's Chihuahua mascot in commercials. As the entire TV channel devoted to the species shows, we are indeed an "Animal Planet," and Anderson's book brings the dimensions of that fact delightfully and interestingly to light.

Judy Kuriansky, Ph.D.
Series Editor, Practical and Applied Psychology

Notes

INTRODUCTION

1. The American Pet Products Manufacturers Association (APPMA) is the nation's leading nonprofit trade organization for the pet industry. They have been tracking statistics for more than a decade. Each year, the organization conducts extensive research to gauge the size of the pet products industry. Unless otherwise stated, data in this chapter were found in the 2007–2008 APPMA *National Pet Owners Survey*.

2. Robert D. Putnam, *Bowling alone: The collapse and revival of American community* (New York: Simon and Shuster, 2001).

3. Ibid.

4. Ching-Ching Ni, Friends in need: Transients say pets offer companionship, unconditional love, and a bit of hope, *Los Angeles Times*, February 21, 1995.

5. Fletcher, a guide dog living in Auckland, New Zealand, was accused of being careless in the crosswalk and he was blamed for an accident involving his charge, Gillian Walker, a 43-year-old sports therapist who suffered several injuries (including a broken leg), when struck by a motorist. A judge later ruled in favor of Walker and Fletcher, saying that the driver caused the crash, http://www.dogsinthenews.com.

6. Dr. Serpell is chief of the section on Behavior and Human-Animal Interactions, professor of Humane Ethics and Animal Welfare, and Director of the Center for the Interaction of Animals and Society at the University of Pennsylvania School of Veterinary Medicine. He is one of the most prolific and respected investigators in the field of human-animal interactions, and he has published some of the most influential work in the area.

7. J. A. Serpell, *In the company of animals: A study of human-animal relationships* (Cambridge: Cambridge University Press, 1996), 126.

8. Caroline Knapp wrote the most engrossing and engaging autobiographical account of life with her dog, Lucy, in *Pack of two: The Intricate bond between people and pets*. Her book remains a standout in a crowded field of similar books. Lucy demonstrated that even one dog can fill your life with profound and unique benefits, which Knapp articulates better than anyone I have read. It is a joyful, uplifting book.

9. Edward O. Wilson, ed., *Biophilia*, reprint (Cambridge: Harvard University Press, 1986).

10. Meghan Daum, Animal passions: Watching out for sparrows, pets, turkeys, and the people who love them, *Los Angeles Times*, November 26, 2005.

CHAPTER 1

1. Linda P. Case, *The dog: It's behavior, nutrition & health* (Iowa State University Press, 1999), 3.

2. Mary Elizabeth Thurston, *Lost history of the canine race* (Kansas City: Andrews and McMeel), 122.

3. Harriet Greenwald, personal communication, July 14, 2007.

4. Australian Broadcasting Corporation, *Animal attraction* (February 10, 2001).

5. Capture myopathy is a stress-induced condition that often develops after restraint of wild animals. Stress causes anaerobic metabolism, which results in chemically stored energy, lactic acid and cramping, and muscle damage. Affected animals may die immediately from lactic acidosis. The clinical signs of capture myopathy include sudden death within twenty-four hours, depression, rapid shallow breathing, and failure to recover from anesthesia. Death can occur after several hours of symptoms, or from cardiac arrest. The animal may also appear to recover, but has heart damage and dies at the next stressful event. Capture myopathy can occur both during physical and chemical restraint. It occurs in most animals, but especially in ungulates (hoofed animals). It has been reported in birds and even fish. There is no treatment for capture myopathy, and therefore, prevention is critical. Excerpted from http://www.deer-library.com and http://www.merckvetmanual.com.

6. Susan Milius, Social cats: Science pokes under the sofa, bats around a few ideas, *Science News Online*, September 15 (2001), http://www.sciencenews.org/.

7. Animal, domesticated, in *Britannica Student Encyclopedia* (2005), http://www.britannica.com.

8. Pit bull is an unfortunate, broad, and confusing term used to describe several breeds of dogs with similar physical characteristics. The American Staffordshire terrier, the English bull terrier, the American bulldog, and the Perro de Presa Canario often fall under this appellation.

9. Johnny Johnson, Pit bulldog kills infant, *Daily Sentinel*, July 16, 2004.

10. J.A. Serpell, ed., *The domestic dog: It's evolution, behavior, and interactions with people* (Cambridge: Cambridge University Press, 1995), 15.

11. Marion Schwartz, *A history of dogs in the early America* (New Haven, CT: Yale University, 1997), 2.

12. Serpell, ed., The domestic dog: It's evolution, behavior, and interactions with people, 8.

13. Ibid., 10.

14. Rick Weiss, Who let the dogs in? And when? New studies ponder origins of pets' domestication, *Washington Post*, November 22, 2002.

15. Wolf origins: The evolution of the wolf, http://www.sdnhm.org/.

16. Weiss, Who let the dogs in? And when? New studies ponder origins of pets' domestication.

17. Sarah Ives, U.S. presidential pets: Then and now, *National Geographic News*, February 12, 2004, 5.

18. Schwartz, *A history of dogs in the early America*, 11.

19. Serpell, ed., *The domestic dog: It's evolution, behavior, and interactions with people*, 14.

20. J. A. Serpell, ed., Pet keeping and animal domestic: A reappraisal, in *The walking larder: Patterns of domestication, pastorialism and predation* (London: Unwin Hyman, 1989), 10–21.

21. Hazel Muir, Stone age cats made great pets, *New Scientist*, April 17, 2004.

22. Schwartz, *A history of dogs in the early America*, 2.

23. National History Museum, Los Angeles, CA (http:www/nhm.org).

24. Muir, Stone age cats made great pets, 13.

25. "Analysis: New evidence suggests humans may have domesticated cats more than 9,000 years ago," *All things considered*. National Public Radio, April 8, 2004.

26. Katherine C. Grier, *Pets in America: A history* (Chapel Hill: University of North Carolina Press, 2006), 192.

27. Ibid., 41.

28. Ibid., 39.

29. Ibid., 251.

30. Linton Weeks, Your next pet may not be fur in the future. Or could be a copy cat, *The Washington Post*, April 24, 2005.

31. A. Libin & E. Libin, Robotic psychology. In *Encyclopedia of Applied Psychology* (Oxford: Elsevier, 2004), 295–298.

32. A paraphrased quote from Thomas Edison printed on sweatshirts from North Carolina Network for animals, now known as North Carolina Justice for Animals. The original quote is, "Until we stop harming all other living beings, we are still savages."

33. The current member states of the EU are as follows: Italy, Luxemburg, the Netherlands, Germany, France, the United Kingdom, Spain, Portugal, Sweden, Greece, Austria, Belgium, Denmark, Finland, and Ireland (as of 2003).

34. The Convention is based on the *principle that pet animals should neither be abandoned, nor be caused unnecessary pain, suffering, or distress. It stipulates minimum standards to which national governments should give effect, with respect to pet animals kept in households, or in any establishment for trading or commercial breeding and boarding, or in animal sanctuaries. It also makes provision with respect to stray animals and humane education programs.* http://www.animallaw.info/.

35. http://www.pfma.com. (Pet Food Manufacturers Association)

36. Paul Clapham, Pets in transit, *Horticulture Week*, July/August 2005.

37. Tracy Wilkinson, Rome's pet ordinance has tails and tongues wagging, *Los Angeles Times*, November 9, 2005.

38. Christine Orr, Import of dog and cat fur to the EU, *Journal of Animal Welfare Law*, November 2005, 15–18.

39. David McNeill, Furtility rate, *South China Morning Post*, August 21, 2004.

40. Dog lovers mad over chihuahua thefts, *Daily Times* (Pakistan), http://dailytimes.com.pk/.

41. McNeill, Furtility rate.

42. A. L. Podberscek, Good to pet and eat: The consumption of cats and dogs in South Korea. Paper presented at the 14th Annual Conference of the International Society for Anthrozoology "Exploring Human–Animal Relationships," July 11–12, 2005.

43. Anthony Podberscek, personal communication, March 2, 2006.

44. Animal Welfare Institute, http://www.awionline.org.

CHAPTER 2

1. Linda Hines, Historical perspectives on the human-animal bond, *American Behavioral Scientist* 47(1) (2003).

2. James A. Serpell, *In the company of animals: A study of human–animal relationships* (Cambridge: Cambridge University Press, 1996), xvii.

3. http://www2.asanet.org/sectionanimals/.

4. http://www.animalsandsociety.org/.

5. http://www.anthrozoology.org.

6. Les Prix Nobel en 1973, Editor Wilhelm Odelberg [Nobel Foundation], Stockholm, 1974 (http://www.nobelprize.org).

7. Linda M. Hines, *American Behavioral Scientist* 47(1) (September 2003), 7–15.

8. Leslie Irvine, *If you tame me* (Philadelphia, PA: Temple University Press, 2004), 18–29.

9. Edward O. Wilson, ed., *Biophilia*, reprint (Cambridge: Harvard University Press, 1986).

10. Irvine, *If you tame me.*

11. Sue-Ellen Brown, The human animal bond and self-psychology: Toward a new understanding, *Society & Animals: Journal of Human-Animal Studies* 12(1) (2003).

12. J. A. Serpell, *In the company of animals: A study of human-animal relationships*, 127.

13. Ibid., 126.

14. McConnell is author of *The other end of the leash: Why we do what we do around dogs* (New York: Ballantine Books, 2002), xvi.

15. Brian Hare and Michael Tomasello, Human-like social skills in dogs? *Trends in Cognitive Sciences* 9(9) (2005).

16. Carol Marzuola, Dog sense: Domestication gave canines innate insight into human gestures, *Science News Online* 162(21) (2002).

17. Adam Miklóski and K. Soproni, A comparative analysis of animals' understanding of the human pointing gesture, *Animal Cognition* 9(2) (2006).

18. K. Soproni, A. Miklóski, J. Topál, Vilmos Csányi, Dogs' (*Canis familiaris*) responsiveness to human pointing gestures, *Journal of Comparative Psychology*, 2002, 116(1) 27–34.

19. Adam Miklóski, Enikö Kubinyi, József Topál, Márta Gácsi, Zsófia Virányi, Vilmos Csányi, A simple reason for a big difference: Wolves do not look back at human, but dogs do, *Current Biology* 13(9) (2003).

20. Adam Miklóski, József Topál, and Vilmos Csányi, Comparative social cognition: What can dogs teach us? *Animal Behaviour* 67 (2003).

21. Stacey Schultz, Pets and their humans, *U.S. News & World Report*, October 30, 2000.

22. Miklóski, Topál, and Csányi, Comparative social cognition: What can dogs teach us?

23. J. A. Serpell, ed., *The domestic dog: It's evolution, behavior, and interactions with people* (Cambridge: Cambridge University Press, 1995), 118.

24. Colin Woodard, Clever canines: Did domestication make dogs smarter? *The Chronicle of Higher Education*, April 15, 2005.

25. Eric Louis and R. S. Wilcox, It's how you say it: Dog owners use non-verbal vocal cues to communicate their emotional state—poster abstract. *ISAZ 14th Annual Conference*, July 11–12, 2005, Niagara Falls, NY.

26. Woodard, Clever canines: Did domestication make dogs smarter?

27. Thomas Lewis, Fari Amini, and Richard Lannon, *A general theory of love* (New York: Vintage Books, 2000), 63.

28. Adam Miklóski, Enikö Kubinyi, József Topál, Márta Gácsi, Zsófia Virányi, Vilmos Csányi., A simple reason for a big difference: Wolves do not look back at human, but dogs do.

29. Adam Miklóski, R. Polgardi, József Topál, Vilmos Csányi, Intentional behavior in dog-human communication: An experimental analysis of "showing" behaviour in the dog, *Animal Cognition* 3(3) (2000).

30. Ibid.

31. Hare and Tomasello, Human-like social skills in dogs?

32. Schultz, Pets and their humans.

33. Sebastian E. Heath, Phillip Kass, Alan Beck, Larry Glickman, Human and pet-related risk factors for household evacuation failure during a natural disaster, *American Journal of Epidemiology* 153(7) (2001).

34. New Orleans couple mourns fate of their dog, by Mike Stobbe, Associated Press State and Local Wire, September 3, 2005, Atlanta, GA.

35. Couple reunited with pets left at N.O. hospital, by Mike Stobbe, Associated Press State and Local Wire, September 7, 2005.

36. Paul Schwartzman, He'll never let go of sassy again, *Washington Post*, September 30, 2005; and Craig Peel, personal communication, October 15, 2005.

37. S. Staats, D. Miller, and M. J. Carnot, The miller rada commitment to pets scale, *Anthrozoös* 9 (1996).

38. Angus Phillips, Incredible journey, *National Geographic*, January 2002.

39. Associated Press, Orlando pastor opens dog-friendly church, *Sun-Sentinel*, September 4, 2005.

40. Javier Erik Olvera, Pit bull owners frets as aurora mulls ban, *Rocky Mountain News* (*Denver, CO*), August 8, 2005.

41. Mimi Scott, phone interview, July 28, 2005.

42. Bill Hendrick, Leap to help goes to dogs; Neiman Marcus worker fired after act to aid pooches," *Atlanta Journal-Constitution* (*GA*), August 26, 2005.

43. Michael de la Merced, Assault victim hopes to find beloved pets, *Star-News* (*Wilmington, NC*), June 25, 2005. Information about the dogs whereabouts as of late 2005, received in an unconfirmed e-mail from an anonymous source.

44. J. Bowlby, Nature of the child's tie to his mother, *Journal of Psycho-Analysis* 39 (1958).

45. J. Topál, A. Miklósi, V. Csányi, and A. Doka, Attachment behavior in dogs (Canis Familiaris): A new application of Ainsworth's (1969) strange situation test, *Journal of Comparative Psychology* 112(3) (1998).

46. L. Beck and E. A. Madresh, Romantic partners and four-legged friends: An extension of attachment theory to relationships with pets, *Anthrozoos* (in press, expected in 2008.)

47. J. Bowlby, Nature of the child's tie to his mother.

48. Beck and Madresh, Romantic partners and four-legged friends (in press).

49. Lisa Keating, Pets can tell us something about ourselves as well, *Nevada Appeal* (November 2005).

50. Anthony L. Podberscek, Elizabeth S. Paul, and James A. Serpell, eds., *Companion animals and us: Exploring the relationships between people and pets* (New York: Cambridge University Press, 2000), 170.

51. Ibid., 173.

52. Anthony Walsh, *The science of love: Understanding love and it's effects on mind and body* (Amherst, NY: Prometheus Books, 1991), 38.

53. Lewis, Amini, and Lannon, *A general theory of love*, 26.

54. Ibid., 5.

55. Ibid., 11.

56. Stephen B. Levine, What is love anyway? *Journal of Sex & Marital Therapy* 31 (2005).

57. Robert J. Sternberg and Michael L. Barnes, eds., *The psychology of love* (New Haven, CT: Yale University Press, 1988).

58. C. S. Lewis, *The four loves* (Fort Washington, PA: Harvest Books, 1971).

59. Lewis, Amini, and Lannon, *A general theory of love*, 37.

60. Mary Carmichael, Jamie Reno, and Hilary Shenfeld, Animal emotions, *Newsweek*, July 21, 2003.

61. News Release, American Association for the Advancement of Science (AAAS), Annual Meeting, February 16, 2005.

62. Samuel D. Gosling, A dog's got personality: A cross-species comparative approach to personality judgments in dogs and humans, *Journal of Personality and Social Psychology* 85(6) (2003).

63. Amanda Jones and Samuel D. Gosling, Temperament and personality in dogs (Canis Familiaris): A review and evaluation of past research, *Applied Animal Behavior Science* 95 (2005).

64. E-mail communication, July 30, 2007.

65. Rupert Sheldrake, *Dogs that know when their owners are coming home* (New York: Crown Publishers, 1999), 2.

66. Ibid., 24.

67. Bella English, Love me, love my dog first, *Denver Post*, March 12 (2006), http://www.denverpost.com/.

68. Lynsay Clutter, Hero dog, owner on national TV (Indianapolis, IN: 2006), http://www.wthr.com.

69. Hero pup, *People*, November 21, 2005.

70. *Dog saves woman from 'gator*, CBS NEWS, April 14 (2005), http://www.cbsnews.com/.

71. News brief, *Russian Life*, November/December 2002.

72. Rodrique Ngowi, Stray dog rescues abandoned baby, *Seattle Times*, May 10, 2005.

73. Superpets! *People*, September 4, 2006.

74. David M. Dosa, A day in the life of Oscar the cat, *The New England Journal of Medicine* 357(4) (2007).

75. Ray Henry, Oscar the cat predicts patient's deaths, *Kansas City Star* (2007), http://www.kansascity.com.

76. Lewis, Amini, and Lannon, *A general theory of love*, 42–43, 62.

77. Ibid., 63–64.

78. Ibid., 61.

CHAPTER 3

1. Gary R. VandenBos, editor, *APA dictionary of psychology*, American Psychological Association, 2007, Washington, DC., 689.

2. Lynda Mae, Leah E. McMorris, and Jennifer L. Hendry, Spontaneous trait transference from dogs to owners, *Anthrozoos* 17(3) 2004.

3. Suzanne B. Johnson and Warren R. Rule, Personality characteristics and self-esteem in pet owners and non-owners, *International Journal of Psychology* 26(2) (1991).

4. Anthony L. Podberscek, Elizabeth S. Paul, and James A. Serpell, eds., *Companion animals and us: Exploring the relationships between people and pets* (New York: Cambridge University Press, 2000), 162.

5. Stanley Coren, *Why we love the dogs we do* (New York Simon & Schuster, 1998), 191–199.

6. Podberscek, Paul, and Serpell, eds., *Companion animals and us: Exploring the relationships between people and pets*, 162.

7. Coren, *Why we love the dogs we do*, 66–87.

8. Stanley Coren, Do people look like their dogs? *Anthrozoos* 12(2) (1999).

9. Michael M. Roy and Nicholas J. S. Christenfeld, Do dogs resemble their owners? *Psychological Science* 15(5) (2004).

10. R. B. Zajonc P. Adelmann, S. Murphy, P. Niedenthal, Convergence of the physical appearance of spouses, *Motivation and Emotion* 11 (1987).

11. Tom Fitzgerald, Probing questions: why are babies so cute? http://www.rps.psu.edu/.

12. Katie Brophy, What's it "aawww" about? *Ladies' Home Journal*, May 2006.

13. Brian Hare and Michael Tomasello, Human-like social skills in dog? *Trends in Cognitive Sciences*, 9(9)2005.

14. The Humane Society of the United States, press release, February 21, 2006, http://www.hsus.org.

15. Mimi Avins, Doggone it, that's good advice, *Los Angeles Times*, July 29, 2006.

16. American Kennel Club, Sit! The popularity of small dogs is here to stay, http://www.akc.org.

17. The American Pet Products Manufacturers Association, *2007–2008 APPMA National Pet Owners Survey* (Greenwich, CT: APPMA, 2007).

18. Ibid.

19. Place them in a cup and place the cup in the freezer. Being coldwater animals, they basically go to sleep and die a painless death.

20. Patricia K. Anderson, Assistant Professor of Anthropology, Western Illinois University, e-mail communication, November 19, 2006.

21. Thomas Lewis, Fari Amini, and Richard Lannon, *A general theory of love* (New York: Vintage Books, 2000), 63.

22. Culum Brown, Not just a pretty face, *New Scientist*, June 12, 2004.

23. APPMA, *National pet owners survey 2007–2008* (Greenwich, CT: APPMA, 2007).

24. Fish are actually the third most popular, but are not considered animals. Consequently, the breakdown is dogs, cats, and birds.

25. Catherine A. Loughlin and Peter W. Dowrick, Psychological needs filled by avian companions, *Anthrozoös* 6(3) (1993).

26. Erich Jarvis, Avian brains and a new understanding of vertebrate brain evolution, *Nature Reviews Neuroscience* 6(2) (2005).

27. http://www.alexfoundation.org/. Dr. Pepperberg will continue exploring the depths of the avian mind with Griffin and Arthur, two other young African grey parrots who have been a part of the ongoing research programs that are part of the Alex Foundation.

28. Patricia K. Anderson, A bird in the house: An anthropological perspective on companion parrots, *Society & Animals: Journal of Human-Animal Studies* 11(4) (2003).

29. Joanna Burger, *The parrot who owns me* (New York: Random House, 2001).

30. Anderson, A bird in the house: An anthropological perspective on companion parrots.

31. Carl Zimmer, Looking for personality in animals, of all people, *New York Times*, March 1, 2005.

32. *Parrot squawks on woman's affair*, BBC News, January 17 (2006), http://www.bbc.co.uk/.

33. Alex Kirby, Parrot's oratory stuns scientists, http://news.bbc.co.uk; Aimee Morgana, The N'kisi project, http://www.sheldrake.org/nkisi/.

34. Gerald P. Koocher, e-mail communication, December 21, 2005.

35. United Poultry Concerns, Chicken companions, http://upc-online.org/.

36. Anderson, A bird in the house: An anthropological perspective on companion parrots.

37. APPMA, *National pet owners survey 2007–2008* (Greenwich, CT: APPMA, 2007).

38. Simon N. Stuart, Janice S. Chanson, Neil A. Cox, Bruce E. Young, Ana S. L. Rodrigues, Debra L. Fischman, Robert W. Waller, Status and trends of amphibian decline and extinctions worldwide, *Science* 306 (2004): 1783–1786.

39. J. B. Jensen and C. D. Camp, eds., *Human exploitation of amphibians: Direct and indirect impacts* amphibian conservation (Washington, DC: Smithsonian Institution, 2003).

40. What is the biggest frog? http://www.AllAboutFrogs.org.

41. There are more than 200 identified zoonotic diseases, including West Nile Virus and Rabies. For more information visit http://www.who.int/zoonoses/en/; http://research.ucsb.edu/connect/pro/disease.html; or www.vetmed.wisc.edu/pbs/zoonoses/.

42. Jonathan Mermin et al., Reptiles, amphibians, and human *salmonella* infection: A population-based, case-control study, *CID* 38(Suppl. 3) (2004).

43. P. S. Mead, L. Slutsker, and V. Dietz, Food-related illness and death in the United States, *Emerg Infect Dis* 5 (1999).

44. Gina Spadafori, The Pet Connection, http://www.veterinarypartner.com.

45. Debora Carvalko, personal communication and email, April 2005–February 2006.

46. Roxanne Khamsi, Fearless iguanas too cool for their own good, NewScientist.com, November 29 (2006), http://www.newscientist.com/.

47. Ibid.

48. Melissa Kaplan, email communication, November 28, 2006. Melissa Kaplan is the author of "Iguanas for Dummies" and moderates an Internet site on reptiles and amphibians, http://www. anapsid.org.

49. Centers for Disease Control and Prevention, Reptile prescription, http://www.cdc.gov/healthypets/pdf/reptile_petscription.pdf.

50. Alan Beck and Aaron Katcher, *Between pets and people: The importance of animal companionship* (West Lafayette, IN: Purdue University Press, 1996), 41–42.

51. Jon Katz, The world's smartest cow, slate.com, April 28 (2006), http://www.slate.com/.

52. Sarah G. Gassen, Adopt a rodent, *Arizona Daily Star*, March 10, 2006.

53. Eileen Mitchell, A hare-raising tale, *San Francisco Chronicle*, April 5, 2006.

CHAPTER 4

1. Alan Beck and Aaron Katcher, *Between pets and people: The importance of animal companionship* (West Lafayette, IN: Purdue University Press, 1996), 41.

2. J.A. Serpell, ed., *Pet keeping and animal domestic: A reappraisal*, in *The walking larder: Patterns of domestication, pastorialism and predation* (London: Unwin Hyman, 1989).

3. Beck and Katcher, Between pets and people: *The importance of animal companionship*, 42.

4. Ibid., 47.

5. Pet Project, *Courier News* (Bridgewater, NJ), November 22, 2005.

6. Norman B. Anderson and P. Elizabeth Anderson, *Emotional longevity: What really determines how long you live* (New York: Viking, The Penguin Group, 2003), 81–100.

7. Beck and Katcher, *Between pets and people: The importance of animal companionship*.

8. Petlovingpeople.com, How your pets can hook you up this valentine's holiday, http://www.free-press-release.com/, February 22, 2006.

9. Julie Hinds, Animal attraction, *Monterey County (CA) Herald*, 2006.

10. Craig Wilson, And they call it puppy love: Animal lovers make meeting on the Internet their pet project, *USA Today*, February 13, 2006.

11. MSNBC, *If only my dog were a man!* http://www.msnbc.msn.com/.

12. Bob Reeves, Pets provide spiritual lessons, *Lincoln Journal Star*, March 11, 2006.

13. Mary Lou Randour, *Animal grace: Entering a spiritual relationship with our fellow creatures* (Novato, CA: New World Library, 2000), xxi, 38–42.

14. APPMA, *2007–2008 APPMA National pet owners survey 2007–2008* (Greenwich, CT: APPMA, 2007).

15. Reuters, *Pets becoming more common at work*, MSNBC, June 21 (2006), http://www.msnbc.com/.

16. Kristen Levine, Make Friday a dog day at the office, *Tampa Tribune*, June 18, 2005.

17. Ibid.

18. Carolyn Jones, Powered by pooches, *San Francisco Chronicle*, February 21, 2006.

19. *The New Oxford American Dictionary*, 2nd ed. (New York: Oxford University Press).

20. Claire Miller, Bird brains: Tweet! *Washington Post*, July 24, 2006.

21. H. Ellengren, Genomics: The dog has its day, *Nature*, December 8, 2005, 745–746.

22. Brief Communications, Dogged approach: Greyhounds pound the ground around a bend, *Nature*, December 8, 2005, 754.

23. Animal Planet, http://corporate.discovery.com/.

24. *Fatal attraction*, September 1987, Paramount Pictures.

25. Honda, Media newsroom, http://www.hondanews.com/.

26. Ingrid Trevino, Selected zoonotic diseases of companion animals (Iowa State University College of Veterinary Medicine, Center for Food Security & Public Health, 2006).

27. Kate Douglas, Mind of a dog, *New Scientist*, March 4, 2000.

28. Adam Miklóski, József Topál, and Vilmos Csányi, Comparative social cognition: What can dogs teach us? *Animal Behaviour* 67 (2003).

29. Patricia B. McConnell, *The other end of the leash* (New York: Ballantine Books, 2002), xviii.

30. J.A. Serpell, ed., *The domestic dog: Its evolution, behavior, and interactions with people*. (Cambridge: Cambridge University Press, 1995), 154.

31. Ibid., 154–158.

32. Ibid., 117.

33. McConnell, *The other end of the leash*, xxii–xxiv.

34. J. Topál, A. Miklósi, V. Csány, Dog–human relationship affects problem-solving behavior in the dog, *Anthrozoös*, 10(4) (1997), 212–224.

35. Adam Miklóski, Enikö Kubinyi, József Topál, Márta Gácsi, Zsófia Virányi, and Vilmos Csányi, A simple reason for a big difference: Wolves do not look back at human, but dogs do, *Current Biology*, 13(9) (2003), 763–766.

36. Á. Miklósi, J. Topál, and V. Csányi, Comparative social cognition: What can dogs teach us? *Animal Behaviour* 67 (2004), 995–1004.

37. Karin Winegar, Relating to animals and their ways, naturally, *Star Tribune (MN)*, January 13 (2006), http://www.startribune.com/.

38. Susan Kruglinski, A doctor's best friend, *Discover*, March 2006, 15.

39. Serpell, ed., *The domestic dog: It's evolution, behavior, and interactions with people*, 181.

40. Douglas Haldeman, interview, February 2006.

41. Cognitive dissonance is a psychological term to describe what occurs when we behave in ways that conflict with the ideals we believe we hold; here there is a disconnect: I say "*believe* we hold" because at face value it seems to me (not a psychologist) that if we truly held the ideals, we would act in ways consistent with them. I guess cognitive dissonance reflects our ability to compromise, I mean compartmentalize, our principles. For instance, one of my favorite examples of cognitive dissonance in action involves people who profess to love dogs and cats, but wear fur. I do not understand how a person can love one adorable, furry animal, and keep it safe by all means necessary, when it is called a companion animal, but refuse to be affected when another equally adorable, furry animal is tortured and killed so that a person can wear its skin for adornment. The weather does not get *that* cold and new high-tech fabrics are lighter with as much, if not more, protection from the cold than fur. How a person who has ever loved or kissed a puppy or a kitten can turn a blind eye to the anal electrocution of a mink or the head-bashing of a seal pup, I doubt I will ever understand. Most people refused to talk to me about this. The most I could get was, "I don't want to think about it" or "That's what they are bred for," which given the history of slavery in this country, does not carry much weight. Another example of cognitive dissonance is people who know smoking kills, but they keep doing it.

CHAPTER 5

1. Colin Woodard, Clever canines: Did domestication make dogs smarter? *The Chronicle of Higher Education*, April 15, 2005.

2. Jillian S. Jarret, Honoring all creatures great and small: Pets blessed on Saint Francis Feast Day, *Washington Post*, October 12, 2006.

3. Maslow's motivational hierarchy, commonly referred to as a hierarchy of needs, is "the hierarch of human motives, or needs, as described by Abraham Maslow." "The physiological needs are (air, water, food, sleep, sex, etc.) are the base; followed by safety and security; then love, affection, and gregariousness (the love needs); then prestige, competence, and power (the esteem needs); and at the highest level, aesthetic needs, the need for knowing, and self-Dactualization," according to the APA *Dictionary of Psychology*.

4. Jon Katz, *The new work of dogs: Tending to life, love, and family* (New York: Random House Trade Paperbacks, 2004).

5. Jenalia Moreno, Puppy love, at a price, *The Washington Post*, July 11, 2005.

6. Pet products industry is the term that defines businesses that provide goods and services related to companion animals and I will use it in this chapter.

7. APPMA, *National Pet Owners Survey 2007–2008* (Greenwich, CT: APPMA, 2007).

8. Moreno, Puppy love, at a price.

9. APPMA, *National Pet Owners Survey 2007–2008* (Greenwich, CT: APPMA, 2007).

10. Mindy Fetterman, Pampered pooches nestle in lap of luxury, *USA Today*, February 11–12, 2005.

11. Randi Schmelzer, As pet industry prospers, ads get more humanized, *Adweek*, May 9, 2005.

12. Moreno, Puppy love, at a price.

13. Tom Enart, Grooming and spa products lend the sweet smell of success to pet industry, *PR Newswire*, October 11, 2005.

14. Traveling on planes? Just carry her right on, *The News & Observer*, February 19, 2006.

15. Jetpets.com, Animal transport, http://www.jetpets.com/.

16. 10 great places to relax, loosen your collars, *USA Today*, January 13, 2006.

17. Valerie Strauss, Dispatch from a city for dogs: Canines lapping up luxury in Miami Beach, *Washington Post*, September 5, 2006.

18. http://www.loewshotels.com.

19. Strauss, Dispatch from a city for dogs: Canines lapping up luxury in Miami Beach.

20. Kitty Bean Yancey, Walking tours let the pooch tag along, *USA Today*, February 24, 2006.

21. Arline Bleecker and Sam Bleecker, e-mail message to author, April 2, 2006.

22. Carlos Mejias, personal communication, November 16, 2007.

23. http://www.otsfd.com.

24. http://www.cratehaven.com/.

25. Liz Seymour, Chill out and warm up to pet climate control, *The Washington Post*, July 26, 2007; and http://www.komfortpets.com.

26. Press package; CatGenie; PetNovations; Suite 811; 989 Old Eagle School Road; Wayne, PA 19087.

27. David Barry, Many happy returns, *The Washington Post*, December 4, 2005.

28. Ibid.

29. Dana Brewington, interviews and e-mail communication, May through September 2007, http://www.do-rites.com.

30. *The New Oxford American Dictionary*, 2nd ed. (New York: Oxford University).

31. J. A. Serpell, Anthropomorphism and anthropomorphic selection—Beyond the "cute response," *Society & Animals* 11(1) (2003).

32. Kim Mitchell, Do you pamper your pet? *Daily Times*, December 3, 2005.

33. National Geographic Channel, *Dog whisperer* returns for a new season of rehabilitating dogs—and training owners—with renowned dog behavior expert Cesar Milan, news release, December 12, 2005, http://www.ngcdogwhisperer.com/.

34. Denise Flaim, Bad doggie medicine? *Newsday*, May 23, 2006.

35. Bringing pets to church, *The Early Show*, 7:00 A.M. EST CBS, May 25, 2005. Harry Smith and Hannah Storm; personal communication with the Rev. Molly McGreevy, July 2007.

36. Bringing pets to church, *The Early Show*, CBS.

37. J. Maselko, Religious service attendance and decline in pulmonary function in a high functioning elderly cohort, *Annals of Behavioral Medicine* 32(3) (2006).

38. Ibid.

39. Diana Bellettieri, Pet owners count their blessings in Croton Falls, *The Journal News* (Whiteplains, NY), December 19, 2005.

40. Neil Schneiderman, Personal e-mail communication, May 2007.

41. Anthony L. Podberscek, Elizabeth S. Paul, and James A. Serpell, eds., *Companion animals and us: Exploring the relationships between people and pets* (New York: Cambridge University Press, 2000), 90–95.

42. Amanda Long, Rub-a-dog: Canine massage, *The Washington Post*, September 30, 2007.

43. Alex Beam, Meanwhile: It's a dog's life for pampered kids, *International Herald Tribune*, March 5, 2006.

44. Susan Scott Schmidt, Down doggies; Yoga for your hounds? Sure it's called "doga," *Pittsburg Post-Gazette*, April 27, 2004.

45. Susan Gilmore, Lawyer breaking new legal ground on animal issues, *Seattle Times*, February 7, 2006.

46. Laura Parker, When pets die at the vet, grieving owners call lawyers, *USA Today*, March 15, 2005; Anemona Hartocollis, Custody battle is settled: Cat will go back to its first owner, *New York Times*, January 21, 2006.

47. Jenny Hunsperger, Divorces can be cat-astrophic, dog-gone sad, *Arizona Citizen* December 1, 2005.

48. Anemona Hartocollis, The furry, 4-legged centerpiece of a custody battle in court, *New York Times*, December 15, 2005.

49. Parker, When pets die at the vet, grieving owners call lawyers.

50. Gilmore, Lawyer breaking new legal ground on animal issues.

51. Christina Ianzito, Party animal: Dog day afternoon, *Washington Post Magazine*, October 15, 2006.

52. Pamela Weiler Grayson, A dog of a date, just as scheduled, *The New York Times* October 29, 2006.

53. Don Fernandez, Ruff life, *The Atlanta Journal Constitution*, August 7, 2005.

54. Ibid.

55. Dog almighty! *Toronto Star*, June 18, 2006.

56. Mitchell, Do you pamper your pet?

57. Meeta Agrawal, Dog crazy, *Life Weekend Magazine*, February 24, 2006.

58. Barry, Many happy returns.

59. Petgrads.com, Pet Gadgets, http://www.petgrads.com/.

60. http://www.uspcak9.com/ (United States Police Canine Association); http://www.napwda.com/ (North American Police Work Dog Association); http://www.npca.net/ (National Police Canine Association).

61. John Horton, Tiny Midge embarks on police career 8-lb pup to sniff drugs for Geauga Sheriff, *Plain Dealer* (Cleveland, OH), November 8, 2006.

62. Michael Brick, Undercover agent in fur snares a fake veterinarian, *New York Times*, February 9, 2006.

63. Jon Zemke, Police dog was special to community, *The Detroit News*, February 28, 2006, http://www.detnews.com.

64. Kim North Shine, Beat goes on: Long tail of the law, *Detroit Free Press*, December 8, 2005.

65. Michael Alison Chandler, Bomb-dog noses pressed into transit duty, *Washington Post*, September 29, 2005.

66. National Search and Rescue Dog Association, The history of UK search and rescue dogs, http://www.nsarda.org.uk/.

67. Ibid.

68. Virginia Search and Rescue Dog Association, http://www.vsrda.org/.

69. FEMA, Canine's role in urban search and rescue, http://www.fema.gov/, April 26, 2007.

70. Mary Ann Ford, More than a friend, March 1 (2006), http://www.pantagraph.com/.

71. Michael G. Lemish, *War Dogs: A history of loyalty and heroism* (Dulles, VA: Brassey's Inc., 1996), 5–9, 12, 41–51, 73–78, 227, 229–230, 232.

72. Ron Aiello, telephone interview, October 2, 2007.

73. Book on King "MOO" available from author at 402 Division St., Union City, MI 49094.

74. Jean Aymar, Tysons pet spa works to equiop the dogs of war, *Washington Post*, July 24, 2005.

75. Aiello, October 2, 2007.

76. Donna St. George, Wounded sergeant fights for a "best friend," *Washington Post*, November 20, 2005.

77. Donna St. George, Update: Dog and handler, wounded in Iraq explosion, sign on to the new life together, *Washington Post*, November 15, 2006.

78. Diane McCartney, A sympathetic ear, *Wichita (KS) Eagle*, April 16 (2006), http://www.mywire.com/; Intermountain Therapy Animals, Reading assistance education dogs, http://www.therapyanimals.org/.

CHAPTER 6

1. M. A. Beck and A. H. Katcher, A new look at pet-facilitated therapy, *Journal of the American Veterinary Medical Association* 184 (1984).

2. Florence Nightingale, *Notes on nursing: What it is, and what it is not*, first American edition, D. Appleton & Company, 103 ed. New York: 1860; reprint, paperback edition by Michigan Historical Reprint Series Scholarly Publishing Office, 2006.

3. Office of Medical Applications of Research; The health benefits of pets, workshop summary; 1987, September 10–11, Bethesda, MD: National Institutes of Health.

4. Ira Perelle and Diane A. Granville, Assessment of the effectiveness of a pet-facilitated therapy program in a nursing home setting, *Society & Animals* 1(1) (1993).

5. J. H. Davis, Animal facilitated therapy in stress mediation, *Holistic Nurse Practitioner* 2(3) (1988).

6. B. Levison, The dog as co-therapist, *Mental Hygiene* 46 (1962): 59–65.

7. The health benefits of pets, workshop summary; September 10–11, 1987, Bethesda, MD: National Institutes of Health.

8. A. H. Katcher and E. Friedmann, Potential health value of pet ownership, *Compendium of continuing education for the veterinarian* 2 (1980); E. Friedmann and A. H. Katcher, Animal companions and one year survival of patients after discharge from a coronary care unit, *Public Health Report* 95(4) (1980).

9. Deborah L. Wells, Domestic dogs and human health: An overview, *British Journal of Health Psychology* 12 (2007).

10. J. A. Serpell, Beneficial effects of pet ownership on some aspects of human health and behavior, *Journal of the Royal Society of Medicine* 84(12) (1991).

11. Alison Hatch, The view from all fours: A look at an animal-assisted activity program from the animals' perspective, *Anthrozoos* 20(1) (2007).

12. Wells, Domestic dogs and human health: An overview.

13. K. Cole, A. Gawlinkski, and N. Steers, Animal assisted therapy decreases hemodynamics, plasma epinephrine and state anxiety in hospitalized heart failure patients. Paper presented at the American Heart Association's Scientific Sessions, Dallas, TX, November 15, 2005.

14. Sadia Latifi, New study suggests a hug can lower blood pressure, reduce stress, *Knight Ridder Business Tribune*, August 9, 2005.

15. Wells, Domestic dogs and human health: An overview.

16. Anita All and Gary Loving, Animals, horseback riding, and implications for rehabilitation therapy, *Journal of Rehabilitation* 65(3) (1999).

17. Therapeutic horseback riding, *Good Morning America*, September 26, 2006, Jake Tapper (reporter), Diane Sawyer and Robin Roberts (anchors), American Broadcasting Companies, Inc.

18. Information from newsletters of the Yellow Ribbon Fund, an organization in Bethesda, MD, dedicated to helping injured soldiers and their families when they are at Walter Reed Army Medical Center and the National Naval Medical Center, http://www.yellowribbonfund.org/.

19. Anne Krueger, Barbara Hey, and Andrea Reynes, Horse Wisperings, *Natural Awakenings*, November 2006.

20. http://www.medicinehorse.org.

21. http://www.guidehorse.org/.

22. Minihorse named Panda is quite the guide animal, http://www.orlandosentinel.com January 28, 2007, by Associated Press.

23. Information about Petie from three sources: Jody Rohlena, A pony tale, *Reader's Digest*, January 2007; *People Magazine*, September 27, 2004, 108; and http://www.VictoryGallop.org/.

24. Rahkia Nance, Riding out cerebral palsy, *The Examiner (Washington, DC)*, July 19, 2005.

25. Premarin (PREgnant MARe urINe) or PMU foals are the "by products" of the hormone replacement therapy drug Premarin, which is prescribed to women with natural or induced menopause. Premarin is made from the urine of approximately 60,000 pregnant mares (female horses), and their foals are usually shipped to slaughterhouses for their meat, which is marketed overseas to European and Asian countries for human consumption. When the mares can no longer conceive, they too are generally shipped for slaughter and replaced on the "pee lines." The mares and foals vary in breed.

26. Amy Orndoff, Dog at work, *Washington Post*, January 18, 2007.

27. Leah Eckberg Feldman, A bond of love, *Ladies' Home Journal*, June 2006.

28. Orndoff, Dog at work.

29. Emily Murphy, "I'm known as the kid with the dog, *USA Today*, August 15, 2005.

30. Thomas Fields-Meyer and Susan Mandel, Healing hounds, *People*, July 17, 2006.

31. Jan Goodwin, Monkey do, *Reader's Digest*, May 2007.

32. Carolyn Willis et al., Olfactory detection of human bladder cancer by dogs: Proof of principle study, *BMJ* 329(7468) (2004).

33. Michael MacCulloch, Diagnostic accuracy of canine scent detection in early- and late-stage lung and breast cancers, *Integrative Cancer Therapies* 5(1), 30–39 (2006).

34. American family dogs trained to detect seizures. *Good Morning America*, July 6, 2004, Diane Sawyer (anchor), American Broadcasting Companies, Inc.; http://www.heavenscentpaws.com/.

35. American family dogs trained to detect seizures, Diane Sawyer.

36. Wringley May Have Sniffed Out a Brain Tumor, *People*, September 4, 2006.

37. Norra Macready and Gary Vogin, Pets may protect children from allergies, *WebMD Medical News*, March 9 (2000), http://www.webmd.com/.

38. D.R. Ownby, C. J. Cole, and E. L. Peterson, Exposure to dogs and cats in the first year of life and risk of allergic sensitization at 6 to 7 years of age, JAMA 288(8) (2002).

39. J. Gern et al., Effects of dog ownership and genotype on immune development and atopy in intancy, *Journal of Allergy and Clinical Immunology*, February 113 (2004), 307–314.

40. Warren Robak, AIDS patients with pets, less depression: Press release, May 6, 1999.

41. Karlyn Barker, Helpers step in for ailing pet owners; volunteers assist with care so animals aren't surrendered, *The Washington Post*, March 20, 2005.

42. Ralph Holcomb et al., Use of an aviary to relieve depression in elderly males, *Anthrozoos* 10(1) (1997).

43. Christine R. McLaughlin, Furry friends can aid your health, *Discovery Health* (2005), http://health.discovery.com/.

44. Another dog saves owner from heart attack, *The Scoop*, March 15 (2001), http://www.dogsinthenews.com.

45. Elaine Wirrell, Adam Kirton, and James Zhang, Seizure-alerting and -response behaviors in dogs living with epileptic children," *Neurology* 62 (2004).

46. Kevin Helliker, Benefits of a Canine Running Mate, *Wall Street Journal*, April 17, 2007.

47. Hayley Cutt et al., Dog ownership, health and physical activity: a critical review of the literature," *Health & Place* 13 (2007).

48. Shalev Abraham and Dror Ben-Mordehai, Snakes: Interactions with children with disabilities and the elderly—some psychological considerations," *Anthrozoos* 9(4) (1996).

49. Help your heart by fighting loneliness, *The Johns Hopkins Medical Letter*, October 2006.

50. Marian R. Banks and William A. Banks, The effects of group and individual animal-assisted therapy on loneliness in residents of long-term care facilities, *Anthrozoos* 18(4) (2005).

51. Odean Cusack, *Pets and mental health* (Binghampton, NY: Haworth Press, 1998), 43.

52. Joan Tucker et al., Playing with pets and longevity among older people, *Psychology and Aging* 10(1) (1995); Ruth Parslow et al., Pet ownership and health in older adults: Findings from a survey of 2,551 community-based Australians aged 60–64, *Gerontology* 51(1) (2005).

53. Thomas F. Garrity et al., Pet ownership and attachment as supportive factors in the health of the elderly, *Anthrozoos* 3(1) (1989): 35.

54. J. M. Siegel, Stressful life events and use of physician services among the elderly: The moderating role of pet ownership, *Journal of Personality and Social Psychology* 58 (1990).

55. Masahiko Motooka et al., Effect of dog-walking on autonomic nervous activity in senior citizens, *Medical Journal of Australia* 184(2) (2006).

56. Corrine Olson, Dog pal enlivens nursing home, *Sioux Falls (SD) Argus Leader*, March 14, 2006.

57. Personal communication with daughter of Paul Klaassen, June 11, 2007.

58. Personal Interview with Vera Persons, July 2007.

59. Katherine L. Anderson and Myrna R. Olson, The value of a dog in a classroom of children with severe emotional disorders, *Anthrozoos* 19(1) (2006).

60. B. W. Davis et al., Assistance dog placement in the pediatric population: benefits, risks, and recommendations for future application, *Anthrozoos* 17(2) (2004).

61. Lana Kaiser et al., Can a week of therapeutic riding make a difference? A pilot study, *Anthrozoos* 17(1) (2004).

62. Barbara L. Flom, Counseling with pocket pets: Using small animals in elementary counseling programs, *Professional School Counseling* 8(5) (2005).

63. Janet Romaker, Canine counselors find role at school, *Toledo Blade*, March 18, 2007.

64. Earl O. Strimple, A history of prison inmate-animal interaction programs, *American Behavioral Scientist* 47(1) (2003).

65. Safe harbor program helps Lansing inmates, KETV.com, November 30 (2005), http://www.ketv.com/; http://www.safeharborprisondogs.com/.

CHAPTER 7

1. Personal communication with publicist of the American Veterinary Medical Association, July 20, 2007.

2. Dell Rae Moellenberg, Pet owners likely to use alternative and complimentary medicine on their pets, according to Colorado State University, *Colorado State News*, October 17 (2006), http://newsinfo.colostate.edu.

3. Robert Marchant, A dog's (Lucky) life in Bedford, *Journal News*, February 19, 2006.

4. Faith McDuffie, A rescue story: The power of technology, caring *(Raleigh, NC) News & Observer*, February 7, 2007.

5. Special surgery on a two-paw cat? Of course" *(Raleigh, NC) News & Observer*, February 19, 2006.

6. Damon Darlin, Vet bills and the priceless pet: What's a practical owner to do? *New York Times*, May 13, 2006.

7. First Coast News, Clinic uses human procedures to help ailing dogs, November 29 (2005), http://www.firstcoastnews.com/.

8. Surgery for Lance's lab, *People*, October 10, 2005.

9. Kristi L. Gustafson, A dog's life comes into focus, *Albany (NY) Times Union*, June 4, 2004; Dr. Michael Buenau, e-mail communication and interviews, May 19–25, 2007.

10. Eileen Mitchell, When your canine gets cancer, *The San Francisco Chronicle*, May 13, 2006.

11. Elizabeth Lowe, Tequila gets a shot—at life, *Burton News*, January 1, 2006.

12. Carl T. Hall, Man's best friend shares most genes with humans, *San Francisco Chronicle*, December 8, 2005.

13. Emily Singer, Prozac for your dog, *(MIT) Technology Review*, March 30 (2007), http://www.technologyreview.com/.

14. Darlin, Vet bills and the priceless pet: What's a practical owner to do?

15. Pets Best, Founder of U.S. pet insurance industry launches pets best, October 17 (2005), http://www.mywire.com/.

16. Humane Society of the United States, A safe cat is a happy cat (brochure number PM 2276).

17. Linda Wilson Fuoco, Bill would keep dogs safer in cars, no ears flapping in the wind, *Pittsburg Post-Gazette*, October 6, 2005.

18. Jennifer Wing Rothhacker, Sweet moment with cinnamon timeless, *The Charlotte Observer*, April 18, 2005.

19. Elizabeth Hume, Fire district given oxygen masks for pets, *Sacramento Bee*, January 18, 2006.

20. Rezendes Allison, Supporting emergency preparedness, *Journal of the American Veterinary Medical Association* 230(11) (2007).

21. Josh Noel, She fights off coyote to rescue her pooch, *Chicago Tribune*, April 4, 2006.

22. Personal communication, Jon Silver, June 25, 2007.

23. http://www.faiththedog.net/; scripture from II Corinthians, 5:7, King James *Holy Bible*.

24. Faith has been the focus of many national broadcasts and articles and Stringfellow has published two books about her family's amazing dog: *With a little Faith* (2nd ed.) and *Faith alone: Stories of an amazing dog*.

25. Carol McAlice Currie, Smokers care for their cat, ironically, more than themselves, *Statesman Journal (Salem, OR)*, December 9, 2005.

26. G. K. Kakesako, Kaneohe marines return from Iraq, *Honolulu Star Bulletin*, April 10, 2005. Kopelman tells Lava's story in *From Baghdad, with love: A marine, the war, and a dog named Lava*.

27. Jeanne Marie Laskas, A soldier's best friend, *Ladies' Home Journal*, September 2006.

28. Marc Bekoff and Carron A. Meaney, eds., *Encyclopedia of animal rights and animal welfare* (Westport, CT: Greenwood Press, 1998), 1.

29. Dianne Feinstein, Feinstein announces animal enterprise terrorism act signed into law (Congressional Quarterly, Inc., 2006).

30. Susan E. Lindt, She's not afraid of a dog fight (2006), http://www.local.lancasteronline.com; www.dogsdeservebetter.com; and telephone conversation with Tammy S. Grimes, July 2007.

31. Vanessa Juarez, Stray dog seeks love, *Newsweek*, March 21, 2005.

32. Samantha Glen, *Best friends: The true story of the world's most beloved animal sanctuary* (New York: Kensington Books, 2001); telephone conversation with Barbara Williamson, Media Relations Manager (June 2007); http://www.bestfriends.org/.

33. Molly Selvin and Abigail Goldman, A dog's life: What's it worth? *Los Angeles Times*, March 30, 2007.

34. Telephone conversation with Julie E. Lewin, June 30, 2007; and Julie E. Lewin, *Get political for animals and win the laws they need* (National Institute for Animal Advocacy, 2007).

35. Charles Abott, House votes to ban horse slaughter for food, *Washington Post*, September 7, 2006.

36. John M. Hubbel, Stray cats, dogs escape the budget as money-saving plan to kill animals sooner draws howls of protest, *Chronical Sacremento Bureau*, June 26, 2004.

37. Pam Belluck, Battered wives' pets suffer abuse, too, *New York Times*, April 1, 2006.

38. Emily Bazar, Laws shield pets from domestic violence, *USA Today*, 2006.

39. Michelle O'Donnell, Cute and furry, some say. A beaten dog, a court finds, *New York Times*, September 1, 2006.

40. Trouble, the $12 million dog, *People*, September 17, 2007.

41. Jeff Kosseff, A tax break to care for your pets if you die? *The Oregonian* (Portland), June 4, 2007.

42. Deborah Yao, Barking up the right tree (2006), http://www.ocala.com; Bide-a-Wee, Retirement Home, http://www.bideawee.org/retirement.asp/, May 14, 2007.

43. Jenn Shreve, Fido's first cell phone, *Wired News*, December 6 (2005), http://www.wired.com/.

44. Associated Press, Pet microchips are high-tech tags, *Indianapolis Star (IN)*, December 26, 2005.

CHAPTER 8

1. Laurel Langoni, Carolyn Butler, and Suzanne Hetts, *The human-animal bond and grief* (Philadelphia, PA: W.B. Saunders Co., 1994), 30.

2. Centers for Disease Control and Prevention, Deaths: Final data for 2003, *National Vital Statistics Report* 54(13) (2006).

3. Paul T. Clements, Kathleen M. Benasutti, and Andy Carmone, Support for bereaved owners of pets, *Perspectives in Psychiatric Care* 39(2) (2003).

4. Christine Morley and Jan Fook, The importance of pet loss and some implications for services, *Mortality* 10(2) (May 2005): 127–143.

5. Ibid., 32.

6. Wallace Sife, *The loss of a pet* (New York: Wiley Publishing, Inc., 1998).

7. Barbara Meyers, Anticipatory mourning and the human-animal bond, in *Clinical dimensions of anticipatory mourning: Theory and practice in working with the dying, their loved ones, and their caregivers*, Therese A. Rando, ed. (Champaign, IL: Research Press, 2000).

8. Deb Acord, A dog's life, *Colorado Springs Gazette*, March 12, 2006.

9. Meyers, Anticipatory mourning and the human-animal bond.

10. Theresa A. Fuess, Where do I go when my pet dies? Pet Columns from the University of Illinois College of Veterinary Medicine, October 13 (1997), http://www.cvm.uiuc.edu/.

11. Margaret S. Stroebe, Wolfgang Stroebe, and Henk Schut, grief and loss, Encyclopedia of Psychology, Alan E. Kazdin, eds. (Oxford University Press 2000).

12. Clements, Benasutti, and Carmone, Support for bereaved owners of pets.

13. Tamina Toray, The human-animal bond and loss: Providing support for grieving clients, Journal of Mental Health Counseling 26(3)(2004), 246.

14. Clements, Benasutti, and Carmone, Support for bereaved owners of pets.

15. Gary R. Vandebos, *APA Dictionary of Psychology*, American Psychological Association, 2007, Washington, DC.

16. Christine Morley and Jan Fook, The importance of pet loss and some implications, *Mortality (Abingdon, England)* 10(2) (2005).

17. J. Quakenbush and L. Glickman, Social work services for bereaved pet owners: A retrospective case study in a veterinary teaching hospital, in *New Perspectives on Our Lives with Companion Animals*, A. Katcher and A. Beck, eds. (Philadelphia: University of Pennsylvania, 1983).

18. Morley and Fook, The importance of pet loss and some implications, 130.

19. Langoni, Butler, and Hetts, *The human–animal bond and grief*, 38.

20. Tamina Toray, The human–animal bond and loss: Providing support for grieving clients, *Journal of Mental Health Counseling* 26(3) (2004), 250.

21. Dave Ford, Losing a "best friend"; grief-filled companions have a place to turn after death of a pet, *San Francisco Chronicle*, September 26, 2003.

22. Clements, Benasutti, and Carmone, Support for bereaved owners of pets.

23. Sarah Newman, Loss of an animal friend can be heart-breaking, *St. Louis Post-Dispatch*, March 3, 2006.

24. Gary R. VandenBos, *APA Dictionary of Psychology*, American Psychological Association, 2007,Washington, DC.

25. K. Shear et al., Treatment of complicated grief: A randomized controlled trial, *Journal of the American Medical Association* 293(2005).

26. Meyers, Anticipatory mourning and the human-animal bond, 557.

27. Morley and Fook, The importance of pet loss and some implications, 130.

28. Langoni, Butler, and Hetts, *The human–animal bond and grief*, 44.

29. Michael D. Mullins, Sorrow in community after homeless man loses best friend, *Hoboken Reporter (NJ)*, March 25, 2007, and http://www.portauthoroitypolicememorial.org.

30. Neil Graves, Hero dog has his day—cops honor pup killed at trade center, *The New York Post*, April 25, 2002.

31. Toray, The human–animal bond and loss: Providing support for grieving clients.

32. Tom Hallman, Grief that nuzzles on the soul, *Oregonian*, February 6, 2005.

33. Fuess, Where do I go when my pet dies?

34. Carol Morello, For pets, religious rites of passage, *Washington Post*, September 4, 2005.

35. Ibid.

36. India Cooke, email communication, July 5, 2007.

37. Rolan Tripp, New options for memorializing pets, *Bradenton Herald*, June 6, 2006.

38. Barbara Whitaker, Building a stairway to paradise, for your beloved pet, *New York Times*, January 14, 2007.

39. Amit R. Paley, Eternal restlessness over MD pet cemetery, *Washington Post*, December 27, 2005.

40. Cameron W. Barr, Pet owners grieving all over again, *Washington Post*, January 11, 2005; Roadside America: Guide to uniquely odd tourist attractions, http://www.roadsideamerica.com/.

41. Tina Firesheets, Pet cemetery, *News-Record*, December 11, 2005.

42. Andrew Herrman, Want to spend eternity with pet?: 2 cemeteries make it possible, *Chicago Sun-Times* (IL), January 30, 2006.

43. Whitaker, Building a stairway to paradise, for your beloved pet.

44. James Langton, Woman who turns pets into pillows faces death threats, *Sunday Telegraph (London)*, April 10, 2005.

45. David Casstevens, People say, "Oh, he was just a dog." No. He was a person who loved me, *Fort Worth Star-Telegram (TX)*, June 11, 2006.

46. Clements, Benasutti, and Carmone, Support for bereaved owners of pets.

47. Langoni, Butler, and Hetts, *The human–animal bond and grief*, 55.

CHAPTER 9

1. Cesar Milan via assistant Gayle, e-mail communication, March 17, 2006.

2. J. A. Serpell, Anthropomorphism and anthropomorphic selection—Beyond the "cute response," *Society & Animals* 11(1) (2003).

3. Although many sites attribute this number to the HSUS, their own site devoted to puppy mills, www.stoppuppymills.com says: "For many reasons, The HSUS does not publish a list of known puppy mills. There are literally thousands of puppy mills in existence all over the country, and most of them are not required to register with any one agency. There are so many unregulated puppy mills that to publish a list of the known or 'problem' mills may give the public a false impression that any establishment that is not on the list is 'safe.' Nothing could be farther from the truth, however. In fact, some problematic puppy mills have been known to change their names and locations frequently to evade their reputations." (August 2006)

4. Jon Mooallem, The modern kennel conundrum, *The New York Times Magazine*, February 4, 2007. Unless otherwise stated, the information on puppy mills comes from this article.

5. Truth about puppy mills: What will it take to stop bad breeders? July 11, 2007. http://www.network.bestfriends.org/.

6. John Mercure, I-team: Puppy mills, in *You News TV* (WTMJ-TV, April 25, 2007).

7. Kelli Ohrtman, Operation freebird, *Best Friends Network*, July 17 (2007), http://network.bestfriends.org/News/16953.html.

8. http://www.petstorecruelty.org/Birdmills.htm; http://www.phoenixlanding.org/.

9. Jon Mooallem, The modern kennel conundrum

10. Ibid.

11. Elisabeth Rosenthal, Cat lovers lining up for no-sneeze kitties, *New York Times*, October 6, 2006.

12. Rick Weiss, In a furry first, a dog is cloned in South Korea, *Washington Post*, August 4, 2005.

13. Fergus Walsh, First cloned horse unveiled in Italy, *BBC News*, June 8 (2003), http://bbc.co.uk/.

14. Maggie Shiels, Carbon kitty's $50,000 price tag, *BBC News*, April 27 (2004), http://bbc.co.uk/.

15. Is it possible for someone to have too many pets? February 9 (2006), http://hometownlife.com.

16. Lynn Tryba, Trash menagerie, *People* 35(6) (2002).

17. Arnie Arluke, Randy Frost, Carter Luke, Edward Messner, Jane Nathanson, Gary Patronek, Health implications of animal hoarding, *Health and Social Work* 27(2) (2002).

18. http://www.peta.org.

19. http://www.banpoundseizure.org, hosted by the American Anti-vivisection Society.

20. Charles Siebert, New tricks, *New York Times Magazine*, April 8, 2007.

21. S. Staats, D. Miller, M. J. Carnot, and K Rada, The Miller Rada commitment to pets scale. *Anthrozoös* 9 (1996), 88–94.

22. M. D. Salman et al., Human and animal factors related to the relinquishment of dogs and cats in 12 selected animal shelters in the United States, *Journal of Applied Animal Welfare Science* 1(3) (1998).

23. S. A. Segurson, J. A. Serpell, and B. L. Hart, Evaluation of a behavioral assessment questionnaire for use in the characterization of behavioral problems of dogs relinquished to animal shelters, *Journal of the American Veterinary Medical Association* 227(11) (2005).

24. M. Gácsi, J. Topal, A. Miklósi, A. Doka, Csányi, Attachment behavior of adult dogs (*Canis familiaris*) living at rescue centers: Forming new bonds, *Journal of Comparative Psychology* 112(3) (1998).

25. Siebert, New tricks.

26. University of Edinburg, Dogs on the scent of better behaviour, *Newswise*, April 22 (2004), http://www.newswise.com/.

27. Francy Blackwood, No-kill nation: The movement to find homes for all adoptable dogs and cats is spreading across the county, *Animal Watch* 23(4) (2003).

28. Bill Hewitt, Should strays be killed, *People*, November 6, 2006.

29. Blackwood, No-kill nation: The movement to find homes for all adoptable dogs and cats is spreading across the county.

30. http://www.maddiesfund.org.

31. Siebert, New tricks.

32. Sandra Marquez, The Angel of "doggy death row," *People*, February 13, 2006.

33. http://www.southbendtribune.com.

34. Jesse Katz, What's a dog worth? *L.A. Times*, May 1, 2006.

35. Critics howl over Calif. pet-fixing bill, MSNBC, June 27, 2007. http://www.msnbc.msn.com.

36. Sharon L. Peters, The fix is in for pet control, *USA Today*, July 5, 2007.

37. Tami L. Harbolt, *Bridging the bond: The cultural construction of the shelter pet* (West Lafayette, IN: Purdue University Press, 2003), 88.

38. Charlie L. Reeve, S. G. Rogelberg, C. Spitzmüller, N. Di Giacomo, The caring-killing paradox: euthanasia-related strain among animal-shelter workers, *Journal of Applied Social Psychology* 35(1) (2005).

39. Karin Brulliard, Euthanasia a strain for animal care workers, *Washington Post*, September 26, 2005.

40. Tami L. Harbolt, *Bridging the bond*, 28–30.

41. Holly E. Hazard, *The violence connection* (Washington, DC: Doris Day Animal Foundation, 2004), 3.

42. Ibid., 9.

43. http://www.aspca.org.

44. Linda Merz-Perez and Kathleen M. Heide, *Animal cruelty: Pathway to violence against people* (Walnut Creek, CA: AltaMira Press, 2004), 19–59.

45. Associated Press, Georgia teens admit to killing dog in oven, Atlanta, GA, *Pantagraph.com (Bloomington, IL)*, January 26, 2007.

46. Josh Loftin, A chocolate lab puppy was injured when his owner wired his mouth to stop his barking, *Deseret Morning News (Salt Lake City, UT)*, January 25, 2006.

47. Associated Press, Armed bandits strangle Oakland pet, *KTVU.com (Oakland, CA)*, March 1 (2006), http://www.ktvu.com/.

48. Karin Brulliard, VA man who killed cat gets suspended sentence, *Washington Post*, January 11, 2006.

49. Mark Maske, Falcons' Vick indicted in dogfighting case; Star QB alleged to have been highly involved, *Washington Post*, July 18, 2007.

50. Hanna Gibson, *Dog fighting detailed discussion*, Animal Legal and Historical Center, Michigan State University College of Law, http://www.animallaw.info.

51. http://www.HSUS.org.

52. Hazard, The violence connection, 7.

53. http://www.api4animals.org/. The Animal Protection Institute.

54. *Jack Hanna's Animal Adventures*, CNN, September 3, 2006.

55. Margaret Ebrahim and John Solomon, Exotic pets in U.S. may pose health risk, *Kansas City Star (MO)*, November 27, 2006.

56. *Fox 5 Morning News*, WTTG Washington, DC, July 29, 2006.

57. Howard Baskin, Last refuge, *Tampa Tribune*, February 13, 2005.

58. Animal Protection Institute, Exotic pets and the law, *Animal Issues* Winter 2005.

59. Siebert, New tricks.

60. Jon Mooallem, *The Modern Kennel Conundrum*.

61. Leo K. Bustad, *Compassion: Our last great hope* (Renton, WA: The Delta Society, 1990), 130.

62. Ibid., 134.

63. Ibid., 135.

64. David B. Chamberlain (excerpted), Historical perspectives on pain, experiments in infant pain, http://www.birthpsychology.com/healing/historical.html.

65. Frans De Waal, Suspicious minds, *New Scientist* 186(2502) (2005).

66. Harbolt, *Bridging the bond*, 25.

Bibliography

Abraham, Shalev, & Ben-Mordehai, Dror. (1996). Snakes: Interactions with children with disabilities and the elderly—some psychological considerations. *Anthrozoos, 9*(4), 182–187.

Adam, Kirton, Wirrell, Elaine, & Zhang, James. (2004). Seizure-alerting and response behaviors in dogs living with epileptic children. *Neurology, 62,* 2303–2305.

Adams, Maureen. (1999). Emily Dickinson had a dog: An interpretation of the human–dog bond. *Anthrozoos, 12*(3), 132–141.

Alger, All, Anita, & Gary Loving. (1999). Animals, horseback riding, and implications for rehabilitation therapy. *Journal of Rehabilitation, 65*(3), 49–57.

Allison, Rezendes. (2007). Supporting emergency preparedness. *Journal of the American Veterinary Medical Association, 230*(11), 1601.

Anderson, Norman B., & Anderson, P. Elizabeth. (2003). *Emotional longevity: What really determines how long you live.* New York: Viking, The Penguin Group.

Anderson, Patricia K. (2003). A bird in the house: An anthropological perspective on companion parrots. *Society & Animals: Journal of Human-Animal Studies, 11*(4), 393–418.

Animal Legal Defense Fund. *Blind to the suffering: The horror of animal hoarding.* Petaluma, CA.

APPMA. (2007). *National pet owners survey 2007–2008.* Greenwich, CT: APPMA.

Arluke, Arnold, & Sanders, Clinton R. (1996). *Regarding animals.* Philadelphia, PA: Temple University Press.

Banks, Marian R., & Banks, William A. (2005). The effects of group and individual animal-assisted therapy on loneliness in residents of long-term care facilities. *Anthrozoos, 18*(4), 396–408.

Beck, Alan, & Katcher, Aaron. (1996). *Between pets and people: The importance of animal companionship.* West Lafayette, IN: Purdue University Press.

Beck, Alan M., & Katcher, Aaron H. (2003). Future directions in human–animal bond research. *American Behavioral Scientist, 47*(1), 79–93.

Beck, L., & Madresh, E. A. (in press). Romantic partners and four-legged friends: An extension of attachment theory to relationships with pets. *Anthrozoos.*

Beck, M. A., & Katcher, A. H. (1984). A new look at pet-facilitated therapy. *Journal of the American Veterinary Medical Association, 184,* 414–421.

Blackwood, Francy. (2003). No-kill nation: The movement to find homes for all adoptable dogs and cats is spreading across the county. *Animal Watch, 23*(4), 22.

Bonner, John. (2007, May 2). Problem pets can now pop Prozac. *New Scientist*, 18.

Bowlby, J. (1958). Nature of the child's tie to his mother. *Journal of Psycho-analysis*, 39, 350–373.

Brodie, Sarah, & Biley, Francis. (1999). Review: An exploration of the potential benefits of pet-facilitated therapy. *Journal of Clinical Nursing*, 8, 329–337.

Brophy, Katie. (2006, May). What's it "Aawww About?" *Ladies' Home Journal*, 18.

Brown, Brown, Kenneth. (2006). Pastoral concern in relation to the psychological stress caused by the death of an animal companion. *Mental Health, Religion & Culture*, 9(5), 411–422.

Brown, Sue-Ellen. (2003). The human animal bond and self-psychology: Toward a new understanding. *Society & Animals: Journal of Human-Animal Studies*, 12(1), 67–86.

Burger, Joanna. (2001). *The parrot who owns me*. New York: Random House.

Bustad, Leo K. (1990). *Compassion: Our last great hope*. Renton, WA: The Delta Society.

ButlerCarlisle-Frank, Pamela, & Flanagan, Tom. (2006). *Silent victims: Recognizing and stopping abuse of the family pet*. Lanham, MD: University Press of America.

Carmichael, Mary, Reno, Jamie, & Shenfeld, Hilary. (2003, July 21). Animal emotions. *Newsweek*, 44–47.

Case, Linda P. (1999). *The dog: It's behavior, nutrition & health*. Ames, IA: Iowa State University Press.

CaCenters for Disease Control and Prevention. (2006). Deaths: Final data for 2003. *National Vital Statistics Report*, 54(13), 1.

Clements, Paul T., Benasutti, Kathleen M., & Carmone, Andy. (2003). Support for bereaved owners of pets. *Perspectives in Psychiatric Care*, 39(2), 49–54.

Coren, Stanley. (1998). *Why we love the dogs we do*. New York: Simon & Schuster.

Coren, Stanley. (1999). Do people look like their dogs? *Anthrozoos*, 12(2), 111–114.

Coren, Stanley. (2002). *The pawprints of history: Dogs and the course of human events*. New York: Free Press.

Cusack, Odean. (1998). *Pets and mental health*. Binghamton, NY: Haworth Press.

Cutt, Hayley, Giles-Corti, Billie, Kniuman, Matthew, & Burke, Valerie. (2007). Dog ownership, health and physical activity: A critical review of the literature. *Health & Place*, 13, 261–272.

Davis, Bw, Nattras, K., O'brien, S., Patronek, G., & Maccolin, M. (2004). Assistance dog placement in the pediatric population: Benefits, risks, and recommendations for future application. *Anthrozoos*, 17(2),130–145.

Davis, J. H. (1986). Children and pets: A therapeutic connection. *Latham Letter*, 7(4), 1.

De Waal, Frans. (2005). Suspicious minds. *New Scientist*, 186(2502), 48.

Dosa, David M. (2007). A day in the life of Oscar the cat. *The New England Journal of Medicine*, 357(4), 328–329.

Eckberg Feldman, Leah. (2006, June). A bond of love. *Ladies' Home Journal*, 84–86.

Ellengren, H. (2005). Genomics: The dog has its day. *Nature*, 438, 745–746.

Feinstein, Dianne. (2006). Feinstein announces animal enterprise terrorism act signed into law. Congressional Quarterly, Inc., Washington, D.C.

Fields-Meyer, Thomas, & Mandel, Susan. (2006, July 17). Healing hounds. *People*, 101–102.

Flom, Barbara L. (2005). Counseling with pocket pets: Using small animals in elementary counseling programs. *Professional School Counseling*, 8(5), 469–471.

Friedmann, E., & Katcher, A. H. (1980). Animal companions and one year survival of patients after discharge from a coronary care unit. *Public Health Report*, 95(4), 307–312.

Gácsi, M., Topál, J., Miklósi, A., Dóka, A., & Csány, V. (1998). Attachment behavior of adult dogs (*Canis familiaris*) living at rescue centers: Forming new bonds. *Journal of Comparative Psychology*, 112(3), 219–229.

Garrity, Thomas F., Stallones, Lorann, Marx, Martin B., & Johnson, Timothy P. (1989). Pet ownership and attachment as supportive factors in the health of the elderly. *Anthrozoos*, 3(1), 35–44.

Glen, Samantha. (2001). *Best friends: The true story of the world's most beloved animal sanctuary*. New York: Kensington Books.

Goodwin, Jan. (2007, May). Monkey do. *Reader's Digest*, 178–183.

Gosling, Samuel D. (2003). A dog's got personality: A cross-species comparative approach to personality judgments in dogs and humans. *Journal of Personality and Social Psychology*, 85(6), 1161–1169.

Grier, Katherine C. (2006). *Pets in America: A history*. Chapel Hill: University of North Carolina Press.

Grim, Get a dog. *Shape*, 96.

Hamilton, Anita. (2005, December 12). Curbing the puppy trade. *Time*, 61–63.

Harbolt, Tami L. (2003). *Bridging the bond*. West Lafayette, IN: Purdue University Press.

Hare, Brian, & Tomasello, Michael. (2005). Human-like social skills in dogs? *Trends in Cognitive Sciences*, 9(9), 440–444.

Hart, L. A., Hart, B. L., & Mader, B. (1990). Humane euthanasia and companion animal death: Caring for the animal, the client, and the veterinarian. *Journal of the American Veterinary Medical Association*, 197, 1292–1299.

Hatch, Alison. (2007). The view from all fours: A look at an animal-assisted activity program from the animals' perspective. *Anthrozoos*, 20(1), 37–50.

Hazard, Holly, E. (2004). *The violence connection*. Washington, DC: Doris Day Animal Foundation.

Heath, Sebastian E., Kass, Phillip H., Beck, Alan M., & Glickman, Larry T. (2001). Human and pet-related risk factors for houseould evacuation failure during a natural disaster. *American Journal of Epidemiology*, 153(7), 659–665.

Henry, Bill C. (2004). The relationship between animal cruelty, delinquency, and attitudes toward the treatment of animals. *Society & Animals*, 12(3), 185–207.

Hergovich, Andreas, Monshi, Bardia, Semmler, Gabriele, & Zieglmayer, Verena. (2002). The effects of the presence of a dog in the classroom. *Anthrozoos*, 15(1), 37–50.

Hewitt, Bill. (2006, November 6). Should strays be killed. *People*, 99.

Hines, Linda. (2003). Historical perspectives on the human–animal bond. *American Behavioral Scientist*, 47(1), 7–15.

Holcomb, Ralph, Jendro, Connie, Weber, Barbara, & Nahan, Ursula. (1997). Use of an aviary to relieve depression in elderly males. *Anthrozoos*, 10(1), 32–36.

Ianzito, Christina. (2006, October 15). Party animal: Dog day afternoon. *Washington Post Magazine*, 16.

Irvine, Leslie. (2001). The power of play. *Anthrozoos*, 14(3), 151–160.

Irvine, Leslie. (2004). *If you tame me*. Philadelphia, PA: Temple University Press.

Jagoe, Andrew, & Serpell, James. (1996). Owner characteristics and interactions and the prevalence of canine behaviour problems. *Applied Animal Behaviour Science*, 47, 31–41.

Jarvis, Erich. (2005). Avian brains and a new understanding of vertebrate brain evolution. *Nature Reviews Neuroscience*, 6(2), 151–159.

Jensen, J. B., & Camp, C. D. (Eds.). (2003). *Human exploitation of amphibians: Direct and indirect impacts*. Edited by R. D. Semlitsch, Amphibian Conservation. Washington, DC: Smithsonian Institution.

Jerome, Richard, & Erwin, Steve. (2006, February 20). Is this the face of a drug smuggler. *People*, 87–88.

Johnson, Suzanne B., & Rule, Warren R. (1991). Personality characteristics and self-esteem in pet owners and non-owners. *International Journal of Psychology*, 26(2), 241–252.

Jones, Amanda, & Gosling, Samuel D. (2005). Temperament and personality in dogs (*Canis familiaris*): A review and evaluation of past research. *Applied Animal Behaviour Science*, 95, 1–53.

Juarez, Vanessa. (2005, March 21). Stray dog seeks love. *Newsweek*, 53.

Kaiser, Lana, Spence, Linda J., Lavergne, Annique G., & Vanden Bosch, Kerrie L. (2004). Can a week of therapeutic riding make a difference? A pilot study. *Anthrozoos*, 17(1), 62–72.

Katcher, A., & Beck, A. (Eds.). (1983). *New perspectives on our lives with companion animals*. Philadelphia: University of Pennsylvania Press.

Katcher, A. H., & Friedmann, E. (1980). Potential health value of pet ownership. *Compendium of Continuing Education for the Veterinarian*, 2, 117–121.

Katcher, A., & Wilkins, G. (1993). Dialogue with animals: Its nature and culture. In S. R. Kellert and E. O. Wilson (Eds.), *The biophilia hypothesis* (pp. 173–197). Washington, DC: Island Press.

Katz, Jon. (2004). *The new work of dogs: Tending to life, love, and family*. New York: Random House Trade Paperbacks.

Kay, William J. (Ed.). (1988). *Euthanasia of the companion animal: The impact on pet owners, veterinarians, and society*. Philadelphia, PA: Charles Press Publishers, Inc.

Kay, William J., Nieburg, Herbert A., Kutscher, Austin H., Grey, Ross M., & Fudin, Carole E. (Eds.). (1984). *Pet loss and human bereavement*. Ames: Iowa University State Press.

Keating, Lisa. (2005). Pets can tell us something about ourselves as well. *Nevada Appeal*, 1–2.

Kellert, Stephen R., & Wilson, Edward O. (Eds.). (1993). *The biophilia hypothesis*. Washington, DC: Island Press.

Kinosian, Janet. (2006, November). No pet left behind. *Reader's Digest*, 27–32.

Knapp, Carole. (1998). *Pack of two: The intricate bond between pets and people*. New York: Random House.

Kopelman, Jay, & Roth, Melinda. (2006). *From Baghdad, with love*. Guilford, CT: The Lyons Press.

Krueger, Anne, Hey, Barbara, & Reynes, Andrea. (2006, November). Horse wisperings. *Natural Awakenings*, 36–37.

Kübler-Ross, Elisabeth. (1969). *On death & dying*. New York: Simon & Schuster/ Touchstone.

Lange, Karen E. (2002, January). Wolf to woof. *National Geographic*, 2.

Langoni, Laurel, Butler, Carolyn, & Hetts, Suzanne. (1994). *The human–animal bond and grief*. Philadelphia, PA: W.B. Saunders Co.

Laskas, Jeanne Marie. (2006, September). A soldier's best friend. *Ladies' Home Journal*, 112–114.

Lemish, Michael G. (1996). *War dogs: A history of loyalty and heroism*. Washington, DC: Brassey's.

Levine, Stephen B. (2005). What is love anyway? *Journal of Sex & Marital Therapy, 31*, 143–151.

Levison, B. (1962). The dog as co-therapist. *Mental Hygiene, 46*, 59–65.

Lewin, Julie E. (2007). *Get political for animals and win the laws they need*. USA: National Institute for Animal Advocacy.

Lewis, C. S. (1971). *The four loves*. Fort Washington, PA: Harvest Books.

Lewis, Thomas, Amini, Fari, & Lannon, Richard. (2000). *A general theory of love*. New York: Vintage Books.

Lindblad-Toh, Kerstin, Wade, C., Mikkelsen, T., Karlsson, E., Jalte, D., Kamal, M., Clamp, M. (2005). Genome sequence, comparative analysis and haplotype structure of domestic dog. *Nature, 438*, 803–819.

Litonjua, Augusto, Milton, Donald, Celedon, Juan, Ryan, Louise, Weiss, Scott, & Gold, Diane. (2002). A longitudinal analysis of wheezing in young children: The independent effects of early life exposure to house dust endotoxin, allergens, & pets. *Journal of Allergy and Clinical Immunology, 110*(5), 736–742.

Loughlin, Catherine A., & Dowrick, Peter W. (1993). Psychological needs filled by avian companions. *Anthrozoös, VI*(3), 166–172.

Mae, Lynda, Mcmorris, Leah, E., & Hendry, Jennifer L. (2004). Spontaneous train transference from dogs to owners. *Anthrozoos, 17*(3), 225–243.

Marquez, Sandra. (2006, February 13). The angel of "doggy death row." *People*, 111–113.

Marzuola, Carol. (2002). Dog sense: Domestication gave canines innate insight into human gestures. *Science News Online, 162*(21).

Maselko, J. (2006). Religious service attendance and decline in pulmonary function in a high functioning elderly cohort. *Annals of Behavioral Medicine, 32*(3), 245–253.

Masson, Jeffrey. (1997). *Dogs never lie about love*. New York: Crown Publishers.

McConnell, Patricia B. (2002). *The other end of the leash*. New York: Ballantine Books.

McCulloch, Michael, Jezierski, Tadeusz, Broffman, Michael, Hubbard, Alan, Turner, Kirk, & Janecki, Teresa. (2006). Diagnostic accuracy of canine scent detection in early- and late-state lung and breast cancers. McNicholas, June, Gilbey, Andrew, Rennie, Ann, Ahmedzai, Sam, Dono, Jo-Ann, & Ormerod, Elizabeth. (2005). Pet ownership and human health: A brief review of evidence and issues. *BMJ, 331*, 1252–1255.

Mead, P. S., Slutsker, L., & Dietz, V. (1999). Food-related illness and death in the United States. *Emerging Infectious Diseases, 5*, 607–624.

Mehrabian, A. (1971). *Silent messages—A wealth of information about nonverbal communication*. Belmont, CA: Wadsworth.

Mermin, Jonathan, Hutwagner, Lori, Vugia, Duc, Shallow, Sue, Daily, Pamela, Bender, Jeffrey, et al. (2004). Reptiles, amphibians, and human *salmonella* infection: A population-based, case-control study. *CID, 38*(Suppl 3), S253–S61.

Merz-Perez, Linda, & Heide, Kathleen M. (2004). *Animal cruelty: Pathway to violence against people*. Walnut Creek, CA: AltaMira Press.

Meyers, Barbara. (2000). Anticipatory mourning and the human–animal bond. In Therese A. Rando (Ed.), *Clinical dimensions of anticipatory mourning: Theory and practice in working with the dying, their loved ones, and their caregivers* (pp. 537–564). Champaign, IL: Research Press.

Miklóski, Adam, Kubinyi, Enikö, Topál, József, Gácsi, Márta, Virányi, Zsófia, & Csányi, Vilmos. (2003). A simple reason for a big difference: Wolves do not look back at human, but dogs do. *Current Biology, 13*(9), 763–766.

Miklóski, Adam, Polgardi, R., Topál, József, & Csányi, Vilmos. (2000). Intentional behavior in dog–human communication: An experimental analysis of showing behaviour in the dog. *Animal Cognition, 3*(3), 159–166.

Miklóski, Adam, Pongrácz, P., Lakatos, G., Topál, József, & Csányi, Vilmos. (2005). A comparative study of the use of visual communicative signals in interactions between dogs (*Canis familiaris*) and humans and cats (*Felis catus*) and humans. *Journal of Comparative Psychology, 119*(2), 179–186.

Miklóski, Adam, & Soproni, K. (2006). A comparative analysis of animals' understanding of the human pointing gesture. *Animal Cognition, 9*(2), 81–93.

Miklóski, Adam, Topál, József, & Csányi, Vilmos. (2003). Comparative social cognition: What can dogs teach us? *Animal Behaviour, 67*, 995–1004.

Millan, Cesar, & Peltier, Melissa Jo. (2006). *Cesar's way: The natural everyday guide to understanding & correcting common dog problems.* New York: Harmony Books.

Mokdad, Ali H, Marks, James S., Stroup, Donna F., & Gerberding, Julie L. (2004). Actual causes of death in the United States, 2000. *Journal of the American Medical Association, 291*(10), 1238–1241.

Mooallem, Jon. (2007). The modern kennel conundrum. *The New York Times Magazine, 78*, 43–49.

Moran, Victoria. (1990, October). Compassionate living. *Animal's Agenda, 43.*

Morley, Christine, & Fook, Jan. (2005). The importance of pet loss and some implications. *Mortality (Abingdon, England), 10*(2), 127–143.

Moseley, Alexander, & Mowbray, Melton. (2005, October 29). Animals aren't people. *New Scientist, 22.*

Motooka, Masahiko, Koike, Hiroto, Yokoyama, Tomoyuki, & Kennedy, Nell L. (2006). Effect of dog-walking on autonomic nervous activity in senior citizens. *Medical Journal of Australia, 184*(2), 60–63.

Muir, Hazel. (2004, April 17). Stone age cats made great pets. *New Scientist, 13.*

Nieburg, Herbert A., & Fischer, Arlene. (1996). *Pet loss: A thoughtful guide for adults and children.* New York: HarperCollins Publishers.

Nightingale, Florence. (2006). *Notes on nursing: What it is, and what it is not.* First American Edition D. Appleton & Company, p. 103. New York, 1860. Reprint, Paperback edition by Michigan Historical Reprint Series Scholarly Publishing Office.

Odendaal, Johannes. (2002). *Pets and our mental health: The why, the what, and the how.* New York: Vantage Press.

Ownby, D. R., Cole, C. J., & Peterson, E. L. (2002). Exposure to dogs and cats in the first year of life and risk of allergic sensitization at 6 to 7 years of age. *JAMA, 288*(8), 963–972.

Parslow, Ruth, Jorm, Anthony, Christensen, Helen, Rodgers, Bryan, & Jacomb, Patricia. (2005). Pet ownership and health in older adults: Findings from a survey of 2551 community-based Australians aged 60–64. *Gerontology, 51*(1), 40–47.

Phillips, Angus. (2002, January). Incredible journey. *National Geographic, 28–29.*

Podberscek, Anthony L., Paul, Elizabeth S., & Serpell, James A. (eds.). (2000). *Companion animals and us: Exploring the relationships between people and pets.* New York: Cambridge University Press.

Pongrácz, P., Miklóski, Adam, & Csányi, Vilmos. (2001). Owners beliefs on the ability of their pet dogs to understand human verbal communication: A case of social understanding. *Cahiers de Psychologie Cognitive/Current Psychology of Cognition, 20,* 87–107.

Pongrácz, P., Molnar, C., Miklóski, Adam, & Csányi, Vilmos. (2005). Human listeners are able to classify dog (*Canis familiaris*) barks recorded in different situations. *Journal of Comparative Psychology, 119*(2), 136–144.

Putnam, Robert D. (2001). *Bowling alone, the collapse and revival of American community.* New York: Simon & Schuster.

Pycior, Helena. The first dog at war: Fala, President Franklin D. Roosevelt, & World War II—Poster abstract, Deptartment of History, University of Wisconsin-Milwaukee, ISAZ 14th Annual Conference, July 11–12, 2005, Niagara, NY.

Quakenbush, J., & Glickman, L. (1983). Social work services for bereaved pet owners: A retrospective case study in a veterinary teaching hospital. In A. Katcher and A. Beck (Eds.), *New perspectives on our lives with companion animals* (pp. 377–389). Philadelphia: University of Pennsylvania.

Randour, Mary Lou. (2000). *Animal grace: Entering a spiritual relationship with our fellow creatures.* Novato, CA: New World Library.

Reeve, Charlie L., Rogelberg, S. G., Spitzmüller, C., & Digiacomo, N. (2005). The caring–killing paradox: Euthanasia-related strain among animal-shelter workers. *Journal of Applied Social Psychology, 35*(1), 119–143.

Rohlena, Jody. (2007, January). A pony tale. *Reader's Digest,* 126–129.

Roy, Michael M., & Christenfeld, Nicholas J. S. (2004). Do dogs resemble their owners? *Psychological Science, 15*(5), 361–363.

Sable, Pat. (1995). Pets, attachment, and well-being across the life cycle. *Social Work, 40*(3), 8.

Salman, M. D., New, J. G., Scarlett, J. M., Kass, P. H., Ruch-Gallie, R., & Hetts, S. (1998). Human and animal factors related to the relinquishment of dogs and cats in 12 selected animal shelters in the united states. *Journal of Applied Animal Welfare Science, 1*(3).

Schultz, Stacey. (2000, October 30). Pets and their humans. *U.S. News & World Report,* 53.

Schwartz, Marion. (1997). *A history of dogs in the early America.* New Haven, CT: Yale University.

Segurson, S. A., Serpell, J. A., & Hart, B. L. (2005). Evaluation of a behavioral assessment questionnaire for use in the characterization of behavioral problems of dogs relinquished to animal shelters. *Journal of the American Veterinary Medical Association, 227*(11), 1755–1761.

Serpell, J. A. (1989). Pet keeping and animal domestic: A reappraisal. In J. Clutton-Brock (Ed.), *The walking larder: Patterns of domestication, pastorialism and predation.* London: Unwin Hyman.

Serpell, J. A. (1991). Beneficial effects of pet ownership on some aspects of human health and behavior. *Journal of the Royal Society of Medicine, 84*(12), 717–720.

Serpell, J. A. (Ed.). (1995). *The domestic dog: It's evolution, behavior, and interactions with people.* Cambridge, UK: Cambridge University Press.

Serpell, J. A. (1996). *In the company of animals: A study of human–animal relationships.* Cambridge, UK: Cambridge University Press.

Serpell, J. A. (2003). Anthropomorphism and anthropomorphic selection—Beyond the "cute response." *Society & Animals, 11*(1), 83–96.

Shear, K., Frank, E., Houck, P. R., & Reynolds, C. F. (2005). Treatment of complicated grief: A randomized controlled trial. *JAMA, 293,* 2601–2608.

Sheldrake, Rupert. (1999). *Dogs that know when their owners are coming home.* New York: Crown Publishers.

Siebert, Charles. (2006, October 8). *New York Times Magazine,* 42–49, 64, 71.

Siebert, Charles. (2007, April 8). New tricks. *New York Times Magazine,* 46–51.

Siegel, J. M. (1990). Stressful life events and use of physician services among the elderly: The moderating role of pet ownership. *Journal of Personality and Social Psychology, 58,* 1081–1086.

Sife, Wallace. (1998). *The loss of a pet.* New York: Wiley Publishing, Inc.

Soennichsen, Susan, & Chamove, Arnold S. (2002). Responses of cats to petting by humans. *Anthrozoos, 15*(3), 258–265.

Soproni, K., Miklóski, Adam, Topál, József, & Csányi, Vilmos. (2002). Dogs' (*Canis familiaris*) responsiveness to human pointing gestures. *Journal of Comparative Psychology, 116*(1), 27–34.

Staats, S., Miller, D., & Carnot, M. J. (1996). The Miller Rada commitment to pets scale. *Anthrozoös, 9,* 88–94.

Sternberg, Robert J., & Barnes, Michael L. (Eds.). (1988). *The psychology of love.* New Haven, CT: Yale University Press.

Strimple, Earl O. (2003). A history of prison inmate–animal interaction programs. *American Behavioral Scientist, 47*(1), 70–78.

Stringfellow, Jude. (2006). *With a little faith.* Philadelphia, PA: Xlibris Corp.

Strobe, M., Stroebe, W., and Schut, H. (2002). Grief and loss, *Encyclopedia of Psychology,* Alan Kazdin, eds. Oxford, England: Oxford University Press.

Stuart, S., & Chanson, J. S., Cox, N., Young, B., Rodriques, A., Fischman, D. (2004). Status and trends of amphibian decline and extinctions worldwide. *Science, 306,* 1783–1786.

Sussman, Marvin B. (Ed.). (1985). *Pets and the family.* New York: Haworth Press.

Talbot, Margaret. (2006, September 4). The baby lab. *The New Yorker,* 90–101.

Teitelbaum, Steven L. (2002). Animal rights pressure on scientists. *Science, 298*(5598), 1515.

The Health Benefits of Pets. (1987, September 10–11). Workshop Summary. Bethesda, MD: National Institutes of Health, Office of Medical Applications of Research.

Thurston, Mary Elizabeth. (1996). *The lost history of the canine race: Our 15000-year love affair with dogs.* Kansas City, MO: Andrews and McMeel.

Topál, J., Miklósi, Á., & Csányi, V. (1997). Dog–human relationship affects problem-solving behavior in the dog. *Anthrozoos, 10*(4), 214–224.

Topál, J., Miklósi, A., Csányi, V., & Doka, A. (1998). Attachment behavior in dogs (*Canis familiaris*): A new application of Ainsworth's (1969) strange situation test. *Journal of Comparative Psychology, 112*(3), 219–229.

Toray, Tamina. (2004). The human–animal bond and loss: Providing support for grieving clients. *Journal of Mental Health Counseling, 26*(3), 244–259.

Tryba, Lynn. (2002). Trash menagerie. *People, 35*(6), 22.

Tucker, Joan, Friedman, Howard, Tsai, Catherine M., & Martin, Leslie R. (1995). Playing with pets and longevity among older people. *Psychology and Aging, 10*(1), 3–7.

Usherwood, James R. (2005). Biomechanics: No force limitation on greyhound sprint speed. *Nature*, *438*, 753–754.

VandenBos, Gary R. (2007). *APA dictionary of psychology*. Washington, DC: The American Psychological Association.

Voigt, Kevin. (2007, May 2). ID chips increasingly a pet issue. *New Scientist*, 18.

Walsh, Anthony. (1991). *The science of love: Understanding love and its effects on mind and body*. Amherst, NY: Prometheus Book.

Weisman, Avery. (1991). Bereavement and companion animals. *Omega: The Journal of Death and Dying*, *22*(4), 241–248.

Wells, Deborah. (2004). The facilitation of social interactions by domestic dogs. *Anthrozoos*, *17*(4), 340–352.

Wells, Deborah L. (2007). Domestic dogs and human health: An overview. *British Journal of Health Psychology*, *12*, 145–156.

Willis, Carolyn, Church, Susannah, Guest, Claire, Cook, Andrew, Mccarthy, Noel, Barnsbury, Anthea, Church, Martin, & Church, John. (2004). Olfactory detection of human bladder cancer by dogs: Proof of principle study. *BMJ*, *329*(7468), 712–714.

Wilson, Edward O. (1986). *Biophilia* (Reprint ed.). Cambridge, MA: Harvard University Press.

Winerman, Lea. (2006). A dog's life. *Monitor on Psychology*, *37*, 18.

Zajonc, R. B., Adelmann, P. K., Murphy, S. T., & Niedenthal, P. M. (1987). Convergence of the physical appearance of spouses. *Motivation and Emotion*, *11*, 335–346.

Index

Activism, 153–58, 203
Adoption, pet, 104
Adoptions, 50, 116, 134
Advertising, 85
Agape love, 39
Aging pet, retirement home for, 160–61
Aiello, Ron, 115
Air travel, 90, 146
Allergies, 11, 57, 68, 71, 134, 138
The Allie Program, 140
Alterego Needs, 21, 22
American Animal Hospital Association, xxiii, 166
American Boarding Kennels Association (ABKA), 87
American Canine Hybrid Club, 184
American Horse Slaughter Prevention Act, 159
American Humane Association (AHA), 74
American Indians, domestication of dogs by, 7
American Kennel Club, 182, 184
American Pet Products Manufacturing Association (APPMA), xxii, 207n1
American Psychological Association (APA), 18–19, 166
American Red Cross, 114
American Society for the Prevention of Cruelty to Animals (ASPCA), 194
American Sociological Association (ASA), 18
Americans with Disabilities Act (ADA), 136–37

Amphibians: human exposure to diseases from, 58; as not companion animal, 56–57
Anand, K. J. S., 198
Anderson, Norman, 68
Angel Airs, 175–76
Animal Assisted Activities (AAA), 120, 121–22, 137, 138
Animal Assisted Therapy (AAT), 120, 137, 138
AnimalAttraction.com, 68
Animal cruelty, 158–60
Animal Legal Defense Fund, 103
Animal Planet (TV program), 74, 205
Animal Society for the Prevention of Cruelty to Animals (ASPCA), 156
Animal Waste Specialists, 93
Animal welfare movement, 14
Anthropodenial, 199
Anthropomorphism, 95, 199
Anthrozoology, 19
Anticipatory grief, 169–70
The APPMA National Pet Owners Survey, 84–86
Arachnids, as companion animals, 5
Armstrong, Lance, 144, 202
Arnold, the pig, 12
Asthma, 134
Attachment theory, 35
A2L Technologies, 71
Automobile design, dog-friendly car, 74–75
Automobile travel, 147

Avian intelligence, 52
Avian Learning EXperiment, 52–53

Backyard breeders, 80
Barbaro, 10, 165
Barnes, Michael, 39
Bart (dog), 148
Basic Animal Rescue Training Program
    (BART), 148–49
Baskin, Carole, 196
Baxter, Nancy, 140
Behrens, Chris, 29
Bekoff, Marc, 40
Benji dog, 49–50
Bennett, Chelsea, 41
Bennett, Valerie, 31–32
Bereavement, 138, 166–70, 176
Best Friends Animal Sanctuary, 156–57
Beta fish, 87
Big Cat Rescue, 196
Biophilia, 20, 201
Bird mills, 183–84
Birds, 10, 89; behavior therapy for, 96; bird
    mills, 183–84; canaries, 10, 11; mental
    health benefits of, 135; parakeets,
    10–11, 53; parrots, 10, 11, 52–55;
    research on hearing/learning songs, 73;
    in sanctuaries, 157; susceptibility to
    capture myopathy, 3; travel with, 89
Bisno, Jay, 9
Bloom, Troy, 33–34
Blueston, Marc, 104
Blumenauer, Earl, 160
Body language, 25, 26, 27
Bond. See Human-animal bond
Borchelt, Peter, 105
Bosch, Michael, 41
Bowlby, J., 35
Brachycephaly, 78
Breakaway Adventures, 91
Breeding, 78–80; dog fanciers, 79, 80;
    for-profit breeders, 79, 80; negative
    consequences of, 78–79;
    not-for-the-profit breeders, 79
Brewington, Dana, 93–94
Broca, Paul, 37
Brotman, Patti, 160

Brotman, Richard, 160
Buenau, Michael, 144, 145
Burger, Joanna, 53
Burials, ceremonies, and memorials,
    175–79
Burns, Bill, 41
Burros, 157
Bustad, Leo, 197–98

Cadaver dogs, 113
Callous behavior by others, 168–69
Canaries, 10, 11
Cancer, detecting, 131–33, 135
Canidae family, 5
Canis familiaris. See Dogs
Capture myopathy, 3, 208n5
Carmack, Betty, 168
Carvalko, Debora, 59–60
Carville, James, 106
CatGenie, 93
Cat litter, 1, 93
Cats: association with religion, 8; as bait
    animals, 195; behavior therapy for, 96;
    designer, 185; domestication of, 7–8;
    dominant hierarchies and, 3; feral, 4,
    154; lifespan of free-roaming, 147;
    numbers of, compared with dogs, 9,
    50–51; obesity in, 76; origins of, 7;
    police work and, 110–11; robotic, 12; in
    sanctuaries, 157; sense of hearing, 7;
    sense of sight, 7; travel with, 89;
    violence against, 194; as work animals, 1
Cemetery, pet, 161, 176–77
Centers for Disease Control (CDC), 58
Cheatham, Valerie, 34–35
Cheers, Ann, 178, 179
Cherry, Frank, 162
Chickens, 10, 55–56, 192
Children, and companion animals, 71–72,
    139–40, 202, 204
Chimpanzees, 25, 52
China, 7, 8, 15
Chiper (dog), 129–30
Chuckie (dog), 178
Church. See "Religious ceremonies"
Cinnamon (dog), 147–48
Clark, Jeff, 147

Clark, Mark, 148
Cleo (dog), 133
Cloning, 185–86
Clothing, for animals, 107–8
Cockatiels, 53
Cody (dog), 108
Cognitive dissonance, 80, 107, 157, 164, 216n41
Cohen, Dan, 68
Communication, interspecies, 25–30; with cats and dogs, 25–27
Community Led Animal Welfare (CLAW), 17
Companion Animal Placement, 172
Companion Animal Related Emotions (CARE), 174
Companion animals: concept of being committed to, 33; effect on pet owner health, 73, 134–37; as family members, 66–67; Golden Age for, 82–84; history of, 5–13; human influence on, 75–78; increase in numbers of, xxi–xxii; influence on humans, 72–75; as miracle workers, 40–43. See also Companion animals, factors in choosing; Individual animal
Companion animals, factors in choosing, 44–65; birds, 52–56; "cuteness," 48–49; farm animals, 62–63; fish, freshwater, 51–52; horses, 61–62; passing fancy, 49–50; personality of pet owner, 45–48, 202; reptiles and amphibians, 56–61; small animals, 63–65
Companion animal versus pet, xix
Compassion fatigue, 193
Complicated grief, 170–73
Consumer spending, on companion animals, 84–95; cleaning/removing animal waste, 93; custom furniture, 92–93; designer crates, 92; doggie disposable diapers, 93–94; grooming, 86, 89; natural products, 92; pet sitting, 86–89; pet sitting, in-home, 88; travel and vacation, 89–90; travel crates, 92–93
Consumption, of companion animals, 16

Contraception, animal, 193
Convention on International Trade in Endangered Species (CITES), 53
Cook, Jane, 148
Cooke, India, 175–76
Coppinger, Raymond, 6
Coren, Stanley, 46
Cowing, Kerri, 107
Coworker, companion animal as, 70–71
Cows, 2, 62–63
Coyotes, 5, 149
Cremation, pet, 177–78
Cruelty to animals, 14, 158–60, 193–95
Cruikshank, Stacy, 106
Csáyni, Vilmos, 27, 28, 77–78, 82
Cue-reading ability, 26
Cupp, Richard, 104–5
Custom furniture, 92–93
Cute factor, 48–49
Cyprus, domestication of cat in ancient, 7–8

Dailey, Sonya, 4
Dalmatians, movie-driven popularity of, 50
Damko, Jennifer, 116
Dana, Jamie, 117, 152
Darwin, Charles, 39
Death: types of loss, 163–66. See also Grief
Declawing, 14, 79
Deer, 3
Deers, Jamie, 203
Delta Society, 18, 118, 120, 197
Designer cats, 185
Designer dogs, 184–85
Devoicing, 79
De Waal, Frans, 198–99
DINC (dual income, no children) families, and companion animals, xxii
Dire Wolf (Canis dirus), 6
Disaster plans, 159
Disenfranchised grief, 168–69
Divorce, and pets, 103–4
Dog Bar, 91
Dog fanciers, 79, 80, 114–15
Dogfighting, 14, 195, 201, 203
Dog Genome, 145–46, 203

Dogs: behavior therapy for, 96; Benji dog, 49–50; cadaver, 113; designer, 184–85; as diagnostician, 133–34, 135; dog-friendly car, 74–75; doggie disposable diapers, 93–94; domestication, 7; as exercise partner, 136; genetic mapping of, 73–74, 145–46, 203; as healing the healer, 135; herding, 47, 109; human world as natural environment of, 82; instinctual actions over training, 4; lapdogs, 47; medicine and, 123–24, 128–30, 131–33; military working, 113–17, 152, 203; numbers of, compared with cats, 9, 50–51; obesity in, 76; police work and, 109–11; problem-solving abilities of domestic, 77–78; as reading tutors, 116, 118; rescues by, 41–42; robotic, 11; in sanctuaries, 157; search and rescue, 111–13; sense of hearing, 25, 109; sense of sight, 25, 109; sense of smell, 25, 26, 42, 109, 118, 131, 202; as shape shifter, 6; small, as bait animals, 195; speech and, 26–27; toy breeds, 7, 47, 50, 67, 136; travel with, 89; as work animal, 1, 118
Dogs Deserve Better (DDB), 155–56
Dogs for Defense, 114–15
Doka, Kenneth J., 168
Domestication: criterion for, 2–3; "tame" vs., 3–4
Domestic cat (Felis catus). See Cats
Dooling, Robert, 73
Do-Rite Disposable Dog Diapers, 94
Dosa, David, 42
Dowling, Corinne, 192
Drent, Piet, 54
Ducks, 10, 19–20
Ducommun, Debbie, 63
Durney, Margie, 33

Ear cropping, 79
Ear docking, 14
Efland, Jaye Ruth, 151–52
Egypt, 7–8
Elderly persons, and pets, 137–39
Emotional disclosure, 68
Empathy, 37, 72, 127, 139, 180

England, 14, 109, 153
Entin, Alan, 107–8
Equine Assisted Therapy, 124–26, 128
Estate planning, 160
European Convention for the Protection of Pet Animals, 14, 209n34
European Union (EU), 14, 209n33
Europeds, 91
Euthanasia, 15, 146, 159, 164–66, 191–93
Evolution, Convergent, 25
Exotics, 195–97
Eye contact, 27–29

Facial expressions, 29–30, 43
Faith (dog), 150
Fala (presidential dog), 13
Fancy rats, 63–64
Farm animals: chickens, 10, 55–56, 192; cows, 2, 62–63; goats, 2, 26, 157; hens, 56; roosters, 10, 56; in sanctuaries, 157
Feathered Kids (Fids), 54
Federal Emergency Management Agency (FEMA), 112, 148–49
Felidae family, 7
Feral cats, 4, 154
Ferrets, 87, 89; behavior therapy for, 96; pet cemeteries and, 177; travel with, 89
Fire safety, 148
Fischbacher, Siegfried, 4
Fish, 90; goldfish, 51, 87; travel with, 89; tropical, 11
Fleming, Scott, 71
"Flooding," 97
Florin (dog), 33, 34
Fontanez, Frederick, 160
Foxes, 5, 49
Foxy (dog), 171, 172
France, domestication of cat in, 8
Free-roaming animals, 146–47
Fritchey, John, 160
Frogs, 56, 57
Fuel source, companion animal as, 72
Functional referential communication (FRC), 28
Fur industry, 15, 157

Galli, Cesare, 185–86
Garrard, Paul, 106–7

Gaze, as social interaction component, 28–29

Geckos, 5, 205

Genetic mapping, of *Canis familiaris*, 73–74

Genetic Savings & Clone, 186

Gerbils, 11, 64, 98, 140

Goats, 2, 26, 157

Golden Age for companion animals, 82–84

Goldfish, 51, 87

Goodall, Jane, 54

Gorilla, as not domesticable, 3

Gosling, Samuel, 40

Grace (dog), 26, 28, 29, 34, 88, 89, 90, 103, 107, 178, 179

Grandin, Temple, 78

Gray Wolf, 6

Greece: cruelty to animals in, 15, 203; dogs in ancient, 6–7

Green, Nancy, 183

Grenick, Leslie, 154–55, 192

Grief, 162–63; of animal in multi-animal homes, 168; anticipatory, 169–70; complicated, 170–73; disenfranchised, 168–69; helping ease, 179–80; processing, 173–75

Grier, Katherine, 197

Grimes, Tammy Sneath, 155–56

Groome, Jerry, 177

Grooming, 86, 89

Guardian versus Owner, xix

Guide animals, 120, 123, 126–27, 128, 136, 184, 207n5

Guide Horse Foundation, 127

Guide Horse Program, 127

Guilder (dog), 33, 34

Guinea pigs, 11, 31–32, 64, 140, 192

Hasbro, 85

Haggerty, A. J., 27

Haldeman, Douglas, 79, 80

Hallundbaek, Hans B., 99

Hamsters, 11, 13, 64, 140, 159, 204

Hanks, Peter, 62–63

Hanna, Jack, 195–96

Harley-Davidson, 85

Harlow, Harry, 35

Haven, Wallace, 184

Health insurance, for companion animals, 146

Hearing loss research, 73

Heaven Scent Paws, 132–33

Heenan, Jane, 99

Helmsley, Leona, 160

Helping Hands, 131

Hens, 56

Herding dogs, 47, 109

Hermit crabs, 87

Hernandez, Cindy, 41

Hierarchy of needs, 3, 216n3

Hillman, Kathleen, 107

Hilton, Paris, 203

HIV/AIDS, persons with, 134

Hoarders, 186–87

Homeless persons, and companion animals, xxii, 171–72

Honda Japan, 74–75

Horn, Roy, 4

Horse: medicine and, 124–28

Horses: behavior therapy for, 96; as companion animals, 3; cruelty to, 14, 158–59; domestication of, 9; euthanasia of, 165–66; factors in choosing, 61–62; as food source, 9, 10; pet cemeteries and, 177; Premarin foals, 128, 220n25; protection of, 9–10; racehorses, 9–10; in sanctuaries, 157; wild, 4; as work animals, 9

House Rabbit Society, 65

Human-animal bond (HAB), 95–108, 197–99, 201, 202; animal law, 102–4; attachment, 35–36; beginnings/growth of, 18–21; clothing for animals, 107–8; commitment and, 32–35; companion animal miracle workers, 40–43; emotions/personality of animals and, 39–40; evolutionary facet of love and, 38–39; gifts and gadgets, 108; love/empathy and, 36–38; mental health, 96–97; parties for animals, 105–6; psychology of, 21–22; relationship qualities of, 30–39; risk-taking and, 31–32; for sound body, 101–2; for sound spirit, 97–101; work animals (*See* Work animals)

Human development and behavior research, 73
Humane Alliance, 193
Humane Society Legislative Fund (HSLF), 158
Humane Society of the United States (HSUS), 16, 157, 158, 182, 187, 189, 191, 225n3
Humane USA, 158
Human Society International (HSI), 16
Hurricane Katrina, 31–32, 41, 112, 201, 203
Hurricane Rita, 203
Hynes, Charles J., 110
Hypoallergenic cat, 185

Idealizing Needs, 21, 22
Identification chips, 161
Iguanas, 5, 58–61
Independent Animal Rescue (IAR), 154–55
Instincts, tamed animal reverting to, 4–5
International Companion Animal Welfare Conferences, 17
International Fund for Animal Welfare (IFAW), 17
International Society for Anthrozoology (ISAZ), 19
Interpersonal Adjective Scales (IAS), 47, 202
Irvine, Leslie, 20–21
Irwin, Steve, 205
Isabella (cat), 139
Israel, dogs in ancient, 6
Italy, 14–15

Jackal, 5
James, John, 162
Jangsem, 99, 100
Japan, 15–16
JetPets, 90
John Paul Mitchell Systems, 85
Johnson, Lyndon B., 13
Jones, Jordan, 42

Kalinoski, Carol, 143–44

Kaplan, Laurie, 145
Kaplan, Melissa, 58, 59, 61
Karp, Adam, 105
Karreman, Manfred, 15
Katz, Jon, 62–63, 83, 158
Keeton, David, 115
Kennedy, John F., 13
Klaassen, Paul, 138
Knapp, Caroline, 207n8
K-9 police officers, 109–11
K-9 Sirius, 172–73
Koocher, Gerald, 54–55
Kopelman, Joy, 152
Kraemer, Lillian, 98
Kübler-Ross, Elizabeth, 173–75
Kuhse, Michael, 33
Kurland, Jeffrey, 48

Laboratory animals, 11
Labradoddles, 184
Lacks, Ciccy, 149
LaFarge, Stephanie, 73
Laikia (astronaut dog), 13
LaMura, A. R., 176
Lane, Glenn, 175
Lapdogs, 47
Larkin's Run, 87
Lassie, 12, 13, 205
Latte (dog), 29, 30
Lauver, Robin L., 176
Leslin, Karen, xxii
Levine, Stephen, 38–39
Lewin, Julie E., 158
Lewis, C.S., 39
Libin, Alex, 11, 12
Libin, Elena, 11, 12
LifeGem diamonds, 178–79
Lifestyle pets, 185
Lim, David, 172–73
Limbic brain, 37–38, 40, 43, 52
Limbic resonance, 43
Lingle, Mark, 99
Lizards, 57, 58, 59, 60, 202
Lopez, Derek, 160
Lorenz, Konrad, 19–20
Loss, types of, 163–66

Love, 16, 19, 20, 22, 35, 36–40, 68, 71, 80, 84, 85, 86, 88, 99, 101, 124, 134, 139, 147, 150
Lucky (dog), 144, 145

Macaws, 53, 54–55
Maitlin, Marty, 106
Malpractice, 103, 104–5
Mammals, small, as companion animals, 11
Margay (dog), 48
Maslow, Abraham, 3, 216n3
Matchmakers, companion animals as, 68–70, 204
Maturation rate, as domestication criterion, 2–3
McCann, Christine, 134
McConnell, Patricia B., 25, 26, 75, 76
McGlynn, Brian, 68–69
McGreevy, Molly, 98
McRobert, Scott, 60
Medical treatments for companion animals, 142–46; costs of, 143–44, 146
Medicine, pets as: accidental therapists, 134–37; animal-assisted activities, 120, 126–37, 201–2; animal-assisted therapy, 120, 123–26; beginnings of, 120–21; children and, 139–40, 202, 204; dogs, 123–24, 128–30, 131–33; elderly persons, 137–39; evolution of research on, 121–22; horses, 124–26, 126–28; incarcerated persons, 140–41; monkeys, 131; special populations, 137–41
Memorial funds, 103
Mertens, Petra, 96
Methane fuel, 72
MeToo (dog), 149, 150
Miacid family, 1, 6, 7
Mice, 11, 63
Middle East, domestication of cat in ancient, 8
Midge (dog), 110
Miklóski, Adam, 28
Milan, Caesar, 96–97, 181
Military working dogs (MWD), 97, 113–17, 152, 203
Miller, Andrea, 69
Miller, Gail, 68

Miller, Laura Hinson, 69
Mimicry, 11, 22, 26, 27, 52, 67, 102, 125
Mirroring Needs, 21, 22
Mister Ed, 205
Mobile grooming, 89
Moore, Barbara, 56
Moose, as not domesticable, 3
Morgan, Vicky Lynn, 85
Morgana, Aimee, 54
Morphic fields, 4
Morris, Julie, 191
Motivational hierarchy, 3, 216n3
Motor function studies, 74
Movies, animals in, 74
Mr. Chips (dog), 93–95
Mulrenin, Ed, 33
Murphy, Darcy, 42

National Association of Pet Funeral Directors, 176
National Association of Professional Pet Sitters, 88–89
National Institute for Animal Advocacy, 158
National Parks, 21
National Shelter Outreach, of ASPCA, 191
Neal, Clifford, 178
Nichols, Lydia, 26
Nightingale, Florence, 135
Noah's Ark Pet Cemetery, 175
North Shore Animal League in America, 17, 151

Obesity, in cats and dogs, 76
Obsessive compulsive disorder (OCD), 186
Off the Leash (television program), 74
Olsen, Janet, 148–49
OPI (nail products), 85
Oscar (cat), 42
Overpopulation, 187–88

Pampering, 16, 32, 67, 75, 82–108
Pandas, 2–3
Parakeets, 10–11, 53
Parrots, 10, 11, 52–55
Peel, Craig, 32, 201

Pennebaker, James, 68
People for Ethical Treatment of
   Animals (PETA), 103, 157, 177, 185,
   191
Pepperberg, Irene, 52–53, 213n27
Perpetual Pet, 179
Perretta, Peter, 86
Personality, of pet owner: choosing
   animals as companions, factors in,
   45–48; influence on companion animal,
   76–77
Persons, Vera, 139
Pet Animal Welfare Statute (PAWS),
   183
PetáPotty, 93
PetCell, 161
PETCO, 89
Petey (dog), 98
Petfinder.com, 156
PetFriendly.com, 91
Petie (horse), 127, 128
PetMobility, 161
Pet Owner Survey, xxiii
Pet resort, 86
Petronek, Gary, 186
Pets-DC, 134–35
Pet sitting, 86–89; in-home, 88
PetsMart, 89
PetSmart, Inc., 85
Pet stroller, 108
PetsWelcome.com, 91
Phila love, 39
Pigeons, 10
Pit bulls, 4, 33–34, 42, 99, 208n8
Play dates, 105–6
Polar bear, as not domesticable, 3
Political image boosters, pets as, 13,
   203
Pollock, Cindy, 56
Poop-Freeze, 93
Popularity, of cats and dogs, 22–30
Positive punishment, 97
Potbellied pigs, 42, 87, 159
Pound-seizure, 189
Pratte, Deborah, 104
Premarin foals, 128, 220n25
Prentiss, Gary, 35

Prenuptial agreement, pet, 104
Presidential dogs, 13
Primus, April, 193
Protection, of companion animals:
   activism, 153–58, 203; health insurance,
   146; individual efforts, 158–60; medical
   treatments, 142–46; medical treatments,
   costs of, 143–44, 146; prevention,
   146–49; rehabilitation, after medical
   treatment, 144; safety gizmos and
   gadgets, 161; separation anxiety, 146; in
   your absence, 160–61
PSYETA (Psychologists for the Ethical
   Treatment of Animals), 19
Puggle, 184
Puppy mills, 80, 155, 182–83, 225n3
Puppy showers, 106
Pythons, 5, 57, 58

Rabbits, 10, 13, 64–65; as bait animals,
   195; behavior therapy for, 96;
   euthanization of, 159, 192; pet
   cemetaries and, 177; rabbit mills, 183;
   rescues by, 42; resorts for, 87; in
   sanctuaries, 157; travel with, 89
Racehorses, 9–10
Rainbow Bridge, 199
Rambo, Ryan, 41
Randour, Mary Lou, 70
Rats, 11, 63–64
Raymond, Jennifer, 56
Reading Education Assistance Dogs
   (R.E.A.D.), 118
Reif, Amanda, 105–6
Reinkemeyer, Michele, 132–33
Relationships, 1, 6, 8, 9, 18, 19, 20,
   21–24, 29; qualities for successful,
   30–31
Religious ceremonies, 14, 33, 34, 47, 74,
   90, 97–101
Replacements Ltd., 71
Reproduction, in captivity, 2
Reptiles: exposure of disease from, 58; as
   not companion animals, 57–58, 72;
   popular appeal of, 58–59
Reptiles, as companion animals, 5
Reptiles and amphibians, 56–61

Rinpoche, Zopa, 99–100
Rin Tin Tin, 12–13, 205
Ritz Carlton, 90
Roberts, Mary C., 152
Robotic cats, 12
Robotic dogs, 11
Robotics studies, 74
Rocco (dog), 151, 152
Rodden, Rick, 111–12
Rodents, 63–64
Roeder, Larry, 203–4
Rome, ancient, 2, 7, 8
Roosevelt, Franklin, 13, 203
Roosters, 10, 56
Ross, Helen, 152
Russia, domestication of cat in, 8
Ryals, Brenda, 73

Salmonella, 58
Santorum, Rick, 183
Saul, Betsy, 156
Saul, Jared, 156
Save a Bunny, 64, 65
Schaaf, March, 64, 65
Schaffer, Jill, 175
Schlismann, Bob, 99–100
Schmaltz, Larry, 71
Schmidt, Russell, 152
Schneiderman, Ellie, 100–101
Schneiderman, Neil, 100–101
Scott, Mimi, 34
Scott, Stephanie, 33–34
Search and rescue dog (SAR), 111–13
Secondhand smoke, 152
Self psychology, 21–22
Seneca Hill Animal Hospital, Resort &
    Spa, 87–88
Separation anxiety, 146
Serpell, James, 5, 18, 22–23, 76, 77, 207n6
Shapiro, Dorothy M., 176–77
Sheldrake, Rupert, 40–41, 54
Shelters, 188–91; kill vs. no-kill, 190–91,
    193; waiting period, at animal, 159
Silver, Jon, 149–50
Simmons, Al, 143
Sinatra, Stephen, 135

Sir Roudy Bushreid of Winterset (dog),
    100, 101, 106
Size, as domestication criterion, 3
Smythe, Joshua, 68
Snakes, 5; euthanization of, 192; as exotic
    animals, 57; health benefits of
    interaction with, 136; as not companion
    animal, 57–58
Social connectors, companion animals as,
    67–68
Social fields, 40–41
Social interaction, 23–25
Social support, 20, 21, 67–70
Society and Animals Forum, 19
Society for the Prevention of Cruelty to
    Animals (SPCA), 190, 191
Songbirds, 10
South Korea, 16
Squirrels, 11
Staats, Sara, 189
Starter pets, 72
Sterilization, 185, 193
Sternberg, Robert, 39
Stevenson, Tom, 147
Storge love, 39
Stormont, Leana, 103
Support group, pet loss, 169
Sweetland, Mary Beth, 185
Sylvia (parrot), 55
Szot, Steven, 193

Tail docking, 14
Tail nicking, 79
Take Your Dog to Work Day, 71
Tamed animal, reversion to instincts, 4–5
"Tame" vs. domestication, 3–4
Taylor, Chris, 54
Teacher, companion animal as, 70, 204–5
Teddy (dog), 90, 91
Teeth cutting, 79
Television programs, animals on, 74
Terry, Jon, 178
Therapeutic riding. See Equine Assisted
    Therapy
Therapy, animal-assisted, 123–26
Thirst Alert, 108
Tigers, 4

Toy dogs, 7, 47, 50, 67, 136
Traisman, Enid, 174
Trap/neuter/release (TNR), 154
Travel crates, 92–93
Trigger, 12–13
Tropical canine pancytopenia (TCP), 115
Tropical fish, 11
Turtles, 5, 46, 57, 58, 159, 194–95
Types of loss: euthanasia, 164–66

United States Police Canine Association,
    111
United States War Dog Association
    (USWDA), 116

Vargas, Ralph, 171–72
Ventral-ventral contact, human/dog,
    77
Veron, Marty, 87–88
Vetere, Bob, 92, 158, 184–85
Veterinary medicine, 142, 147, 163, 165,
    166, 179, 180
Vick, Michael, 201, 203
Vincent, Kathy, 143
Virtual animals, 11–12
Viverravidae, 11

Waldrip, Jewel, 63
Walker, Gillian, 207n5
Walker, Tre, 67
Wal-Mart, 89
Walsh, Anthony, 37
Walsh, Susan, 159–60

War Dog Centers, 114
Waste, cleaning/removing animal, 93
Webb, Jimmy, 135
Wells, Chip, 135
Wells, Stephen, 103
White, Harold, 175
Wiggins, Jerry, 47
Wild Bird Conservation Act, 53
Wilson, Cherie, 68, 69
Wilson, Edward O., 20
Wireless technology, 161
Wise, Stephen, 103
Wolf (canis lupus), 5, 6; intelligence of,
    78; male care for pups, 77; value of
    human face to, 28; vocal
    communication by, 27
Worden, J. W., 173
Work animals, 109–18; cadaver dogs, 113;
    military working dogs, 97, 113–17, 152,
    203; police work, 109–11; reading tutor,
    116, 118; search and rescue, 111–13;
    sense of smell and, 118; transition to
    companion animals, 1
World Society for the Protection of
    Animals, 203–4
World Trade Center, attacks on,
    112

Yoga, 101–2
Young, Megan, 185

Zebra, as not domesticable, 3
Zoonotic diseases, 58, 61, 75, 196

About the Author

P. ELIZABETH ANDERSON is a national award-winning author and journalist with more than 17 years experience in clinical research and 30 years in activities to promote and protect companion animals. She has written for publications of Duke University Medical Center, the National Institutes of Health, the Centers for Disease Control and Prevention, and the U.S. Public Health Service. Prior to writing this book, she was a writer and editor for the Humane Society of the United States. She co-authored an earlier book, *Emotional Longevity*, with her husband, Dr. Norman B. Anderson, CEO of the American Psychological Association.